IRELAND
A Social and Cultural History
1922–2002

Terence Brown is Professor of Anglo-Irish Literature at Trinity College, Dublin where he is also a Fellow of the College. He is a member of the Royal Irish Academy and of the Academia Europaea. Among his publications are: *Louis MacNeice: Sceptical Vision*; *Northern Voices: Poets from Ulster*; *Ireland's Literature: Selected Essays* and *The Life of W. B. Yeats: A Critical Biography*. He has lectured on Irish literature and culture in many parts of the world.

IRELAND

A Social and Cultural History
1922–2002

TERENCE BROWN

HARPER PERENNIAL

Harper Perennial
An imprint of HarperCollins*Publishers*
77–85 Fulham Palace Road,
Hammersmith, London W6 8JB

www.harpercollins.co.uk/harperperennial

This edition published by Harper Perennial 2004
9 8 7 6 5 4 3 2 1

First published in Great Britain by
Fontana 1981

A catalogue record for this book
is available from the British Library

ISBN 0-00-712756-1

Typeset in PostScript Linotype Galliard by
Rowland Phototypesetting Ltd,
Bury St Edmunds, Suffolk

Printed and bound in Great Britain by
Clays Ltd, St Ives plc

For Sue, again.

Contents

Preface to the Second Edition

A new edition of a book written over twenty years ago offers various opportunities. One is the chance to correct errors that marred the earlier version. I have accordingly corrected a number of such errors and am grateful to those who brought some of them to my attention (in particular to Eamon Cantwell who directed me to a dissertation which convincingly identified the editor of the *Catholic Bulletin* in the 1920s).

Another opportunity that I have taken is to recast material so that where it read in 1981 and 1985, when earlier versions of this work appeared, as referring to recent events or to the present, it now refers clearly to the past. This has involved here and there some changes of emphases and, especially in Part III, the incorporation of some additional information. I should say however that this new edition is by no means presented as a re-written version of the book I originally published in 1981. In the preface to that volume I reflected on the difficulties of the task I had set myself then in composing a work of synthesis when so much primary research on twentieth-century Ireland remained to be done. Of course since that date, as I note in this edition, the field of Irish Studies has burgeoned and more works on the social and cultural history of the period have appeared. However, reading through my own work for the purposes of bringing it up to date in the sense that it now covers the period 1922–2002, I was sufficiently happy with the general thesis I had propounded in 1981 to allow it substantially to stand. Therefore what this book does now offer is a volume not in three parts but in four. Part IV deals with the period 1980 to 2002 (incorporating in chapter eleven some material which first saw the light of day in a postscript to the 1985 version of the text), where the first edition had 1979 as its date of termination. This section of the book is now quite lengthy, addressing as it does the quite remarkable events of the 1980s and 1990s when Ireland went from near bankruptcy to economic resurrection, when the "peace process" was inaugurated and the problem of Northern Ireland was confronted by the governments of Britain and Ireland with sustained determination. It was a period too when the Catholic church experienced crises of proportions that would have seemed unimaginable in earlier decades, as Irish society entered on a phase of profound self-questioning in an era of revelations and remembering. I trust this book will allow readers to consider developments of the last two decades of the twentieth century in the context of what had gone before and will take its place as a contribution to the ongoing debate about Ireland's present and future.

T.B.

Trinity College, Dublin, 1 March 2003

Preface

The main focus of this work is the intellectual and cultural history of Ireland since independence. It will quickly be evident, however, that I am also interested in establishing the main outlines of the social history of independent Ireland since the Treaty of 1921. I trust that my reasons for entertaining these dual ambitions will be clear from my text, but it may be as well to indicate them very briefly here.

It was necessary to establish an outline of modern Irish social history for this study since to fail to do so would be to suggest that high culture – intellectual endeavour and debate, the arts – has a life completely independent of the social reality in which it occurs of a kind which I do not believe it possesses. Ideologies, ideas, symbols, literary and cultural periodicals, even lyric poems are social facts, just as potato crops, tractors, and new industries are, and they can be fully understood only within the material world in which they come to life. So a recurrent preoccupation of this book in its first two parts is the analysis of how, for much of the period, certain ideas, images, and symbols provided Irish people with part of their sense of national identity. For this was a post-colonial society beset by manifold problems, but anxious nevertheless to achieve an independent and distinctive life. Part

III of this book looks at how these conceptions and aspirations fared in the new social order that has been in the making in the last twenty years, following the economic revival of the early 1960s. But what also concerns me throughout is how social and cultural change are involved with one another. So the modernization of the last two decades in Ireland is seen to be in part the result of social and cultural factors that had been in the making since about the period of the Second World War, when the framework that had held together since independence began to disintegrate.

It is this concern to measure change and account for it that determines the structure of the book. Part I explores in detail the social and the cultural life of the Irish Free State in its first decade. Despite some signs of change, there was a conservative continuum with pre-revolutionary Ireland, and minorities and critics in the new order had little chance to make their will felt. Part II considers both how and why that continuity was sustained well into the modern period, but detects social and cultural evidences of major change in embryo and analyzes the possible causes of these. Part III presents the social and cultural history of the last two decades in the Republic of Ireland as a period of striking change when set against the picture that Parts I and II have painted of the earlier years of independence.

In Ireland intellectual, cultural, and social history are each infant disciplines. The writer who aspires to provide a study synthesizing the three areas is faced therefore with many insurmountable difficulties, not the least that much basic research has simply not yet been attempted. As a result, this book is very much a provisional and speculative sketch, with few pretensions to completeness in most areas. It is of course the danger of such sketches, particularly of recent and contemporary history, that they become mere caricatures. But without such attempts to chart the field, more fundamental research may not proceed as it must do if more assured works are to result in the future. It is as a preliminary mapping of the territory that I hope this book may prove useful.

I am grateful to the work of those scholars and critics who

have, despite the perils, ventured into the turbulent seas of twentieth-century Irish historical research. My considerable indebtedness to them is clearly evident in my notes and references. Some of them are my colleagues in Trinity College, and I am happy to record here my gratitude to them too for their efforts to respond to my often naive inquiries in the last few years. I am also grateful to Miss Geraldine Mangan and Miss Dee Jones, who typed the manuscript at various stages of its production. To my wife, Suzanne, who arranged many things so that this work might be completed, my gratitude is expressed in the dedication.

T.B.

Trinity College, Dublin, 1977–80

PART I

1922–32

CHAPTER 1

After the Revolution: Conservatism and Continuity

Canonical texts of Irish separatist nationalism have often stressed the social and cultural advantages to be derived from Ireland's independence from the United Kingdom. A free Ireland would embark upon a radically adventurous programme to restore the ancient language, to discover the vitality residual in a nation devastated by a colonial power, and would flower with new social and cultural forms, testaments to the as yet unrecognized genius of the Gael. Patrick Pearse, a martyr to the separatist cause in the Rising of Easter 1916, had prophesied in a vibrant flight of not entirely unrealistic idealism:

A free Ireland would not, and could not, have hunger in her fertile vales and squalor in her cities. Ireland has resources to feed five times her population; a free Ireland would make those resources available. A free Ireland would drain the bogs, would harness the rivers, would plant the wastes, would nationalize the railways and waterways, would improve agriculture, would protect fisheries, would foster industries, would promote commerce, would diminish extravagant expenditure (as on needless judges and policemen), would beautify the cities, would educate the workers (and also the nonworkers, who stand in direr need of it), would, in short, govern herself as no external power –

nay, not even a government of angels and archangels could govern her.[1]

That the revolutionary possibilities of an independent Ireland as envisaged by Pearse were scarcely realized in Southern Ireland in the first decades of the Irish Free State, which came into being following the Treaty of 1921, should not perhaps surprise. The dissipation of revolutionary aspiration in post-revolutionary disillusionment is by now a commonplace of modern political history. That, however, a revolution fought on behalf of exhilarating ideals, ideals which had been crystallized in the heroic crucible of the Easter Rising, should have led to the establishment of an Irish state notable for a stultifying lack of social, cultural, and economic ambition is a matter which requires explanation. For the twenty-six counties of Southern Ireland which made up the Free State showed a prudent acquiescence before the inherited realities of the Irish social order and a conservative determination to shore up aspects of that order by repressive legislation where it seemed necessary.

One explanation presents itself readily. The stagnant economic conditions which the Free State had inherited made nation-building of the kind Pearse had envisaged most difficult to execute. The beautification of the cities and the education of the workers could not proceed without an economic miracle that faith might generate but works in the form of major investment and bold enterprise would have had to sustain. Neither faith nor works could easily flourish in the insecure economic environment of the Irish Free State in the 1920s, in the aftermath of a civil war.

By 1920 the boom years of the First World War, when agricultural prices had been high, had given way to an economic recession made the more severe by the turbulent years of revolution and fratricidal strife which followed, until a measure of stability was restored in 1923, when the Civil War, which had broken out after the departure of the imperial power, drew to its unresolved close. The first years of the Free State, brought into existence by the Constitution of the Irish Free State Act in 1922 and approved in October of that year, were dogged by intense economic difficulty. This fact may in part account for the timorous prudence of the economic policies adopted by the new Irish administration which emerged after the election of August 1923. From the outset the government was confronted by harsh realities of a kind that might have discouraged the most vigorous of nation-builders. A serious strike of port workers lasted for six months in 1923 (cattle exports dropped by 60 percent during the strike); there was poor weather in 1923 and 1924. The summers "were harsh, gloomy and sunless, while the autumn and winter months were characterized by continuously heavy rains which kept the soil sodden throughout and caused extreme discomfort to grazing cattle."[2] Indeed, not until 1925 was there a fine June to cheer the many farmers of agricultural Ireland.

The economy that the Free State government had inherited and for which it assumed responsibility in these inauspicious circumstances had several major inherent defects. It was stable to the point of stagnantion: a developed infrastructure of railways and canals was not matched by an equivalent industrialization; the economy supported too many unproductive people – the old and young and a considerable professional class; there were few native industries of any size and such as there were (brewing, bacon-curing, creameries, biscuit-making, and woollens and worsteds) were productive of primary commodities and unable to provide a base for an industrial revolution. The gravest problem, however, was the country's proximity to the United Kingdom with its advanced industrial economy, so that, as the historian Oliver MacDonagh has succinctly stated, "the Free State . . . was not so much . . . an undeveloped country, as . . . a pocket of undevelopment in an advanced region, such as the Maritime Provinces constitute in Canada as a whole or as Sicily does in Italy."[3]

Throughout the 1920s the government maintained a strict hold on the public purse, balancing the budget with an almost penitential zeal. Despite the protectionism that the Sinn Féin party had espoused in the previous decade as part of its economic plans for an independent Irish Republic, few tariffs were raised to interfere with free trade. The economic nationalism of the prerevolutionary period gave way to a staid conservatism that did little to alter the economic landscape. The government maintained agricultural prices at a low level to the detriment of industrial development. Accordingly, in the 1920s there were only very modest increases in the numbers of men engaged in productive industry, and the national income rose slowly. The need to restrict government spending meant that many social problems remained unsolved. The slum tenements in the city of Dublin are a telling example. Frequently adduced as a scandalous manifestation of British misrule in Ireland (they deeply disturbed that English patriot, the poet Gerard Manley Hopkins, when he worked as a professor of classics in Dublin in the 1880s) and also frequently investigated by official bodies, the tenements of Dublin might well have provided the opportunity for a piece of showpiece reconstruction to a newly independent nationalistic government. In fact, the opportunity so afforded was ignored. Conditions remained desperate. The 1926 census showed that in the Free State over 800,000 people were living in overcrowded conditions (overcrowding being more than two persons per room), many of them in north Dublin City. In the state in 1926 there were 22,915 families living in overcrowded conditions in one-room dwellings, 39,615 families living in two rooms, and, telling statistics indeed, 24,849 persons, living in 2,761 families with nine persons in each, resided in two-room dwellings. Infant mortality figures in Dublin, drawn from the census, tell their own sorry tale. In North Dublin City the average death rate per 1,000 children between one and five years was 25.6, while in the more salubrious suburb of Drumcondra the figure was 7.7 per 1,000 children. A contemporary observer remarked that "the story these tables tell is sordid and terrible, and calls for immediate and drastic action."[4] In fact, no real action was taken until 1932, when a bill designed by the Fianna Fáil Minister for Local Government was introduced envisaging a central role for the government in alleviating the situation. Perhaps poor housing was so endemic a problem in Dublin in the 1920s that it was difficult to imagine a solution.

Other kinds of enterprise were within the imaginative scope of the Free State government of the 1920s. These were to have a considerable effect on social life, particularly in rural areas. In the absence of significant private investment in necessary projects, the Cumann na nGaedheal (the ruling party) administration slipped paradoxically into a kind of state intervention that was quite foreign to its ideological cast of mind. Such enterprises as the Agricultural Credit Corporation and the Electricity Supply Board were the first of the many institutions which, established by successive governments and eventually known as the semi-state bodies, ventured where private capital would not. Indeed, the construction between 1925 and 1929 of a large power station on the river Shannon, under the direction and control of the Electricity Supply Board, was one of the very few undertakings in the first decade of independence which might be said to represent a fulfilment of earlier separatist ambition.

It would be wrong, however, to attribute the devastating lack of cultural and social innovation in the first decades of Irish independence simply to the economic conditions of the country. Certainly the fact that at independence there was no self-confident national bourgeoisie with control over substantial wealth, and little chance that such a social class might develop, meant that the kinds of experiment a revolution sometimes generates simply did not take place. But pre-revolutionary experience had shown that artistic, social, and cultural vitality did not necessarily require great economic resources, since in a society almost equally afflicted by economic difficulties cultural life had flowered and social innovation been embarked upon. Indeed it was to those years of cultural and social activity and to the political and military exploits that accompanied them that the new state owed its existence.

An explanation for this social and cultural conservatism of the new state is, I believe, to be sought in the social composition of Irish society. The Ireland of twenty-six countries which comprised the Free State after the settlement of 1921 was an altogether more homogeneous society than any state would have been had it encompassed the whole of the island of Ireland. The six Northern counties which had been separated by the partition of 1920 from the rest of the country contained the island's only large industrial centre where a large Presbyterian minority expressed its own distinctive unionist sense of an Irish identity. Episcopalian Anglo-Ireland, its social cohesion throughout the island fractured by partition, remained powerful only in the six counties of Northern Ireland. In the twenty-six counties the field lay open therefore for the Catholic nationalist majority to express its social and cultural will unimpeded by significant opposition from powerful minorities (in Chapter four of this section I discuss the fate of those who attempted opposition). When it is further recognized that much of the cultural flowering of earlier years had been the product of an invigorating clash between representatives of Anglo-Ireland (or those who thought of themselves as such) and an emergent nationalist Ireland at a time when it had seemed to sensitive and imaginative individuals that an independent future would require complex accommodations of Irish diversity,[5] it can be readily understood why the foundation of the Irish Free State saw a reduction in adventurous social and cultural experiment. The social homogeneity of the twenty-six counties no longer demanded such imaginatively comprehensive visions.

When finally it is understood that this homogeneous Irish society of the twenty-six-county state was predominantly rural in complexion and that Irish rural life was marked by a profound continuity with the social patterns and attitudes of the latter half of the nineteenth century, then it becomes even clearer why independent Ireland was dominated by an overwhelming social and cultural conservatism. As Oliver MacDonagh remarked, peasant proprietorship, outcome of the land agitation of the previous century "more than any other single force . . . was responsible for the immobility of Ireland – politics apart – in the opening decades of the . . . century."[6] The revolution that dispatched the colonial power from the South of Ireland in 1922 had left the social order in the territory ceded to the new administration substantially intact. It was a social order largely composed of persons disinclined to contemplate any change other than the political change which independence represented.

The twenty-six counties of independent Ireland were indeed strikingly rural in the 1920s. In 1926, as the census recorded, 61 percent of the population lived outside towns or villages. In 1926 53 percent of the state's recorded gainfully employed population were engaged in one way or another in agriculture (51,840 as employers, 217,433 on their own account, 263,738 as relatives assisting, 113,284 as employees, with 13,570 agricultural labourers unemployed). Only one-fifth of the farmers were employers of labour. A majority were farmers farming their land (which had mostly passed into their possession as a result of various land acts which had followed the Land War of the 1880s) on their own account or with the help of relatives. Roughly one-quarter of the persons engaged in agriculture depended for their livelihoods on farms of 1–15 acres, a further quarter on farms of 15–30 acres, with the rest occupied on farms of over 30 acres. Some 301,084 people were employed in various ways on farms of less than 30 acres; 121,820 on farms of 30–50 acres; 117,255 on farms of 50–100 acres; 61,155 on farms of 100–200 acres; and only 34,298 on farms of 200 acres and over. As can readily be seen from these figures, small and medium-sized farms were the predominant feature of Irish agriculture.

In this rural world, at least since the Famine years of the 1840s, two phenomena had been observable as aspects of the social organization of the countryside – a high average age of marriage accompanied by an extraordinary degree of apparent premarital chastity and the massive haemorrhage of emigration. Some simple statistics highlight these. The 1926 census revealed that in Ireland there was a larger proportion of unmarried persons of all ages than in any other country in which records were kept. In 1926 80 percent of all males between the ages of twenty-five and thirty years were unmarried, with 62 percent of males between thirty and thirty-five years, 50 percent of males between thirty-five and forty, and 26 percent of males between fifty-five and sixty-five also unmarried. The figures for women, while not quite so amazing, were also very high. In the age group 25–30 years 62 percent, 30–35 years 42 percent, 35–40 years 32 percent, and 55–65 years 24 percent were unmarried. These figures reflect a pattern of rural practice (the highest figures relate to rural districts) which had obtained, it seems, since the Famine. It was the 1840s, too, which saw the beginning of the modern Irish diaspora with its perennial emigration, which by the early 1920s meant that 43 percent of Irish-born men and women were living abroad:

1,037,234	in the United States
367,747	in England and Wales
159,020	in Scotland
105,033	in Australia
93,301	in Canada
34,419	in New Zealand
12,289	in South Africa
8,414	in India.

This figure of 43 percent compared remarkably with other European countries with traditions of emigration – Norway with 14.8 percent, Scotland with 14.1 percent, and Sweden with 11.2 percent (in 1921) – and most strikingly with most other European countries, where about 4 percent of their populations were overseas. The continuous Irish diaspora, under way since the Famine, kept the population of the country as a whole almost stable throughout most of the modern period.

Various reasons have been suggested for the strange marital abstemiousness of the Irish countryman and woman in the period. It has been argued, for example, that the influence of a French Jansenist professorship at the major Irish seminary, St. Patrick's College, Maynooth, had an unduly puritanical influence on the Irish priesthood and people in the decades following the French Revolution and that this abstemiousness was somehow attractive to a Celtic people whose religious tradition had included masochistic excesses of penitential zeal and whose mythology and imaginative literature had combined male solidarity with heroic idealism.[7]

Rather than attributing the patterns of rural life in Ireland (marital abstemiousness and emigration) to some innate perversity of the Celtic personality, one is much more impressed with the arguments of the social historians who have shown that these patterns have their origin mainly in the economic and social realities of Irish farming life in the post-Famine period. The argument is as follows. The Famine, in which the Irish rural population, particularly in the congested districts of the west of Ireland, suffered terribly, confronted the small farmer with the abject insecurity of his position and the economic folly of the mode of life tradition had bequeathed him. He did not own the land he worked, and he was likely to be asked to subdivide it to accommodate the domestic and social ambitions of his sons as they sought the early marriages common in the two or three generations following 1780, when, as K. H. Connell reports, "peasant children, by and large, married whom they pleased when they pleased."[8] In the years following the Famine Irish rural life was characterized not by the agreeable carelessness of earlier decades in matters of land and marriage, but by a calculating sensitivity to the economic meaning of marriage and in due course during the Land War in the 1880s by a political will to achieve individual economic security.

Rather than exhibiting that disinclination to bow to the "despotism of fact" that Matthew Arnold had promoted in his *On the Study of Celtic Literature* in 1867 as a distinguishing feature of the Celtic imagination, the Irish tenant farmer displayed in the post-Famine period an almost Darwinian capacity to adapt in the interests of survival and an attention to the despotism of fact that would have gratified Jeremy Bentham or Mr. Gradgrind. Fathers held on to their land as long as was possible, eventually supported agitation for land reform, which in due course came, chose which one of their sons would inherit the farm, discouraged the early marriages of their children, determined that the holdings would remain intact without subdivision, and faced the prospect that most of their offspring would be forced to emigrate, if not with equanimity then with a resigned consciousness that no other course was possible.

Irish rural life was like a raft afloat in the calm after a great storm. The Famine had betrayed so many that the survivor, conscious of the frailty of his craft and of the likelihood of future buffetings, calculated its precise seaworthiness and supported a social order that allowed no significant role in the countryside for those sons and daughters who could neither inherit the land nor make an appropriate marriage. For them emigration was the only possible route to a life without the frustrations and indignities of their position as helpers about the farm they neither owned, nor, accidents apart, would ever own.[9] So, in the first two decades of independence, emigration was much less a reflection of demoralization in the countryside than a measure of continuity in Irish life and an indication of how powerfully the values that had taken hold in the second half of the nineteenth century still held sway.

Some historians have doubted the apocalyptic simplicity of this thesis, suggesting that the Famine rather confirmed and extended to the smaller farmers a way of life that had already established itself in the economy of the wealthier or strong farmers of pre-Famine Ireland.[10] Be that as it may, even as late as the 1930s two American anthropologists, C. M. Arensberg and S. T. Kimball, found in County Clare a society and mode of life that preserved substantially intact the values and assumptions, the social and cultural forms that can most readily be accounted for in terms of an economic necessity made all the more stringent by the appalling depredations of the Famine. In the 1930s the prudent social values, reflected in postponed marriage and emigration, that had characterized the world of some larger, wealthier farmers even before the Famine, seemed dominant in smaller and larger farms alike.

County Clare, a remote county that had suffered much in the famines of the 1840s, may seem altogether too unrepresentative an Irish county to bear the weight of such a generalization, but in fact much of the farming life of the country in the early years of independence was similar to that found in Clare in the 1930s. Only in the cattle trade based on farming in Leinster in the east of the country and in dairying in central Munster to the south was agricultural activity highly commercialized. Throughout much of the rest of the country subsistence and mixed agriculture of the kind found in Clare, where farmers farmed on their own behalf with the help of relatives, was predominant.

Nor was it that the anthropologists in Clare had come upon a region which, having escaped by reason of its isolation the tides of modernization, exhibited traditional social patterns in extreme form. Rather the society they encountered there was obviously touched by modernizing forces – it was literate, open to mass communications, served by roads and railway, involved, often to an intense degree, in the democratic process, with a history of revolutionary political activity[11] – suggesting the degree to which the values and assumptions of the Irish countryside could be sustained despite a good deal of social and political change. It is therefore reasonable to believe that the life of most farmers in Ireland working their land with family help bore a close if not complete resemblance to what Arensberg and Kimball found in County Clare, even in districts closer to the cities, the centres of modernizing influence. That such literary records of Irish rural life in the twentieth century as we possess from different parts of the country bear out this belief is further confirmatory evidence. Patrick Kavanagh's autobiographical works, *The Green Fool* (1938), for example, and that searing indictment of the sexual frustration of the Irish countryman *The Great Hunger* (1942), set in County Monaghan in the east of the country, display striking resemblances in the ways of life they record to the picture the anthropologists paint of life in the distant west.

Arensberg and Kimball employed the term "familism" to describe the social structure they observed in the Irish countryside in the 1930s. They employed this term to characterise the mode of life of mostly small farmers engaged in raising cattle, sheep, and pigs, whose wives were responsible, in a strict division of labour, for the domestic economy of the house, for the poultry, milking, and dairying. The father was the dominant figure in the family, making all economic decisions, not even allowing his fully grown sons to handle money when produce was to be sold at the local fair in the town. A male child was exclusively looked after by his mother until his first communion was taken in the church at seven years of age. Then he came under the charge of his father and was in the company of his older brothers during that extraordinary "boyhood" which might well last until his fortieth or fiftieth year if he was the favoured heir and had not been forced into emigration or a job in the town.

Daughters of the household learned the ways of farm domesticity from their mothers until the time came for them to receive offers of marriage or to seek a life elsewhere. Marriage was a complicated process in which a matchmaker played a part in the subtle economic valuations that were necessary before the favoured son who would inherit the farm could be allowed to introduce a new bride to the household. Sometimes the introduction of the new woman to the household was effected at the moment when it was possible for the farmer to hand over the main responsibility for the farm to his heir (the old age pension allowed for this possibility when the farmer turned seventy), and when this occurred it was perhaps easier to avoid the tensions which must often have developed between mother and daughter-in-law. The centre of the house was the kitchen, and when the old couple "retired", they ceased sleeping in that room and moved to a small room at the west of the house, where the family heirlooms, pictures, and religious symbols were displayed. As the anthropologists report, "They move in among the symbols of family unity, among the religious symbols of the house, into surroundings of a certain religious or sacred character."[12] Their hierarchical position was maintained. The father could still occupy the nearest chair to the fire with the older men when they came to visit, and the old couple achieved an almost patriarchal status as the grandchildren were born. The society was strictly hierarchical, and the family unit was its fundamental organizing principle.

Co-operation in farming work between different farmers did exist in a system known as "cooring," but this was not a sign of any collectivist impulse. Rather, it was a deeply felt system of obligation in the exchange of services and implements between individual households. The only interruption to this strictly famil- ist social system was the help proffered to individuals who could not be expected to reciprocate in any way. A widow, for example, trying to keep her farm together with the help of hired hands, could expect a local family to help her out at harvest time, but again the impulse was not at all collectivist, but, in such instances, charitable. In Arensberg and Kimball's succinct summary, 'Econ- omic endeavour, both upon the individual farms and in the form of co-operation between farms, is controlled through the operation of social forces springing from the family.'[13]

The sons and daughters who could find no significant role in this system had a limited number of choices open to them. They might seek jobs in a nearby town, they might aspire to join one of the professions, or they might emigrate. An option firmly closed to them was the choice of finding a fulfiling role at home, for by the 1920s it was increasingly unlikely that they could final rural occupations that would allow them to stay in the district of their birth. Many of the rural trades and crafts that had flourished in nineteenth-century Ireland had declined in the face of compe- tition from mass-produced goods, and the craftsmen and women of the countryside instead of being absorbed, as such people were in other European countries, by an industrial revolution in which their technical abilities were useful, had been forced into emi- gration. So even if the sons and daughters of farmers had been willing to accept the loss of social status entailed in following a rural trade, the opportunities to do so were rapidly diminishing and a future as a craftsman or craftswoman would have seemed as bleak as that of an unmarried son or daughter about the farm.

A job in the town usually meant the grocery trade to which a young man became indentured as an assistant until such time as he was able to set up business on his own account, often upon marriage to a farmer's daughter. The farmer helped with the initial capital required in the form of a dowry. Daughters were also so indentured and might have hoped in time to make a sound marriage within the trade. As exact an awareness of economic responsibilities attended the marital arrangements in the world of provisions and weighing scales as it did in the world of acreage and cattle. The values and familist social structures of the farm world were transferred to the shop and town, thereby ensuring that the cultural and political influence of the small and strong farmers in the country was augmented by that of the grocers and small traders of the town.

For those sons and daughters of farmers who chose to enter one of the professions through attendance at a seminary, at a college of the National University, or at a teachers' training college, the chances were slim that they could make their lives in their native parishes or indeed that they could even pursue their careers in a rural setting. By the 1920s only a few opportunities remained for a rural professional life in the priesthood and in the legal, medical, and teaching professions. If a boy or a girl wished to avoid emigration, a move to an Irish town or city was almost imperative where, in the trades, professions, and state service, they bore with them the values so indelibly etched upon their personalities by a rural Irish childhood.

The combined force of these two social groups in modern Ireland, the farmers and the tradesmen, together with such of their offspring as could find roles in the professions, was enormously influential in fashioning the political, social, and cultural moulds of the independent state. Their economic prudence, their necessarily puritanical, repressive sexual mores and nationalistic conservatism, encouraged by a priesthood and hierarchy drawn considerably from their number, largely determined the kind of country which emerged in the first decades of independence.

The role of the Irish Catholic church in directing Irish life into the narrow channels of a Jansenistic puritanism has, as was mentioned, been proffered by commentators as one explanation for the fact that so many people for so long in Ireland were able to behave as if those troublesome but exhilarating manifestations of human nature, passion, sexual aspiration, and the erotic principle itself, had been quite excised from the Irish experience. While social historians have been able to provide alternative, rather more credible accounts of a process whereby a society of farmers and shopkeepers developed, resolutely determined to restrain sexuality in the interests of economic realism, the contribution of the church as the institution which aided the process must also be assessed.

A study of the main developments within Irish Catholicism in the late nineteenth and early twentieth centuries is a prerequisite for any informed understanding of the social and cultural history of modern Ireland. The great nineteenth-century struggles in the Irish church between the centralizing, apparently ultramontanist party led by that organizational genius, the first Irish Cardinal, Paul Cullen, and older, local, more independent forms of Catholicism had been resolved in favour of a church loyal to Rome. Concurrent with this political conflict within the nineteenth-century Irish Catholic church had occurred a remarkable devotional revolution whereby continental expressions of piety were introduced to an Ireland which adopted them with an astonishing enthusiasm, so that the texture of modern Irish religious life owes much to the period 1850–75 when that revolution was in large part effected. It was in those twenty-five years that the great mass of Irishmen and women were confirmed in loyalty to the modern Roman church and were provided with the symbols and institutions which might maintain and express that loyalty, which was a source of wonder to many a commentator on modern Irish affairs. The celebration of the mass was regularized (in pre-Famine Ireland the shortage of churches had led to a practice known as "stations", whereby the priest celebrated mass in various houses in his parish), and new devotions were introduced – the rosary, forty hours, perpetual adoration, novenas, blessed altars, *Via Crucis*, benediction, vespers, devotion to the Sacred Heart and to the Immaculate Conception, jubilees, triduums, pilgrimages, shrines, processions, and retreats. It was the period when popular piety began to express itself in beads, scapulars, religious medals, and holy pictures, and open religious feeling, as one historian has commented, was "organized in order to communalize and regularize practice under a spiritual director."[14] This organization included societies, confraternities, and sodalities. A programme of church-building was undertaken (in 1865 there were 1,842 churches, in 1906 2,417),[15] and sound investments were made in land and property so that by the beginning of our period, reflecting on the piety of the people and on the rich inheritance of buildings and investment bequeathed by the nineteenth-century church, it should have been possible for the Irish hierarchy to feel serenely confident about its position in Irish life.

The hierarchy in the first few years of the Irish Free State, despite the inheritance of the nineteenth century, was nevertheless rather pessimistic about the future. The troubled years from 1912 to 1923 had often placed the hierarchy in very difficult political positions. During the Civil War the bishops had antagonized the republicans through their support of the Free State government, and they were disturbed by what they thought were signs of an unravelling moral fabric in a society which had experienced revolution and warfare and which was riskily open to the influence of rapidly developing mass media. Their concern was premature, however, for the great majority of the faithful were to remain loyal to the church practice of the devotional revolution until the late 1960s. Neither the political stance of the hierarchy during the Civil War nor the influence of an increasingly libertarian climate outside Ireland disturbed the religious devotion of Ireland's Catholic believers. That it was maintained well into the modern period is attributable not only to the power of the church's apologetic but also to the ways in which Irish Catholicism was precisely adapted to Irish social reality in the period.

Crucial to the institutional and popular achievements of the church in the period following the Famine until the 1960s was the role played by Catholicism in confirming a sense of national identity. The church, with her formally regularized rites and practices, offered to most Irishmen and women in the period a way to be Irish which set them apart from the rest of the inhabitants of the British Isles, meeting the needs thereby of a nascent Irish nationalism at a time when the Irish language and the Gaelic culture of the past were enduring a protracted decline. And the Catholic faith was peculiarly suited to play a role in that nationalist awakening. Bound up in the past with the traditional Gaelic way of life to which the Famine had largely put paid, historically associated with the repression of the eighteenth century, when the native priesthood had heroically resisted the proscription of their faith, permeated with that profound sense of the supernatural which had characterized the countryside for centuries, Catholicism was richly endowed with attributes appropriate to its modern role in the nation's life. Strengthened by the Roman vigour of the devotional revolution, given a distinct tincture of Victorian respectability by the new discipline imposed on popular expressions of piety, the Catholic faith of the majority of the Irish people became therefore intimately linked with national feeling. Accordingly, from the years of the devotional revolution onward Irish Catholicism increasingly became a badge of national identity at a time when the church also felt able to propound doctrines that enshrined the rights of private property. In a nation where nationalist aspiration was so often rooted in the farmer's rigorous attachment to his land, all this was to help ensure the church's continued role in Irish life, even though at difficult moments during the Land War and the War of Independence ecclesiastics felt obliged to oppose the tactics employed by political activists.

It is true, one must point out, that nationalist ideologues, at least from the time of the Young Irelanders of the 1840s, always strove to define Irishness in more comprehensive terms than the merely religious, seeking national distinctiveness in language and culture. But despite brief periods when enthuasiasm for Gaelic revival showed some signs of translating itself into a major social force, transcending sectarian divisions (in the first decade of the twentieth century), Irish nationalists sometimes found themselves acutely embarrassed by the lack of immediately obvious marks of Irish identity apart from a devout, loyal Catholicism. Indeed, some of the strenuous efforts made on behalf of the Irish language were perhaps partially rooted in such embarrassment.

By contrast, few efforts were required for most of the twentieth century to develop Catholicism as a mark of national distinctiveness; the church was incontrovertibly part of Irish reality and the practice of religion an evident feature of national life. In 1926, 92.6 percent of the population of the Irish Free State were returned as Catholic in the census. From all the impressionistic evidence available, we can assume that the great majority of their number were regular in their duties and obligations. Sir Horace Plunkett must be representative of the many writers who have looked on Irish piety in the twentieth century and wondered. "In no other country probably," he wrote in 1904, "is religion so dominant an element in the daily life of the people as in Ireland."[16]

The Irish church was also successful because in spite of its ultramontanist tendencies, it was a national church in the sense that it drew its bishops from its priesthood and its priesthood in the main from the people. It therefore offered opportunities in the late nineteenth and twentieth centuries for preferment and power in a society that had hitherto had little chance to avail itself of the one or to exercise the other.

This statement requires some expansion. Almost all observers of religious life in the latter half of nineteenth-century Ireland are agreed that during this period, significant numbers of the sons of farmers and shopkeepers were entering the national seminary at Maynooth, County Kildare, to study for the priesthood, as they were in other ecclesiastical colleges in the country. Furthermore, literary and journalistic sources suggest that the social tone of Maynooth in this period and in the early twentieth century was somewhat boisterous and uncultivated, dominated as it was by young men from the land, and that the education provided was rather less than culturally enlarging in its anti-intellectualism and sexual prudery, confirming the rural values in which so many young men had been reared. It seems many a farmer's son emulated William Carleton's hero Denis O'Shaughnessy, taking the

road to Maynooth with more success than he. Gerald O'Donovan's interesting novel *Father Ralph* allows us a glimpse of
Maynooth in the 1890s (it is important to remember that priests
trained in this period would have exercised their ministry well
into the 1930s). The novel, largely autobiographical, recounts
the progress of a young boy of a wealthy Catholic family (they
have houses in Dublin and in the country) from days of cloistered
piety as a child to the tough practicalities of priesthood in a
depressed Irish village. Ralph O'Brien at Maynooth discovers the
intellectual poverty of the theological education offered in the
1890s.

> During the few free days before the arrival of the general body of
> students Ralph . . . explored the College: the poky, ill-supplied
> divisional libraries, without catalogue, order, or classification,
> or any book that one wanted to read; the rather fine College
> library, not quite as despicable as the admirer of Marie Corelli
> found it, but still pitifully unrepresentative of any general
> culture.[17]

Ralph finds theological speculation of any kind dismissed by
professors and students alike, all religious mystery apparently
comprehended in a facile scholasticism. The best among them
have a simple uninquiring faith, while the worst employ orthodoxy as a means of personal advancement in the church. For the
religious thinker there is nothing:

> After a lecture in dogmatic theology by Father Malone, who
> demolished all the thinkers of four centuries with an axiom
> culled from Aquinas, delivered in a loud self-satisfied voice and
> accompanied by much table-thumping, Ralph often sat in his
> room, limp and confused, hopeless of his own future and of
> the future of the Church. . . .
>   Ralph once ventured an opinion contradictory of Dunlea's
> notes. The Professor flushed angrily, but said suavely – "What
> is good enough for St Thomas and me ought to satisfy you Mr
> O'Brien. I'd advise you to read my notes carefully. They contain
> everything necessary to be known on the subject."
>   That evening during study Ralph read these meagre notes,

the fine flower of Maynooth teaching, a superficial application of a knowledge theory to religion that carried no conviction. If this book was the best Maynooth could do, why had he wasted the best years of his life there? It reduced God to a series of abstractions, unreal and meaningless.[18]

The upper-class Ralph O'Brien also finds himself socially ill at ease in a church that appears to be dominated by the acquisitive prudery of farmer and shopkeeper. Both *Father Ralph* and a later O'Donovan novel, *Vocations* (1921), describe a social order in which church, farmer, grocer, and gombeen publican comprise a corrupt and corrupting alliance, intent on social advancement.

O'Donovan, a supporter of the Irish cooperative movement founded by Sir Horace Plunkett, and keenly interested in rural renewal, presents the church as an institution dedicated neither to spirituality nor the intellectual enhancement of the faith, but to material and social advantage. Other much less tendentious commentators suggest that his portrait of Maynooth as intellectually deficient and the church as lacking a constructive social vision was not wholly unfounded. Canon Sheehan, the priestly novelist and a really sympathetic observer of Irish ecclesiastical life, remembered in an unfinished manuscript his own days at Maynooth in the 1870s, where he was distressed by a prevailing careerism evident in such current phrases as "respectable position in the Church," "high and well-merited dignities," "right of promotion," "getting a better parish," "a poor living," concluding:

Only too soon will the young Levite learn to despise the self-effacement, the shy and retiring sensitiveness, the gentleness and humility that are such bright and beautiful ornaments of a real priestly character: and only too soon will he set his heart upon those vulgar and artificial preferments which the world prizes, but God and His angels loathe and laugh at.[19]

It was his judgment too that

. . . the general verdict on our Irish Ecclesiastical Colleges is that they impart learning but not culture – that they send out learned men, but men devoid of the graces, the "sweetness and light" of modern civilization.[20]

Considering their future careers, Sheehan could remark, "It may be questioned whether, in view of their mission and calling, this is not for the best," but in 1897 he was moved to call for a Christian cultural revival in Ireland led by a well-educated priesthood, writing in terms that suggest the enormous changes such a revival would require:

> Some of us, not altogether dreamers and idealists, believe it quite possible to make the Irish race as cultured, refined, and purified by the influence of Christian teachings as she was in the days of Aidan and Columba. . . .
> But to carry out this destiny, Ireland needs above all the services of a priesthood, learned, zealous, and disciplined into the solidarity of aim and principle, which alone can make it formidable and successful.[21]

Sheehan admired the unshakable piety of the Irish poor in a way that O'Donovan could not easily do. He valued "the gentle courtesy, the patience under trial, the faces transfigured by suffering – these characteristics of our Celtic and Catholic peasantry," and he felt himself keenly alive to "the self-sacrifice, the devotion to duty, the fidelity to their flocks, which have always characterized the Irish priest."[22] Nevertheless, his comments on the social ambition of the clergy and their lack of humane culture tend to confirm rather than contradict O'Donovan's much more astringent analysis.

A church without intellectual or cultural ambitions of any remarkable kind was unlikely to attract to its service the most creative and imaginative members of society. Rather, it offered career opportunities to many who might have found intellectual or cultural demands upon them even more difficult to meet than the obedience, discipline, and administrative ability that were required of them by a powerfully authoritative church. Accordingly, in the first decades of the Irish Free State the church was unhappily notable in the main for lack of interest in artistic and cultural activity. The early years of the Catholic Revival in the later nineteenth century had, it is true, stimulated a good deal of architectural enthusiasm in the church, as many churches were built, some in the Hiberno-Romanesque style at the one time expressing the general medievalism of late Victorian culture and, more strikingly, attempting to establish a continuity with pre-Conquest Ireland which gratified nationalist sensibilities, but by the 1920s this style had become rather hackneyed and most church architecture and art (with the exception of some stained glass) were undistinguished. An exhibition of Irish ecclesiastical art during Dublin Civic Week in 1929 drew from George Russell's paper, the *Irish Statesman*, the regretful conclusion that "none of the Churches has thought it important to give their clergy an education in good taste as well as in dogmas," and, that where some "natural good taste or love of the arts" does exist in the churches, "that appreciation is individual. It owes nothing to a traditional policy of the Churches."

> One comes away with the feeling that quality is of no importance, beauty is of no importance, anything is good enough for God and for his worshippers. We have bright brass vulgarities, a gaudy lustre seeming to be the only thing required, not exquisite craftsmanship, but commercialized work turned out with no more reverence than one would turn out boots or shoes.[23]

Lest it be thought such a melancholy estimate of Irish ecclesiastical art was solely a response of the theosophist George Russell, it can be noted that a correspondent of the *Irish Independent* in 1932, casting about for examples of modern Irish churches which, because of their undoubted beauty and use of Irish art might reflect glory on the Irish church in the year of the Eucharistic Congress in Dublin, could think of only two, the Honan Hostel Chapel in Cork (1916) and Loughrea Cathedral (1904).

If then the Irishman was faithful to his church because it secured for him a sense of national identity, gave spiritual sanction to his hold on the land, and provided for his sons and daughters respected positions in society without the need for developed intellectual or cultural endowments, it is important to recognize that there was a further altogether more remarkable element in the attachment, which accounts for an important strand in modern Irish cultural history. For many Irish men and women the church was an international institution which allowed their small country a significant role on a world stage. This sense of belonging to a worldwide religious community was curiously linked to the internationalism of Irish nationalist feeling in the early twentieth century. For the phrase "the Irish race" that resounds through many nationalist utterances in the first two decades of the century was understood to refer not only to the inhabitants of the island but to the "nation beyond the seas," "the Greater Ireland," that vast number of Irish Catholic men and women scattered abroad (in the United States alone in 1920 there resided over four million people who could claim at least one Irish-born parent) who comprised an Irish diaspora. Indeed, it may not be unjust to see in both Irish nationalism and Catholicism of the period an effort to provide a counterweight to the international vision of British imperialism. If Britain had its material empire, the Irish could assert their dignity in terms of a patriotism and a Catholic spirituality which both transcended the island itself. Nationalist and Catholic propaganda of the period often echoes the rhetoric and tones of Victorian and Edwardian imperial celebration, and the Ireland that escaped the most cataclysmic effects of the First World War on the Victorian and Edwardian frames of mind continued to think in this oddly imperial manner until well into the 1930s. In this mode of thought, Ireland as a Catholic nation has a peculiar destiny in human affairs.

A writer in 1937, for example, reminiscing on St. Patrick's College, Maynooth, managed a rhetoric which suggests the return of a Victorian British imperial official to his public school, seeing on the playing fields of Eton or in Rugby Chapel the destiny of nations:

In this place of memories one is apt for many fancies. To see the oak stalls in the College Chapel, darkening a little with the

years, is to think of all who have been students there before my
time and since. With no effort I can slip from the moorings of
Past and Present, and see in this moment all rolled in one. The
slowly moving line of priests down through the College Chapel
is never-ending; it goes into the four provinces of Ireland; it
crosses the seas into neighbouring England and Scotland, and
the greater seas into the Americas and Australia and Africa and
China; it covers the whole earth; it goes wherever man has
gone, into the remotest regions of the world; it is unbroken, it
is ever renewing itself at the High Altar in Maynooth. . . . Some
there were who prayed for a place in that endless line. They
had counted the weeks and the days, even to an ordination day
that never dawned for them. "Each in his narrow cell for ever
laid", they are the tenants of the plot, sheltered by yew trees,
beyond the noises of the Park. A double row of little marble
headstones, a double row of graves all facing one way; they lie
like soldiers taking their rest.[24]

That such feeling, in a book that another writer, celebrating the
hundred and fiftieth year of the college, called "a sort of second
breviary . . . the Maynooth classic,"[25] represented a significant
element in the imaginative life of the early decades of independence is evidenced by the fact that Eamon de Valera, on 6 February 1933, shortly after his accession to executive power, chose to
open a new high-power broadcasting station at Athlone with a
speech to the nation which made special reference to Ireland's
historic Christian destiny. He was responding in the speech to
the accusation that modern Irish nationalism was insular and
intolerant. He began with an evocation of the glories of Ireland's
Christian past. The new broadcasting station would, he informed
his listeners, who in fact included many dignitaries in Rome,

. . . enable the world to hear the voice of one of the oldest, and
in many respects, one of the greatest of the nations. Ireland has
much to seek from the rest of the world, and much to give
back in return. Her gifts are the fruit of special qualities of mind
and heart, developed by centuries of eventful history. Alone

among the countries of Western Europe, Ireland never came under the sway of Imperial Rome. . . .

Because she was independent of the Empire, Ireland escaped the anarchy that followed its fall. Because she was Christian, she was able to take the lead in christianizing and civilizing the barbarian hordes that had overrun Britain and the West of Europe. This lead she retained until the task was accomplished and Europe had entered into the glory of the Middle Ages.[26]

An opportunity now existed, declared de Valera, for Ireland to repeat her earlier triumph:

During most of this great missionary period, Ireland was harassed by Norse invaders. Heathens and barbarians themselves, they attacked the centres of Christianity and culture, and succeeded in great measure in disorganizing both. That Ireland in such circumstances continued the work of the apostolate in Europe is an eloquent proof of the zeal of her people, a zeal gloriously manifested once more in modern times in North America and Australia and in the mission fields of Africa and China.[27]

The broadcast concluded with a call to Ireland to undertake the new mission "of helping to save Western Civilization" from the scourge of materialism:

In this day, if Ireland is faithful to her mission – and please God she will be, if as of old she recalls men to forgotten truths, if she places before them the ideals of justice, of order, of freedom rightly used, of Christian brotherhood – then indeed she can do the world a service as great as that which she rendered in the time of Columcille and Columbanus, because the need of our time is no whit less.

You sometimes hear Ireland charged with a narrow and intolerant nationalism, but Ireland today has no dearer hope than this: that, true to her holiest traditions, she should humbly serve the truth, and help by truth to save the world.[28]

Undoubtedly this idealistic vision of the Irishman's burden helped to reconcile many a young man to the sacrifices of priesthood as he contemplated the depressing secular opportunities of independent Ireland. Indeed, since the 1920s Ireland has sent numerous missionaries abroad to serve the church not only in the English-speaking world, but in Africa, Asia, and South America. By 1965 there were to be ninety-two mission-sending bodies in Ireland,[29] and by 1970 the Irish church maintained "6,000 missionaries – 4,000 of them in full-time socio-economic occupation – in twenty-five African, twenty-six Asian and twenty-six Latin-American countries – evidence of a primitive energy or expansive potential in the religious life of a people."[30]

A clear demonstration of the internationalism of Irish Catholic life was provided by the remarkable enthusiasm generated in Ireland by the Eucharistic Congress of 1932. Dublin had experienced a great demonstration of popular piety in 1929, when the centenary of Catholic Emancipation had brought half a million people to a mass celebrated in the Phoenix Park, but the month of June 1932 saw an even more extraordinary manifestation of Irish Catholic feeling in Dublin. Crowds gathered in such numbers that it is tempting to see in the occasion itself a triumphant demonstration by the Irish Catholic nation in honour of the victories won in the long years of struggle since emancipation which had reached a climax in independence. Special buildings were erected to accommodate the great influx of pilgrims; 127 special trains brought the pious to the city. For the entire week of the congress the *Irish Independent*, the most clerically minded of the national dailies, was in a state of very great excitement as it hailed the arrival of church dignitaries, including eleven cardinals from forty countries. The arrival of the papal legate, Cardinal Lauri, was headlined by the *Independent* as "The Greatest Welcome in Irish History." There were special candlelit masses held in the Phoenix Park, for men, for women, and for children. Four thousand people were received at a state reception in St. Patrick's Hall in Dublin Castle and twenty thousand people attended a garden party in the grounds of Blackrock College at the invitation of the Irish hierarchy. The week culminated with a mass in the Phoenix Park, where a crowd of over a million people heard

Count John McCormack sing Franck's *Panis Angelicus* and a papal message broadcast. For a moment Dublin must have seemed the centre of Christendom and Ireland truly a part of a worldwide community.

> Those million people came from the remotest districts in Kerry and from the mountain fastnesses of Donegal; from Canada and the United States, from the Argentine and other South American countries; from the Fiji islands, from Australia and New Zealand; from India; from Malta; and from all the countries of Europe.[31]

Writing in the *Round Table* a correspondent reported, "It was essentially an Irish celebration, a hosting of the Gael from every country under the sun."[32]

The church, therefore, provided for the needs of the Irish people in these particular ways. Occupying a role in Irish life that made it an integral part of that life, it enjoyed the unswerving loyalty of the great mass of the people. In the 1920s it used that authoritative position in Irish society to preach a sexual morality of severe restrictiveness, confirming the mores and attitudes of a nation of farmers and shopkeepers, denouncing all developments in society that might have threatened a rigid conformism in a strictly enforced sexual code.

The hierarchy was much distressed in the 1920s by the threats posed to what it sought to confirm as traditional Irish morality by the cinema, the English newspaper, and the cheap magazine, by the new dances that became fashionable in Ireland as elsewhere in the postwar period, by provocative female fashions, and even by the innocent company-keeping of the countryside at parties and ceilidhes. All occasions of sin were to be forsworn in the interests of an intensely regular life. A joint pastoral of the Irish hierarchy issued in 1927 expressed the Irish church's mind directly.

> These latter days have witnessed, among many other unpleasant sights, a loosening of the bonds of parental authority, a disregard for the discipline of the home, and a general impatience

under restraint that drives youth to neglect the sacred claims of authority and follow its own capricious ways. . . . The evil one is ever setting his snares for unwary feet. At the moment, his traps for the innocent are chiefly the dance hall, the bad book, the indecent paper, the motion picture, the immodest fashion in female dress – all of which tend to destroy the virtues characteristic of our race.[33]

Pearse's programme for an independent Ireland, with which we began, had envisaged an economic, social, and cultural flowering as a necessary effect of freedom. I have suggested that economic stagnation combined with social and religious conservatism in a highly homogeneous, essentially rural society to ensure that the first decades of independence in the Irish Free State could scarcely meet Pearse's ambitions for a free Ireland (though the Pearse who precipitated the Irish revolution by his courageous self-sacrifice in 1916 would, one suspects, have found both partition and the treaty entirely repugnant, acceptance of the Free State a betrayal of the separatist faith). Undoubtedly another force was at work – the influence exerted on the country by the terrible inheritance of the civil war which followed the Treaty of 1921. In a small country made disastrously smaller by a border that had set six of its counties adrift, memories of those tragic months and the bitterness they fed perverted much goodwill and idealism, soured many personal relationships, tore at the heart of aspiration. And it would be wrong too to ignore the fact, to which J. H. Whyte alerted us, that it might be wise to see Irish cultural and social conservatism reflected most obviously in the Censorship of Films Act of 1923, the Censorship of Publications Act of 1929, and the motion of 1925 making divorce legislation impossible as merely a more extreme form of a general phenomenon "among the more traditionally-minded people all over the world"[34] in the aftermath of the Great War. But the fact remains that Irish repressiveness, whatever its cause, was extreme in those first crucial decades and that it severely stunted the cultural and social development of a country which a protracted colonial mismanagement had left in desperate need of revival in both spheres.

By the 1920s the depressed state of cultural and social life in most of Ireland was a theme of some ancestry in the writing of social commentators. Sir William Wilde in 1853 in his *Irish Popular Superstitions* had lamented the decline of folk tradition in the wake of the Famine, sketching a grim picture of rural desolation:

The old forms and customs, too, are becoming obliterated; the festivals are unobserved, and the rustic festivities neglected or forgotten; the bowlings, the cakes and the prinkums (the peasants' balls and routs), do not often take place when starvation and pestilence stalk over a country, many parts of which appear as if a destroying army had but recently passed through it.[35]

Later, such writers as Sir Horace Plunkett in *Ireland in the New Century* (1904), W. P. Ryan in *The Pope's Green Island* (1912), and Filson Young in *Ireland at the Cross Roads* (1903) reflected on the dismal conditions of Irish civilization. By the 1920s the attractions of the dance hall and the craze for jazz that so disturbed the bishops had done much to put the remnants of Gaelic ways into the shadows. In the 1920s George Russell, the poet, visionary, and social activist, in his journal the *Irish Statesman* (of which we shall hear more) frequently expressed his profound depression at the spectacle of an Irish rural world without cultural hope or energy. Writing in 1924 he declared:

Nothing in Ireland so wakens in us the sense of stagnant or defeated life as to walk at night in a country district and to find here and there little knots of young men by a gate, seated on a wall, under the shelter of a tree, sometimes silent, sometimes engaged in desultory conversation, sometimes playing cards or pitch and toss. Life is in a backwater with them. Every now and then one drops out of these groups. He has gone to America. The sense of stagnation or depression becomes a little deeper with those who remain, and then another and another breaks away, flying from the stagnant life to where they believe life has fullness. The vast majority of those who go acquit themselves well in their new surroundings. They adjust themselves rapidly to American standards and become energetic and progressive citizens. Their stagnant life in rural Ireland was not due to any lethargy, mental or physical. They had no opportunity for vital expansion. Where, in the vast majority of cases, could they meet except in the lanes? There was no village hall, no library, no gymnasium, no village choir, no place to dance except the roadside.[36]

In his columns Russell and others lamented the lack of book-shops in the country and doubted "whether a single literary man in Ireland could make the income of an agricultural labourer by royalties on sales of his books among his own countrymen, however famous he may be abroad."[37] Sean O'Casey, for example, regretted the absolute gulf between Ireland's working class and the world of high culture, enquiring rather plaintively, "And why should the docker reading Anatole France or the carter reading Yeats be a laughter-provoking conception?"[38] Stephen Gwynn, the essayist, pondering whether an Irish writer had any sense of an audience, could reach no hopeful conclusion, opining sadly "men – and women – in Ireland read very little," and, "talk is their literature."[39]

One of the places in which that literature was produced was the public house, a meeting place Russell, the tee-totaler, appar-ently could not bring himself to mention in his evocation of the deprivations of rural life. In his omission he neglected one of the more notable aspects of the Irish scene. In 1925 the Irish government commissioned a report on various matters relating to alcohol in the state. Their report presented a picture likely to give pause to the most libertarian. In the commission's opinion there were 191 towns or villages where the number of public houses was excessive. Russell commented indignantly even as the commission was about its work:

It is merely absurd that a country struggling desperately to find its feet should attempt to maintain in proportion to its population, twice as many licensed houses as England and three times as many as Scotland. The statistics for individual towns are still more startling. In Charlestown and Ballaghadereen every third house is licensed to sell liquor; Ballyhaunis, with a total population of a thousand, has a drink shop for every twenty of its inhabitants, and Strokestown and Mohill run it close with one for every twenty-six. We wish Mr. Kevin O'Higgins had informed the Commission how many of these towns can boast a book-shop, a gymnasium, a public swimming-bath, or a village hall. Throughout the greater part of a rural Ireland such things are still looked on as ridiculous luxuries, and the mark of social progress is demonstrated by the opening of two public houses where one would normally suffice.[40]

Russell would have found it difficult, as an ascetic idealist, to see anything but stagnation and cultural deprivation in a country where the only social expressions of large numbers of the population appeared to be talk, drink, and sociability. He saw, too, in emigration primarily social disintegration, not the painful dedication of the family to the inherited plot. He was surely right, however, in detecting in the extraordinary dependence on alcohol in the country and in the perennial emigration, sure signs of social waste, of opportunities neglected, and possibility frustrated.

In 1925 an American journalist travelled throughout Ireland and in his volume of observations managed a greater optimism about the country's cultural future than Russell could achieve as the 1920s progressed. He wrote in hope, recognizing, however, that cultural life in Ireland depended much on isolated individuals:

At Enniscorthy it came to me very conclusively that scattered all about Ireland there is a small, highly-educated intellectual middle class which does not coincide with the moneyed people nor with the fox-hunting people at all – a class which, quietly living its own life and unobtrusively going its own way, is not often observed by the stranger. Nevertheless, it adds a very necessary leaven to the mind-life of Ireland, and it does not, as one of the ladies at the hotel said of herself "live to bloom unseen." For those good and excellent people scattered over the face of Ireland, whose habits of mind force them to a certain solitude, may accept as a rather enheartening certainty the thought that when they sit alone playing Wagner instead of bridge or reading Joseph Conrad instead of someone's palm, they are taking a place with honor in the community life of their country. There will be shy people at the gate to listen, and there will be those in the library to receive the book. Ireland will grow slowly into its new life . . . and there will be an increasing number of those who will look up eagerly toward better things.[41]

Some of what follows in this book reflects on the experience of such solitary people and on their work to generate cultural and intellectual revival. Their experience did not bear out the confidence of this prophecy. The repressiveness, conservatism, and deprivation of Irish life in general, like the country's economic poverty, did not, unhappily, admit of such inevitable amelioration.

CHAPTER 2

An Irish Ireland:
Language and Literature

Political life in the newly independent Irish Free State, even in the immediate aftermath of a revolution, reflected in obvious ways the essential conservatism of the predominantly rural Irish electorate. Law and order were rigorously maintained and the books carefully balanced. The party in power, composed in the main of elements of the Sinn Féin party that had accepted the Treaty of 1921, quickly won the support of those sections of the Irish community most likely to benefit from stability – the businessmen and merchants, the larger farmers and shopkeepers, the remnants of Anglo-Ireland anxious for security, and the kind of middle-class men and women who had earlier put their trust in respectable politicians of the Irish parliamentary party. The ruling Cumann na nGaedheal party had the support of the major national dailies, the *Irish Independent, Cork Examiner*, and *Irish Times* and of the churches. As the IRA and the republican diehards maintained an opposition that always threatened and occasionally generated violence, a general shift to the right was widely accepted by an Irish public that sought peaceful stability after a period of intense uncertainty. As one historian succinctly stated it, "Cumann na nGaedheal's basic attitude differed little from that of the British Conservative Party between 1895 and

1905: a well-governed Ireland would receive positive economic benefits from its association with Britain and quickly forget old passions and hatreds.''[1] The government emphasized the benefits in terms of national prestige to be derived from membership of the Commonwealth while pressing ahead with the diplomatic arrangements that helped define the possibilities in that dominion status which had constituted in Michael Collins' view a stepping-stone to freedom.

Perhaps it is less than just to regret the social and cultural pusillanimity of the Free State government in the 1920s, anxious as it was to provide a sound, conservative administration in perilous times. That the state managed to survive at all is in itself remarkable. A viciously fought civil war had left in its wake a recalcitrant minority implacably opposed to the elected government. At least until 1927 when Eamon de Valera, who had led the anti-Treaty faction into the Civil War, accepted the role of parliamentary opposition for the political party he had founded in 1926, Fianna Fáil (Warriors of Fál, or Ireland), the threat from the IRA to the new institutions of the state could by no means be discounted. After the assassination in 1927 of one of the government's most active young ministers, Kevin O'Higgins, it seemed necessary to pass an extreme Public Safety Act, as it did once again following republican violence and intimidation in 1931. Furthermore, the government was forced in 1925 to absorb that drastic shock to nationalist sensibility and aspiration, the leak of the *Boundary Commission Report* on the border between the Irish Free State and Northern Ireland. That report, if it had been accepted by the British government would, it appeared, have proved a crippling blow to nationalist hopes that the Northern semi-state established against the Irish majority's wishes in 1920, would be required to cede so much territory to the Irish Free State that it would become untenable. Rather, it transpired that the Free State itself might lose a portion of its territory to Northern Ireland, gaining little. In seeking to prevent the publication and acceptance of the report, the Free State government found itself a scarcely enthusiastic signatory in

London in December 1925 to a tripartite agreement accepting the territorial status quo, thereby providing much ammunition to those who saw the establishment of a thirty-two-county republic as the only legitimate if unrealizable Irish political ideal.

The resolve and courage (which extended in such difficult conditions to the creation of an unarmed police force to replace the old Royal Irish Constabulary) with which the Free State government managed the affairs of state, establishing and protecting democratic institutions, must in fairness be reckoned to its credit. That little that was remarkable was attempted in the social or in the cultural spheres is perhaps not surprising, since survival occupied most people's minds. Yet the revolution had been fought for more than administrative efficiency and a balanced budget, and it is impossible not to feel some sympathy for those diehard republicans who thought the revolution betrayed in the 1920s, while one admires the stern-minded determination of the government in its efforts to establish and maintain public order.

But it could scarcely have been otherwise. A government with its "power-base firmly established among instinctively conservative and prosperous middle-class elements of society,"[2] was, in a society marked by a general conservatism, hardly likely, whatever one might have hoped, to have embarked upon many social, economic, and cultural experiments in such difficult times. That the government did in fact strenuously commit itself in such unlikely conditions to one radical policy – the apparently revolutionary policy of language revival – must seem initially, in such a context, difficult to explain. This particular commitment, however, quickly becomes comprehensible when one realizes that the government, anxious to establish its legitimacy in the face of the republican's uncompromising zeal, had, in language revival, a cause of unexceptionable nationalist authenticity. However, the government's dedication to the cause of language revival was by no means simply self-interested. Indeed to suggest that its espousal of this policy was anything more than very slightly opportunistic would be to ignore how profoundly the Irish revolutionary movement that had led to the independence of the Free State

had been affected by the revivalist ideology of the Gaelic League
and the enthusiasm it generated.

The Gaelic League (founded in 1893 to propagate knowledge
of and interest in the language) had been a nursery for active
members of Sinn Féin and the Irish Volunteers of 1916. The
ideology so ably broadcast by the League had moreover achieved
a measure of acceptance in the country at large. Accordingly,
when a Free State government was formed it contained members
of the Gaelic League and individuals sympathetic to the aims of
what had been perhaps the best-supported, most vital cultural
movement of the preceding thirty years. In fact, the state's first
Minister for Education, Eoin MacNeill, who had been the chief
of staff of the Irish Volunteers when the Easter Rising took place
(against his advice as it happened), was professor of early Irish
history at University College, Dublin, and a Gaelic scholar who
had become known in the early years of the century as a devoted
worker for the Gaelic League. It was in fact he who had copro-
posed a series of recommendations on education at an Ard-Fheis
of the League in 1913 which had sought to have Irish taught to all
pupils in National Schools and to exclude from teachers' training
colleges individuals who lacked sound knowledge of the language.

The first Dáil in 1919, after the major Sinn Féin electoral
successes of 1918, had created a Ministry for Irish, and as the
new state was founded, the Gaelic League could be reasonably
sure that any government emerging from only a section of the
former Sinn Féin party would have the revival of Irish as one of
its central concerns. So, an announcement of the government's
achievements and policies published in November 1924 included
amid much matter on farming, drainage, rates, electricity, and
railways, the following declaration:

> The Organisation and the Government are pledged to co-
> ordinate, democratize and Gaelicize our education. In each of
> these aims great progress has already been made. It is now
> possible for the child of the poorest parents to pass from one end
> of the educational ladder to the other, and the Irish language has
> been restored to its own place in Irish education. In addition,

the condition of that important class, the Secondary Teachers, has been improved. The Organisation and Government intend to devote special attention to the problem of safeguarding the Language in the Gaeltacht by improving economic conditions in the Gaeltacht and developing Educational Institutions therein.[3]

The references to democratization referred here to the government's replacement of the intermediate and national education commissions by civil servants, thus, as one educational historian has it, "substituting for an academic and professional oligarchy, an unfettered bureaucracy"[4] and the adoption of a system of government support for secondary schools on the basis of capitation grants for each child following approved courses. A system of incremental salary scales was also introduced, making teachers less dependent on local managements. The twenties saw, however, very little change in the Irish educational system, and certainly the claims that Irish education was being democratized ring rather hollow. For the state was content to maintain almost the entire educational structure bequeathed to it by the imperial authorities with its class-conscious, religiously managed secondary schools, its technical sphere generally thought socially inferior to the more academic institutions, and its universities almost the sole preserve of students from propertied or professional backgrounds. What was effected was a strengthening of the control of education by a central bureaucracy.

The gaelicization of education was, in contrast, systematically attempted. It was determined that all teachers leaving training colleges should be expected to have a knowledge of Irish; preparatory boarding schools were established to prepare young people for careers in the teaching profession which would emphasize the language; school inspectors were required to study Irish, and no further appointments were offered to individuals who lacked proficiency in Irish; Irish was made compulsory for scholarships in the Intermediate and Leaving Certificates in the secondary schools; and financial and other encouragements were offered to schools and individuals alike to use Irish more frequently. But it was in the primary or National Schools that the linguistic policy was prosecuted most vigorously. In its initial stages this linguistic effort was presided over by Professor Eoin MacNeill, whose commitment to education as a means to revive Irish civilization (which for him included the Irish language) was made clear in a series of articles published while he was Minister for Education, in the *Irish Statesman* in 1925. There he asserted:

> Nationality, in the best sense, is the form and kind of civilization developed by a particular people and distinctive of that people. So understood, nationality needs no apologist. . . . I believe in the capacity of the Irish people, if they clear their minds, for building up an Irish civilization. I hold that the chief function of an Irish State and of an Irish Government is to subserve that work. I hold that the principal duty of an Irish Government in its educational policy is to subserve that work. I am willing to discuss how this can best be done, but not discuss how it can be done without.[5]

The National School teachers were enlisted in this crusade, their role to clear the minds of the nation's children through intense exposure to the Irish language.

Eoin MacNeill himself had a much more sophisticated understanding of the relationship of language to society than many others who supported revival, and he well understood that to depend on the schools alone to revive Irish would be unwise. But it was his ironic fate, busy as he was with other matters of state, to preside over the legislative steps that made such a dependence possible. In the absence of any coherent social and economic policy, particularly in relation to the Irish-speaking districts that remained, this dependence was, as events were to prove, almost entirely misguided. The schools alone could not perform a linguistic miracle while the social order was undisturbed by any revolutionary energies.

Theoretical justification for this linguistic onslaught on the schools was supplied by the very influential professor of education at University College, Dublin, Father T. Corcoran, SJ. His claim to eminence in historical studies was work on the hedge schools of penal times (when education for Catholics was offered in barns and even out-of-doors by many dedicated spirits) and on the apparently baneful influence on the Irish language of the British-imposed National School system of the nineteenth century. It was his simplistic belief that what the National Schools had wrongfully done, they could now undo. He was certain that the National Board of Education had been "fatal to the national use of ver-nacular Irish"[6] as he sought to 'reverse a change that was made fully practicable only by the prolonged misuse of the schools.'[7] In 1920 the Irish National Teachers' Organization (INTO) at its annual congress, conscious that the Gaelic League had already set out a series of proposals for the gaelicization of the National Schools, responded by establishing a conference to consider its own position. Professor Corcoran, "while declining to act as a member . . . intimated that it would have at its disposal the benefit of his advice and experience."[8] He was available therefore as a consultant to the congress when it suggested in 1921 that all singing in the National Schools should be in Irish, that instruction in history and geography, which were taught from the third stan-dard onward, should be through Irish, and that one hour a day should be spent in direct language acquisition. Such draconian measures meant that other subjects had to be eliminated from the programme. So, in Irish National Schools, drawing, elementary science, hygiene, nature study, and most domestic studies were dispensed with in favour of the language. Furthermore it was proposed that all teaching in the first two, or infant grades, should be in Irish. The new programme was accepted and set in motion in April 1922.

Patrick Pearse, in a famous phrase, had once castigated the imposition of an educational programme on children by an exter-nal authority as "the murder machine." Professor Corcoran was disinclined to see any analogy in the policies he encouraged. He was persuaded that because non-English-speaking immigrants to the United States could be taught English in grade schools, although it was not the language of the home, so in Ireland children from English-speaking homes could receive instruction in all subjects in Irish at school. The obvious point that European immigrants' children in the United States were being introduced to the language of the wider community while in Ireland children certainly were not, apparently did not weigh with him. Nor indeed, one imagines, did the fact that children might endure some emotional and mental distress in their efforts to cope with the linguistic obstacle course he was setting them, for his vision of the educational experience had little room for such concepts as pleasure or the joy of learning. His dismal creed was formulated in dispiriting terms: "All true education must progressively combine effort with mere interest: it is the effort that enobles and makes worthily human."[9] Policies were developed to retrain teachers to take part in this educational enterprise; special courses were arranged for teachers to increase their knowledge of Irish; individuals whose mother tongue was Irish were encouraged to enter the teaching profession at the Irish-speaking preparatory colleges, even if they displayed few other pedagogic aptitudes. As Professor Corcoran had it: "From the national point of view, even mediocre quality in a boy or girl of fourteen years, if the Irish vernacular command is present, makes that prospective teacher highly valuable."[10]

So, despite a government-appointed conference which reported in 1926 and expressed some doubts about fundamental aspects of the experiment, the major educational innovation of the 1920s was the effort to gaelicize the National Schools, thereby, it was hoped, achieving a revival of Irish as a vernacular language. By 1928 there were 1,240 schools in the country where the teaching of infants in the first two grades was entirely through Irish, 3,570 where teaching was through English and Irish, and only 373 where the teaching was through English alone.

Opposition to this *Kulturkampf* from those who were in essential sympathy with revivalism and its underlying ideology was not significant. Only a few voices were raised to suggest that this demand that children should shoulder most of the burden of language revival might prove counterproductive. Such opposition as there was, as we shall see, tended to originate, not in doubts about the feasibility of the programme nor indeed in deeply felt sympathy for the children actually participating in it, but in apprehensions of a more general kind that the policy might have a deleterious effect on Irish culture as a whole. Michael Tierney, professor of Greek at University College, Dublin, and member of the Dáil, who had served on the government's commission appointed in 1925 charged with a study of the Gaeltacht (the Irish-speaking areas) sounded a warning in 1927. While believing that the efforts to revive the language presented "the greatest and most inspiring spectacle of our day,"[11] he counseled with exacting realism:

> The task of reviving a language . . . with no large neighbouring population which speaks even a distantly related dialect, and with one of the great world-languages to contend against, is one that has never been accomplished anywhere. Analogies with Flemish, Czech, or the Baltic languages are all misleading, because the problem in their cases has been rather that of restoring a peasant language to cultivated use than that of reviving one which the majority had ceased to speak. Still less has it proved possible to impose a language on a people as its ordinary speech by means of the schools alone.[12]

It was Osborn Bergin, Gaelic scholar and professor of early Irish at the same university, who somewhat wryly pointed out what was happening:

> Today the people leave the problem to the Government, the Government leaves it to the Department of Education, the Department of Education to the teachers and the teachers to the school-children. Only the very young are unable to shift the burden to someone else's shoulders, so perhaps they will learn to carry it, and save our faces. After all, infants, before the age of reason can do marvels with language, so they may not notice the weight.[13]

The decline in membership of the Gaelic League in the 1920s suggests that Bergin was correct in this cold-eyed analysis, for in

1924 there were 819 branches of the League in existence while by 1924 there were only 139. A sharp drop of this kind cannot be accounted for only in terms of the dislocation of the Civil War; it seems that many members of the League felt their work was at an end since the state could now be entrusted with the task they had hitherto adopted as their own. It may be indeed that a cultural movement of the kind the League had been, like a religion of the dispossessed, really thrives only under pressure and that the elevation of the language to semiofficial status in the state was a concealed disaster. It is worth noting that a body, Comhaltas Uladh, whose prime concern was the encouragement of the language in Ulster, was one of the few lively sections of the League in the late 1920s as it concerned itself with that part of the country where members of the Northern Ireland government ignored, when they were not openly hostile to, the language movement.

It should be made quite clear that most members of the Gaelic League and the many that gave their willing or tacit support to the government's revival policy and strategy in the 1920s would have rejected the suggestion of imposition contained in Professor Tierney's warning. To comprehend why this is so it is necessary to consider the ideological assumptions of the Gaelic League and of that cultural force known as the Irish Ireland movement which supported its aims in the first two decades of the century. For those assumptions had been made generally available through much effective propaganda and were influential in creating a cultural context in the 1920s in which the government's Irish revival policy could be implemented with a significant measure of popular support and without any great sense of imposition.

The classic text in the Gaelic League's ideological armoury was Douglas Hyde's famous speech, delivered before the National Literary Society in Dublin on 25 November 1892, "The Necessity for De-Anglicizing Ireland." In this Hyde, the son of a Church of Ireland clergyman, who became an enthusiastic worker for Gaelic revival, had identified an Irish cultural imperative, the need to "build up an Irish nation on Irish lines," decrying a central ambivalence in Irish society, "imitating England and yet apparently hating it." His appalled conviction in that lecture was that "within the last ninety years we have, with an unparalleled frivolity, deliberately thrown away our birthright and anglicized ourselves," so "ceasing to be Irish without becoming English." Central to the structure of Hyde's argument in his lecture is that the true, essential Irish reality is the Gaelic, the reality deriving from ancient Ireland, "the dim consciousness" of which "is one of those things which are at the back of Irish national sentiment." An obvious rejoinder to such a view of late-nineteenth-century Ireland might have been that since the seventh century, a time he particularly venerated, frequent invasions have produced a composite civilization or indeed a mosaic. Hyde outlined, in anticipation of such an argument, the very powerful myth of Ireland's assimilative capacities, a myth that has maintained its potency in Irish life to the present day. The passage where he expands on this popular myth is worth examining:

> What we must endeavour to never forget is this, that the Ireland of today is the descendant of the Ireland of the seventh century, then the school of Europe and the torch of learning. It is true that North men made some minor settlements in it in the ninth and tenth centuries, it is true that the Normans made extensive settlements during the succeeding centuries, but none of these broke the continuity of the social life of the island. Dane and Norman drawn to the kindly Irish breast issued forth in a generation or two fully Irishized, and more Hibernian than the Hibernians themselves, and even after the Cromwellian plantation the children of numbers of the English soldiers who settled in the south and midlands, were after forty years' residence, and after marrying Irish wives, turned into good Irishmen, and unable to speak a word of English, while several Gaelic poets of the last century have, like Father English, the most unmistakably English names. In two points only was the continuity of the Irishism of Ireland damaged. First, in the north-east of Ulster, where the Gaelic race was expelled and the land planted with aliens, whom our dear mother Erin, assimilative as she is, has

hitherto found it difficult to absorb, and the ownership of the land, eight-ninths of which belongs to people many of whom always lived, or live, abroad, and not half of whom Ireland can be said to have assimilated.[14]

We note here how major social changes in the distant past are themselves assimilated in a sentimental metaphor ("Dane and Norman drawn to the kindly Irish breast") but that the more recent complications of Irish history do not admit of such simple resolution. For Hyde cannot avoid recognizing that contemporary Irish experience demonstrates not the assimilative power of Irish reality but the degree to which Ireland has been assimilated by the English-speaking world. So he must implicitly condemn the class with which he, as a Protestant English-speaking descendant of the aliens, might most readily be associated, the Anglo-Irish Ascendancy, remaining untroubled later in his lecture that the contribution of Daniel O'Connell and St. Patrick's College, Maynooth to the decline of Gaelic might be seen as tending to refute his theory about Ireland's assimilative capacities.

Such thinking became the staple of Gaelic League propaganda and of the writings of that most energetic proponent of Irish Ireland, the pugnacious journalist and editor of the *Leader* newspaper, D. P. Moran, well into the 1930s. The true Ireland is Gaelic Ireland; Gaelic Ireland has extraordinary assimilative powers, and it must, as the receptive centre of Irish reality, receive English-speaking civilization, as it has developed in Ireland, into itself. Otherwise Ireland would lose her essence, cease to be, in any worthwhile sense. In his powerful polemic *The Philosophy of Irish Ireland*, Moran stated the case clearly: "The foundation of Ireland is the Gael, and the Gael must be the element that absorbs. On no other basis can an Irish nation be reared that would not topple over by the force of the very ridicule that it would beget."[15]

There was, it is important to stress, a vigorously idealistic and humanistic aspect to much of the revivalist activity in the first three decades of the century. Certainly there were those who supported revival from motives of the crudest kind of racial chauvinism and many for whom the language was merely a nationalistic rallying cry, a way of stamping the new state with a distinctive imprint, but thinkers like Douglas Hyde, D. P. Moran, Eoin MacNeill, and in the 1920s, Daniel Corkery, the novelist, short story writer, and critic, all of whose writings were influential in arousing interest in the language and the civilization they thought it enshrined, had each a concerned awareness of the psychological distress suffered by countless individual Irish men and women because of colonial oppression. Irish people could not be themselves, they argued, could not express the vital life of their own country. They were mute in their own language, ignorant of the most appropriate, perhaps the only, vessel capable of bearing that life into the future. They languished as provincial Englishmen, aping metropolitan manners in a most vulgar fashion, or they were driven in frustration to the spiritual and emotional sterilities of permanent political agitation. D. P. Moran summed up Ireland's cultural paucity in a trenchant sentence: "Ireland has invented nothing of importance during the century except the Dunlop tyre."[16] And even Moran, who one suspects wished for cultural revival mostly because it would underpin economic resurgence, was conscious of the individual enhancement possible in a cultural awakening:

> When the people go back into their national traditions, get permeated by their own literature, create a drama, resurrect their customs, develop their industries; when they have a language to bind them together and a national personality to guard, the free and full development of every individual will in no wise endanger or weaken any political movement.[17]

Eoin MacNeill, equally sure why the national life should be fostered, was clear why he espoused the cause of national freedom. It was so that the Irish people might live their own lives in their own way:

> For my own part, if Irish nationality were not to mean a distinctive Irish civilization, I would attach no very great value to Irish

national independence. If I want personal liberty to myself, it is in order that I may be myself, may live my own life in my own way, not that I may live the second-hand, hand-me-down life of somebody else. . . . If I want national freedom for my people, it is in order that they may live in their own way a life which is their own, that they may preserve and develop their own nationality, their own distinctive species of civilization.[18]

Daniel Corkery too, at his most imaginatively ample, suggests that he shared Patrick Pearse's grasp of the simple educational fact that integrated creative personalities cannot be fostered without a "creative and integrated community with a special and continuing experience of its own."[19] So his urgent concern in his polemical critical works *The Hidden Ireland* (1924) and *Synge and Anglo-Irish Literature* (1931) (which led him, as we shall see, to a narrow exclusivity of mind) to promote an Irish literature which would truly relate to a vital Irish world, has to be seen in part as an educationalist's desire for books in the schools that would touch the quick of actual life:

What happens in the neighbourhood of an Irish boy's home – the fair, the hurling match, the land grabbing, the *priesting*, the mission, the Mass – he never comes on in literature, that is, in such literature as he is told to respect and learn.[20]

The Irish Ireland movement at its best, therefore, was aware, in a mode of thought reminiscent of many nineteenth-century English and European Romantic social critics, of the creative possibilities for the individual in a healthy social environment. Independence of mind, integrity of personality, confident possession of identity, liberality of thought, and artistic self-expression were the fruits that could be expected from cultural regeneration of which linguistic revival was the neccessary catalyst.

Such idealism commended itself to many Irish men and women in the new state who felt it only right that Irish children should learn their ancestral language in the schools, encountering there "texts . . . which did not automatically reflect the fashions and clichés of the English-speaking world, but brought the pupils into contact with a world of ideas which was at once alien and, mysteriously, intimately their own."[21] The children in their Irish-speaking National Schools were not in a spiritual sense enduring any imposition. They were encountering the language of the essential Gaelic strand in Irish life, the language of the past, and their own language which would eventually, the most optimistic hoped, absorb English and the cultural life associated with it, as so much had been absorbed by Ireland down the centuries.

It might have been thought, therefore, that the government's language policy would have been successful for it was pursued in a society where considerable numbers of people were ready to see in the policy no imposition but a rediscovery of a necessary past. And had the efforts to revive Irish in the 1920s been conducted primarily on the basis of the kinds of humanism which generated the original enthusiasm of the Gaelic League, together with a committed sense in the country as a whole of the need for genuine social as well as linguistic renewal, the policy might have met with real success. In such a context certain basic practical problems (the fact that there were several dialects of the language in the country and the Gaelic and Roman script were very different) might have been addressed with decisive energy. As it was, in the absence of a revolutionary social policy attending the efforts for linguistic revival and making it possible (for no language policy could have had much chance of success which did not tackle the depressed economic conditions of the Irish-speaking districts, and indeed of the slums of Dublin), conservative and authoritarian tendencies in the language movement quickly began to cloud the radical humanism which for many had been the most attractive aspect of its ideology. Instead of participating as one element in a general transformation of the social order, the revival movement soon came to be characterized by the reaction and dogmatism of the disappointed and despairing. For almost all that the revivalist had to encourage him or her as time went on was the language policy in the schools and a faith in the assimilative powers of Irish reality that contemporary social fact did little to confirm. Indeed, the linguistic profile of the country even in the 1920s suggested that rather than proving to be an assimilative centre of the Irish experience, Gaelic Ireland was being absorbed into the English-speaking world.

There were some signs, however, which suggested that revival might be possible. The fact, though, that revivalists had some superficial causes for optimism, in retrospect, makes the essential weakness in their position all the more poignant. The census of 1926 had revealed that a striking increase in the numbers of those who claimed a knowledge of Irish had recently taken place in Dublin County Borough and Dublin County (from 11,870 in 1911 to 23,712 in 1926 and from 5,873 in 1911 to 15,906 in 1926, respectively), but some reflection would have cast cold water on the optimism generated by such figures.[22] Undoubtedly some of the rise was due to the fact that since independence school-children had been required to study Irish, and that before independence the language had been introduced into the second-ary school curriculum; it was not wholly due to the direct efforts of the Gaelic League. And there was no guarantee that such people would continue to use Irish in their daily lives as adults.

Much more telling were the figures from north-western, western, and south-western areas of the country. These included the counties with the highest proportions of Irish-speakers (in Galway 47.4 percent of the population claimed to know Irish, in Mayo 36.8 percent, in Clare 30.3 percent, in Waterford – exclud-ing the County Borough – 30.1 percent, in Cork – excluding the County Borough – 21.1 percent). Despite the high incidence in these counties of persons claiming knowledge of the language the figures in fact revealed a serious decline in the numbers of Irish speakers in those regions. In Galway for example, between 1911 and 1926 the numbers of such persons had declined from 98,523 to 80,238, in Cork from 77,205 to 60,616, in Mayo from 88,601 to 63,514, in Kerry from 60,719 to 49,262. Though some of these reductions were undoubtedly attributable to emi-gration of Irish-speaking persons, in itself a lamentable fact, it was probable that a real loss of the language was occurring *in situ*. Even in those districts which were designated fíor-Gaeltacht areas by the Gaeltacht Commission, where 80 percent and over of the population claimed knowledge of Irish, the period 1911–26 showed a decrease from 149,677 claiming knowledge of the language to 130,074 – an actual loss of 19,603 or 13.1 percent. What is even more striking is that in those areas the Gaeltacht Commission designated breac-Gaeltacht, partly Irish-speaking (i.e., with 25–79 percent of the population claiming knowledge of Irish), the period 1911–26 saw a reduction of 47,094 persons claiming knowledge of the language, a loss of 28.7 percent. Such statistics suggest that what many witnesses told the commission was occurring: Irish-speaking parents were bringing up their children through the sole medium of English. The figures that the commission itself produced in its 1926 report revealed that in 1925 there were only 257,000 Irish-speakers altogether in the seven Irish-speaking and partly Irish-speaking areas identified by the commissioners. Of these, 110,000 resided in the partly Irish-speaking districts.

From the census figures, and the figures supplied in the Gaeltacht Commission report, it would have been difficult therefore to avoid the conclusion that English was making inroads and emigration effecting its slow attrition. While the effects of official language policy could be seen among schoolchildren and signs of Gaelic enthusiasm were evident among some well-educated adults in the English-speaking areas (when broken down by occupations the professional class boasted the largest percentage of Irish-speakers – 43.5 percent of this group claiming knowledge of the language), the protracted decline of the Gaeltacht had gone unchecked. That decline meant that overall in the years 1881–1926 the number of Irish-speaking persons in the country had dropped by 41 percent.

Eventually the fact that the ideology of the Gaelic League and the Irish Ireland movement flew in the face of social reality was to prove signally destructive of its best intentions. Committed to a view of Irish reality which was to become increasingly untenable, in a society where the population seemed unwilling to consider let alone to inaugurate a period of radical social change, the revivalists could do nothing but dogmatize and appeal for more stringent enforcement of linguistic sanctions. As they did so the popular appeal of the whole revival enterprise could not but lessen. Even in the 1920s there were signs that this unfortunate process was at work.

The language policy throughout the 1920s was often defended in the crudest possible terms. J. J. Walsh, the Minister for Posts and Telegraphs, informed a meeting in 1926: "There was no doubt that a country without a language was not a country at all. At best it was a province," declaring roundly:

> They were told that the teaching of Irish was compulsory, but the teaching of everything else in school-life was equally so. They knew that the majority of children learned because there was no alternative. Therefore the talk of ramming the subject down their throats was all nonsense. . . . This country had for centuries been dosed with compulsory English to the entire exclusion of their native tongue, and the people who now complain of compulsory Irish were whole-hog backers of that English policy.[23]

D. P. Moran in his editorials in the *Leader* issued a repetitive barrage of dogmatic statement, which was echoed in periodicals such as *Fáinne an Lae* (The Dawning of the Day), and intensified by anti-Protestant bigotry, in the zealous pages of the *Catholic Bulletin*. That monthly periodical had been established in 1911 chiefly to warn the Catholic faithful of the dangers of immoral literature, but it quickly became dedicated to waging cultural and psychological war against the malign influence of Protestant Anglo-Ireland. Professor T. Corcoran was a frequent anonymous contributor. The direct, brutal tone of the following passage is characteristic of the journal's literary style. Here the *Bulletin* in 1924 editorializes on a suggestion that modern Irish nationality is a synthesis:

> The Irish nation is the Gaelic nation; its language and literature is the Gaelic language; its history is the history of the Gael. All other elements have no place in Irish national life, literature and

tradition, save as far as they are assimilated into the very substance of Gaelic speech, life and thought. The Irish nation is not a racial synthesis at all; synthesis is not a vital process, and only what is vital is admissible in analogies bearing on the nature of the living Irish nation, speech, literature and tradition. We are not a national conglomerate, not a national patchwork specimen; the poetry or life of what Aodh de Blacam calls Belfast can only be Irish by being assimilated by Gaelic literature into Gaelic literature.[24]

The intemperance here is in part that of anti-Protestant bigotry (the *Bulletin* knew that the remnants of Protestant Anglo-Ireland would be offended by such Irish Ireland dogma) but it is also, one suspects, as so often in Irish Ireland propaganda, the fruit of frustration.

In the more thoughtful attempts of Irish Ireland's writers to propose a genuinely Irish philosophy of national life one can hear conservative and authoritarian notes drowning the radical strains of their message as, in an increasingly hopeless linguistic situation, they sought to protect the language without any broad social vision of how this could be done. This revealed itself in two ways: in a tendency to venerate national life at the expense of individual expression and in a highly prescriptive sense of Irish identity. The work of Daniel Corkery in the 1920s and early 1930s supplies a fascinating example of how the humanistic ideals of Irish Ireland could be swamped by a conservative's vision of the nation's life in just the way I am suggesting.

Before the War of Independence Daniel Corkery had been a moderately well-known Irish novelist and short story writer who had espoused the cause of Gaelic revival with quiet conviction. His novel *The Threshold of Quiet* (1917) is a sensitive study of provincial frustration, concentrating on the dismal, unfulfilled lives of a group of young Corkmen. A gravely earnest reflection on the quiet desperation of lives lived without achievements of any major kind, it is a fine expression of his serious-minded, pedagogic cultural and social concern. The War of Independence and particularly the death of his close friend Terence MacSwiney, the mayor of Cork, after a long hunger strike, seems to have affected Corkery deeply, sharpening his didacticism and quickening his sense of national outrage and need. In the 1920s and early 1930s his writings became increasingly polemical and dogmatic as, from his position as professor of English at University College, Cork, he sought to direct the course of Irish writing and education into properly national channels. Corkery justified the rigour of his stance in the following terms:

> In a country that for long has been afflicted with an ascendancy, an alien ascendancy at that, national movements are a necessity: they are an effort to attain to the normal. The vital-minded among the nation's children answer to the impulse: they are quickest to become conscious of how far away everything has strayed from the natural and native. They search and search after that native standard that has been so long discarded: they dig and dig; and one may think of them as beginning every morning's work with . . . "I invoke the land of Ireland."[25]

One notes here how political history is allowed to justify a unity of national purpose which might interfere with individual perception and expression. A search for the "native standard" is necessary if the country is to become "normal." So in the contortions of his cultural study of the dramatist John Synge, *Synge and Anglo-Irish Literature* (as the critic labours to discover why despite his origins in the alien Ascendancy Synge nevertheless manages to be a good dramatist), one finds the humanistic strain in Corkery's thinking, his educationalist's concern for enhancing individual experience, drowned by notes of a nationalist's celebration of the nation's will. In denying Anglo-Irish writers of the Literary Revival artistic membership of the Irish nation, he comments:

> If one approaches "Celtic Revival" poetry as an exotic, then one is in a mood to appreciate its subtle rhythms, and its quiet tones; but if one continues to live within the Irish seas, travelling the roads of the land, then the white-walled houses, the farming life, the hill-top chapel, the memorial cross above some peasant's grave – memorable only because he died for his country –

impressing themselves as the living pieties of life must impress themselves, upon the imagination, growing into it, dominating it, all this poetry becomes after a time little else than an impertinence.[26]

Key words here are "must impress themselves," "growing into it, dominating it." The truly national imagination will, in Corkery's sense of things, be consciously or unconsciously submissive to the great forces of the Irish being, will be dominated by them. His criticism of much Anglo-Irish writing is that the great forces "that work their will in the consciousness of the Irish people have found little or no expression in it."[27] "Work their will" is a telling phrase, and it does not surprise that when Corkery casts about in his book for a representative Irish Ireland moment he chooses not some individual activity, nor some occasion of personal expression but a crowd of 30,000 people at a hurling match in Munster, comprising a body of sentiment that he feels Anglo-Irish writers could not comprehend. In such passages Corkery exhibits how easy it is for a sensitive humanist with a proper appreciation of the individual to allow himself the gratification afforded in the contemplation and veneration of the national will and of the people imagined as a mass movement.

D. P. Moran had, as we noted, assured his fellow countrymen in *The Philosophy of Irish Ireland* that the nation he envisaged would stimulate "the free and full development of every individual." At revealing moments in his writings Corkery made evident that he was unwilling in the country's abnormal state to allow such liberty to writers. Rather, they must obey a national imperative, must in the interests of a truly Irish identity allow the nation to work its will on them, must serve as the seedbeds of the future. Such thinking has an authoritarian ring to it. It is the intellectual equivalent of Irish Ireland's propagandist dogmatism coexisting uneasily with the educationalist's vision of humane fulfilment that also stirs Corkery's imagination.

Furthermore Corkery was sure, like most of his fellows in the movement, what Irish identity would be like if it was allowed a fertile soil in which to flower. Various supporters of the movement differed about this, but they shared the conviction that they knew. D. P. Moran was vigorously certain that to be truly Irish would be to cultivate masculinity, in a "racy Irish atmosphere" where the Celtic note of melancholy would be derided as an alien absurdity. He aspired to "making the people sober, moderate, masculine and thereby paving the way for industrial advancement and economic reform."[28] Eoin MacNeill, by contrast, made more of the noble, natural piety of the people and was disinclined to venerate the masculine virtues or berate weakness. But his sense of Irish identity was no less developed. His vision was of a historic Irish rural Christian civilization, chaste and learned, which must be allowed to express its rich life in the present. Corkery felt able to identify with even greater precision the forces which preoccupy a properly Irish racial mind. They are, as he defines them in *Synge and Anglo-Irish Literature*, (1) religion, (2) nationalism, (3) the land. Unless, his exclusive creed asserts, a writer is imaginatively absorbed by at least one of these preoccupations he is, Corkery assures us, not to be considered an Irish writer; he does not express the reality of Irish life. Irish identity, therefore, poses no problems for Corkery. His conception of an essential Irish mind, as of an authentic Irish literature, is equally categorical – it must express a clear-sighted sanity, an intellectual order where wit controls intensity of feeling, realism tempers imagination, intelligence the affections; the truly Irish mind must exhibit the virtues of classicism:

> This core of hardness is scarcely ever lacking to the Gaelic poet; track him right down the centuries, and one never finds it missing. It is intellectual in its nature: hard-headed and clear-sighted, witty at its best, prosaic when not eager; and to its universality in the truly Gaelic world is due the fact that one can turn over the pages of the Gaelic book of poetry, century after century, without coming on any set of verses that one could speak of as sentimental.[29]

Such intellectual assurance with its implicit prescriptive zeal is a characteristic of Irish Ireland's writings, and it suggests the degree to which in desiring a flowering of the Irish intellect the writers knew what to expect. That individual blooms of creativity are unlikely to obey such prescriptive imperatives is a signally salutary fact that Irish Ireland weighed rather too little.

I have argued that a genuinely radical and attractive humanism had fired much of the pre-revolutionary enthusiasm for the Irish language and its revival and that some of this feeling survived into the post-independence period. I have argued further that in the early years of the Irish Free State the proponents of Gaelic revival and the supporters of Irish Ireland, in general possessing no real social programme, tended to express the need for language revival in terms of conservation and of a despairingly authoritarian control of a society that was becoming increasingly anglicized. The revival attempt, therefore, despite its apparent radicalism, can be seen as rather more a reactionary expression of the deep conservatism of mind that governed public attitudes in the period than as a revolutionary movement. This, I think, becomes even clearer when we consider the relationship between the Irish Ireland ideology and the exclusivist cultural and social pressures which bore fruit in the enactment of the Censorship Bill of 1929.

A recurrent intellectual motif in the writings of Irish Ireland's thinkers is the provision of historical accounts of Ireland's European uniqueness. The authentic Gaelic life which must be the basis of an Irish resurgence in the twentieth century, the argument runs, is a way of life that has traditionally escaped the universalizing forces that have disturbed local life throughout most of the rest of Europe. Ireland, it seems, escaped the imperial, legalistic dominance of Rome and the essentially artificial cosmopolitanism of the Renaissance. It is true that Gaelic Ireland was threatened by the inheritors of Renaissance and Enlightenment civilization, by the Anglo-Irish Ascendancy, but Ireland, driven underground, did not absorb the alien values. The hidden Ireland survived beyond the power of the Protestant Ascendancy's Big Houses and the British government official, maintaining its essential character and a brotherhood of feeling with the local life of pre-Renaissance, pre-Reformation Catholic Europe.

There was, therefore, in the Irish Ireland movement a cultural equivalent of the political doctrine of Sinn Féin (Ourselves) in an imaginative attachment to the local and a belief that history had allowed that local life a protracted protection from alien influences. It was a short step from such thinking to the belief that cultural protectionism might enable Ireland to sustain her unique identity and to a draconian censorship as means of providing that protection.

Of course, not all those associated with the Irish Ireland movement took that step, and it would be quite wrong to identify the Irish Censorship of Publications Act of 1929 solely with cultural exclusivism. Many countries in the early twentieth century felt that the accelerating pace of publications, particularly of cheap newspapers and magazines, created a social problem that they could not ignore. A Committee of Enquiry on Evil Literature set up by the Free State Minister for Justice in 1926, which prepared the way for the eventual bill, found it could seek guidance from the example of eleven countries and states where statutes relating to obscene publications were in force. The problem such publications created had indeed been the subject of an international convention for the suppression of the circulation of and traffic in obscene publications, organized by the League of Nations in 1923. A responsible government in the 1920s in almost any country would have felt that there was nothing unusual about the enactment of a bill to censor certain publications and to protect populations from pornography.

It was clear, too, from the report of the Committee of Enquiry on Evil Literature and from the Dáil and Senate debates on the issue that efforts were made by the legislators to distinguish the merely pornographic from works which might possess literary merit. Indeed, a good deal of the firepower of the bill was aimed not at literary works but at the many imported popular newspapers and magazines that were considered unsavory and at works which recommended, or provided information on, birth control.

There were signs, nevertheless, that an Irish Censorship Bill might represent something more stringent than a government's rational attempt to suppress the more vicious forms of pornographic publication. These perhaps account for the alarm that the mere proposal of the bill aroused (as we shall see) in the minds of most Irish writers of the time. Much of the public demand for the bill was orchestrated not by members of the political parties but by Irish Vigilance Societies (the Irish Vigilance Association had been founded in 1911 by the Dominican Order) and by the Catholic Truth Society of Ireland (founded in 1899, among whose aims was the effort "to combat the pernicious influence of infidel and immoral publications by the circulation of good, cheap and popular Catholic literature").[30] It might reasonably have been feared that such bodies, in a country where the mass of the population was encouraged by the church to observe a peculiarly repressive sexual code, would press for a censorship policy expressing not literary and aesthetic but strict Catholic moral values.

Furthermore, a prevailing note sounded in the writings and speeches of those calling for a censorship bill was the notion that all evil in literary and journalistic matters derived from abroad, particularly from England. It was, therefore, the business of an Irish legislature to protect Irish life from the impure external influences and to help build up a healthy, clean-minded Catholic Irish civilization. It must protect that supposedly distinctive Irish religious life and practice that, sometimes associated with the Irish language and the Gaelic way of life, comprised national identity. It was at this point that the interests of those who sought censorship from moralistic impulses alone and the interests of those, like the Irish Irelanders, who desired cultural protectionism, met and often overlapped. An example of such an overlap is provided in the demand by a certain Father R. S. Devane, SJ, for a tariff on imported literature and journalism. Father Devane was a Dublin priest who had been strenuous in his efforts to arouse public support for the cause of censorship of indecent and obscene publications. He had met with Kevin O'Higgins, the

Free State's Minister for Justice, in 1925 to put, on behalf of an organization to which he belonged, the Priests' Social Guild, the case for a censorship bill, and he was the only private individual who presented evidence before the Committee of Enquiry on Evil Literature established by O'Higgins in 1926. In 1927, in the Jesuit periodical *Studies*, Father Devane went a step further, arguing for high tariffs on imported publications in the following terms:

> We are at present engaged in an heroic effort to revive our national language, national customs, national values, national culture. These objects cannot be achieved without a cheap, healthy and independent native press. In the face of English competition such a press is an impossibility. . . . Against such propaganda of the English language and English ideas the present effort at national revival looks very much like the effort to beat back an avalanche with a sweeping brush.[31]

Here cultural protectionism of the Irish Ireland kind is proposed, but the cultural impulses coexist with a particular vision of morality embodied in the one word "healthy." The Reverend M. H. MacInerny, OP, editor of the Dominican magazine *The Irish Rosary* and an active member of the Vigilance Association since 1912, in a comment on Father Devane's suggestion clearly grasped the twin impulses, moral and cultural, that fired Father Devane's demand for tariffs as well as censorship. Agreeing with "every word" in Father Devane's article, he continued:

> By all means let legislative effect be given, without undue delay, to the unanimous recommendation of the Commission on Evil Literature; this will at once bar out a great mass of prurient and demoralizing publications. For economic, national and cultural reasons of the highest moment, the Oireachtas ought to pass a resolution imposing a heavy tariff on the remainder of what Father Devane calls the "popular" class of imported publications.[32]

That such individuals represented public opinion on the matter, inasmuch as the public interested itself in literary and cultural affairs at all, there can be little doubt. The only outspoken opposition to such thinking came from writers themselves and had little effect. Indeed, there were those in the country who, far from attending to the writers' criticisms of the proposed bill, merely thought they deserved to be silenced and that they were understandably fearful of the just deserts that awaited them. Such, certainly, was the attitude of the *Catholic Bulletin*, which had long waged a battle against Irish writers on the grounds of their alien immorality and pagan un-Irish philosophy. Indeed that periodical, in an even more obvious fashion than Father Devane's article, suggests that a good deal of Irish Ireland enthusiasm in the period was generated less by idealistic cultural imperatives than by a desire to advance Catholic power and social policy in the country through the defeat of Protestant Ireland and the anglicized culture associated with it, in ideological warfare. For the periodical, edited until 1922 by Seán Ua Ceallaigh, who was president of the Gaelic League between 1919 and 1923 and thereafter by Patrick Keohane with Professor Timothy Corcoran as a guiding spirit, combines much anti-Protestant invective and hatred of Freemasonry with a celebration of an Irish Ireland life that comprises staunch Catholic as well as Gaelic elements. With an almost entertaining virulence of phrase, the *Bulletin* had excoriated the work of Yeats, Russell, Joyce, and Gogarty as the machinations of a new Ascendancy exploiting Ireland for squalid foreign gold. The periodical greeted W. B. Yeats's receipt of the Nobel Prize for Literature in 1923 with that xenophobia which characterized its attitudes to most Irish writing in English and which fueled the fires of its demand for censorship.

> The Nobel Prize in Literature is the occasion. Senator Gogarty directs attention to the fact that on this issue there was recently a tussle between the English colony in Ireland and the English of England, for the substantial sum provided by a deceased anti-Christian manufacturer of dynamite. It is common knowledge that the line of recipients of the Nobel Prize shows that a reputation for paganism in thought and word is a very considerable advantage in the sordid annual race for money,

engineered as it always is, by clubs, coteries, salons, and cliques. Paganism in prose or in poetry has, it seems, its solid cash value: and if a poet does not write tawdry verse to make his purse heavier, he can be brought by his admirers to where the money is, whether in the form of an English pension, or in extracts from the Irish taxpayer's pocket, or in the Stockholm dole.[33]

The *Bulletin* was, of course, an organ of extremist propaganda but its attitudes were not unknown in other areas of Irish society, if their expression was customarily rather less inflamed. People like those who had denounced Synge's treatment of Ireland in *The Playboy of the Western World* could still be found ready to object to any unflattering literary portrait of their country.

D. P. Moran in the *Leader* added his eloquent Irish Ireland voice to the demand for a firm censorship policy, and critics at a rather more theoretical level were at work on studies that might provide ideological ammunition for cultural protectionism. The writings of Daniel Corkery, in *The Hidden Ireland*, and later in his study of Synge, where he made residence in Ireland a union card in a closed shop of Irish letters, did nothing to encourage an openness to foreign literary and cultural influences. Rather, Corkery's cultural nationalism and prescriptive zeal seem to suggest that no great disservice would be done the nation if the writings of certain authors became unavailable. Other critics were earnest in their desire to see in much modern writing, especially in works by suspect Irish writers, a shallow cosmopolitanism that vitiated imaginative power. So Seorsamh O'Neill, in an article published in 1924 in the *Irish Statesman* characteristic of many such which appeared in various periodicals in the 1920s, lamented the tragedy of George Bernard Shaw's imaginative aridity, asserting that "compared with men of equal or even less vitality whose minds are rooted in their national and local cultures Shaw's mind is two-dimensional, mechanical, lacking in depth and imaginative insight." O'Neill associated such literary rootlessness, as he concluded his essay, with the anticipated threat of television and with international culture – "the pilings round our lives of a rag-heap of odds and ends which through lack of assimilation will remain a pile of meaningless and bewildering refuse, even though it be gathered from the ends of the earth."[34]

In writings of this kind the cultural exclusivism of the Irish Ireland movement helped created a climate of opinion in which authors whose work might encounter moral disapproval could also be suspected of a lack of national authenticity or will. The nation need not disturb itself over much if their writings should fall foul of a censor. In this way the thinking of the Irish Ireland movement must be associated with the conservative climate of opinion in which the Censorship Bill of 1929 was enacted and put to work even where, in individual cases, supporters of the movement may not have espoused the cause of censorship at all or as vigorously as did D. P. Moran in his *Leader* editorials. None of them rose to decry censorship as a reactionary offence to the revolutionary humanism that had originally generated their move-ment. No voice was raised to wonder if so positive an enterprise as linguistic and cultural renewal could be stimulated by so negative a practice as censorship.

If Irish writers of the 1920s had cause to take alarm in part because of the source of the demands for censorship (the Catholic Vigilance Association and the Catholic Truth Society) and in part because of the atmosphere of national self-righteousness and cultural exclusiveness in which a censorship bill would be enacted, certain incidents also served to concentrate their minds on the kind of future which might await their work. Among these the Galway public library board putting Shaw's works under lock and key, the stopping of trains and the burning of their cargoes of imported newspapers (which D. P. Moran thought evidence of the need to pass a censorship bill as quickly as possible), and the public demonstrations in favour of censorship were disturbing enough, but the unhappy experience of the Carnegie Libraries' Trust in Ireland following an imprudent if scarcely pornographic publication by one of the members of its Advisory Committee must have seemed like a suspiciously nasty portent indeed.

The Carnegie Trust had made itself responsible in 1921 for establishing and financing, with the help of a local rate, centres for the distribution of books in many parts of Ireland. The playwright Lennox Robinson was secretary and treasurer to the Advisory Committee, which included among its members Lady Gregory and George Russell (Æ). In 1924 Robinson contributed a harmless short story on a religious theme, "The Madonna of Slieve Dun," to a literary paper which the writer Francis Stuart and his wife had begun to edit and publish with some friends. The periodical came to the attention of President Cosgrave, who, it was rumoured, intended to suppress it. The story about a young girl who imagines herself another Madonna provoked a Jesuit member of the Advisory Committee to tender his resignation and a first-rate row blew up when W. B. Yeats, who had also published his sexually adventurous poem "Leda and the Swan" in the paper *To-Morrow*, entered the fray on Robinson's behalf. To no avail, however, because the unhappy outcome of the literary contretemps was the suspension of the committee and the dismissal of its secretary and treasurer, the unfortunate Robinson.[35]

The bill, when it eventually appeared, was apparently a much less draconian legislative tool than had been feared. The Minister for Justice was willing to make amendments to the bill when it was presented to the Dáil, and the bill itself failed to implement the Committee on Evil Literature's recommendation that there should be recognized associations in the country charged with bringing dubious publications to the attention of the Censorship Board. What Oliver St. John Gogarty, the poet, wit, surgeon, and senator, had feared as "the most monstrous proposal that has ever been made in this country,"[36] since it implied that the Irish should make use of their "recently won liberty to fill every village and hamlet with little literary pimps who will be recognized," was not to be part of the legislative process. No one at the time of the bill's enactment foresaw that the customs would fulfil the function of public watchdog, referring books upon suspicion to the board in large numbers, thereby filling the role that the Committee on Evil Literature envisaged for the recognized associations. Even the *Irish Statesman*, which had waged a protracted campaign against the bill, was able to express relief that it had turned out rather better than expected. J. J. Horgan in an essay on affairs in the Irish Free State in the *Round Table* probably expressed the general satisfaction of those who had been disturbed by the possibilities of an Irish censorship when he wrote in March 1929, "The debates on this measure in the Dáil have been more courageous than was to be expected." In May 1930 he reported on the earliest effects of the new legislation, recounting with relish how in some respects the act was proving counterproductive, where it was having any effect at all:

> The first result of the new Censorship of Publications Act has been the banning of seventeen books by the Minister for Justice on the advice of the Censorship Board. The only three of any importance are Mr Aldous Huxley's *Point Counter Point*, Miss Radclyffe Hall's *Well of Loneliness* (which has already been banned in England), and Mr Bertrand Russell's *Marriage and Morals*. The remainder of the books censored are principally the works of Dr Marie Stopes and writers of her ilk on the subject of birth control. It is interesting to record that one bookseller who had six copies of Mr Huxley's book which he could not sell, sold them all on the day the censorship of that volume was announced, and also received orders for twelve additional copies.[37]

The Minister for Justice, Horgan informs us, was rather concerned that lists of banned books were being published in the daily press, thus conferring upon them a certain notoriety. He also regretted, it appears, that few people were bringing objectionable works to the Censorship Board's attention. On this latter point Horgan observed with what seemed like sage equanimity:

> The fact is that very few people in Ireland read any modern books at all, and that those who do are not likely to take the trouble of acting as literary informers to the Censorship Board. In any event, to attempt a censorship of modern literature, even in one language, is not unlike trying to drink a river.[38]

That for almost forty years the Censorship Board would make this epic attempt seemed in 1930 an improbability. That it was in a large part successful is a cultural fact of twentieth-century Ireland that as yet has not been comprehensively analyzed.

Twenty years after the enactment of the bill the writer and critic Arland Ussher, who had been involved in the fight against censorship in the 1920s, managed a retrospective detachment, providing a measured assessment:

> We were wrong and over-impatient – unjust also, to the men who were re-building amid the ruins. . . . We . . . concentrated our indignation on their Acts for prohibiting divorce and for prohibiting the sale of "evil literature" – measures which might have been expected from any Irish Catholic government, and which, considering the social atmosphere of Ireland, did little more than register prohibitions that would in any case have been effective, in fact if not in form.[39]

Other individuals who perhaps suffered more directly from the fact and the form of the prohibitions could not afford such an olympian historicism. In the 1920s Dermot Foley was a librarian who had left his native Dublin to take up a post as a librarian in Ennis, County Clare. In an essay published in 1974 he told how the wave of national enthusiasm that had inspired the War of Independence, "a spirit of optimism and participation so powerful that it survived the terrible realities of a civil war," broke, in his case in County Clare, against the harsh rocks of puritanical philistinism. He remembered the effects of the Carnegie Trust row:

> An incident that was treated as farce by sensible people nearly foundered the whole library movement. Its consequences hit me in Clare. In Irish Revival terms, thereafter books were tainted and it was left to the Censorship Board to expose libraries as seed-beds of corruption. It became a statutory, inexhaustible beanfeast for the bigots and obscurantists, and in due time made a dog's dinner of defenceless people who, above all things, badly needed a bit of leadership to lift them out of the morass of ignorance they had for so long endured.[40]

For Foley the greatest crime perpetrated by censorship was not the undoubted injury done to Irish writers, not the difficulty experienced by educated men and women in getting hold of banned works, but the perpetuation of cultural poverty in the country as a whole, left without the leaven of serious contemporary literature.

> My library was whipped into serving up an Irish stew of imported westerns, sloppy romances, blood-and-murders bearing the *nihil obstat* of fifty-two vigilantes, and anything escaping them was lying in unread bundles on the shelves of musty halls and schools.[41]

So the Censorship of Publications Act gave a licence to Irish Grundyism which had its censorious way in literary matters for almost four decades of Irish independence.

CHAPTER 3

Images and Realities

A commonplace of Irish Ireland cultural analysis in the 1920s was that Ireland without the Irish language was spiritually deficient, even impoverished, the central impulse of a genuine separatism terribly thwarted. Indeed national existence was in serious jeopardy. Undoubtedly many of those who thought in this fashion were quite genuinely moved by a pained vision of the cultural deprivation complete anglicization could entail, appalled by the idea that the langauge could die in an independent Ireland, and truly fearful for the future. Some few others, however, were perhaps more concerned with the advance of Catholic power in the new state and were prepared to use the revival of Irish and a celebration of a narrow conception of the Gaelic way of life as a weapon to discomfort Protestant, anglicized Anglo-Ireland. Both groups, whether consciously or unconsciously, undervalued what was in fact the inheritance that the nineteenth and early twentieth centuries had bequeathed to the citizens of the new state. For newly independent Ireland was endowed with a repository of myths, images, and motifs, literary modes and conventions cultivated to a degree that might indeed have been the envy of most emerging states in a century of infant, fragile nationalisms. The antiquarian literary and cultural activity of the preceding one hundred years had offered Irishmen and women a range of modes of thought and feeling that could help confirm national identity and unity. So, when these imaginative assets are reckoned together with the social and national binding powers of an overwhelmingly homogeneous religious belief and practice, which provided a primary sense of identity, it can readily be seen that the new state was rich in integrative resources in spite of the vision of national fragility that Irish Ireland employed as an ideological weapon.

Throughout much of the nineteenth century Irish nationalism had accreted an iconography and a symbolism. Motifs such as shamrocks, harps, round towers, celtic crosses, and sunbursts had become associated with patriotic feeling, and national sentiment had expressed itself in song, ballad, and rhetoric. The new state could draw on this repository of national motifs and feeling as it wished – the harp, for example, became the state's official symbol. Furthermore, at the end of the nineteenth century a feeling had developed that these familiar symbols of Irish identity had become hackneyed and vulgar. A new literary and cultural enthusiasm had sought what were thought to be more appropriately heroic emblems for a nascent nationalism. The new state inherited therefore both the more traditional symbols of national identity and the modes and motifs that were the fruit of the Literary Revival which had come to vigorous life when, from the 1880s onward, scholars, poets, playwrights, historians, and folklorists rescued much from the Gaelic past and reinterpreted that past in the interests of a raised national consciousness. It had indeed been that literary and cultural activity which, as the critic Ernest Boyd noted in 1922, had done "more then anything else to draw the attention of the outside world to the separate national existence of Ireland."[1]

The new literature that began to be produced in the eighties and nineties of the nineteenth century primarily affirmed the heroic traditions of the Irish people, directing their attention to the mythological tales of their past, to the heroes and noble deeds of a vanished age. When such literary antiquarianism had managed to suggest a continuity of experience between past and present a powerful propagandist weapon had been forged. Such occurred most notably in the poems and plays of W. B. Yeats, where the figure of Cuchulain, the mythological hero of the eighth-century epic, the *Táin Bó Cuailnge*, and the figure of Cathleen ni Houlihan became associated with contemporary possibilities in a manner that suggested that the heroic could yet again dominate the Irish world. The heroic ideal, as presented in Yeats's poems and plays, in Standish O'Grady's versions of the mythological literature, in the translations of Lady Gregory, and in the many poems by minor poets of the Celtic Movement, entered the consciousness of twentieth-century Ireland as a metaphor of political hope. When, indeed, such heroic aspiration was allied with Catholic notions of sacrificial chivalry, which as Paul Fussell shows in his stimulating study *The Great War and Modern Memory* were prevalent in Europe before and during the 1914–18 war, the result was the fervent patriotic religiosity of Pearse's writings and his self-immolating political passion.

The 1920s saw a reduction in such heroic imagining. The business of reconstruction following civil war apparently lacked the exhilaration of a liberation struggle and could not be conceived of in such resonant terms. The dominant literary modes of the most adventurous writers became realistic if not indeed satiric. The efforts to write a modern Irish epic in English based on the matter of Ireland, which had absorbed many poets since Samuel Ferguson first set his hand to the task with the composition of *Congal* (published in 1872), seemed no longer likely to prove fruitful. In 1925 the young poet Austin Clarke published the last of his three attempts to write an epic based on mythological materials and subsequently abandoned the mythological past for a more personal, lyrical relationship with the Hiberno-Romanesque period in Irish history which received expression in his volume *Pilgrimage* in 1929. In such a transition, undoubtedly rooted in Clarke's own personality, one may perhaps detect a more general intimation of the failing powers of the mythological and heroic vision of the 1920s in the depressed aftermath of the

Civil War. While the struggle against England continued, the image of Cuchulain as the Hound of Ulster and the Fenian heroes as an exemplary Irish militia bore on contemporary experience with a striking pertinence, charging the work of even minor writers with national significance. In the wake of the Civil War, in a period of prudent recovery, images of heroic life began to seem like Irish stage properties, employed in literature when ceremony demanded. There was a general sense that the heroic age had passed. So P. S. O'Hegarty could review a biography of the patriot and freedom fighter Michael Collins in 1926 with a certainty that Ireland would not see his like again. Collins had embodied for O'Hegarty the energy of the mythic past, which the poet Alice Milligan had recreated in her poem "The Return of Lugh Lamh Fada": "That comes nearer than anything I know, than any words I can pen, to rendering how Michael Collins. came to Ireland in the post-1916 years and what he meant to her. . . . He stands out in the red years a veritable Lugh, outstanding, gigantic, efficient."[2] But the present could not contain him.

As the heroic strain in Anglo-Irish writing, which Yeats had employed for the purposes of high art as well as potent propaganda, and lesser poets had found appropriate to patriotic utterance began to dissipate in the drab unadventurous atmosphere of the 1920s, serious poets and writers like Yeats and his younger contemporaries began to turn to new ways of interpreting their experience. The heroic images and symbols drawn from the sagas that had earlier vitalized genuine art and political action began to achieve a ceremonial status in the public mind, became mere icons of received political and historical wisdom, were discharged of their energizing currents in anniversary and collected editions of various poets' work and in the schoolroom textbook.

In August 1924 the efforts to revive the Tailteann Games in Dublin, initiated, legend bore witness, by the Irish mythical hero Lugh Lamh Fada (Lugh of the Long Hand) around 1600 B.C. and continued until the twelfth century, were not entirely successful, for they did not manage to command universal support in the bitter aftermath of the Civil War. In 1929 Æ sadly bore

witness to the declining power of the heroic vision in Irish life.
Reflecting on the work of Standish O'Grady, while declaring "the
figure of Cuchulain amid his companions of the Red Branch
which he discovered and refashioned for us is, I think, the greatest
spiritual gift any Irishman for centuries has given to Ireland," he
admitted ruefully, "I know it will be said that this is a scientific
age, the world so full of necessitous life that it is a waste of time
for young Ireland to brood upon tales of legendary heroes."[3] By
1935, when a statue by Oliver Sheppard, which portrays the
figure of Cuchulain, was erected in the General Post Office,
scene of the Easter Rising in Dublin, this process was almost
complete, provoking from Yeats in his poem "The Statues," not
a simple celebration of the heroic energy of the Celtic past and
of the Easter Rising but a troubled question and an ambiguous
affirmation:

> When Pearse summoned Cuchulain to his side,
> What stalked through the Post Office? What intellect,
> What calculation, number, measurement, replied?
> We Irish, born into that ancient sect
> But thrown upon this filthy modern tide
> And by its formless spawning fury wrecked,
> Climb to our proper dark, that we may trace
> The lineaments of a plummet-measured face.

If the heroic vision of an Ireland the poet imagined "terrible
and gay" was wrecked, as Yeats thought, by the "formless spawn-
ing fury" of the modern world or more probably by the mediocre
dullness of the new democratic Irish State, the image of Ireland
as a rural, almost pastoral nation, which had also preoccupied
the writers of the Literary Revival, maintained its hold. In the
1920s it was the notion of the virtuous countryman that writers,
artists, and commentators accepted as the legacy of the Literary
Revival period, rather than the heroic aristocratic figures of the
mythological cycles. A vision of rustic dignity and rural virtue
was popularized in speeches, poems, plays and paintings. In the
writings of Yeats and Synge rural figures had been employed as

images of wildness, pagan exuberance, earthy intuitive knowledge of deep-rooted things, but for many years less imaginative, more piously patriotic writers had produced countless poems in which peasants and farmers had appeared not to reveal human possibility but to exhibit the unspoiled simplicity of the essential Irish, who had for many violent centuries endured the ravages of climate and oppression. Poems of this kind had exploited conventional properties, such as the bog, hazel trees, streams, currachs, the hearth, primitive cooking utensils, ploughing, sowing, and rough weather, employing a verse technique that owed its simple repetitions and structure to folk song and its assonance and internal rhyme to the native Gaelic poetic tradition. They remained popular in the 1920s, and new poets took up the tradition, ready to exploit the prevailing literary fashion. They celebrated a version of Irish pastoral, where rural life was a condition of virtue inasmuch as it remained an expression of an ancient civilization, uncontaminated by commercialism and progress. In so doing they helped to confirm Irish society in a belief that rural life constituted an essential element of an unchanging Irish identity.

The social reality of the countryside was more dynamic; unheroic, hardly bucolic, and involved with change in ways which were eventually to disrupt it entirely. Indeed any study of the social profile of Irish society in the 1920s as the new state began to exercise its authority must impress upon the student the overwhelming nature of the problems that a government would have faced if it had attempted real social reorganization in the countryside. For example, overcrowding in housing was not simply confined to urban areas but was endemic in many rural counties as well, particularly in the west of the country. Most of the rural population lived in three-room dwellings, and this was true for each size of family from two to eleven persons. The three-room dwellings referred to in the census of 1926, from which these facts were adduced, were most frequently the whitewashed Irish thatched cottages, single-storey dwellings, seldom more than one room deep, with a kitchen, where a family ate, entertained themselves, met for gossip and talk with neighbours, a sleeping area, and a parlour for important family occasions. This form of dwelling, much loved of poets and playwrights as the heart of Irish pastoral with its permanently burning turf fire as image of its primeval vitality, was the setting throughout much of the country for a scarcely idyllic way of life in which thousands of Irish parents sought to raise their children in dignity despite the difficult circumstances. In 1926 (reckoning on current estimates in other European countries that defined families having more than two persons per room as living in overcrowded conditions) County Mayo had 43 percent of its population in such conditions, Donegal 40.8 percent, Kerry 38.9 percent, Galway 31.4 percent, and Sligo 30 percent, revealing that rural Ireland as well as urban was faced by a serious housing problem.

Between 1911 and 1926 the housing of the rural population had, however, improved somewhat, though clearly emigration had played its part in ameliorating the problem in a cruel way. There had been a decrease of 42 percent in one-room dwellings, a decrease of 33.9 percent in two-room dwellings, a decrease of 5.8 percent in three-room dwellings, and an increase of 34.1 percent in four-room dwellings. Despite such improvements, the overcrowding in Irish housing was aggravated by the high fertility rate of those Irishmen and women who did marry. As outlined in chapter one, Irish social patterns were characterized both by late marriage and by the large numbers of men and women who chose to remain single or to emigrate. What seems remarkable by contrast with this evidence of Irish inhibition and repression is the fact that the practice of raising large families also characterized Irish social life, particularly in the west of Ireland. The reasons for this apparent anomaly in the Irish character have troubled demographers, and the explanations are necessarily complex.[4] Be that as it may, in 1926 the figures for Irish fertility showed that married women under forty-five years of age in the state reared on an average 18 percent more children under five years of age than in Northern Ireland, 36 percent more than in Canada, 41 percent more than in Denmark, 44 percent more

han in Australia, 70 percent more than in the United States, and
35 percent more than in England and Wales.

Implicit in idealized literary portraits of Irish rural life in the
early decades of the twentieth century was the assumption that
a traditional culture still intact, inherited from a rich past, would
surely compensate the Irish countryman for any discomforts he
might be forced to endure in his humble but heroic condition.
Again, the social reality was less exhilarating than the writers
presumed. Certainly Irish rural life, particularly in the west of the
country, retained aspects of the traditional Irish civilization that
predated the Famine and the fairly general loss of the Irish language in the nineteenth century.[5] The old tales and legends were
still remembered by *seanachais* (storytellers) in parts of the west, a
repository of ballad, song, and historical legend had been handed
down, the people still observed ancient pre-Christian shibboleths
about fairy-thorns, holy wells, the rites of the agricultural year,
the calendar customs, magic cures, pishogues (or superstitions),
and the lore of the countryside. Folk festivals, folk drama, and
mummers and local saints' days still enlivened the work year.
Homes were furnished with the chairs, stools, settle beds, kitchen
dressers, bins, cooking utensils, the woven wickerwork baskets
and cradles, the artifacts wrought from the ubiquitous osier, that
were all the staple images of the Abbey Theatre's rural sets. Cooking was often still performed on the open hearth, where food
was suspended over turf fires and the housewife baked her family's
daily bread. Milk was churned at home, sometimes in the ancient
dash-churn which came in various forms in different parts of the
country and, since the previous century, in horse or donkey driven
dash-churns which lightened this heavy domestic load on the
woman of the house. Ropes were still twisted from local materials,
from straw, hay, rushes, bogwood, horsehair. The traditional
tools of Irish agriculture were still employed, the spades mostly
produced in spade-mills established in the nineteenth century,
but sometimes even the ancient wooden implement was used.
Grain was harvested sometimes with the sickle, more usually with
the scythe, and then threshed with a flail, though in some few

places this task was performed using the ancient method o
beating the grain with a stone. The hiring fair, where youn
agricultural labourers bearing their own spades sought to be hire
by wealthier farmers for the season of May to November, wa
still a feature of Irish rural life well into the 1930s. Traditiona
means of transport and carriage still dominated the rural scene
the horse or donkey-drawn cart, even, where the land was poo
and rough, the sledge or slidecar. Women could still be seer
carrying huge burdens on their heads as they had been fo
centuries.

When Irish writers turned to rural Ireland to discern there ar
unsullied tradition, they naturally highlighted those aspects o
that life which suggested an undying continuity, an impervi
ousness to change, an almost hermetic stasis that transcended
history. In so doing they were popularizing a notion of tradition
that ignored the degree to which Irish rural life by the early
twentieth century was as involved with the processes of history
and social change as any other. For the Irish countryman o
the late nineteenth and early twentieth century, while forced by
economic circumstances as much as by inclination to retain ways
of life that the writers could proclaim as time-honoured traditions.
also showed himself adept in acts of adaptation, innovation, and
even exploitation. He was ready to use horse-driven threshing
machines, prepared to experiment with steam, and in the 1930s
he began to welcome the tractor, which would render the agricultural labourer increasingly redundant, into his rural world. By
the 1920s the countryman and his family had willingly accepted
mass-produced articles of clothing, boots, and shoes. Their diet
represented not a traditional set of recipes and ingredients but
an intelligent adaptation to post-Famine agricultural conditions,
substituting for the milk and potatoes of pre-Famine times, grain,
eggs, and occasionally meat as the staples and by the 1920s a
ready acceptance of town bakers' bread, which on important
occasions replaced the breads cooked on the cottage fire. The
bicycle had introduced a new mobility to the Irish countryside,
and life in the long dark winters was made more agreeable by

the widespread use of commercially produced paraffin oil lamps which replaced the traditional rushlights.

Indeed, not only was some social change evident in the countryside in signs of adaptation and modernization but aspects of rural Ireland's life, the sports of hurling (which was of great antiquity) and football (which had been long played in Kerry), had been enlisted in support of the nationalist cause which in fact brought the rural world increasingly into contact with large-scale national organization and political movements.

Perhaps even more suggestive of the way the world of the towns and the cities was penetrating the countryside in the late nineteenth and early twentieth centuries in Ireland was the readiness with which rural dwellers quickly adapted to notions of respectability and social conformity that derived from the town. As living conditions improved somewhat and more and more small farmers abandoned the practice of keeping their livestock with them in the cottage (a practice once widespread in the peasant societies of Europe) and as numbers of them moved to the houses with loft bedrooms and slated roofs provided by the Congested Districts Board (founded in 1891) and by the commission which took over its work in 1923, and as others in the relative affluence of the years 1914–18 expanded their houses or converted them to two-storeyed structures or even built the two storeyed stone houses that date from this period all over the country, the life of the countryman became socially more akin to that of his town cousins than it had been even in the recent past. The parlour in the country cottage or small house, as in the shopkeeper's house in the town, became the place where the best pieces of furniture were displayed, where, as photography became popular, the family portraits were exhibited, where even a gramophone might appear and collections of china ornaments would rest on sills behind the ubiquitous lace curtains. On the wall would hang, gazing at the lares and the penates of the home, pictures of the pope and of Irish patriots and heroes that were the mass-produced icons of country- and town-dweller alike.

The towns to which the countryside was beginning to approximate in fashion and social forms were in 1926 mainly the many small collections of shops which served as service centres for the inhabitants of small surrounding rural districts. They had most developed[6] on the basis of the distance that could easily be traversed in the course of a day, spread out evenly across the Irish countryside about ten miles apart. Their population was in each case under 3,000. Larger towns of 3,000–10,000 persons were normally about thirty miles apart; the regional capitals, Dundalk, Athlone, Waterford, Limerick, Tralee, Galway, Sligo, Derry, are at least sixty miles apart. Small towns and villages which were either rebuilt after the ravages of the seventeenth-century wars or were laid out by paternalistic landlords in the eighteenth or early nineteenth century were the commonest elements of the Irish urban scene. Often near a large demesne, where the country house may have been converted into a convent or monastery, they usually comprised a main street with two- or three-storey houses on either side, where shopkeepers both resided and did their business. Sometimes there was a market-place or a town square and perhaps a small market hall. Some of the larger towns boasted a courthouse built in the classical style. The only recent buildings in such towns would have been the workhouses that were built in Ireland in the 1840s and 1850s under the Poor Law system, National Schools, hospitals, military barracks, railway stations, and the Catholic churches that were built in the post-Famine period declaring by size if not by their position in the towns that they had overtaken the Church of Ireland houses of worship in social importance. By the 1920s many of the towns were in a state of some dilapidation since often they depended on rural areas which were enduring population decline for their economic life blood. Indeed these many small and medium-sized towns in Ireland were to see little physical change or population increase until the 1960s.

The life of most of these towns was by the 1920s thoroughly anglicized and considerably modernized. As Neil Kevin (Don Boyne) wrote of Templemore, Country Tipperary, his native town, in 1943:

The fact that the overwhelming majority of the people in Ireland are in step with the rest of the English-speaking world is not deducible from the literature that is written about Ireland. . . .

Modernized countryside has not yet become "typically Irish" in print, though, out of print, it certainly is. The country town with a wireless-set in the houses of rich and poor, with a talkie-cinema, with inhabitants who wear the evening clothes of London or New York and dance the same dances to the same music – this town has not yet appeared in Irish literature, but it is the most typical Irish country town.[7]

The main activity of such towns was commerce conducted by family-owned concerns in shops retailing specific goods. Change which dated from about the First World War was at work in this world as it was on the small farm:

But recently a draper's life had consisted in moving and dusting, and dressing-out vast piles of tweed, cutting up innumerable lengths of grey calico and army grey shirting, measuring and trimming great quantities of single-width coarse frieze for conversion into the everlasting suits that farmers wore on Sundays, and like quantities of thick white flannel, which their wives made into sleeveless waistcoats or bawneens. Heaps of smelly corduroys, nailed boots, and wide-awake hats, all one model, had made up the stock-in-trade. The day had nearly drawn blood that put twenty pounds in the safe. And, suddenly, there was this new era of readymades, artificial silks, general fancies, and light footwear.[8]

The traders who sought respectability discouraged haggling over prices and warily eyed their competitors as they dispensed credit to the farm community that could not have existed without it. A concern with social class absorbed their excess energies directing the better-off traders to ally with members of the various professions to found tennis and golf clubs, establishing these as the symbols of polite social improvement. Life for the successful shopkeepers and the professional classes was comfortable if unadventurous. Income tax was low at three shillings in the pound in the 1920s, as were costs in general. Domestic help was readily available. Indeed, the census of 1926 reveals that nearly two-thirds of girls between thirteen and fifteen years of age who did not take up agricultural employment became domestic servants, helping to create a total of 87,000 such persons in the state as a whole. It was easy for well-placed, relatively prosperous people to ignore the social inequalities and problems of a society where the proportion of boys of sixteen and seventeen years who had no gainful employment was 28 percent, three times the proportion of such people in Scotland, England, and Wales, and the very large numbers of people, single women in particular, who were dependent on the productive work of others as they devoted themselves to the care of relatives. Of 899,000 females of twenty years and over recorded in the 1926 census, no less than 233,000, or over one-quarter, were widowed or single and without gainful employment. It allowed them to ignore a society where the number of orphans, widows, and aged persons was abnormally high, particularly in the west of the country. It allowed them also to feel a sense of class superiority to the landless labourers they saw in the marketplaces of their towns on hiring days.

Those Irish writers, painters, and polemicists therefore who chose to identify and celebrate an ancient rural national tradition in Ireland were required to ignore much of contemporary Irish social reality – the existence even in country districts of professional men and women for example (the 1926 census recorded 55,441, including 14,145 professed clergymen and nuns, 2,051 medical doctors, 16,202 teachers, 5,341 sick nurses in the state as a whole) or the increasingly modernized countryside that was reducing the numbers of farm labourers through redundancy – directing attention by contrast wholly to the tiny regions in the west of the country, where they could affirm that a vestige of ancient Gaelic aristocracy remained:

> The racial strength of a Gaelic aristocratic mind – with its vigorous colouring and hard emotion – is easily recognized in Irish poetry, by those acquainted with the literature of our own people. Like our Gaelic stock, its poetry is sun-bred. . . . Not with dreams – but with fire in the mind, the eyes of Gaelic

poetry reflect a richness of life and the intensity of a dark people, still part of our landscape.[9]

There was something poignant in fact about the way in which so many Irish imaginations in the early twentieth century were absorbed by the Irish west, almost as if from the anglicized rather mediocre social actuality with its manifest problems, its stagnant towns and villages, they sought inspiration for vision in extremities of geography and experience. They looked to the edge of things for imaginative sustenance.

The 1920s saw the confirmation of the west, of the Gaeltacht, and particularly of the western island as the main locus of Irish cultural aspiration. John Wilson Foster has argued cogently that the image of the western island in pre-revolutionary Ireland had served as:

> . . . a new creation myth for an imminent order . . . as the Gaelic Revival and new nationalism gained momentum, especially after the founding of the Gaelic League in 1893, western islands such as the Arans and Blaskets focused the place of impending awakening, providing a symbolic and it was hoped actual site where Ireland would be born again . . . The western island came to represent Ireland's mythic unity before the chaos of conquest: there at once were the vestige and symbolic entirety of an undivided nation.[10]

After the War of Independence and the Civil War in a politically divided island with a border truncating the country, the image of the creative unity of the west, the vision of heroic rural life in the Gaeltacht or on a western island served as a metaphor of social cohesion and an earnest of a cultural unity that transcended class politics and history. Islands of Gaelic-speaking people in a sea of anglicization, the Gaeltacht and the western island represented that ideal unity which nationalist ideologues had envisaged and prophesied, but which reality had failed to provide. Douglas Hyde advised an audience at a heady meeting in Dublin's Mansion House in 1926, after the publication of the Gaeltacht Commission's report:

Remember that the best of our people were driven by Cromwell to hell or Connacht. Many of our race are living on the seaboard where Cromwell drove them. They are men and women of the toughest fibre. They have been for generations fighting with the sea, fighting with the weather, fighting with the mountains. They are indeed the survival of the fittest. Give them but half a chance and they are the seeds of a great race . . . it will save the historical Irish Nation for it will preserve for all time the fountain-source from which future generations can draw for ever.[11]

Before the 1920s most literary studies of the Irish-speaking districts and of the west had been cast as voyages of discovery. John Millington Synge's classic *The Aran Islands* (1907) is both representative and apogee of the tradition. In such treatments the structural movement of the work is a journey from the bourgeois world of self to an almost prelapsarian innocence and community which the writer can enter or, as in John Synge's work, employ to highlight his own Romantic, melancholic alienation. In 1941 Seán O'Faoláin remembered his own introduction to the western island in 1918 in terms that powerfully evoke the imaginative attraction of this region to generations of Irish men and women. It was a release from self into community, and escape from prose to poetry, from complexity to simplicity:

It was like taking off one's clothes for a swim naked in some mountain-pool. Nobody who has not had this sensation of suddenly "belonging" somewhere – of finding the lap of the lost mother – can understand what a release the discovery of Gaelic Ireland meant to modern Ireland. I know that not for years and years did I get free of this heavenly bond of an ancient, lyrical, permanent, continuous immemorial self, symbolized by the lonely mountains, the virginal lakes, the traditional language, the simple, certain, uncomplex modes of life, that world of the lost childhood of my race where I, too, became for a while eternally young.[12]

Recollecting such bliss, the writer admitted to a "terrible nostalgia for that old content, that old symbolism, that sense of being as woven into a pattern of life as a grain of dust in a piece of homespun."[13]

In the 1920s a number of literary works were published which attempted a more realistic treatment of the western island and the Gaeltacht, in a tradition that had begun with the short stories of the Irish-language writer Pádraic Ó Conaire and of Seumas O'Kelly. These were works of fictional realism written by men who know the Gaeltacht intimately. Novels such as Peadar O'Donnell's *Islanders* (1928) and *Adrigoole* (1929) and Liam O'Flaherty's *Thy Neighbour's Wife* (1923) are works therefore not of romantic discovery but essays in rural naturalism and social criticism. What is striking about the work of both these writers, who wrote their novels with a vigorous socialist concern to unmask social injustice in the Irish countryside through literary realism, is that they both seem tempted by the vision of an Irish rural world that exists beyond political reality. At moments the Irish rural scene in both their works is allowed to occupy the same primal, essentially mythic territory as it does in the conceptions of purely nationalist ideologues. In both O'Donnell's and O'Flaherty's writings there are passages of epic writing therefore which obtrude in their realistic settings. At such moments class politics and social analysis give way before an apprehension of the west as a place of fundamental natural forces, of human figures set passively or heroically against landscapes of stone, rock, and sea in a way that makes their works less radical than they perhaps thought they were. There is implicit therefore in their writings a sense that Gaelic Ireland in the west is the authentic heroic Ireland in a way that confirms rather than contradicts the conventional image of the west as "certain set apart." The power of this conventional image was perhaps so great that it affected as intelligent a social commentator as Peadar O'Donnell and overwhelmed the turbulent anger of Liam O'Flaherty's social criticism.

So in the 1920s the sense of the western island and of the west as specially significant in Irish life became a cultural commonplace. Even an English visitor in 1924 fell under its spell:

The West is different. Its spirit was used by the intellectuals in the late struggle but it was never theirs. It seems to come from some primitive elemental force which smoulders on, like a turf fire, long after such movements have spent themselves. It is a permanent factor to the existence of which no Irish statesman can safely shut his eyes.[14]

The Northern Protestant naturalist R. Lloyd Praeger could declare:

If I wished to show anyone the best thing in Ireland I would take him to Aran. Those grey ledges of limestone, rain-beaten and storm-swept, are different from anything else. The strangeness of the scene, the charm of the people (I don't refer to the rabble that meets the steamer), the beauty of the sea and sky, the wealth of both pagan and Christian antiquities . . . all these help to make a sojourn in Aran a thing never to be forgotten.[15]

When in November 1927, forty fishermen were drowned in a storm off the west coast, even the *Irish Statesman* which had, as we shall see, its own reasons to reject the primacy of Gaelic civilization in Irish life, responded to the disaster in elegiac terms, aligning the journal uneasily with all those who thought the west the cradle of Irish civilization:

But the trawlers in which modern fishermen elsewhere go out to sea seem safe almost as the land compared with these frail curraghs which visitors to the west of Ireland see dancing on the waters. As one watched these curraghs and the fishermen on that rocky coast seemed almost like contemporaries of the first men who adventured on the seas, their Gaelic language and their curraghs alike survivals from ancient centuries. These western fishermen are a very fine type, full of character and vitality, and Gaelic enthusiasts from contact with these vestiges of the Gaelic past have tried to conjure up an image of the Gaelic world when the tide of life was high in its heart.[16]

The vision of the western island as the primal source of the nation's being received further confirmation in 1929 with the publication of Tomás Ó Criomhthain's work *An tOileánach* (*The*

Islandman). Works of this kind, in which an islander's reminiscences were recorded in written form by researchers and literary men and are then translated, came in a few brief years to
comprise almost a modern Irish subgenre. *The Islandman* (the
English translation) is one of the finest examples of this type of
work, exhibiting a strong narrative sense and swift economy of
style and discourse. A sense of an almost Homeric, heroically
charged zest emerges from a keenly objective record of island
life.[17] For any who might be inclined to doubt the primal rural
superiority of the western world in Irish reality these accounts
of work, feasting, death, play, fighting, and drinking could be
proffered as ready proof. For in the pages of *The Islandman* it
seems we are seeing island life not through the eyes of literary
discovery or nationalist wish-fulfilment but from the cottages and
currachs of the islands themselves. The work has an exhilarating
freshness about it, an impression of fundamental things, a sense
of origins.

In the difficult years of reconstruction after the Civil War, in
the 1920s and early 1930s, the Free State government made
few conscious attempts other than the encouragement of Gaelic
revival to project a cultural image of the nation despite the
resources they had inherited and might have exploited systematically. A direct espousal of rural civilization was to be the cultural
contribution of Mr. de Valera in the following decade. The
government granted an annual subsidy to the Abbey Theatre in
1925, to an Irish-language theatre, An Taibhdhearc, in Galway
in 1928, and established a publishing venture named An Gúm
in 1926 for the publication of books in Irish. Apart from these
fairly minimal gestures the government seemed content to
approve, where it did not simply ignore, the work of writers who
dwelt in a conservative and nationalistic fashion on rural aspects
of the country's life, while establishing a Censorship Board which
would, it transpired, repress writings which might disturb conventional moral sensitivities.

But almost as if to confirm the symbolic significance of rural
images in the cultural life of the state, in 1927 the Minister

for Finance received the recommendation of the Irish Coinage Committee, established to help implement the Coinage Act of 1926 under the chairmanship of W. B. Yeats. Those recommendations were that the Irish coinage, which was first issued in 1928, should bear the images of Irish animals and wildlife rather than the traditional hackneyed symbols of Ireland, round towers, the shamrock, and sunbursts. There were some objections to this decision from individuals who suggested that animal imagery was insufficiently Christian for the Irish nation's coinage. The choice of birds and beasts as the basis of an Irish coinage's iconography was in part dictated by the committee's desire that the coinage should be a unified series of images, but individual members of the committee were firmly persuaded that the images selected bore intimately on the rural nature of Irish life. "What better symbols could we find for this horse-riding, salmon-fishing, cattle-raising country?"[18] wrote the chairman, W. B. Yeats, and Thomas Bodkin, a governor of the National Gallery of Ireland and a subsequent director, concurred with his chairman:

> Coins are the tangible tokens of a people's wealth. Wealth in the earliest times was always calculated in terms of cattle. Thence comes the word *pecunia*, money, derived from *pecus*, the beast. The wealth of Ireland is still derived in overwhelming proportion from the products of her soil. What, therefore, could be more appropriate than the depiction upon our coinage of those products?[19]

And so Percy Metcalfe's beautiful designs were issued in 1928, giving Ireland a coinage that depicted her agricultural, rural, and sporting life in the images of a woodcock, a chicken, a pig with piglets, a hare, a wolfhound, a bull, a hunter, and a salmon.

Irish painters of the period were also touched by the prevailing rural understanding of Irish identity. As Bruce Arnold has remarked, there is in the work of painters in the 1920s and 1930s, such as Paul Henry, William Conor, Sean O'Sullivan, and Maurice MacGonigal, "often an uncomfortable feeling of strain, a self-consciousness about what 'being Irish' meant."[20] From the painters of this period, whom Arnold has broadly defined as comprising a school of "Irish academic realism," come those pictures of countrymen and women, fishermen, small farmers, turf stacks against cloudy skies, and cottages in secluded places, which seem so representative of the early years of independence. Paul Henry was probably the most popular of these artists, and his simple, often unpeopled landscapes seemed to express for many Irish men and women a sense of essential Irish realities. He was almost the official artist of the Free State – a painting entitled "Errigal Co. Donegal" was used as the frontispiece to the *Irish Free State Official Handbook* published in 1932. It pictures a small Irish village huddling beneath an austere mountain and a clouded sky. This official handbook, in fact, draws heavily for its illustrations on the work of Henry, Seán O'Sullivan, and Maurice MacGonigal, all artists absorbed by the Irish landscape.

So cultural life in the new state was dominated by a vision of Ireland, inherited from the period of the Literary Revival, as a rural Gaelic civilization that retained an ancient pastoral distinctiveness. This vision was projected by artists, poets, and polemicists despite the fact that social reality showed distinct signs that the country was adapting to the social forms of the English-speaking world and that conditions in rural Ireland were hardly idyllic. It is probable, as I have suggested, that this imaginative interpretation of Irish rural life, particularly as lived on the western island, served as an integrative symbol of national identity in the early years of independence. It helped to confirm people in a belief in Irish distinctiveness, justifying that political separatism which a revolutionary movement had made a linchpin of political life in the state. As such, it provided an imaginative consolidation of the new order in which a conservative, nationalist people in a society dominated by farmers and their offspring in the professions and in trade believed that they had come at last into their rightful inheritance – possession of the land and political independence.

But there were other symbolic properties that the new state had enlisted to sustain its sense of its national uniqueness. In addition to the imaginative legacy that the recent past had bequeathed to modern Ireland in powerful images of heroism and idyll, the new Irish state was significantly blessed with a repository of national treasures that had either been unearthed in the preceding century or had entered into the popular consciousness at that time. Many of these treasures were associated with Irish Christianity in the Hiberno-Romanesque period, and they had become charged in the nineteenth century with a national as well as religious symbolism. Great works of art and craft, the Cross of Cong, the Ardagh Chalice, the Books of Kells and Durrow, had become identified with the Celtic genius. Lady Wilde, the mother of the playwright, had written in 1888:

> Early Irish art illustrates in a very remarkable manner those distinctive qualities of Irish nature, which we know from the legendary traditions have characterized our people from the earliest times. . . . All these reverential, artistic, fanciful, and subtle evidences of the peculiar celtic spirit find a full and significant expression in the wonderful splendours of Irish art.[21]

So profound a sense of national significance became attached to the Celtic treasures, which were widely admired after the opening of the National Museum of Ireland in 1890, that its effects permeated Irish design work of all kinds in the twentieth century. Ireland, such work signified in bookplates, medals, jewellery, Christmas cards, Celtic lettering on shopfronts, letterheads, postage stamps, and tombstones, was once the centre of great artistic achievement, was dignified by the peculiar genius of her people, and could become so again.

By the 1920s enthusiasm among artists for Celtic design had perhaps passed its peak, the high point of the movement being the work that the Dun Emer Guild produced in the early years of the century. Nevertheless, at a popular, often rather crude level, Celtic designs continued to be associated with Irish national identity in the first decades of Irish independence. Indeed, the *Official State Handbook* published in 1932 sets the title on a front cover in pseudo-Celtic lettering against a background based on the Book of Kells and contains plates of the National Museum's treasures, as well as reproductions of Irish landscape art. One aspect of the Celtic revival in arts and craftwork, however, maintained standards of unusual excellence well into the 1930s.

Many of the Irish treasures which fired the imaginations of designers and artists in the early twentieth century had been works of Christian art, associated with worship and piety. It does not, therefore, seem surprising that concurrently a group of artists, partly at the urging of that pious but practical patron and playwright Edward Martyn, had established a cooperative, An Tur Gloine (The Tower of Glass)[22] to provide stained-glass windows for Irish churches which made possible the very remarkable work of Harry Clarke, Michael Healy, and Evie Hone. These artists were to produce some of their finest church windows in the 1920s and 1930s. Certainly they had received part of their inspiration from the fairly widespread English and European interest in craftwork and religious art in the late nineteenth and early twentieth centuries, but the sense of Irish antecedents must also have stimulated them in their labours. Once again Ireland was becoming known as a centre of Christian art as Irish missionaries took their knowledge of this modern achievement abroad with them and as Irish stained-glass work received international recognition. As James White and Michael Wynne affirmed in 1961:

By the end of the 1920s standards in stained-glass production had so risen in Ireland that it could safely be claimed that this was one sphere of art in which we as a race had taken a commanding position and in which one could point to an individual Irish school. Could it be that these Irish artists had inherited an instinctive feeling for the gleaming colours and dark sinuous lines which make the Celtic illuminators the most remarkably creative beings produced in our island? This suggestion may seem far-fetched since twelve centuries separate the two groups. Yet comparison throws up many similarities, not least of which was a desire in both cases to suggest the sanctity and holiness of the saints and to see them as removed from the worldly ambience so attractive to artists in other mediums.[23]

In this chapter we have seen how images of heroic nobility lost their imaginative potency in the 1920s and how a largely conservative, rurally based society found its self-understanding expressed in minor literary and artistic works whose claims to attention now are often little more than a conventional rustic charm. It is good, therefore, to reflect for a moment on the achievements of these artists in stained glass who, without compromising high standards, managed both a measure of popular esteem and international reputation before we consider in the following chapter the defeats and distresses endured by those social groups and individuals who in the 1920s and early 1930s found the social and cultural character of newly independent Ireland less than inspiring.

CHAPTER 4

The Fate of the Irish Left and
of the Protestant Minority

It might have been expected that the Catholic nationalist conservatism which dominated Irish society in the first decade of the
Irish Free State's history would have met with some significant
political opposition from two sources – from the forces of organized labour and from the ranks of the Protestant minority in
the state. The former had, as their intellectual inheritance, the
internationally minded writings of the socialist, syndicalist, and
revolutionary James Connolly, executed after the Rising of
1916, and experience of the bitter class conflicts of 1913 in
Dublin, to generate commitment to a view of Irish society which
would emphasize class interests and divisions, rather than a
nationalist vision of social and cultural unity transcending class.
And Protestant Ireland, culturally and emotionally involved with
the English-speaking world and recently represented in Westminster by the Unionist party, was naturally antagonistic to those
definitions of Irish nationality current in the new state which
emphasized the centrality of either Catholicism or the Irish language and the Gaelic past. The fact is, however, that neither
organized labour nor the Protestant community was able to
mount any effective political opposition to the dominant political,

ideological, and cultural consensus of the early years of independence. The reasons for this require analysis.

In 1922 Irish Labour politics were expressed through the trade union movement and the Irish Labour Party. The Labour Party, with admirable if naive political idealism, had chosen not to contest the elections of 1918 and 1921, believing that such restraint would allow the electorate to express itself unambiguously on the national question. So, despite the incorporation of aspects of Labour policy in the Democratic Programme adopted by the First Dáil in January 1919, a number of years were to elapse before the popularity of socialist policies of however diluted a kind could be tested at the polls. As a result, the Labour Party stood on the sidelines of Irish politics throughout the crucial years of the War of Independence until 1922. As the Free State began reconstruction it found itself unable to make much electoral headway. Furthermore, the trade union movement in the 1920s was ill prepared to mount a sustained attack on the conservative basis of the social order, even if it had wished to do so, nor was it able to provide the industrial muscle for a militant labour programme. The movement was split by inter-union struggles, and in the widespread depression, bred of disunity, trade union membership declined steeply. Furthermore, many categories of workers had no union organizations to represent their interests. By the end of the decade, with the Labour Party's role as a responsible parliamentary opposition rendered almost nugatory by the entry of Fianna Fáil to the Dáil in 1927 and with the trade union movement at odds with itself and largely ignored by the government and the civil service as the worldwide economic depression began to make itself felt in Ireland, the likelihood that a consistent, energetic, politically powerful, socialist critique might be developed to challenge the prevailing economic and social orthodoxy was dim indeed. At the end of the first decade of independence, organized labour in Ireland could take comfort only from the fact that the Irish Labour Party was still in existence and that the inspirational force of James Larkin (the labour leader who had played a crucial role in Dublin in 1913), to the fore in the

Workers' Union of Ireland, had kept alive the fitful flames of a revolutionary working-class consciousness in Dublin, which had flared almost two decades earlier. In years when the dominant nationalism often combined, in the wake of the Bolshevik successes in the Soviet Union, with outright antagonism to socialist ideas of politics, that even this little was achieved is a testament to the dedication and will of those few individuals who were prepared to plant socialist seeds for a later harvesting.

The policies and approach adopted by the Labour Party in the 1920s reflected the fact that the social panorama scarcely admitted of revolutionary perspectives. The party, under the leadership of Thomas Johnson, who was concurrently secretary of the Irish Congress of Trade Unions, abandoned the revolutionary syndicalism of James Connolly while continuing to venerate his memory, preferring a cautious use of parliamentary tactics to advance the workers' cause. "I have," Johnson wrote in 1925, "advocated the use by the workers of political means and parliamentary institutions to further their cause. I have opposed the proposition that the workers should rely solely on their economic power to attain their ends. I have acted in the belief that a democratic government would preserve the fundamental rights which have been won and would not lightly cast aside those social obligations which they had inherited from their predecessors."[1] He continued in a passage that very fully expresses the position adopted by the great majority of Labour Party and trade union members in Ireland, throughout the twentieth century:

> Shall the aim be honestly to remove poverty . . . or are we to agitate and organize with the object of waging the "class war" more relentlessly, and use "the unemployed" and the "poverty of the workers" as propagandist cries to justify our actions . . . I do not think this view of the mission of the Labour Movement has any promise of ultimate usefulness in Ireland.[2]

Johnson knew his electorate and suspected how precarious was Labour's hold on Irish life in the Free State. For, lacking a solid base in a large industrial proletariat (only about 13 percent of the workforce was employed in industry of any kind – the island's only real industrial centre was north of the border in Belfast), and, after 1926, in competition in rural areas with the popular reformism of Fianna Fáil, Labour had a difficult enough task in mere survival, without espousing what Johnson feared were ideas "in direct conflict with the religious faith of our people."[3]

The cultural effects of this socialist eclipse in twentieth-century Ireland are not far to seek. The socialist ideas and preoccupations of much of modern Europe had curiously little currency in a country where ideology meant protracted, repetitive debates on the national question with little attention directed, until the 1960s, to class issues and social conditions. Indeed, one of the obvious weaknesses of Irish intellectual life in much of the period was the absence of a coherent, scientific study of society of the kind that in many European countries had its roots in a socialist concern to comprehend the ills of a manifestly unjust social order. For decades, indeed, such issues as the decline of the Irish language were most frequently discussed in terms of culture and nationality, without any serious effort to challenge an economic order which allowed the haemorrhage of emigration from Irish-speaking districts to flow unabated for forty years. Where other Europeans engaged in a conflict about the very nature of man and society, Irish men and women, writers, artists, politicians, workers committed themselves to a vision of national destiny which often meant a turning away from much uncomfortable social reality to conceptions of the nation as a spiritual entity that could compensate for a diminished experience. The counterpoint that a powerful socialist party and working-class movement might have represented in the intellectual and cultural life of the country in the first decades of independence is a possibility we find sounding only fitfully early in the century and suffering an almost complete extinction in the 1920s. There were, in fact, until recently, very few novels and plays of Irish working-class life in twentieth-century writing. Only in the plays of O'Casey was the world of the urban proletariat employed as the material of a committed art. There were no Irish disciples of Brecht, no efforts, apart from O'Casey's later plays written in exile, to produce a literature *engagé* on behalf of socialism; indeed, only in a very few historical studies did the socialist ideas that absorbed so many European minds in the twentieth century find any large-scale Irish expression.

If the left in Ireland was unwilling or unable to pose a politically effective ideological challenge to the governing assumptions of the new state, the Protestant minority was manifestly unable to fill the breach. By 1922 the events of the preceding decade had rendered that once spirited and assured ruling caste nervously defeatist and impotent. Many of its members almost to the eve of revolution had refused to countenance the possibility of Home Rule for Ireland, and even those who had in one way or another so envisaged the Irish future now found themselves overtaken by events which had precipitated an even less desirable resolution of the national struggle. The establishment of the Irish Free State found Protestant Ireland in the twenty-six counties ideologically, politically, and emotionally unprepared for the uncharted waters of the new separatist seas, where they comprised what was seen by many of their nationalist fellow citizens as an ethnic minority.

Ideologically, the Protestants of Ireland, apart from certain few individuals who had been aroused by an enthusiasm for Gaelic revival and the cultural renaissance, had in the decade before independence made almost no effort to comprehend the national-ist cause. A dismissive contemptuousness had often reflected the offensive blend of insecurity and caste snobbery that characterized fairly commonplace Protestant reactions to Irish nationalism. The Irish Ireland movement by turn had not hesitated to reply in kind, proposing a theory of Irish nationality that denied full spiritual communion with the Irish nation to the colonizing, landed Anglo-Irishman with his apparently English accent, manner, and loyalties and his Protestant faith. It was indeed the Irish Ireland movement that had given potent propagandist currency to the term Anglo-Irish itself, to the discomfort of many individuals who had hitherto had no doubts of their fully Irish patrimony. Even those of them who had sought to sympathize with Irish needs and aspirations had found themselves denied a secure hold on their own Irish identity in these years by the propagandist outspokenness of the Irish Irelanders. Accustomed to think of themselves as unambiguously Irish, indeed Irish in one of the best possible ways, they had found themselves swiftly becoming treated in the newspapers, in political speeches, and in polemical pamphlets as strangers in their own land. The Celt and the Irish language were the new orthodoxies comprising an ethnic dogmatism that cast Anglo-Ireland in the role of alien persecutor of the one true faith. Furthermore, the recurrent political and emotional crises of the decade preceding independence had not allowed many Protestant Irishmen and women sufficient leisure and sense of security to devise an intellectual counter to the assaults of Irish Ireland or indeed much opportunity even to consider, had they cared to, the kinds of defence the poet W. B. Yeats had in fact developed in the face of Irish Ireland's assault on what he thought were values Anglo-Ireland most fully possessed. Rather, the trauma of the Home Rule crisis, followed by the Great War in which so many of their sons perished and the savageries of guerrilla war in their own land, had left them without ideological resource, concerned only with economic and actual survival.

The Irish minority, to which the term Anglo-Ireland had recently been attached so uncomfortably, and which hoped for survival in these difficult circumstances, was not a large one in the twenty-six counties of the Irish Free State. Before the partition of the country in 1920, Protestant Ireland had been able to feel a certain security inasmuch as it comprised one-quarter of the population of the entire island. In 1926 the census in the Free State revealed that only 7.4 percent of the population of the twenty-six counties was recorded as professing the Protestant faith. Of these, only a few were the substantially landed Protestant gentry that for generations had intermarried with one another, with the better-born Catholic Irish, and with the English aristocracy and had supplied the empire with politicians, statesmen, soldiers, and sailors and Ireland with a ruling caste, with sportsmen, churchmen, and occasionally patriots. Many of these Irish gentry had resided on large estates in the predominantly rural provinces of Munster and Connacht, where by 1926 they comprised an extreme minority of the population. Indeed in the 1926 census only 2.6 percent of the population of Connacht was returned as Protestant while in Munster the figure was 3.6 percent.

For the rest, the Protestant population of the Irish Free State was made up of inhabitants of the three counties of Ulster that had been included in the state where 18.2 percent professed the Protestant faith and inhabitants of Leinster where 10.1 percent of the population was Protestant. In the Ulster counties of Cavan, Monaghan, and Donegal many of the Protestants were small and medium-sized farmers, whose emotional centre of gravity often lay across the Irish border as bonds of blood and political instinct tied them to a more vigorous and populist Protestant unionism than had commonly been espoused by the Anglo-Irish gentry to the south (the Orange Order remained a strong influence on Protestant life in these counties almost to the present day). In Leinster much of the Protestant population was made up of professional and businessmen (Protestants were particularly well represented in the banking and legal professions and in the biscuit, brewing, distilling, and builders' providers trades), who undoubtedly felt a kinship with the Irish Protestant gentry of the former Ascendancy to whom they were often related, but whose interests would increasingly lie in a prudent accommodation with the new order. Such people and their families, helping to give a distinctive social tone to such fashionable areas in and near Dublin as Rathmines and Rathgar, where in 1926 33.2 percent of the population was Protestant, and Greystones, where 57.4 percent of the population declared themselves to be such, probably shared more in social terms (though they often did not care to admit it) with their Catholic, suburban, middle-class contemporaries than with the landowners of the former Protestant Ascendancy. As time went on and the political climate relaxed, this would allow for their integration into the new Ireland in ways which would not be so easily possible for their landed coreligionists and kin, whose possession of such tracts of the Irish soil as they still owned would always be liable to affront nationalist sensibilities. So what before independence had been a social minority bound together by religious affiliation and Unionist politics became fragmented upon independence: the remaining landowners isolated in the countryside, the farmers of the Ulster counties unsettled in mind and ready to move to the more congenial atmosphere of Northern Ireland, and the Protestant professional and business community concerned about stability and nervously ready to accept the new order if it offered such. What they all shared was a sense of isolation and of political impotence.

Independence marked therefore the end of the Protestant minority's significant political power in the South of Ireland. Indeed, in its fragmented state it is difficult to see how any political party could have represented its interests in specific ways. None attempted the task, and the political associations that had directed the Unionist cause before independence swiftly became defunct. It is true that about seventeen former Southern Unionists were to be granted seats as non-elected members of the Upper House of the Oireachtas, Seanad Eireann (the Senate), but the actual political insecurity experienced by the Protestant community in Ireland at independence can be adjudged the more certainly by the remarkable spectacle of a delegation dispatched by the general synod of the Church of Ireland on 12 May 1922 to wait on Michael Collins to inquire in what may strike one now as plaintive terms indeed, "if they were permitted to live in Ireland or if it was desired that they should leave the country."[4] (It is surely revelatory that it was a church body and not a political party or association that took this step.) Collins's firm assurance that they were welcome to remain and would be protected by his forces must have relieved them as it evidenced in a very important quarter indeed the existence of that republican strand in modern Irish nationalism which owes something to an eighteenth-century vision of an Irish democracy which could offer a secure home to Catholic, Protestant, and dissenter alike. But events in the country itself, over which it is only fair to emphasize Collins and the provisional government's army had a far from satisfactory military control, must have seemed to many Anglo-Irish people to suggest that less idealistic forces might swamp the exemplary conscientiousness of the new administration. Between 6 December 1921 and 22 March 1923, 192 Big Houses were burned by incendiaries as reported in the *Morning Post* of 9 April 1923.[5] Although these attacks on the houses of the former Ascendancy can be understood as part of a political and military strategy (many of the houses were burned by republicans who considered probably rightly that their occupants were supporters of the Treaty party), to Anglo-Ireland itself this must have seemed a veritable *Jacquerie* and a painful demonstration of their isolated vulnerability in an Ireland which no longer appeared to accept them.

The emotional state of Anglo-Ireland in the period was registered in a number of novels which appeared in the 1920s and early 1930s which employed the Big House as a metaphor that might allow the author to explore the socially disintegrated world of the Protestant Ascendancy. In 1925 Edith Somerville published *The Big House of Inver*, a chronicle of passion, vice, enmity, and corruption which destroy the great house of the work's title. In the opening chapters the writer ponders the decline in the fortunes of the house as an emblem of social decay among her Anglo-Irish peers. She is tough-minded and ironic about their plight, convinced that they and their ancestors were in large measure the architects of their own downfall. The Anglo-Irish Big House had been a noble conception: "Inver House embodied one of those large gestures of the mind of the earlier Irish architects, some of which still stand to justify Ireland's claim to be considered a civilized country."[6] Such defiance, she recognizes, comes too late; too many houses have been burned, destroyed before the fire took them, from within. The house that "faced unflinching the western ocean" suffered a fierce blow in the Famine of 1845, but the line of succession had been sullied before that by an act of lustful folly. From this primal sin can be traced subsequent incapacities to outface the blows of fate and history: "The glories and the greatness of Inver therewith suffered downfall. Five successive generations of mainly halfbred and wholly profligate Prendevilles rioted out their short lives, living with country women, fighting, drinking, gambling."[7] The Famine was only the axe that felled the dying tree:

> Many an ancient property foundered and sank in that storm, drawing down with it – as a great ship in her sinking sucks down those that trusted in her protection – not alone its owners, but also the swarming families of the people who, in those semi-feudal times, looked to the Big Houses for help. The martyrdoms, and the heroisms, and the devotion, have passed into oblivion, and better so, perhaps, when it is remembered how a not extravagant exercise of political foresight might have saved the martyrdoms. As for other matters, it might only intensify the embittering of a now outcast class to be reminded of what things it suffered and sacrificed in doing what it held to be its duty.[8]

Such stern resignation to Anglo-Ireland's demise, with its flash of anger at wasted opportunities, was rare in the ranks of her Anglo-Irish contemporaries, but Edith Somerville bears eloquent testimony here to the bitterness and sense of social isolation many of her fellows experienced in the 1920s.

There were those who hoped that resignation was premature, that Anglo-Ireland might have some role to play in the new Ireland even if its political power was broken. One of the most poignant expressions of this hope was the novel published in 1929 by Elizabeth Bowen, *The Last September*. In 1942, writing of her own ancestral home, Bowen's Court, she reflected on the isolation which she felt was a central feature of Anglo-Ireland's experience, made the more severe by the development of the Irish Free State and the depredations of wartime, but a constant of its history.

> Each of these family houses, with its stables and farm and gardens deep in trees at the end of long avenues, is an island – and, like an island, a world. . . . Each of these houses, with its intense, centripetal life, is isolated by something very much more lasting than the physical fact of space: the isolation is innate; it is an affair of origin.[9]

The Last September is set in a Big House at a moment when that innate isolation was intense, during the grim months of the War of Independence in 1920. The heroine, Lois Farquar, orphaned niece to Sir Richard Naylor of Danielstown, becomes conscious, amid the comings and goings of guests, the tennis parties and dances arranged for the British garrison, of a haunting isolation, a sense of space ready to be filled when the transitional years of adolescence are done with, when autumn achieves the definition of winter, when the war that threatens their lives has been resolved.

> Looking down, it seemed to Lois they lived in a forest; space of lawns blotted out in the pressure and dusk of trees. She wondered they were not smothered; then wondered still more that they were not afraid. Far from here, too, their isolation became apparent. The house seemed to be pressing down low in apprehension, hiding its face, as though it had her vision of where it was. It seemed to gather its trees close in fright and amazement at the wide light lovely unloving country, the unwilling bosom whereon it was set.[10]

The basic metaphor of the novel is the emptiness of the spaces in the house and the space between the house and the landscape and society it has been set amidst. Early in the novel Lois walks among the laurel trees in the shrubbery and comes undetected upon a man in a trench coat:

> It must be because of Ireland he was in such a hurry; down from the mountains, making a short-cut through their demesne. Here was something else that she could not share. She could not conceive of her country emotionally: it was a way of living, abstract of several landscapes, or an oblique, frayed island moored at the north but with an air of being detached and drawn out west from the British coast.[11]

She recognizes that, "Conceivably she had surprised life at a significant angle in the shrubbery," and the book suggests, in its constant metaphors of empty space, that perhaps some means can be discovered of filling them with a significance that will relate the isolated Ascendancy world of Lois Farquar to the wide, active countryside that surrounds her house. But the book's expression of hope for such a relationship is muted and rendered plaintive by the valedictory movement of its prose and by the chilly finality of its scrupulously composed social tableaux and vistas. Written with the knowledge of 1929, the whole is contained within the final metaphor of empty spaces filled at the last by fire:

> At Danielstown, half way up the avenue under the beeches, the thin iron gate twanged (missed its latch, remained swinging aghast) as the last unlit car slid out with the executioners bland from accomplished duty. The sound of the last car widened, gave itself to the open and empty country and was demolished. Then the first wave of a silence that was to be ultimate flowed back, confident, to the steps. Above the step the door stood open hospitably upon a furnace.[12]

It was possible, perhaps, to those less sensitive to the emotional isolation so precisely explored by an Elizabeth Bowen, to pretend that while the new order might refer to Kingstown as Dun Laoghaire, Kingstown it remained in polite society and that the National Anthem was still "God Save the King," though Queen Victoria's statue had vanished from the forecourt of Leinster House, former home of the Royal Dublin Society, now the seat of government.[13] Brian Inglis, in *West Briton*, his witty account of Protestant society life in Malahide (a seaside town seven miles north of Dublin) in the period following independence, gives a spirited account of a contentedly vestigial world. He remembers:

> Their social world remained stable; like a prawn in aspic it gradually began to go stale, but it did not disintegrate. All around them "that other Ireland" as George Russell (Æ) had called it, was coming into its force, but they remained almost unaware of its existence.[14]

Accent, social class, and religion still determined membership of the exclusive Island Golf Club. General satisfaction was expressed at the government's impeccably orthodox economic policies.

Indeed, as he recalls: "The State's effort to impose what to us was an alien culture and, worse, an alien language, was almost the only feature of life in the Free State which compelled our attention and aroused our active resentment."[15] Sailing, dancing, hunting, and the club remained to distract Anglo-Ireland and those who felt themselves associated with it from uncomfortable developments, while the thriving condition of the Royal Dublin Society, with its lectures, concerts, and library suggested that the cultural influence of the distinctly Anglo-Irish or Protestant institutions was still strong. Membership of the society, which established itself in new premises in Ballsbridge in Dublin in 1925, increased substantially in the 1920s. In 1919 it could claim 2,221 members; by 1926 that figure had risen to 7,000, and although in 1920–21 only 9,730 attendances were registered at the reduced recitals of that troubled year, by 1925–26 35,780 attendances were registered at recitals and 11,002 at the lectures sponsored by the Society.[16]

By contrast to the Royal Dublin Society, the condition of Trinity College, Dublin in the 1920s is a more accurate indicator of the isolated predicament of the Anglo-Irish and Protestant minority in the new state. That university had long been identified with the Protestant Ascendancy (although in the nineteenth century it had rather served the Irish Protestant middle class than the gentry, who often preferred Oxford and Cambridge for their sons) and in the years preceding independence had endured much nationalist obloquy on account of certain intemperate utterances by some of its best-known fellows, in particular, John Pentland Mahaffy, whose contemptuous attitude to nationalist Ireland was not to be easily forgotten or forgiven. Furthermore, the college was in somewhat straitened financial circumstances. A Royal Commission of 1920 had recommended that the college receive an annual subvention from the public purse, and a sum of £30,000 per annum had been designated for Trinity in the Government of Ireland Act of the same year, but the provisions of that act never became active in the South of Ireland, and although the provost of the college sought to have some such financial arrangement included in the Treaty of 1921, he was unsuccessful.[17] So the 1920s found Trinity financially insecure, intellectually and socially remote for the most part from contemporary Irish concerns, and identified in the popular mind with the former, rejected ruling class. There were those, too, ready to express the profoundest ill-will toward the institution. An Eoin MacNeill, with a certain distress, might regret that the college was responsible, as the chief agent of English culture in Ireland, for that anglicization which had almost destroyed the authentic civilization of the country (the college awarded him an honorary degree in 1928). Others were even more vigorously opposed to the college, ready to see in the large crowds that gathered in College Green, in front of the college, on Armistice Day, the symbol of a surviving Ascendancy attitude to be identified with the college itself. That the first provost to be appointed after the foundation of the Free State was a Gaelic scholar (Dr. E. J. Gwynn was appointed in 1927) and that scholarly material on the Irish language and on Irish literature was published in the college's house journal, *Hermathena*, could do only very little to reduce antagonism toward an institution which had before independence seemed to set its face against the ideal of Irish freedom.

In the 1920s and 1930s Trinity suffered one of its bleakest periods. The buildings and grounds became dilapidated and a little unkempt. A sense of isolation and economic insecurity was not alleviated by much intellectual or imaginative enterprise. Many of the graduates sought their careers abroad, and the college was unable to play its part in the developing life of the Free State in the way the National University, particularly University College, Dublin, did. Indeed, the college in the centre of Dublin bore in its isolation and decline a striking resemblance in social terms to the Big Houses of the countryside – each symbolizing a ruling caste in the aftermath of its power.

Many Anglo-Irish men and women chose simply to leave the country, preferring the secure if duller life of a villa on the English south-east coast to the strains of further anxiety and isolation in Ireland (and their departure meant that much of the fine furniture and many books and paintings that had escaped the fires of the Civil War went for sale and were bought by dealers from abroad). The period 1911–26 saw indeed a striking decline of about one-third in the Protestant population of the South of Ireland as a whole[18] (in the same period the Catholic population declined by 2.2 percent), which must be accounted for not only by the lamentable losses endured by Protestant Ireland in the Great War but by the large numbers of landed families, Protestant professional men, former members of the Royal Irish Constabulary, civil servants, and Protestant small farmers, who felt that the new Ireland was unlikely to provide a satisfactory home for themselves or their offspring. In the early 1930s one witness recorded the fact that in County Clare seventy Protestant landed families had left the country since 1919,[19] leaving only a small remnant of their class and creed behind them. In other counties of the south and west the pattern was similar, if not quite so starkly etched.

A sense of bitterness and betrayal accompanied these men and women into exile, together with a conviction that the new Ireland was, sadly, no place for them. Their feelings and attitude are, in fact, well represented in a volume of reminiscences by P. L. Dickinson published in 1929. Dickinson, a Dublin architect, in his book *The Dublin of Yesterday*, remembers his youth and young manhood in a city he reckons has now fallen into enemy hands. Fairly typical of the professional Dublin man who felt a kinship with Anglo-Ireland and the Protestant Ascendancy (his father was vicar of the important St. Anne's Parish in Dublin, and his family had links with the gentry, while his paternal grandfather had been bishop of Meath), Dickinson had been educated in England before returning to a comfortable Dublin professional life in a social ambiance he found totally agreeable. He had wide contacts in Dublin's literary, artistic, and medical worlds, numbering among his acquaintances John Pentland Mahaffy (he was secretary to Mahaffy in the Georgian Society founded in 1910), W. B. Yeats, whom he met in the Arts Club, where he enjoyed many sociable occasions, George Russell, Pádraic Colum, and Katherine Tynan. A man of broad views (he was sceptical about revealed religion and prepared to view monogamy as only one form of sexual arrangement), he felt by 1929 that Ireland was "largely ruled by a priesthood and atmosphere based on economic conditions of the medieval and early Renaissance period."[20] It was no place for one of his class and outlook. He was particularly oppressed by the Gaelic enthusiasm:

> The Gael was a rung on the ladder, a rung which has long been overstepped. The modern movement in the new political entity – the Irish Free State – the modern movement back towards this Gaelic Hey-Day is pathetic: or if you wish it is comic; certainly it is useless. It cannot last – Ireland is politically and economically and, above all, socially, one with Great Britain; any such retrograde movement as an attempt at the compulsory revival of a dead language only becomes a local racial injury. It hurts every one a little; but it hurts the authors a lot. To those who, like myself have had to leave their native country owing to the acts of their fellow-countrymen, a perfectly dispassionate judgement of the situation must be a little difficult. I love Ireland; few people know it better. There is hardly a mile of its coastline or hills I have not walked. There is not a thought in me that does not want well-being for the land of my birth; yet there is no room today in their own land for thousands of Irishmen of similar views.[21]

All that he now sees in Ireland are "the gestures of the child shaking itself free from its nurse" as he looks on with "a devoted but impotent love."

Some Anglo-Irishmen were unprepared to accept the position of isolated impotence or exile that seemed their lot in the new political dispensation. Men of substance like Lord Midleton and Andrew Jameson, who had played leading parts in the Irish Unionist Alliance which had attempted to project the Unionist cause in the years before independence, were willing to take places in the Seanad, ready to participate in government and to defend their social and economic position in the political arena (in fact, only Jameson was offered a seat). However, it was in the Dáil that the real legislative muscle was exercised, and although the government contained men who realized the new state could gain much from the former Ascendancy, there were also those, like Ernest Blythe, for a time Minister for Finance, who frankly admitted later of such as Midleton and Jameson, "We looked on them as the dregs of landlordism."[22] So a figure like the remarkable Bryan Cooper, Anglo-Irish landowner, former Unionist MP at Westminster and British army officer, who stood and was elected as an independent for the Free State Dáil, where he played a significant role in legislative business, finally in 1927 joining W. T. Cosgrave's ruling party, must be seen, I think, as an exception to the rule that more usually saw Anglo-Irishmen and women quite remote from political life in this period. Cooper was probably unique as Anglo-Irishman in his adaptability and personal attractiveness, so while his participation in the Dáil, which was welcomed by various members of that house, can, as his biographer argues, be seen as proving

> . . . that a man of his birth and upbringing could have, and did have, a place in Ireland and could help to shape the new Irish State. His presence in the Dáil and his power there gave the lie to the pedants in the Kildare Street and Stephen's Green Clubs and gave the lie to the Protestant Bishops and rural Deans[23]

one also suspects that Cooper's genial and attractive personality made smooth his way in an assembly that might not have proved so welcoming to others less happily endowed.

Some few Anglo-Irishmen and individuals who identified with Anglo-Ireland's fate were prepared in the face of isolation, impotence, and the difficulties militating against political participation to contemplate defiance and intellectual defence as proper responses to their predicament. In 1926, in his play *The Big House*, Lennox Robinson nicely caught this mood. The play, which was presented by the Abbey in September of that year at what one reviewer called "one of the most enthusiastic first performances that I can remember at the Abbey Theatre,"[24] offered four scenes from the recent life of a Big House which has sent its sons to their deaths in the Great War and is finally destroyed in the flames of the Civil War. The heroine, Kate Alcock, is perhaps the most interesting character in the play. Daughter of the house, she has sought to identify with the Ireland she has seen developing about her, but at a crucial moment in the play she senses her absolute separation from those with whom she seeks acceptance. A young woman in the village has perished at the hands of the Black and Tans, and Kate visits the bereaved family:

> Oh yes, I threw a bridge across the gulf and ran across it and called Pat, Mick and Larry by their Christian names, and hob-nobbed with priests and creamery managers and Gaelic teachers – but it was only a bridge, the gulf remained and when the moment came they instinctively forced me to stand on the far-ther side. Oh, it wasn't only tonight I've felt it. I've been con-scious of it ever since I've been conscious of anything, but I thought it could be broken down.[25]

The play ends with Kate accepting her Anglo-Irish distinctiveness, defiantly determining to rebuild the gutted family house, con-vinced that "Ireland is not more theirs than ours."[26] Now she glories in her Anglo-Irish difference, rejecting the "democratic snobbishness we went in for:"

> Now I don't want to give up the "they" and "us," I glory in it. I was wrong, we were all wrong, in trying to find a common platform, in pretending we weren't different from every Pat and Mick in the village. . . . We were ashamed of everything, ashamed of our birth, ashamed of our good education, ashamed of our religion, ashamed that we dined in the evenings and that we dressed for dinner, and after all, our shame didn't save us or we wouldn't be sitting here on the remnants of our furniture.[27]

It was inevitable that some would find this kind of speech offen-sive. One correspondent wrote to the *Irish Statesman* pointedly inquiring why the daughters of the Big Houses "grow flat-footed and thin haired, and the sons degenerate, often a little strange in the head," opining that in his view it was because the Ascendancy "barred its windows against the native vitality" until "gradually its teeth grew longer and its feet flatter and its viscera more withered."[28] The *Statesman*'s editor, George Russell (Æ), however, greeted the play with enthusiasm, recognizing it as an energetic salvo in a battle he had been fighting on behalf of Anglo-Ireland in his journal for several years:

> We do not want uniformity in our culture or our ideals, but the balancing of our diversities in a wide tolerance. The moment we had complete uniformity, our national life would be stagnant. We are glad to think we shall never achieve that uniformity which is the dream of commonplace minds and we imagine that many who saw *The Big House* felt a liberating thrill at the last outburst of Kate Alcock.[29]

The *Irish Statesman* had been revived in 1923, when Æ accepted the editorship at the request of Sir Horace Plunkett who was keen that the new state should have a journalistic organ of a high literary and intellectual calibre to act as a leaven in its life. And for the rest of the decade Russell showed that Plunkett had chosen his editor wisely, for the *Statesman* proved to be one of the most remarkable cultural organs modern Ireland has known – humane, politically engaged, and broadly literate. In its early years the periodical threw its weight behind the Cosgrave administration, berating the Republicans who still hoped that the Treaty might be dismantled, for their obdurate fantasizing. Almost from the beginning, however, the *Statesman* was alert to those aspects of Irish intellectual and cultural life that tended to national exclusivism, xenophobia, and cultural imposition. From the first Æ was determined that Irish life should be open to diverse influences from abroad: Ireland should be attentive to contemporary historical developments. Writing in November 1923 on "National Culture", he declared:

> We say we cannot merely out of Irish traditions find solutions to all our modern problems. It is no use reading Wolfe Tone or John Mitchel or Thomas Davis in the belief that they had a clairvoyance which pierced into our times with their complexities, or that by going back to Gaelic Ireland we shall find

images upon which we can build anew. We shall find much inspiration and beauty in our own past but we have to ransack world literature, world history, world science and study our national contemporaries and graft what we learn into our own national tradition, if we are not to fade out of the list of civilized nations.[30]

Accordingly, throughout the 1920s Æ filled the columns of his periodical with international as well as national news and comment, with reviews of most of the major writers writing in the English language, with comparisons of Ireland with such countries as Sweden and Denmark, allowing a sense to emerge of Ireland as one small country among many in an effort to counteract what he felt was a prevailing national narcissism. Æ waged strenuous war against the Irish Irelanders' conception of Gaelic civilization with the Irish language as the matrix of Irish life. He preferred a vision of the national synthesis, believing that the majority of the Irish people were culturally mixed, whatever the polemicist might wish. He certainly approved "the determination to give every Irish child access to the language in which is locked up the history of their race for two thousand years,"[31] but he objected both to "the precise methods by which Irish youth is being rushed back into the Gaelic world"[32] and to the exclusive dogmas of Irish Ireland. "We do not believe," he wrote, "that the Irish people will ever allow their knowledge of English to lapse."[33] Instead of the Irish Irelanders' vision of an absorbent Gaelic reality, Æ vigorously preached a doctrine of national synthesis in which no ethnic group is predominant, no culture the assimilative one. Ireland is a fertile creation of the historic fusion of races, culture, and language.

We wish the Irish mind to develop to the utmost of which it is capable, and we have always believed that the people now inhabiting Ireland, a new race made up of Gael, Dane, Norman and Saxon, has infinitely greater intellectual possibilities in it than the old race which existed before the stranger came. The union of races has brought a more complex mentality. We can no more get rid of these new elements in our blood and culture than we can get rid of the Gaelic blood.[34]

Crucial to the force of Æ's argument here is the distinctiveness and distinction of Anglo-Ireland's contribution to Irish civilization, and it is to this that he frequently turns in his columns, opening them also to writers and critics who could extol the Irish quality of such figures as Swift, Burke, and Berkeley, highlighting too the remarkable achievements of the Anglo-Irish Literary Revival of the preceding four decades. Anglo-Ireland, through its openness to fertilizing ideas from abroad was, and would remain, vital to Irish cultural health. It could fill a crucial social and cultural role, even though its political power was no more. Ireland, he argues,

> . . . has not only the unique Gaelic tradition, but it has given birth, if it accepts all its children, to many men who have influenced European culture and science, Berkeley, Swift, Goldsmith, Burke, Sheridan, Moore, Hamilton, Kelvin, Tyndall, Shaw, Yeats, Synge and many others of international repute. If we repudiate the Anglo-Irish tradition, if we say these are aliens, how poor does our life become.[35]

The frequent debates in the *Statesman* as to what constitutes Irish writing and the arguments about Irish and Anglo-Irish culture, it is important to stress, were disguised debates about politics. The underlying political issues were who should shape the new Ireland and what traditions, if any, should be predominant. As Æ put it frankly in 1925, identifying the cultural debate in which he was engaged with current attitudes which had deprived Anglo-Ireland of real political and national opportunities:

> Those who inherit the national tradition should not be so scared at the suggestion that Irish people lately of another tradition might take an active part in the building up of the new self-governing Ireland. Man for man they are just as good human beings as any of their nationalist fellow-countrymen. It is their misfortune to be on the losing side in the political struggle.[36]

They came, indeed, from a tradition which had supplied a modern Irish literature in English that had attracted the attention of the world.

The Irish Literary Revival was for Æ the chief reason why Anglo-Ireland deserved the respectful attention of all Irishmen. Furthermore, for Æ as to a lesser extent it did for W. B. Yeats, it represented the best hope for a resolution of differences between Irishmen. If, he believed, it could be wholeheartedly recognized by all that men and women of Anglo-Irish stock had contributed through their literary and dramatic works to Irish regeneration and that a genuinely Irish literature had emerged through the fusion of the English language with Gaelic mythology and traditions, then political differences in Ireland might lose their sharp distinctiveness, softened in the beneficent glow of culture. Æ argued that "Anglo-Irish literature only began to take on a quality when writers like O'Grady, Yeats, Hyde, Synge, Lady Gregory, Stephens, Clarke, Higgins, O'Flaherty and others either learned a good deal of the language or studied its cultural content in translations,"[37] and "however hateful and unjust the invasion of Ireland was to the Nationalists, the blending of races and cultures finally brought about a more vital and complicated mentality. Some of the most brilliant intellects in modern times are the product of this fusion of races or cultures."[38] And it was Æ's conviction that "if these names were deleted from Irish history the country would be almost intellectually non-existent as far as the rest of the world was concerned."[39]

It was not easy to sustain the force of this polemic throughout the 1920s. There was a troubling sense that the tide of the Revival as a distinctive intellectual and cultural movement directly associated with Anglo-Ireland had somewhat withdrawn, its energies waning. The closure of the Maunsel publishing company in 1926, the company that had published the work of many of the writers associated with the Revival, was a chilly omen of Ireland's literary future (the firm of Maunsel and Roberts Ltd. was auctioned off in separate lots). Critical works and histories of the movement began to appear which suggested that observers felt the time was ripe for the assessment of a past period. Memorial and collected editions were published in London. For Æ it was imperative that the vitality and vigour of the Anglo-Irish literary movement should not be seen as in decline. He noted that the work younger writers were now producing, many of them those young men whose talents he so assiduously cultivated, tended to realism and psychological subjectivism. The plays of O'Casey, which set the heroic vision of the Easter Rising and the War of Independence against the squalid but vibrant life of Dublin's slum tenements, the harsh portrait of revolutionary violence in O'Flaherty's novel *The Informer*, the spiky satire of Denis Johnston's expressionist play *The Old Lady Says "No!"* which sends the eighteenth-century patriot Robert Emmet abroad in a smugly or foolishly nationalistic and uncomprehending suburban Dublin, all suggested that the new modes were realistic and satiric. Æ absorbed such works into the canon of the Literary Revival, which he felt had been idealistic and visionary, in terms of a dialectical continuity:

> That action and reaction are equal and opposite is an aphorism which is true not only in the material but psychic sphere. Oscillations of emotion take place in literature and the arts. . . . Twenty years ago the literary movement in Ireland was spiritual and romantic, and the reaction from that has brought us to James Joyce and Sean O'Casey.[40]

Some of the young men whose work Æ gladly published in his journal, perhaps because their presence helped to confirm his theory, though he had also an innate literary hospitality, were less than willing to fit easily into their editor's grand schemes (and it is surely germane to note that most of them derived from Catholic backgrounds). Frank O'Connor was ready in youthful iconoclasm to dismiss Yeats from the pantheon of Irish poets in the name of a genuine Gaelic tradition (as distinct from the spurious kind O'Connor was also ready to denounce); Liam O'Flaherty could blithely inform his tolerant editor:

> I don't for a moment claim that your paper is not doing good work. But I do claim that it is not Irish, that it is not national,

and that it is not representative in any respect of the cultural forces, in all spheres, that are trying to find room for birth in this country at present.[41]

O'Flaherty, with others (Austin Clarke, F. R. Higgins), joined in the chorus of those who hated O'Casey's *The Plough and the Stars*, directing their attack at the playwright and his eminent defender, W. B. Yeats. Perhaps Æ might have viewed such literary wars as the manifestation of the necessary emotional and psychic oscillations of his theory, but the fact that those he wished to encompass within a general thesis that would allow for the continuity of Anglo-Irish literature as he understood it had no intention of being so encompassed, made his position difficult. For the younger writers were energetically determined that the new Irish writing would be distinct from the Anglo-Irish tradition they associated with Yeats. There is, therefore, something poignant about Æ's mystified efforts to comprehend the later work of Joyce, the *Work in Progress* that became *Finnegans Wake*, for which clearly he felt a temperamental distaste, within his optimistic theory about the continued vitality of the Irish Literary Renaissance, while younger men like the poet and art critic Thomas MacGreevy hailed the novelist in the columns of Æ's journal as "the most suggestive figure in the history of European art or literature since Leonardo da Vinci."[42] He associated Joyce not with the Anglo-Irish Revival at all but with the great Catholic writers of Europe, with the Dante of the *Divine Comedy*.

The poignancy of Æ's position was compounded by the fact that writers like Joyce, Clarke, O'Flaherty, and MacGreevy himself in fact demonstrated in their work the truth of one element in Æ's polemic on the nature of Irish reality. The historic fusion of races in Ireland and the introduction of the English language to the country had indeed allowed for the birth of a distinctive Irish literature in English, a cultural endowment that could not be gainsaid. But this literature was and would increasingly be a product of the social and linguistic reality of modern Ireland in which English with an Irish colouring was and is the *lingua franca.* It could not therefore, even in the 1920s, and certainly could not as the century progressed, be easily employed as a persistent proof of the cultural necessity of the Anglo-Irish Protestants in the new state, which was the other element in Æ's polemic. In proving the substance of Æ's ideas on the social and cultural reality of modern Ireland as hybrid and a consequence of racial fusion such writers of Catholic middle-class and rural background were, ironically, vitiating the force of his propagandist efforts on behalf of the Anglo-Irish Protestants. At the high point of the Irish Literary Revival they had perhaps seemed crucial. Now they were less so.

There was a further and even deeper poignancy in Æ's repetitive efforts to encourage a synthesis of Anglo-Irish and Gaelic culture as a road to Irish harmony. Neither of the two social groups associated with these traditions, the remnants of Protestant Anglo-Ireland nor Catholic nationalist Ireland, saw themselves or each other simply as media for culture, whether Anglo-Irish or Gaelic. Furthermore, each was concerned to an extent Æ was unable or unwilling to absorb fully with religious belief and affiliation, often linking the latter to economic, social, and political issues. It is arguable, indeed, that what concerned many people in Ireland in the 1920s and early 1930s was not a conflict of Anglo-Irish and Gaelic culture but the tensions between a social majority and a minority, both identified in part by religious affiliations. Such certainly was the impression created by some of the Catholic Action associations and organizations that flourished in the 1920s and early 1930s, all of them determined that Irish life in the independent state should bear a frankly Catholic complexion and that Catholic power should assert itself unambiguously in social and economic terms as it had been unable to do in the past. A tract published by the Catholic Truth Society in 1927 is representative of much of this kind of feeling in its explicitly denominational sense of the social and economic order.

> Once again in the twenty-six Counties the Catholic is substantially in control of the government. The Civil Service and

judiciary, the Army and the Police force are at his disposal. The opportunity of education is again within his reach. The learned professions boast of many distinguished Catholic members. And yet in two important aspects the Catholic still suffers as a result of the penal laws – in the industrial and commercial life, from the handicap of poverty under which he started a century ago; the Protestant continues to maintain an ascendancy in social life. The cultivated pose of superiority of the Protestant oppresses us. Until these blemishes are removed from Irish life the work of emancipation, gloriously initiated a hundred years ago, will not be completed.[43]

People who thought in these aggressive terms were unlikely to be impressed by arguments of the kind that Æ advanced. But even in circles where he might have hoped for a more sympathetic hearing the ground was infertile. Those few individuals, for example, mostly professors and lecturers at University College, Dublin, who comprised a Catholic intelligentsia in the new Ireland, among whom Æ might have hoped to make headway with a cultural message, were in fact inclined to view the literary products of the Revival period which Æ so venerated as showing clear signs of heterodoxy. An almost Chestertonian commitment to a resolute orthodoxy made such persons less than ideal readers for a literature that had often emphasized both the pre-Christian traditions of the island and a cultural unity that transcended denominational differences.[44] It was unlikely therefore in the 1920s that a synthesis of Gaelic culture (which in any case was in crisis because of the precarious condition of the language) with Anglo-Irish literary culture (which most of the Protestants who remained in the country largely ignored) could have done much to soften the sharp divisions between Catholic and Protestant Ireland that the Catholic Truth Society so unembarrassedly identified. Quite simply Catholic nationalist Ireland was in the ascendant, Protestant in decline.

Æ, certainly to his credit, with his eirenic theosophical mysticism, found it difficult to accept how deeply Catholic and Protestant attitudes differed on many topics and how significant these

differences were in a country where a devout attachment to orthodox religion was a central aspect of most people's lives, bound
up with their sense of politics, economics, and identity. In 1926
Church of Ireland Protestants, at their annual synod, expressed
a fear that the revival of Irish would undermine their faith. Æ
would have none of it – "it would be to assume that one who
learns Chinese must gradually cease to be Christian and become
a follower of Confucius or Buddha or Lao-tze"[45] – and while he
may have rightly suspected the synod of a certain bad faith, he
seemed incapable of grasping how much Irish Protestantism was
attached, even if only in a sentimental fashion, to the King James
Bible, to Cranmer's prayerbook, and to the vast repository of
English hymnology. In 1929, as the spectacle of Catholic piety
at the Emancipation celebrations in Dublin struck even his
uninterested eye, the only uncomprehending, defensive comment
he could manage was "Religion is the high culture of the average
man, and especially of the poor, who do not often have opportunity to read the greatest masterpieces of secular literature."[46] Æ's
defence of Anglo-Ireland, which perhaps in its weak position was
beyond defence, was cast in terms that bore only in part on
contemporary Irish social reality. He largely ignored how religion
was often regarded as a badge of social, economic, and national
identity, and this may account for his inability to influence the
country in any profound way, despite the energy and dedication
with which he sought to fulfil an almost prophetic mission. In
attending so vigorously to the cultural debate he was fighting on
one front alone.

Æ's blind spot about the significance of religious feeling in the
country did not totally obscure from him the fact that legislative
developments in the Dáil reflected in crucial areas the social thinking of the religious majority. He was conscious enough of the
threat this posed to what he saw as individual liberties to use his
journal as a weapon in the fight against the motion forbidding
divorce legislation in 1925 and against the worst aspects of the
proposed Censorship Bill in the following years. He also objected
in his last editorial, before the journal closed in 1930, to the rise

of religious secret and semi-secret societies. However, he was disinclined, probably because he still hoped, in an entirely admirable way, that a cultural synthesis might make such differences irrelevant, to see these developments in sharply sectarian terms.

W. B. Yeats, who also made it his business in the 1920s to attempt a full-scale defence of Protestant Anglo-Ireland, was not so troubled by such scruples. Yeats shared in part Æ's vision of an Ireland where differences of religion, race, and wealth might be rendered insignificant by a rebirth of spirituality, and he was equally persuaded that Anglo-Ireland had a role to play in the creation of this regenerate Irish order. In the 1920s he clearly thought, however, that the distinctive Protestant Anglo-Irish tradition he valued as a bulwark against a vulgarized modernity was genuinely threatened and that there would be little point in preaching a doctrine of national synthesis if one of the most important elements that might comprise that synthesis was at risk of suppression. Yeat's defence of Anglo-Irish distinctiveness in the 1920s was therefore defiant and assertive; it was close to the attitude expressed by Kate Alcock at the end of Robinson's *The Big House*: "Ireland is not more theirs than our," he declared. "We must glory in our difference, be as proud of it as they are of theirs."[47]

For Yeats, part of that difference was Protestant Anglo-Ireland's attachment to freedom of conscience and individual liberty. It was no mean task to defend Anglo-Ireland in such terms. Yeats himself as a young man had been scathing in his denunciation of Protestant Ireland's intellectual and political mediocrity (Trinity College, and its professor of English literature – the famous Shakespeare scholar, Edward Dowden – had especially stimulated his impatience), and he had scant regard for the orthodoxies of reputable religious piety. One senses that his celebration of Protestant individualism of mind and conscience was related to the artist's demand for freedom of expression. So, in face of the manifest evidence that Anglo-Ireland with a few remarkable individual exceptions had in the twentieth century scarcely been in the vanguard of those who served human liberty, he developed

private vision, a historical myth, of a great tradition of the
ghteenth-century Anglo-Irish mind, Protestant and freedom-
rving, sceptical, anti-empirical, anti-modern, hostile to the
ulgar levelling of formless revolutionary agitation and mass
emocracy. In the name of an Ascendancy pantheon of philos-
phers and writers, he denounced both the excesses of the Gaelic
nthusiasm and the Catholic democracy he saw about him which
as prepared, at the behest of a majority feeling in the country,
) refuse to countenance divorce and restricted freedom of
xpression. In his notorious speech in the Seanad on the subject
f divorce, he frankly identified himself with Protestant Ireland,
asting his argument against any proscription of divorce in
ggressively sectarian terms that caused great offence in the
hamber and in the country. He was, he argued, defending rights
won by the labours of John Milton and other great men, and
von after strife, which is a famous part of the history of the
'rotestant people."[48] He invoked his own people as "one of
he great stocks of Europe" and listed the resonant names of
Anglo-Irish history in a peroration guaranteed to offend:

> I think it is tragic that within three years of this country gaining
> its independence we should be discussing a measure which a
> minority of this nation considers to be grossly oppressive. I am
> proud to consider myself a typical man of that minority. We
> against whom you have done this thing are no petty people. We
> are one of the great stocks of Europe. We are the people
> of Burke; we are the people of Grattan; we are the people of
> Swift; the people of Emmet, the people of Parnell. We have
> created most of the modern literature of this country. We have
> created the best of its political intelligence.[49]

n 1928 Yeats chose to denounce the proposed Censorship Bill
n even more direct and insulting terms, clearly identifying the
hreat to individual expression in what he saw as religious bigotry,
vhat he had dismissed in 1927 in a letter to Olivia Shakespear
s "the dislike of the more ignorant sort of Catholic for our
chool".[50]

The zealots have been wise in their generation; they have struck at the moment when the country is unprepared to resist. The old regime left Ireland perhaps the worst educated country in Northern Europe. . . . We were helots, and where you have the helot there the zealot reigns unchallenged. And our zealots' idea of establishing the Kingdom of God upon earth is to make Ireland an island of moral cowards.[51]

The Act on the Statute Book, Yeats set himself to the task of opposition, establishing with the help of George Bernard Shaw the Irish Academy of Letters in 1932, precisely because, as the letter inviting the membership of well-known writers stated "There is in Ireland an official censorship possessing, and actively exercising, powers of suppression which may at any moment confine an Irish author to the British and American market, and thereby make it impossible for him to live by distinctive Irish literature."[52] He spoke in extravagant praise in the same year of Liam O'Flaherty's novel *The Puritan* (it was banned by the Censorship Board), which was little more than a propagandist assault on censorship, in which a young man who had belonged to an association opposed to evil literature becomes so unhinged by moral and religious fervour that he commits a horrendous murder.

In defending Protestant Anglo-Ireland, Yeats, unlike Æ, perhaps because he thirsted for drama and opposition, was quite prepared to call a spade a spade, even if it gave deep offence. More astute than Æ, he probably realized that the support for Gaelic revival in much of Ireland was more sentimental than real. He certainly argued against what he saw as the hypocrisy of the revival policy in the 1920s and tried, in an introduction to a translation of an eighteenth-century Irish poem (Brian Merriman's *The Midnight Court*, translated by Arland Ussher and published in 1926), to propose a more inclusive, less puritanical understanding of the Gaelic tradition than was current. Nonetheless, the real target of his propagandist and polemical efforts in the 1920s was not Gaelic revivalism but a vulgar philistinism and religious intolerance he considered the most dangerous threat o religious, intellectual, and artistic minorities in the country: "ignorance organized unders its priests, and unorganized and rgely terrified intelligence looking on helpless and angry."[53]

Neither Æ's argumentative persistence nor Yeats's aggressive lefiance in public speech and newspaper article had any real effect. "he new Ireland, convinced of its Catholic nationalist rectitude n social issues, was prepared to grant Anglo-Ireland the right o remain in the country but was neither to be cajoled (as Æ ttempted) nor browbeaten into great regard for the values of a lefeated caste. The new state with admirable fair-mindedness had ecognized the property and institutional rights of the former ulers. Beyond that, at most, it might offer those Anglo-Irishmen nd women who remained in Ireland after independence toler- nce and a measure of sentimental affection.

It was Yeats the poet rather than Yeats the Protestant Anglo- rish polemicist who provided Anglo-Ireland with almost the only eal dignity it could muster in its harassed circumstances. For Yeats as a poet sensed that the finality of Anglo-Ireland's fate partook of tragedy. He recognized that the destructive fires of evolutionary change were a heroic climax for what he believed vas a noble caste, preferable to the indignities of taxation, pov- rty, and gradual decay which were to be the lot of ancestral nouses elsewhere in an egalitarian century which Yeats detested. n a series of poems written in the 1920s Yeats reflected on he death of the Irish Big Houses in the light of an aristocratic nythology. Houses like Coole Park, the home Lady Gregory had opened to the poet for rest and recuperation, were seats of civility, cultivation, and order. It was Yeats's genius to realize that at the noment of Anglo-Irish collapse he could so celebrate a class that ts demise would be seen not simply as a fact of history but as in event that threatened the death of culture. As the critic Richard Gill has stated:

> Paradoxically, dying as a social actuality, the house was reborn,
> transfigured as a symbol. Divorced from the nagging injustices
> and complexities of its local history, the house came to represent

a humane order of culture and civility, a state of community beyond the circumstances of nation or class.[54]

That symbolic transfiguration allowed Anglo-Ireland to maintain a kind of cultural afterlife in Ireland and beyond, in the writing of the many critics and literary historians who have dwelt on the Yeatsian vision of civilization overwhelmed by the mob as if it were literal fact, and in the impatience that these poems can still occasionally arouse in some Irishmen and women sensing, long after Anglo-Ireland's social and political collapse, in Yeats's metaphor of history a condemnation of their own unromantic condition.

> A spot whereon the founders lived and died
> Seemed once more dear than life; ancestral trees,
> Or gardens rich in memory glorified
> Marriages, alliances and families,
> And every bride's ambition satisfied.
> Where fashion or mere fantasy decrees
> We shift about – all that great glory spent –
> Like some poor Arab tribesman and his tent.
>
> We were the last romantics – chose for theme
> Traditional sanctity and loveliness;
> Whatever's written in what poets name
> The book of the people; whatever most can bless
> The mind of man or elevate a rhyme;
> But all is changed, that high horse riderless,
> Though mounted in that saddle Homer rode
> Where the swan drifts upon a darkening flood.
>
> "Coole Park and Ballylee, 1931"

Yet if, as this chapter has argued, neither the forces of organized labour nor the remnants of the former Protestant Anglo-Irish Ascendancy could muster any effective political or indeed ideological opposition to the social and political orthodoxies of the period, could neither disturb the economic conservatism nor counter the cultural protectionism and Catholic nationalism that characterized a cautious decade of recovery and reconstruction, hen one must also remember a crucial fact. These were but the most distinctive features of a society that in many ways exhibited a remarkably provincial aspect. For much of social and cultural life was markedly similar to that in the United Kingdom. The policy of Gaelic revival might be pursued in schoolrooms across the country, but the language of daily intercourse in most regions remained English, and the English-speaking world increased its hold on daily life in the late 1920s as the film industry introduced its "talkies," which became enormously popular, particularly in Dublin. An Irish-language theatre might be established in Galway in 1928 (An Taibhdhearc) by Micheál MacLiammóir, but reading through the reviews of plays in Dublin for any year in the 1920s quickly sets this remarkable and long-lived venture in a context of a theatrical life that included some Irish-language productions, but in the main, plays in English, some the dramas of the Irish Literary Revival, some few the English translations of modern European works that Micheál MacLiammóir was keen to present, but mostly the realistic plays in English about Irish rural and small town life that became the staple of Abby Theatre productions, and some works that might well have appeared regularly in the English provincial repertory. All this bespeaks a theatre-going public that did not differ greatly from that in the United Kingdom.

On the concert-hall platform, too, an occasional modern work based on Irish folk materials or on a programmatic sense of Irish life might reflect the nationalism of the dominant ideology, but the most popular concerts in a country where orchestral music had achieved no widespread popularity were those where the most familiar works of the classical, romantic, and operatic repertoire were performed by the many visiting artists who included Dublin and sometimes Cork on their tours of provincial centres. A pastoral myth, important to Irish self-understanding, might celebrate the countryside of the western island as a national Eden, but visits there were made from the anglicized towns and from the villas and streets of semi-detached houses in the cities that were advertised in the weekly and daily papers in terms of a suburban felicity indistinguishable from that which tempted city-dwellers throughout the United Kingdom to invest in home-ownership. A dominant social myth might project a vision of a Catholic and Gaelic people newly freed from imperial bondage with a historic mission as an internationally civilizing and Christianizing force but many middle-class men and women in the towns and cities were content to live a comfortable, petit-bourgeois life that bore a closer relationship to the life of similarly placed people in Britain than to any vision of special destiny, gratified not that their government's diplomatic efforts were defining new forms of international relationship at the beginning of the post-colonial period but that it was people like themselves who were receiving invitations to official occasions in Dublin Castle and the Viceregal Lodge, as Dublin welcomed its new diplomatic corps.

Accordingly, even the conservatism of Irish society in the 1920s which we have explored lacked any great positive passion. No architectural splendours can be pointed to as expressions of a confident, assertive self-regard in a society persuaded of its own newly independent traditional strengths. Rather a petit bourgeois state expressing the prudent and inhibiting values of farm and shop allowed the children of the nation to bear the brunt of its ostensibly most adventurous policy, the revival of a language while the opportunities implicit in that independence so eagerly sought went a-begging in a fairly general acquiescence in comfortably provincial modes of social life and art.

The economic realities of independent Ireland were, as I suggested earlier, against any great national resurgence; the general will of the people was also desperately lacking. Too many thought a respectable survival was enough. Pearse had sounded the clarion before the 1916 Rising which challenged a nation to economic, social, and cultural deeds of daring. In 1928 George Bernard Shaw issued an equally demanding warning, couched in characteristically sceptical and astringent terms as Pearse's call had been buoyant with idealism:

Ireland is now in a position of special and extreme peril. Until the other day we enjoyed a factitious prestige as a thorn in the side of England, or shall I say, from the military point of view, the Achilles heel of England? . . . when we were given a free hand to make good we found ourselves out with a shock that has taken all the moral pluck out of us as completely as shell shock. We can recover our nerve only by forcing ourselves to face new ideas, proving all things, and standing by that which is good. . . .

The moral is obvious. In the nineteenth century all the world was concerned about Ireland. In the twentieth, nobody outside Ireland cares twopence what happens to her. If she holds her own in the front of European culture, so much the better for her and Europe. But if, having broken England's grip of her she slips back into the Atlantic as a little grass patch in which a few million moral cowards cannot call their souls their own . . . then the world will let "these Irish" go their own way into insignificance without the smallest concern.[55]

Only the work of a few individual poets, novelists, and artists in the 1920s gave any hint that the dismal obscurity that Shaw feared might not envelop the country. There were the fiercely personal paintings that Jack Yeats executed throughout the 1920s as, in the face of public incomprehension, he brooded on the tragedy of civil war; the defiantly speculative poems of his more renowned brother; the young men beginning to exploit the short story as a means of probing a society that dissatisfied them; MacLiammóir presenting European drama at his Gate Theatre and Irish language drama in Galway; and writers as different as the poet Austin Clarke and the novelist Francis Stuart, each beginning careers that were to take them to searching explorations of Irish life; all of whom gave hope that individual imaginative nerve had not atrophied in what must in general be reckoned a dispiriting decade from the social and cultural point of view. But a state that might not have survived at all had established and protected democratic institutions and given hope to many colonial peoples that they too could achieve similar feats of post-colonial construction.

PART II

1932–58

CHAPTER 5

The 1930s:
A Self-Sufficient Ireland?

The election of 1932 was fought by the government of the Irish Free State in the most inauspicious of circumstances. The twenty-six counties of the Free State had been spared in the years 1929–31 the worst effects of the Great Depression as the country continued to export its livestock and livestock products at relatively stable prices, while the price of imports dropped sharply. But by late 1931 the world economic situation began to have serious repercussions on the Irish economy. Exports started to decline seriously, as did the prices they commanded. The government, forced to economic austerities and responding to a marked recrudescence in politically motivated violence on the part of the IRA by a draconian Public Safety Bill (1931), was in no position to present an appealing face to the Irish electorate. Nor had it ever been natural for the Cumann na nGaedheal administration to attempt a softening of its political profile in the interests of expediency. That sternly responsible body of men had rather preferred to outface the winds of circumstance with stoicism and a forbiddingly austere public aspect. And, as if to remind the electorate of the party's essential nature, almost on the eve of the election the government decided to prosecute the *Irish Press* (the daily newspaper Mr. de Valera had founded as the journalistic organ of the Fianna Fáil party) for seditious libel before a military tribunal. On previous occasions such unbending legalism had served the party well, but the public was now less prepared to accept measures appropriate to the early days of the state and to a civil war, but odiously heavy-handed in a democracy beginning to feel and anxious to express a developing self-assurance. *Dublin Opinion* indeed, an influential humorous magazine, had pilloried the Cosgrave administration in its last months, reflecting a widespread mood.

Eamon de Valera came to power with a small parliamentary majority which largely depended on the support of the Labour Party. This change of power was in fact to install de Valera and his party in the seats of office for the next sixteen years, and the election therefore represented a major watershed in Irish political life. That the transition of power from the party victorious in the Civil War of a decade before to the party representative of much of the defeated republican faction was effected without violence and with a measure of dignity may in part have been because de Valera's narrow majority gave hope that the interruption of Cumann na nGaedheal's rule was only temporary. For no one in the circumstances of 1932 could have envisaged Fianna Fáil's monopoly of Irish political life for the next decade and a half. Nevertheless, the peaceful acceptance of the people's democratic will and the ordered change of government must also stand as evidence of a political maturity in the new state which could not easily have been forecast in 1922 or 1923.

Further evidence of the electorate's developing self-confidence was the fact that de Valera's political manifesto had included economic novelties that might well have given pause to an insecure populace, forcing it to prefer the familiar if unattractive economic doctrines of free trade as practised by W. T. Cosgrave and his ministers to the untried economic nationalism of de Valera's programme. The fact that sufficient of the electorate opted for de Valera (though much of his support came from small farmers and small businessmen, who hoped to benefit in the new order) suggests that there was in the country sufficient national self-confidence, together perhaps with the feeling that economic realities both at home and abroad demanded novel measures, for a change of direction.

This de Valera swiftly set in motion. At the heart of his policy changes was a vision of what he hoped Ireland might eventually become – a genuinely independent, self-sufficient rural republic. Almost immediately de Valera set about reducing what he felt were the more offensive aspects of the Treaty of 1921, seeking to abolish the Oath of Allegiance to the Crown, downgrading the role of the governor general (his power to withhold assent to bills, for example, was removed in 1933), and embarking upon what was to prove an extended campaign in which Ireland withheld certain annuities due to Britain under the terms of agreements entered into by the previous administration.

This last aspect of de Valera's programme became linked with his economic policy, which was to establish national self-sufficiency through the erection of high tariff walls. From the beginning of his first period of office de Valera set himself to the raising of tariffs. A contemporary commentator remarked in horror as the new administration revealed its hand:

> If a Glasgow Communist and a die-hard tariff reformer were merged into a single personality and, having somehow managed to escape certification, became Minister of Finance in the Irish Free State, the result would probably be somewhat similar to the budget introduced in the Dáil . . . by Mr. Seán MacEntee.[1]

Ironically, de Valera's relish for tariffs was made the more easy to satisfy since the British government's response to the withholding of the annuities was to establish tariffs on Irish agricultural produce, provoking in return further Irish tariffs on British goods so that the two countries entered on a state of economic warfare. Speaking in Paris in September 1933 de Valera declared that his policy was to "abolish free trade."[2] By the mid-1930s he had gone a fair distance toward achieving this costly aim. For costly indeed it was. The cattle trade suffered particularly as exports fell from 775,000 in 1929 to 500,000 in 1934, while exports as a whole fell somewhat less

sharply. But de Valera and his party, as well as the many small
farmers and budding small industrialists who supported his policy,
returning him to power with an overall majority in 1933 when he
called a snap election, felt these sacrifices were necessary to achieve
social changes in the country. As F. S. L. Lyons succinctly states it,
the tariff policy, reinforced by the economic war, was

> ... a serious and prolonged attempt to redress the balance
> between the different sectors of the economy – to free the
> countryside from the dominance of the cattleman, to extend
> the area of tillage, to develop home industries and thus provide
> employment for those who might otherwise be obliged to
> emigrate.[3]

Crucial to de Valera's programme was the creation and success
of native industries behind the tariff walls he had so single-
mindedly established. Strenuous efforts were made to encourage
private investment, but despite the protection that the tariff walls
provided, private Irish capital investment proved almost as shy as
it had done under Cosgrave's administration. By default, the state
was forced to increase its involvement in Irish manufacturing
industry, in the building of houses, and in the provision of services
such as air transport through the mechanism that had begun to
provide many rural Irish homes with electric light since the Shannon electrical scheme of the 1920s, the state-sponsored body.
Furthermore, in the countryside the Land Commission built large
numbers of small houses (costing about £350 each) thereby creating employment, while the Housing Act of 1932 brought central
government into the support of local authorities' policies to such
a degree that the Act "amounted to a public works policy."[4]

These various measures were blessed with some modest success.
Employment in industry rose from 110,588 in 1931 to 166,513
in 1938, and industrial output rose by 40 percent between 1931
and 1936.[5] But Irish industry was faced with certain structural
problems that made it unlikely that success could be more than
modest in such a protectionist environment. The home market
was too small to allow new Irish industries to expand to any

significant degree, while increasing their export business was difficult both because as small companies they found it hard to compete in international markets and because their costs were high. That the growth of native industry in the 1930s was scarcely sufficient to compensate in terms of national income for the export losses suffered by traditional Irish export business such as brewing and biscuit-making (which encountered British tariffs) was in itself regrettable enough. That this unremarkable industrial growth was bought at the expense of severe disruption in Irish agriculture as the cattle trade endured a near catastrophe which could not easily be ameliorated by any transition to productive tillage farming makes one question both the wisdom of de Valera's protectionist economics and the reasons why his policies received the undoubted support that they did.

That the economic nationalism of de Valera in the 1930s did receive sufficient support can perhaps be explained by the fact that the protectionist policies pursued were not only in the interests of native industries and the creation of employment but because they also played a part in an economic war against the old enemy, England. The sacrifices demanded could be extolled in a crudely nationalistic rhetoric. In addition, one can perhaps account for their acceptance, particularly among the many small farmers from whom Fianna Fáil received its most fervent support, by the fact that there was in much of the country a deep urge toward self-sufficiency, a conviction that the life of an Irish small farm represented a purity and decency of life that could set Ireland apart from the more commercial societies that surrounded her. In de Valera's own mind, the ideas and attitudes of the Irish Ireland movement, with its emphasis on the national distinctiveness of the Gaelic way of life, extolled in newspaper articles, in pastoral letters in the churches, in poetry, and in literary polemic, became closely identified with the life of the Irish small farm. For de Valera, despite his attempts to encourage Irish industry, enthusiastically shared Irish Ireland's vision of national possibility, preferring an Ireland of frugal, God-fearing country folk to any absorption of the country into industrial Europe. In 1933 in Paris when he set himself to the task of "abolishing free trade", it was in hopes of a rural renewal based on small farm life: "to provide work for the 30,000 young people who formerly would have emigrated, to build 10,000 houses and divide half a million acres within five years. Every thirty acres of land would represent a new family."[6] Ten years later in a famous St. Patrick's Day broadcast to the Irish people, that vision of an Irish idyll could still seem appropriate matter for the nation's reflection:

> That Ireland which we dreamed of would be the home of a people who valued material wealth only as a basis of right living, of a people who were satisfied with frugal comfort and devoted their leisure to the things of the spirit; a land whose countryside would be bright with cosy homesteads, whose fields and villages would be joyous with sounds of industry, the romping of sturdy children, the contests of athletic youths, the laughter of comely maidens; whose firesides would be the forums of the wisdom of serene old age.[7]

The dominant ideology in the country was therefore in favour of achieving and maintaining as much self-sufficient Irish independence as was possible. The prevailing republican creed, which was propounded in schoolrooms, in newspapers, on political platforms, assumed that the ancient Gaelic Irish nation had finally thrown off the thrall of foreign subjugation and that her true destiny lay in cultivating her national distinctiveness as assiduously as possible. Economic nationalism was therefore but one aspect of a prevailing ethos.

The policy of language revival was pursued with perhaps an even greater dogmatism than during Cosgrave's administrations. In 1934 Thomas Derrig, the Minister for Education, demanded swifter progress in the revival of Irish and reached an agreement with the Irish National Teachers' Organization which allowed for a greater concentration on Irish in schools at the expense of standards in other subjects, including English. Rural science ceased to be an obligatory subject in the curriculum. In the face of this intensification of the linguistic crusade in the schools, in

1936 the INTO was prepared at its annual congress to adopt a resolution which recognized a widespread belief that "the use of a teaching medium other than the home language of the child in the primary schools of Saorstat Eireann is educationally unsound."[8] It was, however, unlikely that Derrig would have paid much attention to such opinion. Already in the Dáil in 1935 he had dismissed even Irish parents, as having no right to be consulted on the language policy in the schools – "I cannot see that parents as a body can decide this matter."[9]

The 1930s also saw the elevation of Irish traditional music (a rich inheritance inadequately recognized during the cultural revival in the years before independence) to a position in official esteem, second only to the Irish language as Derrig declared in March 1937 at the Dublin Feis. Irish folk music, in such a view, was an expression of the nation's mind. Accordingly the musical tradition was celebrated in terms that echoed Irish Ireland's attachment to the Irish language. Passages like the following became the staple of cultural polemic:

That set of values which makes the Irish mind different looks out at us clearly from our old music – its idiom having in some subtle way the idiom of the Irish mind, its rhythms, its intervals, its speeds, its build have not been chosen arbitrarily, but are what they are because they are the musical expression, the musical equivalent of Irish thought and its modes.

. . . the Irish idiom expresses deep things that have not been expressed by Beethoven, Bach, Brahms, Elgar or Sibelius – by any of the great composers.[10]

The theme of Irish tradition was staunchly reiterated in reviews of plays, exhibitions, and concerts. An attitude of xenophobic suspicion often greeted any manifestation of what appeared to reflect cosmopolitan standards. An almost Stalinist antagonism to modernism, to surrealism, free verse, symbolism, and the modern cinema was combined with prudery (the 1930s saw opposition to paintings of nudes being exhibited in the National Gallery in Dublin) and a deep reverence for the Irish past.

Devout attachment to the past undoubtedly had its positive aspects in the 1930s. It bore fruit, for example, in the work of the Irish Folklore Commission. In 1927 Ireland's first folklore society, An Cumann le Béaloideas Eireann, had begun its work. In 1930 the government gave a grant to a committee appointed by the Folklore Society and by the Royal Irish Academy, which was constituted as the Irish Folklore Institute. Within a few years this body became the Irish Folklore Commission (1935). Almost at the last moment before swift change overtook the countryside, these bodies, particularly the Folklore Commission, collected and recorded evidence of a vast repository of folklore and folktale before they began to vanish from memory. Equally zealous in its scientific attachment to the past, the Irish Manuscript Commission, from its foundation in 1928, made efforts to see that documentary evidence of Ireland's experience was located, preserved, and published, making known its findings in its periodical publication *Analecta Hibernica*. This publication, together with the commission's facsimiles of important manuscripts and its republication of standard out-of-print historical works, helped in the development of modern, scientific historical studies in Ireland which date only from the early decades of the twentieth century. The establishment of the periodical *Irish Historical Studies* (first published in 1938) was a major turning point, as it provided a focus for disciplined, academic historical research in the country.

Veneration of the past, however, more commonly expressed itself in a crude distaste for the dangerous symptoms of modernism. The mood of much contemporary journalism and comment is caught therefore in this wearyingly representative and complacent passage: "It is . . . a comforting thought that the steady stream of tradition still moves on, indifferent to these squalls, and it is heartening to remember that the gates of Hell shall not prevail against it."[11] The population at large was protected from the incursions of alien modern thought and art forms not only by the admonitory fulminations of such critics, but of course, by the Censorship Board, ably assisted as it was by the zeal of the customs. A list of the books by modern English, European, and

Irish authors banned in the 1930s as being in general tendency indecent now makes surprising reading. Between the years 1930 and 1939 some 1,200 books and some 140 periodicals fell foul of the censors' displeasure. Only the *Irish Times*, a few individuals, and some of the Irish writers who had suffered at the hands of the board mounted any opposition to this apparent act of suppression. By contrast, there were highly influential individuals and bodies ready to complain that the censorship policy had been prosecuted with insufficient rigour. The Catholic Truth Society in 1937 appointed a committee to recommend changes in the Censorship Act. The members, including the future bishops of Kilmore and Galway and a future member of the Censorship Board itself (C. J. Joyce, appointed in 1946), concluded that the act did not allow for sufficient censorship and was tardy in its operations.

It would be unwise perhaps to rest too large a cultural thesis upon the activities of the Censorship Board. We have seen how in the 1920s the passing of a censorship act would have struck most Irish men and women as an entirely rational measure and how prevailing nationalist and moral assumptions met in the demands for action in this area. To explain why the act was implemented in such an all-encompassing fashion, one need look no further than the precise mechanics of its operation as they developed. Customs officials or concerned individuals sent suspicious works to the board, where they were first read by a permanent official who marked passages that he thought infringed the act. The board was then presented with these marked volumes for final judgment. It is likely that in the pressure of business, books were banned simply on the basis of the marked passages, rather than upon consideration of the general tendency of the works. The censorship of so many modern classics in the period might be readily explained therefore in terms of administrative inertia rather than by anything more sinister. And a blasé view of the effect of the censorship would acknowledge that the period between the book's publication and its banning allowed a reader who really wanted to get hold of it ample opportunity to do so. Nevertheless, it must be remembered that the censorship policy was prosecuted in a society where the written word was taken very seriously, where even the religious affiliation of a librarian could be a matter of scandal and controversy.[12] In 1930, in a famous incident, the Mayo Library Committee had refused to confirm the appointment of a Protestant, a woman educated at Trinity College, Dublin, to a position as county librarian. In the Dáil in June 1931, where the issue was extensively debated, de Valera touched on the power that the written word represented:

> If it is a mere passive position of handing down books that are asked for, then the librarian has no particular duty for which religion should be regarded as a qualification, but if the librarian goes round to the homes of the people trying to interest them in books, sees the children in the schools and asks these children to bring home certain books, or asks what books their parents would like to read, if it is active work of a propagandist educational character – and I believe it to be such, if it is to be of any value at all and worth the money spent on it – then I say the people of Mayo, in a country where, I think – I forget the figures – over 98 percent of the population is Catholic, are justified in insisting on a Catholic librarian.[13]

It may well have been that de Valera, in opportunist fashion, was here attempting to suggest that Fianna Fáil was not to be outdone by Cosgrave's party in its respect for religious obligations. But such overt religious discrimination was rare in the Irish Free State, where genuine efforts were made to respect, if not always to accommodate, religious minorities, and it is striking that it was the possibility of unsuitable literature reaching the citizens of Mayo that should have stimulated such an unguarded reaction from the normally cautious de Valera. However, the outspokenness with which de Valera espoused a Catholic position in the controversy was merely an uncharacteristically direct expression of his almost instinctual association of Catholicism with the Irish way of life. For the independent Irish life that independence would allow to develop freely would, in de Valera's view, be Catholic as well as Gaelic. His government, when it came to power, was zealous in its efforts to ensure that Catholic morality should be enforced by legislation and that public life, state occasions, the opening of factories, new housing estates, and the like should be blessed by an official clerical presence. In 1933 a tax was imposed on imported newspapers to the satisfaction of moralists who had inveighed for years against the depredations of the English "gutter press." And in 1935 the sale and importation of artificial contraceptives were made illegal.

It was, it must be stressed, politically expedient for Fianna Fáil to be seen as dutifully recognizing the authority of the hierarchy and attentive to matters of social morality, since many of its members had endured episcopal condemnation when as Republicans they rejected the Treaty of 1921 and had taken up arms against the Free State government. But the frank piety of de Valera's broadcast speeches in the 1930s suggests that he scarcely found the necessary accommodation of the state with the church anything other than gratifying. In a St. Patrick's day broadcast (de Valera had swiftly realized the value of radio as a political instrument) to the United States in 1935 he was unambiguous in his identification of Catholic Ireland with the Irish nation:

Since the coming of St. Patrick, fifteen hundred years ago, Ireland has been a Christian and a Catholic nation. All the ruthless attempts made through the centuries to force her from this allegiance have not shaken her faith. She remains a Catholic nation.[14]

So the 1930s, if anything, deepened the conservatism of Irish life that we have explored in earlier chapters. To cultural and religious protectionism at their most draconian in the censorship policy was added the official encouragement of economic nationalism as a force sustaining the structure of an essentially rural society dominated by the social, cultural, and political will of the farmers and their offspring. In the period 1926 to 1936 the population of towns throughout the country grew only very slightly, some of them even experiencing a loss of inhabitants, while the population as a whole remained almost stable (1926, 2,971,992; 1936, 2,968,420; a decline of 0.12 percent). Only Dublin city increased its population in any marked way from 394,089 to 472,935 while Cork's population rose somewhat, from 78,490 to 93,322, indicating a measure of internal emigration to the cities in a society where the population of most small towns remained almost static. Emigration rates stayed high (at a net figure of about 6 per 1,000 of the population for the period 1926–46, western areas suffering the most) though now England rather than the United States was the customary destination. This change which had been in the making since independence was hastened in 1930, when the United States began to apply stringent immigrant quotas. The percentage of single persons in most age-groups also remained high. Clearly, postponed marriage and emigration allowed Irish society to maintain the social profile established in the second half of the nineteenth century well into the modern period. It is true, emigration had lessened for a brief period in the first half of the decade, particularly when the American Depression and the new regulations closed the door of opportunity in that country, increasing unemployment at home (by 1935 it was 133,000, twice what it had been in 1926), but by the end of the 1930s the rate of emigration had quickened once more, draining off what disenchantment with the social order a rising population of unemployed young people might have generated.

Indeed, apart from the largely unsuccessful effort to shift Irish agriculture from pasturage to tillage and to encourage native industry, Fianna Fáil showed no real evidence of any revolutionary desire to change Irish society fundamentally (as some of their critics had feared they might do) in the 1930s. The party was willing to support some new forms of modest state welfare (unemployment assistance was instituted in 1933) and to become centrally involved in house-building and the creation of employment, but no pressing necessity for a full-scale alteration in the order of things seemed apparent. Some social changes certainly occurred as the inevitable outcome of technical developments abroad. The middle-class family motor-car, for example, began to become more common than it had been in the 1920s. In 1931 there were 4,455 new registrations of private motor vehicles; by 1936 this figure had risen to 8,111 and in 1937 over 10,000 officially registered new motor vehicles took to the roads (in 1937 209 people died in road accidents).[15]

Radio began to become more popular as a form of home entertainment. In the 1920s broadcasts from the national radio station (which began broadcasting from Dublin in 1926 and from Cork in 1927) had been of very low power and had been heard in only a small part of the country. From 1933 onward when the high-powered station had been opened in Athlone, radio broadcasts were much more widely available. The number of licences issued rose sharply in the 1930s from 50,500 in 1935 to 62,200 in 1936 to 100,000 in 1937 (the peak of licences issued in one year was reached in 1941 at 183,000).[16] It must also be remembered that many Irish people saw little reason to purchase a licence in order to enjoy the new benefits of radio ownership, for in 1938 the Post Office in a drive against pirates found 25,000 such. There were probably many more. But despite the increased numbers of radios in the country and the wider availability of Irish broadcasts, the majority of licences issued at the end of the 1930s still went to people in the Dublin region (in 1939, of 166,275 licences issued, 40 percent were to people in Dublin and its neighbourhood; very few were issued to people in Connacht or Ulster). Whether Dublin was simply more law-abiding or more addicted to the pleasures of the new medium than the rest of the country cannot be said. Countryside, town, and city were, however, alike addicted in the 1930s, as were the masses throughout the English-speaking world, to the Hollywood film. In village hall and city cinema in Ireland the 1930s was the decade of an enthusiastic discovery of celluloid dreams from California. But change, even when these technological novelties are admitted, was scarcely a dominant characteristic of years when Irish life continued to find its most appropriate expression in moulds shaped in the late nineteenth century.

The impulse to seek self-sufficiency which characterized the 1930s, representatively expressed in the attitudes and policies of de Valera, was, it is necessary to stress, a noble one. It was idealism that stimulated it into life and sustained it through a decade when the international situation suggested that only a vigorous national self-confidence would allow for survival. At its most positive the urge toward self-sufficiency reflected a belief in Irish life, in its dignity and potential, and in the value of a secure, self-confident national identity. That such idealism could be maintained only by ignoring the dismal facts of emigration, economic stagnation, individual inhibition, and lack of fulfiling opportunity was its crippling flaw, akin to that contradiction at the heart of Irish Ireland's attitudes to the revival of Irish that we noted earlier.

As in the 1920s, it was primarily writers who mounted the most coherent criticisms of the ruling ideology and the prevailing climate and conditions of the period. The most immediate victims of the censorship, it was likely that they should feel a peculiar antipathy to the society that adjudged their work obscene. Among them, such writers as Liam O'Flaherty, Frank O'Connor, and Seán O'Faoláin, all of whom had fought in the liberation struggle and whose works had attracted or were to attract the censor's interdict, expressed a deep disillusionment about the kind of Ireland that independence had inaugurated. Frank O'Connor, writing in 1942, is entirely representative of the distaste they all felt in the 1930s:

> After the success of the Revolution . . . Irish society began to revert to type. All the forces that had made for national dignity, that had united Catholic and Protestant, aristocrats like Constance Markievicz, Labour revolutionists like Connolly and writers like Æ, began to disintegrate rapidly, and Ireland became more than ever sectarian, utilitarian, the two nearly always go together, vulgar and provincial. . . . Every year that has passed, particularly since de Valera's rise to power, has strengthened the grip of the gombeen man, of the religious secret societies like

the Knights of Columbanus, of the illiterate censorships. . . . The significant fact about it is that there is no idealistic opposition which would enable us to measure the extent of the damage.[17]

The writers, particularly Seán O'Faoláin, took it upon themselves to provide that necessary opposition, despite the herculean nature of the task.

A degree of disenchantment might certainly have been expected in the new Ireland as in most post-revolutionary societies. And later O'Faoláin himself, in his autobiography *Vive Moi!* (1965), was to identify his own youthful iconoclasm with that of Stendhal's Julien Sorel, thereby reducing its significance by implication – the attitudes he expressed then were only what might have been expected, the mature O'Faoláin benignly implies. But this late retrospective tolerance on his part does little justice to the substance and quality of O'Faoláin's earlier critical assault on post-revolutionary Ireland, which was both intellectually based and vigorously argued. Rather it tends to soften in memory what was in fact a protracted campaign of opposition waged against their society by Irish writers, in which O'Faoláin played a commanding role.

Seán O'Faoláin, who was born in 1900, the son of a member of the Royal Irish Constabulary in Cork, had been caught up as a youth in the enthusiasm of the Gaelic League, that nursery of freedom fighters, and had graduated to membership of the IRA and action in the War of Independence. By the 1930s, however, following a period of study at Harvard University and of residence in London, he had returned to Ireland determined, as he put it later in his autobiography, to write of his own land, "this sleeping country, these sleeping fields, those sleeping villages." Initially he had hoped that the change of government which had brought de Valera to power in 1932 might do something to disturb the unrealistic dreams of the sleeping country, but he quickly came to believe that de Valera was himself a powerful soporific. For he preached just those nationalistic doctrines of an ancient Gaelic and Catholic nation rooted in the Irish Irelanders' vision of an unbroken Irish tradition which must be restored to its former glory that O'Faoláin considered a romantic distraction from urgent, practical social business that lay to hand. In a series of articles and books, including perhaps his finest work, *King of the Beggars* (1938), O'Faoláin offered a radically different interpretation of recent Irish history. His fundamental thesis was that Gaelic Ireland had died in the eighteenth century and that there was little point in trying to resurrect it. Gaelic Ireland had collapsed under a persecution which it could not endure because it had grown effete and weak, clinging to aristocracy and hierarchy in a world moving inexorably toward democracy. The modern Ireland that the twentieth century had inherited was not the outcome of many centuries of Gaelic and Catholic civilization but the fruit of the democratic victories won by Daniel O'Connell in the nineteenth century. With great vigour O'Faoláin denounced all those who thought otherwise. Daniel Corkery bore the particular brunt of a disillusionment bred of the fact that he had been O'Faoláin's first mentor:

> To us the Irish fisherman and the Irish farmer and the Irish townsman is the result of about one hundred and fifty years of struggle. And that, for history, is long enough for us. To us, Ireland is beginning, where to Corkery it is continuing. We have a sense of time, of background: we know the value of the Gaelic tongue to extend our vision of Irish life, to deepen it and enrich it: we know that an old cromlech in a field can dilate our imaginations with a sense of what was, what might have been, and *what is not*; but we cannot see the man ploughing against the sky in an aura of antiquity.[18]

How O'Faoláin could in fact see him was as the descendant of a vast number of disenfranchised helots whom Daniel O'Connell had taken and moulded into a democratic nation by the force of his practical, utilitarian, unsentimental will. In *King of the Beggars* O'Faoláin presented O'Connell as a more appropriate model for twentieth-century Ireland than any figure drawn from the sagas or the mists of Celtic antiquity. O'Connell – Benthamite, English-

speaking, and philosophic about the loss of Gaelic, liberally conscious of the differing roles of church and state – was a figure to
inspire a new Ireland rather than the heroic ideal of Cuchulain
or of the sacrificial victims of 1916. Ireland's role was now to
cast off the sleep-walking dreams that nationalistic rhetoric and
ideology induced and to recognize her true nature as a nation
fashioned in the mind of the Great Liberator:

> He is interesting in a hundred ways, but in no way more interest-
> ing than in this – that he was the greatest of all Irish realists
> who knew that if he could but once define, he would thereby
> create. He did define, and he did create. He thought a democ-
> racy and it rose. He defined himself, and his people became
> him. He imagined a future and the road appeared. He left his
> successors nothing to do but to follow him.[19]

O'Faoláin's writings were immediately recognized as a powerful critique of prevailing ideology and of the version of history
that sustained it. Professor Michael Tierney, a former Cumann
na nGaedheal TD and professor of Greek at University College,
Dublin, who introduced a series of articles in *Studies*, the Irish
Jesuit periodical, which responded in 1938 to *King of the
Beggars*, admitted the energy and skill of O'Faoláin's work. He
acknowledged:

> He has done us a very valuable service in going to the roots of
> our present society and compelling us to study and ponder on
> our destiny as a people. In many ways the future of our political,
> social and educational systems must depend on whether or not
> we agree with what he has said about the significance of
> O'Connell.[20]

Tierney disagreed with O'Faoláin's analysis – as did the three
other contributors to the *Studies* symposium. It was Tierney who
put the case against O'Faoláin most searchingly. Recognizing
much truth in O'Faoláin's analysis, he questioned in distress:

> The significance of Mr. O'Faoláin's book is that it once more
> raises clearly and frankly the dilemma that inexorably faces
> modern Ireland. Are we bound to rely for all our culture upon

an incongruous mixture of etiolated Catholicism, Puritanical individualism, and commercial utility, or is there no hope of our being able to obtain some light from our vanished Gaelic past to brighten our gloom?[21]

O'Faoláin's reply to those who asked such questions throughout his career was simple and direct. To pose them is to have ideas above one's station, to give in to a massive "inferiority complex with regard to the actuality of the Ireland in which we live." People like Tierney

> . . . hate the truth because they have not enough personal cour-age to be what we all are – the descendants, English-speaking, in European dress, affected by European thought, part of the European economy, of the rags and tatters who rose with O'Connell to win under Mick Collins – in a word this modern Anglo-Ireland.[22]

In his own novels and short stories, as did other writers who published novels and collections of short stories in the 1930s, O'Faoláin tried to attend to the realities of Irish life, allowing an unvarnished portrait to appear. In his short stories, as in Frank O'Connor's and later in Mary Lavin's work, we see an Irish provincial world, in Cork, in the small towns, in the countryside, where inhibition is disguised as economic prudence, land hunger and stolid conservatism as patriotic duty, subservience to church authority as piety. It is a world where intimacies, moments of personal fulfilment, seem wrested from an unyielding oppression. The emotional climate of the Irish short story, particularly in O'Faoláin, O'Connor, and Mary Lavin, is one where passion and encounter are matters of fleeting privacies, where disillusionment dogs individual hope and disappointment enforces bitter submission. The Irish short story of the 1930s and 1940s regis-tered a social reality that flew in the face of nationalistic self-congratulation. Instead of de Valera's Gaelic Eden and the uncomplicated satisfactions of Ireland free, the writers revealed a mediocre, dishevelled, often neurotic and depressed petit-bourgeois society that atrophied for want of a liberating idea.

O'Faoláin's image for it, as it was James Joyce's before him, is the entire landscape of Ireland shrouded in snow: "under that white shroud, covering the whole of Ireland, life was lying broken and hardly breathing."[23]

There was a sense nevertheless in which the writers and the politicians were not in fundamental disagreement. They may have differed on the historical basis of contemporary Irish society and disagreed profoundly in their conscious assessment of the quality of Irish life, but they shared a faith that the Irish future would depend on Irish invention and on a commitment to the essential worth of Irish experience. In de Valera this faith was expressed in a naive, direct idealism, in a version of pastoral and an economic nationalism that could not but attract impatient criticism. In the work of O'Faoláin and the other short story writers, by contrast it was expressed almost unconsciously in the quality of the writing itself. For despite the uncompromisingly bleak portrait of Irish society in the aftermath of civil war that the short story writers provide, the Irish short story – as Seamus Deane has remarked of modern Irish literature as a whole – registers alienation; it is not a literature of alienation.[24] Suggestive of speech in its prose rhythms, and in its ready acceptance of anecdote and discursive digression, it has seemed, although the authors learned in part from the Russian and French practitioners of the form, a literary form intimately involved with Irish life, peculiarly adapted to its rhythms and moods. Reminiscent of the tradition of Gaelic storytelling, it has seemed an art richly receptive to the racy pleasure of Irish conversation. Furthermore, its unquestioning dependence on traditional narrative techniques, eschewing as it does modish experimentation, implies the writers' own innate conservatism. They are of their people in spite of themselves. The Irish short story of the 1930s and 1940s therefore was an enactment of humanist faith in the Irish reality that it explored ostensibly as a condition of hopeless privation. It took for granted that an Irish art would have Ireland as its primary matter, and it addressed itself to its subject in a manner that unselfconsciously bore witness to the vitality of Irish discourse.

There were those in the Ireland of the 1930s who did not share this faith in an Irish self-sufficiency which de Valera urged in speech and in policy and the short story writers perhaps unconsciously made manifest in subject matter and manner. To these others it seemed that Irish survival as a nation could be assured in the midst of international crisis in Europe only if ideologies and modes of social organization currently shaping the experience of modern Europe were also made effective in their own country.

The vocationalist ideas on social organization commended by Pope Leo XII in his encyclical of 1891, *Rerum Novarum*, and reaffirmed in Pius IX's encyclical *Quadragesimo Anno* in 1931 had a special appeal to those who felt that Ireland's Catholic nature must be expressed in her new-won independence. And this could best be managed through a loyal active obedience to papal teaching on the social order. Accordingly the 1930s saw the creation of numbers of organizations, societies, and journalistic organs that encouraged the adoption of vocationalist and corporatist ideals. These shared a sense that the crisis which faced contemporary Europe in the conflict between capitalism and communism could be resolved only by the establishment of a new vocationalist social order in which men and women would organize themselves into guilds or corporations according to their various professions and vocations and where representative government would reflect that vocationalist organization of society. Through such reorganization it was hoped the conflicts between classes and between state and state could be healed in a new era of social harmony and cooperation. In Ireland an organization named Muintir na Tire (People of the Land), founded only a week before the publication of *Quadragesimo Anno*, soon became much more than the agricultural economic cooperative it had been at its inception, as it enthusiastically urged the cause of vocationalism at study weekends and later in the decade at residential congresses. Muintir na Tire reckoned the parish to be the basic unit of social organization, and by the end of the decade fifty Irish parishes were sending their representatives to rural weeks of study. Other organizations spread the vocationalist message at similar occasions, the summer school proving a particularly popular means of evangelism. Intellectuals in periodicals like *United Ireland* and *Studies* commended the concept. In 1938 the *Standard* newspaper was reinvigorated, and its doughty espousal of the vocationalist cause through the vigorous articles of Professor Alfred O'Rahilly of University College, Cork, certainly helped the paper to its circulation of about 50,000 in 1939.[25] The hierarchy added its voice, regularly commending vocationalism in its pastorals, thereby at the least providing a leaven of intellectual content to their repetitive proscriptions of such dangers to the public good and personal morality as provocative fashions, jazz music, mixed bathing, and rural company-keeping.

In September 1933 the vocationalist ideal received what might have proved a powerful impetus in Ireland when the Cumann na nGaedheal party was dissolved and reconstituted together with two other political organizations as Fine Gael. The major partner in this new political grouping was a recently formed (and even more recently banned) body named in menacing fashion the National Guard, which included in its constitution a commitment to the reorganization of society on a vocational basis.[26]

To explain this remarkable turn of events, whereby a party that had resolutely defended and worked the system of parliamentary democracy bequeathed to it a decade before should suddenly accept partnership in a political alliance which might involve a risky flirtation with new, less than fully democratic, forms of social organization it is necessary to consider in some detail the turbulent and spectacular growth in 1932 and 1933 of what came to be known as the Blueshirt movement.

The peaceful transition of power in 1932 (as I have already suggested) may well have been made possible because of the narrowness of de Valera's majority, dependent as it was on the support of the Labour Party. It seemed unlikely that his regime would prove either effective or long-lived. The snap election of 1933 which gave de Valera his overall majority put a swift end to hopes that his power would be only temporary. Furthermore, the intervening months had given many of the former government's members and supporters much to ponder, had the speed of events allowed them leisure for contemplation. Fianna Fáil seemed willing to turn an indulgent blind eye on the increasingly bellicose activities of the IRA (it had released IRA prisoners immediately upon taking office) which became identified, in an upsurge of anticommunist hysteria, with the Red threat. The government party also seemed ready to victimize former public officials of the old regime (though in fact de Valera refused to initiate a spoils system in Irish political life, which must always rest to his credit). In response to these disturbing portents an organization named the Army Comrades Association, which had been founded a week before the election of 1932 as an old comrades' society, swiftly began a change of nature which was to transform it into a strong-arm force ready to flex its muscles against the IRA, the government, and any threat of republican extremism or communism.

Two weeks after de Valera's re-election in 1933 he chose to dismiss the commissioner of the Civic Guards (the chief of police), General Eoin O'Duffy. For O'Duffy, a vigorous organizer and colourful popular personality, who had often been in the public eye (he had been in charge of crowd control during the Eucharistic Congress of 1932), this reverse was the opportunity to move on to greater things that before the summer was over (he was dismissed in February) was to take him to leadership of the Army Comrades Association, renamed the National Guard, and then to overall presidency of the new Fine Gael party when the old Cumann na nGaedheal party sought association with his own apparently powerful movement.

It was inevitable that the National Guard, with its zest for marches and public displays of mass support, its uniform of blue shirts, and its raised arm salute should be immediately associated with contemporary fascist movements of continental Europe. The fact that O'Duffy was also sympathetic to the corporatist ideas of the Italian fascists made it seem all the more likely that the

Blueshirt movement was an Irish expression of a European phenomenon. There is little doubt indeed that it was O'Duffy's apparent sympathy for European corporatist ideology that made him an attractive figure to those intellectuals and ideologues within the Cumann na nGaedheal party (men like Professors Michael Tierney and James Hogan) who had already become convinced of the need for Irish social reorganization on corporatist and vocationalist lines, though they preferred to relate their social ideals to papal utterance rather than to the direct example of Mussolini. And O'Duffy's apparent commitment to individual will as a force in public affairs probably made his movement attractive to the poet Yeats, who composed marching songs for the Blueshirts (though one doubts they were ever used).

General O'Duffy and the Blueshirt movement momentarily seemed poised for major action. By the end of 1934, however, any hopes individuals may have cherished that O'Duffy would prove a regenerative force in Ireland's body politic were dissipated as the movement collapsed in disagreement and operatic posturings. The political inexperience of O'Duffy and his grandiloquent absurdities of speech and manner had swiftly brought home to Cosgrave and the other more sage members of the former government party that nothing was to be gained from such an ill-advised association. Nor had such traditionally minded democratic politicians much taste for social experimentation of a vocationalist kind that had attracted Tierney and Hogan to O'Duffy. Furthermore, de Valera began to move decisively against the IRA in 1935, thereby reducing support for the Blueshirts which had sprung up in part because of fear of de Valera's past association with extreme republicanism. What the movement represented in fact, as Maurice Manning has argued, was not a widespread Irish desire to emulate social and political developments on the Continent but an Irish response to local political conditions. The politics of the Civil War had more to do with the rise and decline of the movement than the social theories of either Pius XI or Mussolini.

Despite the demise of the Blueshirt movement, which had

encouraged vocationalist ideals, the belief that Irish society required restructuring according to vocationalist principles did not die with it. In the Constitution of 1937, promulgated largely because Mr. de Valera wished to redefine the constitutional relationship of the Irish state with the United Kingdom, there are clear signs that the currently fashionable Catholic social thinking influenced certain of its Articles. It is not clear whether de Valera, who was almost single-handedly responsible for the document, was a vocationalist at heart, or whether he was simply responding to the thinking of the church, allowing it certain rights, but not dominance. What is clear to most commentators[27] on the 1937 Constitution is that it is a curious amalgam of ideas, particularly in the area of human rights. Enshrined in its various clauses are ideas familiar from the liberal tradition together with ideas drawn directly from Catholic social thought, including a modicum of vocationalism. Therefore the Constitution asserted that the state recognized "the Family as the natural primary and fundamental unit group of society" and guaranteed its rights "as indispensable to the welfare of the Nation and State," forbidding in further clauses any enactment of laws permitting divorce. The Constitution further limited the state's rights in education, firmly ascribing those rights to the parents. This latter clause in practice meant that the state could not choose to interfere with the church's control of much of Irish education so long as parents wished their children to be educated in denominational schools. The Constitution further recognized in an oddly vague clause, "the special position of the Holy Catholic and Apostolic Roman Church as the guardian of the faith professed by the great majority of its citizens." Vocationalist thinking in particular rather than Catholic social principles in general was expressed in the Articles defining the composition of the Seanad or Upper House. De Valera had set up a commission to report on the possible composition of a future Seanad (he had abolished the old Seanad in 1936). He accepted aspects of a minority report (the signatories included Professors Tierney and O'Rahilly), which recommended a body elected on a vocationalist basis. Part of the body of senators was to be selected from panels of candidates sharing cultural, social, and administrative experience.

As a whole the Constitution of 1937 was a cautious document which did not propose, apart from redefining the state's relationship with Britain, radical change. It affirmed basic Catholic social teaching, recognized property rights in a manner that would not disturb the largely rural, farming electorate, took the liberal tradition of individual rights very seriously, sought to protect religious minorities, and included a measure of idealism in seeking reunification of the national territory, elevating Irish to the status of the first national language. It also committed the state to do its utmost to secure the rural civilization that de Valera so devoutly desired. The fact that it was the relatively powerless Senate that de Valera chose to restructure on semi-vocationalist lines suggests that he was willing to allow Catholic ideas on the vocationalist state expression in his Constitution and in society but not to the extent that a fundamental reorganization of the legislature would be involved. To a large extent indeed the Constitution of 1937 confirmed the state's dependence on a parliamentary system of the British type rather than introducing novel experiments based on European ideas.

Nevertheless, the Constitution of 1937 shows that de Valera had a precise appreciation of the need for the state to take account of the fact that Southern Ireland, the area of the Free State's jurisdiction, was in the main a Catholic society, where the population would expect Catholic social teaching, especially when it touched on marriage and family law, to be expressed juridically. Furthermore, it manifests his understanding that the church had rights defined by herself that an Irish government could usurp only at its peril. De Valera seemed willing therefore to grant the church a role in education and in providing social services that a more revolutionary and secular republicanism might have attempted to wrest from her. In 1939 de Valera acceded to a motion introduced in the Seanad by Michael Tierney and another senator recommending the establishment of a commission to examine how further vocational organization could be encouraged in the country. The commission of twenty-five persons, chaired by the Most Reverend Bishop of Galway, Michael Browne, drew on the expertise of various individuals who had been most vocal in their support of vocationalist ideals. That de Valera considered such a commission worthwhile shows at the least that the idea of restructuring Irish society according to papal teaching still had a fairly wide currency, but de Valera may well have acceded to the suggestion simply because a commission was the best way to appear to act without the need to do so. After it reported in 1943 little more was heard of the corporate state,[28] although a later prime minister, Seán Lemass, who came to power in 1959, was to be influenced by corporatist ideas.

The ideological climate of the 1930s was therefore marked by economic and republican nationalism (the latter expressing itself at its most extreme in the recurrent violence of the IRA which was directed both within and without the state), though the state also presented the same essentially Catholic nationalist aspect that it had done during the Cosgrave administration. Concern for the native language, music, and rural tradition, and antagonism to cosmopolitan values were intensified to a degree which would have gratified the Russian Narodniki. The efforts of some intellectuals, ideologues, and socially active priests and laymen to introduce European ideas of social reorganization which coloured the Constitution of 1937 allowed for a good deal of sociable discussion and debate throughout the decade. They did not, however, interfere with the steady development of Irish society into a stable, deeply conservative, parliamentary democracy where change, if it was to occur, would occur slowly within the framework that the Constitution provided. It was a decade when even some of society's most outspoken critics, young short story writers and novelists who experienced a deep post-revolutionary disillusionment, felt little need for literary experiment, preferring to explore the new Irish world through the traditional forms of the short story and the realistic novel. The only literary journal to survive from an earlier era of literary enthusiasm and the heady days of Dublin's literary salons was the *Dublin Magazine* edited by Seumas O'Sullivan, who, with his wife, the painter Estella Solomons, tried to keep up, with a few others, the tradition of "evenings" for discussion and literary exchange that had so enlivened earlier years. But the *Dublin Magazine* in the 1930s was more notable for its sense of an insecure, self-regarding coterie remembering past glories and for its academic tone than for literary energy and commitment to a coherent, vital editorial policy. That intellectual and imaginative stirring which had once stimulated Edward Martyn to affirm that "the sceptre of intelligence has passed from London to Dublin" had now ended. Once more Dublin was a place to leave.

Occasionally a play, for example Paul Vincent Carrol's *Shadow and Substance* (1937) with its unabashed assault on Irish hypocrisy, might stimulate a brief intellectual frisson at the Abbey, and Micheál MacLiammóir's Gate Theatre in Dublin (employing the remarkable talents of his friend Hilton Edwards as director and designer) might influence the quality of stage design in the Irish theatre but neither managed quite to create that sense of new awakening that had characterized the early years of the Irish Literary Theatre.

In 1938 W. B. Yeats left Ireland for the last time, but not before his play *Purgatory* (performed at the Abbey in August 1938) had provoked conventional taste to a final public flurry of uncomprehending disapprobation of the poet's work. Judicious periods abroad in more congenial intellectual climates had of course always been Yeats's habit – a strategy which over many years had allowed him to survive as an artist in his own country. In the 1930s other, younger men also felt the need to escape the stultifying air of the Free State. For them Paris offered a freedom Ireland could not provide, as it had for generations of Irish artists and writers.

Walter Benjamin in a famous phrase once christened Paris the capital of the nineteenth century. The title bears testimony to the city's power to attract writers, poets, painters, and intellectuals, who, fleeing political persecution or cultural stagnation, found there a cosmopolitan freedom from local constraint entirely necessary to their work. In the early decades of the twentieth century Paris seemed set fair to maintain that cultural dominance of Europe as it remained the lodestar for emigré writers and artists from much of the Continent and from the United States. It was in Paris that James Joyce lived throughout the 1930s at work on *Work in Progress* which was to become *Finnegans Wake* (1939). In Ireland a few young intellectuals, mostly graduates of University College, Dublin, though the most famous of them, Samuel Beckett, was a graduate of Trinity College, were conscious of Joyce's genius and reputation; indeed some of them sought his acquaintance in Paris. They recognized in their veneration of Joyce's work and their sense of the European nature of his achievement that Irish cultural provincialism could be redeemed only if a proper concern with nationality was combined with an acceptance of the riches of European culture. Most of these young men, some of whom settled in Paris for a time in the 1930s (Beckett indeed settled permanently), were members of the very small Irish bourgeoisie that in its urban tastes and values had been overtaken by the populist rural values of the new state. Apart from Beckett, their literary work, that of the poets Denis Devlin, Brian Coffey, and the slightly older Thomas MacGreevy for example, has received limited critical attention in Ireland or elsewhere. Its intellectual, often theological, concerns, its unselfconsciously urban pre-occupations, its modernist experiment, its assured familiarity with European civilization, set their work apart from what most Irish men and women had come to expect from their contemporary writers. For these writers Ireland could be most herself not through a self-absorbed antiquarianism but through acceptance of her position as a European nation with links to the intellectual and artistic concerns of the Continent.

Their highly experimental work therefore represents an important strand in modern Irish literary and cultural history, which because of the prevailing nationalist ideology that celebrates the rising of a peasant people against oppression became almost as hidden an Ireland as Corkery's eighteenth-century Munster. The novelist Mervyn Wall in 1971 reflected on the social origins of his contemporaries. He noted that many of these writers were

> . . . of urban origin, and like myself they probably never had the experience of listening, as had probably O'Faoláin, O'Connor, Kavanagh and others who had been born in the provinces to aged relatives cracking their swollen knuckles over the fire as they told tales of old Land League days, of evictions and of the lucky shot that winged a land agent. I, and I suppose most of my acquaintances, only learnt about small town and rural Irish life through visits to the Abbey Theatre and subsequent reading. Many of the writers . . . had brilliant academic careers. Many came from prosperous families and no doubt from childhood on believed that a secure place in the world awaited them.
>
> It was natural for these people to turn to Europe where culture was, just as the writer of provincial origin nowadays turns to America where the money is. Provincial Ireland has the long tradition of American emigration behind it. Dublin has not. I hate mentioning myself, but by doing so I may make things clearer. My father had the means and leisure to spend a great deal of his time from 1895 onwards travelling all over Europe and even to the West Indies. Our house was full of books that dealt with other lands, and I never heard when young a single place name in Ireland mentioned. All the talk was of Paris, the Italian lakes, Vienna and Dresden.[29]

For a brief period in 1936–38 the periodical *Ireland Today* gave a platform to some of these writers and to intellectuals and critics whose concerns were European as well as Irish. The journal was one of the very few places in Ireland where support for the republican cause in Spain had any overt expression. Indeed it was popular opposition to its stand on this issue that led to its demise in 1938. The journal, as well as reporting on political developments in European countries in vigorously antifascist terms, attended to developments in European cinema, sought to publish intellectual Catholic commentary on social and cultural policies in the Free State and in Europe, and sought out new writing. There was an astringent impatience in its pages, a contempt for all mediocre aspects of Irish life, an iconoclasm that could be directed at the Abbey Theatre and the Gaelic revival alike, and an uncompromising republicanism in some of its social commitments which made it an obvious target for suppression in the interests of a national complacency that thought Ireland had little to gain from modern European culture and nothing certainly from the pretensions of a self-appointed intelligentsia.

As the 1930s ended, however, it became clear to even the most obdurate that the affairs of Europe must become Irish affairs as the war clouds gathered, threatening a storm that might engulf the infant Irish state on its uncontrollable journey. There was a general concern that come what may, the victories won in 1921 should not be thrown away in wartime alliances and risky partisanship. For most Irish men and women survival as a state seemed the highest good that could be expected in the coming crisis. Ireland must seek to survive as a neutral power. Michael Tierney in an article in 1937 caught a mood which by 1939/40 united the country:

> We must be implicated, as far as in us lies, in no more wars to end wars or wars for democracy or for any of the other high-sounding ideals in which war-propaganda is so fruitful. Our course, above all in war-time, must be one of "sacred egoism."[30]

CHAPTER 6

"The Emergency":
A Watershed

I

When Harold Nicolson visited Dublin in March 1942 to fulfil
a number of speaking engagements, he noted in his diary that
Irish neutrality had "taken on an almost religious flavour; it has
become a question of honour; and it is something which Ireland
is not ashamed of but tremendously proud."[1] He sensed the
popularity of a cause that had united the people of independent
Ireland under a leader, de Valera, who exhibited a "deep spiritual
certainty." By the time Nicolson paid his visit to Dublin to discover how invincibly persuaded most Irish men and women were
of the soundness of the policy that had brought obloquy upon
Ireland both in Britain and in the United States, neutrality was
a much less risky stance than it had been just two years earlier
(though of course this was not fully clear at the time). American
troops were already stationed in Northern Ireland preparing for
the invasion of Europe, and Germany was principally occupied
in the war against Russia, so that the threat of German invasion
no longer gave great cause for alarm. While pressure for a full
Irish participation in the war might be exerted economically by
Britain and the United States, the possibility of an anticipatory

invasion by British forces to forestall German occupation of Ireland for strategic reasons had lessened appreciably. The period of greatest danger to Irish neutrality had in fact been the year of June 1940 to June 1941 when German troops came to the very point of an invasion of the United Kingdom which threatened also to engulf Ireland in a general conflagration. In this year de Valera's diplomatic skill, together with his unswerving refusal to place the interests of any other nation above that of his own, allowed him to steer a safe passage through a mine-infested sea, in consultation with two diplomats who managed to view Irish positions on the matter with shrewd sensitivity, Sir John Maffey, the British representative, and the German minister, Dr. Edouard Hempel. De Valera's resolute, cool-headed handling of affairs in these dangerous months won him widespread respect and support in Ireland. The neutrality policy was loyally adhered to by all parties in the Dáil, though in the early months of the war, after the fall of France, dissenting parliamentary voices had sometimes been raised.

Throughout the years of the war de Valera strove to maintain that even-handed diplomatic balance between the belligerents which served him in the tense months of 1940–41, to a degree that suggested pedantic shortsightedness to many people abroad. However, it could not really be doubted that a scrupulous diplomatic care was of the utmost importance to an Irish neutrality that exhibited telling signs of partiality. Some Irish men and women certainly favoured a German victory in the military struggle. Attitudes of respect for Hitler's reconstruction of the German nation combined with an old Irish nationalist conviction that England's difficulty might prove Ireland's opportunity were reflected in a limited sympathy for the German war effort and in the IRA's clumsy attempts to establish contacts with the German intelligence service. The majority of the population, however, probably hoped for British survival and, after America entered the war, for an Allied victory. De Valera himself certainly favoured the Allies' cause; on the practical level Allied airmen who were shot down over Ireland were returned to Britain when Germans in similar straits found themselves spending the rest of the war in Irish internment. The Irish intelligence service and its British counterparts maintained contacts. In addition, over 50,000 citizens of the Irish state volunteered for service in the British armed forces during the course of the war.

But such evidence of Irish partiality in the European conflict did not mean that there was ever any large-scale opposition to de Valera's determined efforts to keep the Irish state uninvolved in the hostilities. When in 1940 Professor Michael Tierney (who had earlier counselled "sacred egoism") recorded that neutrality afforded Ireland "the nightmarish satisfaction of looking on in comparative safety at horrors we can do nothing to prevent"[2] most Irish people would have agreed with his sentiments and would have seen little reason to forsake that comparative safety for the overwhelming risks to their young state that political and military partisanship would involve. And nothing that happened in subsequent years would have changed their minds. A minority, however, thought such safety ignoble, believing that to remain a spectator in such desperate times was to place Ireland in grave moral jeopardy.

Not unnaturally, given links of family and feeling with Britain, most of this minority comprised members of the Anglo-Irish community (though James Dillon, who resigned from Fine Gael on the issue of neutrality, could scarcely be identified with Anglo-Ireland), for whom Ireland's neutrality was a difficult pill to swallow. Many of them were still accustomed to think of British forces as "our army" and "our navy." What others saw as sacred egoism, some of them were inclined to regard as shameful indifference to the fate of their English kin. The poet Louis MacNeice, who had been in Ireland on holiday when war broke out, bitterly expressed this mood when, serving as a fire-watcher during the London blitz, he turned on his native country:

> The neutral island facing the Atlantic,
> The neutral island in the heart of man,
> Are bitterly soft reminders of the beginnings
> That ended before the end began. . . .

But then look eastward from your heart, there bulks
A continent, close, dark, as archetypal sin,
While to the west off your own shores the mackerel
Are fat – on the flesh of your kin.[3]

MacNeice, in common with many others of his Anglo-Irish background, would undoubtedly have been distressed to read the
views of the *Leader* newspaper on the sea battles alluded to in
the above stanzas. It was that organ's stern view that Britain had
brought sea warfare upon herself by her traditional policy of naval
supremacy. The paper's moral outrage was reserved for occasions
when neutral shipping was caught up in a conflict of others'
making. The war therefore heightened that sense of Anglo-
Ireland's isolation from Ireland and from the world that, as we
saw earlier, had in the main characterized its experience since
independence. The Viscount Powerscourt confessed to Harold
Nicolson with mingled gloom and saturnine satisfaction: "Here
I am marooned – the last of the aristocracy with no one to
speak to."[4]

If Anglo-Ireland was marooned, conscious in a new way that
Irish independence had really cut their country loose politically
from Britain, then Irish writers too felt remote from the outside
world. The 1930s had been a trying time for writers who had
chosen to remain in the country. Censorship and an unsympathetic public climate had proved bearable only because markets
for their work had been readily available abroad. The war closed
off many such outlets (literature from neutral Ireland ceased to
be so welcome in London journals and publishing houses, and
the paper shortage was acute), placing Irish writers in positions
of desperate financial insecurity, for no writer could imagine
making a living on Irish sales alone. The poet Patrick Kavanagh
caught their mood in a line from his poem "Lough Derg" (written in 1942) when, contemplating an Irish crowd at the annual
pilgrimage there, he imagined the banal, acquisitive prayers of
the people as "All Ireland . . . froze for the want of Europe."[5] A
new note of real venom came into some of their writings as they

reflected on their own society. Seán O'Faoláin in his *An Irish Journey* (1941) castigated the country's capital for its cultural deficiencies: "The quality of life is weak . . . weak for a capital. . . . Politics, journalism, conversation are generally tawdry, and sometimes far worse."[6] The city stirred him to savagery: "no sooner does any man attempt, or achieve, here, anything fine than the rats begin to emerge from the sewers, bringing with them a skunk-like stench of envy and hatred, worse than the drip of a broken drain."[7] At more controlled moments, he concluded of Ireland in wartime, "Life is so isolated now that it is no longer being pollinated by germinating ideas windborne from anywhere."[8]

In his book *The Emergency* (1978), Bernard Share has suggested that the conventional estimation of the years 1939–45 as a particularly isolated and culturally stagnant period in modern Irish history is something of an exaggeration. He suggests that for British commentators, and for those of Anglo-Irish background, both at the time and since, it was impossible to credit that a country which had apparently opted out of the central struggle of modern times, the war against fascism, could have been anything other than culturally stagnant, since the nation, in its callous self-interest, was morally deficient. He further implies that those Irish writers who also bewailed the cultural isolation of the period were perhaps exaggerating the general condition of the country because of the peculiar pressures on themselves. Share's opinion is that, by contrast, the years of "the Emergency," as the war was known in Ireland, show signs of some cultural and intellectual vitality.

The truth is probably more simple – for the majority of Irish men and women the years of the war represented scarcely more of an experience of cultural isolation and deprivation than had any of the years that had preceded them. The entire period since independence, it must be remembered, had been characterized by an isolationism encouraged by official ideology and protected by censorship. Only those, like the writers, who had objected to that prewar condition, might have been expected to believe that the experience of neutrality deepened it. Most people simply supported neutrality as the only sane policy in a world gone mad, and got on with their lives as best they might.

If the mass of the Irish people were in all probability unconscious of the cultural stagnation some commentators thought must inevitably result as a consequence of neutrality, the economic depredations of the war years were all too evident. Ireland, dependent for some basic necessities on the strained goodwill of the British, quickly took steps to ensure that the population could be fed. A compulsory tillage policy was introduced in 1940 which, during the war years, almost doubled the acreage under crops. Despite this, bread was rationed from 1942 onward following tea, sugar, and fuel, which had already been placed on the rationed list. Coal, gas, and petrol were in very short supply (private motoring became almost impossible by 1942 and was replaced by many resurrected horse-drawn vehicles). By most people, indeed, the war years are remembered as years of severe if not desperate shortages. For some there was wretched poverty – the monthly periodical the *Bell* in 1942 predicted "scurvy, rickets and kindred diseases because we are unable to get a properly balanced diet."[9] For others the unavailability of tobacco seemed the most serious personal consequence of the international crisis.

The economy as a whole entered on a period of decline. Exports fell, and while imports also fell in the generally insecure economic environment, the cost of imports rose strikingly in comparison with the prices gained for exports. The loss of many unavailable imported raw materials reduced industrial potential, and industrial employment declined. Efforts were made to exploit local resources: the turf bogs were tapped in a venture that was in postwar years to become one of the successful semi-state enterprises (Bord na Mona); advertisements appeared in the press on behalf of the Department of Agriculture, urging the population to grow potatoes wherever possible. A lively black market in scarce goods quickly developed.

British visitors to Dublin in the war years, whatever the miseries that high costs and shortages inflicted on the city's poor (and at the outbreak of hostilities an Emergency Powers Order had frozen wages), discovered a city that seemed an island of prewar life in the midst of a sea of international change. They noticed the ready availability of meat for those able to pay for it, they observed that social life continued, given a special dash by a whiff of espionage and by English and European exiles from more stringent austerity. In the early months of the war indeed, as Patrick Campbell recalls, a hint of bohemian excess was generated by the occasion: "Dublin almost seemed to have a special duty, in a world gone grey and regimented, to preserve the gaieties and pleasures that we felt had vanished from everywhere else."[10] Indeed, Peter Kavanagh, the poet's brother, even sensed that Dublin in the war years exuded "a certain international atmosphere"[11], in contrast with the preceding decade.

In some ways, the war years in Ireland were not without their agreeable aspects for many people. As John Ryan testified: "Looking back on it, there was a lot to be said for the times. . . . The goodness of simple things was emphasized rather than diminished by the absence of superfluous luxuries. The country was clean, uncluttered and unhurried."[12] During "the Emergency," about 250,000 men became involved in defence roles of one kind or another, and while service in the regular armed forces or in the reserve in a neutral country had its tediums, the war in Ireland as elsewhere offered release from the normal round of domestic and local responsibilities. Furthermore, service in the Irish armed forces had an important healing effect on Irish life. The *Leader* newspaper had marked its Christmas edition of 1939 by publishing a cartoon which showed de Valera and Cosgrave crossing the floor of the Dáil to shake hands, burying the Civil War hatchet once and for all, invoking the early days of Sinn Féin in a ballad:

> We two have run about the hills
>   For Ireland suffered pain
> We'd then united hearts and wills
>   In old Sinn Féin.
>
> But many a time since then we've fought
>   And maybe will again;

> Now friends for Ireland's sake we ought
> For old Sinn Féin.

Apart from the few diehard republicans in the IRA who tried to make common cause with Germany during "the Emergency," the experience of uniting to defend Irish sovereignty for many certainly helped dissipate the surviving bitterness inherited from the early years of independence which, as the journalist and commentator John Healy remembered, had in prewar days "flared sullenly, if silently, at the sight of the uniform of the National Army."[13]

Others noted how the years of "the Emergency" showed a decided increase in the number of books borrowed from public libraries (by 1944, twenty-four out of twenty-six of the counties of the Irish state had a public library, Westmeath and Longford going without) although public expenditure on these services remained comparatively low and the work of librarians was made difficult because of poor salaries and the endless vigilance of self-appointed moral guardians of the people. In the *Bell* a library assistant reported how even the poems of John Donne fell out of favour in one library, only to be read on request. The optimism of one correspondent to the *Leader* who reckoned that "the Ireland of the future will certainly be more broad-minded and less insular"[14] because of the noticeable increase in a readership for the English classics, was not reckoning with Irish Grundyism. But film societies were founded and the Gate Theatre in Dublin flourished.

Amateur dramatics was a major feature of social life in the war years. Michael Farrell, the novelist, in the *Bell* in February 1942, having spent fifteen months recording the theatre up and down the country "from Belfast to Kerry, from Wicklow to Sligo," could report in a final summary of his findings:

> The striking fact is that dramatic activity in the country is abundant and enthusiastic, and that it is not necessary to list among the difficulties of the Country Theatre a lack of talent. Possibly at no time has there been so much of it; or so much talk of

drama and plans for drama. Clearly, the long lull which followed the palmy and piping days of Redmondite Ireland has given place to a period of greater vigour than ever.[15]

He noted how some towns had recently built new halls specially designed for dramatic purposes, instancing Tralee and Killarney in County Kerry, and that there were two little theatres, in Birr, County Offaly, and Dundalk, County Louth. Elsewhere dramatic performances were staged in town halls and cinemas. Farrell accounted for the revival in amateur dramatics throughout much of the country, which dates from the late 1930s and which flowered during "the Emergency," in two ways. He suggested that the international reputation of the Abbey Theatre had generated new interest in things theatrical throughout the country and that it was that theatre which set standards and governed taste. Furthermore, the exigencies of wartime had made Ireland attractive to Irish and English professional touring companies which in earlier days would have cast their sights elsewhere:

Since the appetite comes in eating, their visits have stimulated the production of local plays. It must be made clear, however, that the revival itself had begun several years ago and that the increased number of visits from touring companies has only been an acceleration of a process not its cause.[16]

To these causes one would only wish to add the fact that local Catholic clergy were occasionally to the fore in the encouragement of amateur dramatics, certainly because they saw the social benefits to be derived from community effort, but also one suspects because they saw in local drama an alternative to the questionable offerings of Hollywood. Be that as it may, the years of "the Emergency" saw a healthy growth in an amateur dramatic movement, with its annual festivals (in Sligo and Dundalk, for example) that was to be so much a feature of social and cultural life in Ireland in the 1950s. In 1953 the Amateur Drama Council of Ireland was formed.

But even the most sympathetic of British observers of Irish neutrality during the war years could not but discern in Ireland's political stance a withdrawal from the realities of contemporary history. Cyril Connolly, for example, writing in *Horizon* in 1942 concluded a sensitive and sympathetic appraisal of the Irish social, cultural, and political scene: "Ireland has chosen to pass he hand."[17] A more acute observer might have acknowledged that Ireland had refused to play the game of nations by the same rule as her neighbours. The period 1939–45, therefore, for most Irish men and women, was not experienced simply as a time when Ireland opted out of history but when her own history and the maintenance of her recently won independence were of primary concern. The cultural isolation of the preceding twenty years was perhaps deepened, but the healing effects on Civil War division in Irish society of a genuine external threat might be set against that in any overall evaluation. For many, the years of the war were simply a continuation of prewar experience, in economically straitened circumstances, with the language, national sovereignty, religion, and protection of Irish distinctiveness as the dominant topics of intellectual and cultural concern in a society still moulded by its essential conservatism, with talk, drink, sport, and other local activities absorbing energies spared from the rigour of daily life.

II

If, then, the experience of many Irish people during "the Emergency" was, despite the international situation, one of continuity with earlier years, there are nevertheless reasons for regarding the period 1939–45 as the beginning of a watershed in Irish life. The developments of those years which allow one to speak of something as striking as a watershed were not, one must stress, in any really direct sense the outcome of the war that was raging on the European mainland. Rather, they were related to changes that were occurring in Ireland itself that would have undoubtedly occurred in peacetime as in war, for they were grounded in the dynamics of the country's post-independence history. In this ense, the period, rather than representing a stretch of time when reland behaved like a historical dropout, was in fact a period vhen the country's own internal historical life was entering on a rucial phase.

In his essay "After the Revolution: The Fate of Nationalism n the New States,"[18] Clifford Geertz identified a tension between wo impulses in newly independent nationalist states in the twen-ieth century. The one is an impulse to answer the question 'Who are we?" by employing "symbolic forms drawn from local raditions." Through these, the new state can "give value and ignificance to the activities of the state, and by extension to the :ivil life of its citizens." Such an impulse Geertz labels "essen-ialism." The other impulse to answer the question of national dentity through discovering the "outlines of the history of our :ime and what one takes to be the overall direction and signifi-:ance of that history," Geertz names "epochalism." New states, 1e argues, frequently exhibit a tension between the two impulses - "to move with the tide of the present and to hold to an inherited :ourse." Geertz's categories and terms are highly illuminatory of :he Irish experience since independence.

The first twenty years of Irish independence were obviously dominated by the first of these impulses. The Irish language, religion, and aspects of rural life that could be identified as embodying Gaelic tradition served as the essentialist symbolic forms, giving significance to the life of the state and its citizens. There had, however, been conscious efforts by the new state almost from its inception to define itself as well, in relation to the movements of contemporary history. Ireland joined the League of Nations in 1923 and was admitted to the League Council in 1930. After the change of government in 1932, de Valera, who was elected president of the council in the same year, continued the effort. He was scrupulous in his observance of his responsibili-ties to the League, refusing, despite great public pressure, to shift from a policy of nonalignment in the Spanish Civil War. He also supported sanctions against Italy following the assault on Abyssinia. Throughout its first twenty years, in fact, the Irish state

played an important role in a contemporary historical movemen
which sought through an international forum to establish nationa
rights and to protect the peace. In this, Ireland, particularly unde
de Valera's direction, was to the fore in pressing the belief tha
small states must not become puppets of the larger powers. Ire
land's voice was heard in contributions to some of the vital issue
of the period. Furthermore, some of those who in the 1930s ha
sought to introduce vocationalism had also, with less success
tried to adapt Ireland to international developments. The tensio
that Geertz identifies as characteristic of newly independent state
was therefore evident in the Irish Free State from the earlies
years of its foundation. Geertz helps us understand how such
tension is expressed in society. He writes:

> The interplay of essentialism and epochalism is not ... a kind
> of cultural dialectic, a logistic of abstract ideas, but a historical
> process as concrete as industrialization and as tangible as war.
> The issues are being fought out not simply at the doctrine and
> argument level – though there is a great deal of both – but
> much more importantly in the material transformations that the
> social structures of all the new states are undergoing. Ideological
> change is not an independent stream of thought running along-
> side social process and reflecting (or determining) it, it is a
> dimension of that process itself.[19]

It is not difficult, in the light of this, to explain why essentialis
conceptions of Irish identity were to the fore in this process i
the first two decades of Irish independence. As we saw earlier
the Irish Free State in those decades was a largely homogeneous
conservative, rural society, in which critics of the dominant ideo
logical consensus could make little headway. Furthermore, the
abstractions of international relations, while attractive to the
juridical mind of a de Valera, could scarcely stir the popula
imagination as could the intimacies of local language, religiou
belief, and tradition. Conservative ideology and the social fabri
were bound up with one another, both expressive of the atavisti
and widespread conviction that the essential Irish reality wa

he uniquely desirable, unchanging life of small farm and country
own in the Irish-speaking west. There was neither competition
rom other equally compelling conceptions of the nation's life,
ior pressure for ideological innovation in the dynamics of social
:omplexities or large-scale rapid change. For despite the degree
:o which much of rural Ireland had been penetrated by modern-
zing influences in the early decades of the century, and the
vays in which change had been at work there since the Famine,
nuch of the social life of the countryside as it had developed
n the late nineteenth century remained apparently intact, as we
:aw, until well into the 1930s. It was only in the early 1940s
:hat things in rural Ireland began to change more rapidly and
ioticeably.

From the period of "the Emergency" onward Ireland has
undergone the experience of a widespread rejection of the con-
litions of rural life similar to that which has characterized most
Western European countries since the end of the nineteenth cen-
:ury.[20] Up to the late 1930s, most commentators are agreed,
:migration reflected in its paradoxical way a commitment to rural
ife, or at the very least to the protection of the inherited plot.
From that date onward the historian, with increasing frequency,
:omes on reports and surveys, on literary and dramatic portraits,
which agree in their discovery of an almost universally demoralized rural scene, where emigration has begun to represent
an outright rejection of rural life. In 1925, as Hugh Brody points
but in his *Inishkillane: Change and Decline in the West of Ireland*,
the Gaeltacht Commission in its studies found little evidence to
suggest that the country people of the Irish-speaking districts
were demoralized, in the sense that they rejected their world.
Certainly the commissioners found much rural poverty and a
highly ambivalent attitude to the Irish language that disturbed
their revivalist sensibilities (most Gaelic-speaking parents seemed
determined that their children would speak English); and there
were areas, too, like the Aran Islands, where the collapsed market
for mackerel had caused much depression and parts of the coast
of Clare where some of the population in the war years had

become used in a way that bespoke social deterioration to makin
a living off flotsam, jetsam, and oil from sunk ships.

But to read through the minutes of evidence presented to th
commissioners is to be struck by how strong a hold the lan
had on the people and how much commitment, even when
circumstances were desperate, there was to survival there. Th
evidence in these documents in fact confirms the authenticit
of Peadar O'Donnell's literary conclusion in his novel *Islander*
(1928), where the hero and heroine at the end of the book rejec
the possibilities of mainland life in the east of the country t
remain on their island even though their life there will be on
of privation and stringency. Indeed in his evidence one Patric
Gallagher, the manager of a rural cooperative in Donegal, clos
to where O'Donnell set his novel, told the commissioners tha
the people in the Rosses in County Donegal "looked upon th
little holding at home as a place to come to for a few months i
the winter, some place in which to build a nest, while they loo
to Scotland, the Lagan and America as the place in which to ear
the money to keep the rest."[21] In 1948, when it was widel
accepted that emigration had reached crisis proportions, a com
mission was appointed to prepare a report on the matter. It
conclusions (the report was published in 1956) reveal that th
countryside now viewed emigration in a new way. Throughou
the report it is implied that the conditions of rural life are now
quite unacceptable to many country people. The report solemnl
reminds its readers of the data with regard to sanitation in th
1946 census, which revealed that four out of every five farm
dwellings had no special facilities, such as a flush lavatory, chemi
cal closet, privy, or dry closet and that only one out of every
twenty farm dwellings had an indoor lavatory. It noted tha
"through the cinema and the radio, and above all by direct experi
ence either personal or through relatives, people in such con
ditions are, more than ever before, becoming aware of the
contrast between their way of life and that in other countries
especially in urban centres."[22] The report remarked on the lack
of social contacts and insufficient facilities for recreation and

intellectual pursuits, detecting in fact "a psychological and economic malaise."[23] In summary the commissioners stated of the
rural conditions they had studied:

> We were impressed by the unanimity of the views presented to
> us in evidence on the relative loneliness, dullness and generally
> unattractive nature of life in many parts of rural Ireland at pre-
> sent, compared with the pattern of life in urban centres and
> with that in easily accessible places outside the country.[24]

The reasons why this change in rural consciousness occurred
are not hard to find. The report itself sensed that modern communications had interfered with rural satisfaction. Furthermore,
the availability of work in Britain's war economy had given many
Irish emigrants the opportunity to earn good wages quickly.
Indeed, John Healy, remembering his boyhood in Charlestown,
County Mayo in the 1930s, in his *The Death of an Irish Town*,
suggests that this latter development was highly disruptive of the
social fabric of County Mayo. For instead of the rural emigrant
departing for a protracted exile from which he or she sent back
remittances to sustain the homestead, or for the rigours of short-
term, ill-paid employment, the towns were now visited by
returned workers with spending money in their pockets. The rural
emigrants' returning to local towns thereby disturbed the balance
of the social hierarchy in such towns with their assumed superiority to the small farmers who depended upon credit facilities,
infecting them with the dissatisfaction that had already begun to
take its toll of the countryside. Such is Healy's remembrance of
the period, and certainly from the 1940s onward Irish emigration
was increasingly from the country towns as well as from the
countryside. In 1940 a writer in the *Leader* caught the hint of
this infection in the small town air when he published a short one-
act drama entitled *The Microbe – a Rural Tragedy*. The microbe of
the title is the affliction that visits the young in Bailebeag, a small
country town, disturbing their contentment. "I refuse," declares
the daughter of a shopkeeper who has passed the examination for
entry to the Civil Service, "to stagnate down here on a farm."[25]

Perhaps films and magazine advertisements and the ready avail-ability of jobs in Britain had merely put a superficially attractive gloss on economic necessity in this period. Perhaps, as has been argued, the quickening pace of emigration that dates from the years of "the Emergency" can be accounted for in terms of increasing mechanization and of a "steadily increased hegemony of commodity economy"[26] which had been at work in Irish rural society since the Famine and in that sense was nothing new. But what cannot I think be doubted is that since the early 1940s larger numbers of people (particularly young women) than in earlier decades left rural and small-town Ireland because they believed a more attractive life awaited them elsewhere. The lure of the urban world, glimpsed in film and magazine, made emi-gration less awesome, gave a sense of possibility to what in the past would have been experienced only as the workings of an implacable fate.

In the next two decades emigration, principally to Britain, would account for a major decline in rural population. In the intercensal period 1936–46 an estimated net emigration of 187,000 was recorded. By the period 1951–56 this would rise to 197,000 (a larger figure in less than half the time) and for 1956–61 the figure would be 212,000. As Hugh Brody con-cludes, the country-dweller's "determination to stay on the land seemed to have broken."[27] By 1965–68 when Damian Hannan came to study attitudes to emigration among young people in County Leitrim, almost all traces of the familialist values which had once played so crucial a role in rural life seemed to be absent. Hannan stated, on the basis of findings among respondents to a questionnaire to school-leavers, five-sixths of whom had con-sidered emigrating: "results suggest that family obligations do not have the precedence in migration decisions that was expected" and "where respondents believed they could not fulfil their aspirations locally, increasing levels of family obligations made no difference to their migration decisions."[28]

In 1942, at the beginning of this starkly new phase in Ireland's social history, the poet Patrick Kavanagh published his harrowing poetic account of a particular rural life, *The Great Hunger*. The work is a record of the diminished experience of a small farmer, Patrick Maguire, in County Monaghan. Maguire's life is claimed by the forces of Land, Mother, and Church (a variation on Corkery's troika of forces which must be reflected in a truly national literature). In thrall to these forces, Maguire's vital energies are withered in an all-encompassing negation. Kavanagh's poem is an outraged cry of anger, an eloquently bleak riposte from the heart of the rural world to all those polemicists, writers, and demagogues who in de Valera's Ireland sought to venerate the countryman's life from the study or political platform. There is a harsh authenticity in this work, where sexual starvation is imaginatively associated with the great famines of the 1840s, which reveals the uncompromising directness of Kavanagh's social criticism. Acutely conscious of the realities of Irish life, Kavanagh overwhelms the reader of this work with a sense of the desolation of a rural existence in Ireland. The same energetic directness of mind which dominates *The Great Hunger* was to characterize Kavanagh's later social criticism, when he turned his impassioned intelligence on the Irish urban scene in the late 1940s and early 1950s. In 1942, however, he wrote of the world of his own childhood and young manhood in the parish of Inniskeen, County Monaghan. The poem, which must rank as a major work by an Irish poet in the twentieth century, discovers in one small parish a deprivation and mute despair which in Ireland as a whole were to drive thousands of young men and women off the land to the industrial suburbs of Birmingham and to London. Indeed, if there is a case for viewing a major work of art as an antenna that sensitively detects the shifts of consciousness that determine a people's future, *The Great Hunger* is that work. Maguire's life and the dismal fate that befell countless Maguires in the hundred years following the Famine, were no longer acceptable.

Patrick Maguire, the old peasant, can neither be damned nor
    glorified:
The graveyard in which he will lie will be just a deep-drilled
    potato-field

Where the seed gets no chance to come through
To the fun of the sun.
The tongue in his mouth is the roof of a yew.
Silence, silence. The story is done.

He stands in the doorway of his house
A ragged sculpture of the wind,
October creaks the rotted mattress,
The bedposts fall. No hope. No lust.
The hungry fiend
Screams the apocalypse of clay
In every corner of this land.[29]

Many Irish men and women in the early years of this new phase
in Irish social history contrived to ignore the bleak facts of rural
disintegration that it represented. Many continued to write,
speak, and sermonize on the features of Irish identity that only
rural people authentically possessed. But for some the ideological
challenge of the new social reality could not easily be set aside.
Very quickly ideological and intellectual innovation began to be
evident as aspects of the social process of change set in motion
by new attitudes in the country.

For the Gaelic revivalist the crisis in Irish rural life of the 1940s
from which the countryside did not begin to recover until the
late 1960s and Ireland's entry to the EEC in 1973 posed a
challenge of a precise and unignorable kind. Indeed it was in the
ranks of the revivalists that some of the first signs of ideological
change based on a perception of social change can be detected.
It had been the hope that had fired the Irish-language policy of
the first two decades of independence that the rural Gaelic-
speaking districts of the western seaboard would be consolidated,
and their populations increased. Furthermore, Irish in the schools
in English-speaking areas would gradually expand knowledge of
the language so that the partly Gaelic-speaking areas would
enlarge, thereby reversing overall the decline in knowledge of the
language that had set in in the nineteenth century. In the 1940s
it became clear to most people who thought about the matter

that the policy was failing in its purposes, for neither had emigration from Irish and partly Irish-speaking districts been checked – indeed it was increasing alarmingly – nor had the language in the schools policy been as successful as had been hoped. The revival policy was not creating a situation where an eventual linguistic exchange might occur throughout the country. Rather, it was evident that the Irish language was nearing the point of extinction. The point began to be made in Dáil and Seanad speeches which criticized the policy frankly. The *Leader* newspaper was equally frank when in 1940 it opined, "people today lack faith in the possibility of language revival." That newspaper astutely associated the crisis in the fortunes of the language with the "decay that has overtaken rural Ireland." The editor sadly warned: "There is no use, therefore, in blinking the fact that the last reservoirs of living and vigorous Irish on whose continuance depends the success of what we are trying to do in the Gaeltacht are vanishing before our eyes."[30]

There were signs of that loss of faith in the country that gave enthusiasts for the language great cause for concern. In 1940 University College, Dublin, the largest college in the National University of Ireland, appointed a new president. The Gaelic League protested about his knowledge of Irish. As if to add real injury to insult, the same college appointed a Mr. W. J. Williams to its chair of education in 1943. Again the Gaelic League felt obliged to protest. The college made clear, however, despite the Gaelic League's vigorous objection, that even in so crucial an appointment as the most influential chair of education in the country, academic criteria counted for more than strictly national requirements. After a brief but very ill-tempered controversy Professor Williams was confirmed in his appointment.

In the National Schools too the early 1940s produced sure signs that things were changing. The teachers began to voice outright criticisms of the dependence on the schools for language revival. Educational values were being ignored in the drive for a revival conducted on purely nationalist lines. Certainly the Irish National Teachers' Organization (the INTO) had, as we saw earlier, readily cooperated with the Department of Education in the early years of the drive to restore the national tongue. But by 1936 the organization's executive responded to what its historian has described as

> . . . a growing body of opinion even among staunch supporters of the revival movement, that the teaching of ordinary school subjects through the medium of Irish in the English-speaking areas and the all-Irish programme for infants in those areas, was not alone detrimental to the educational development of the children, but a hindrance to the progress of the language.[31]

In response, the executive encouraged the wide discussion of the issue at branch and county committee level. The result was a resolution, which we have already noted, at the annual Congress in 1936 which led eventually to the *Report of the Committee of Inquiry into the Use of Irish as a Teaching Medium*. This report appeared in 1941 (an *Interim Report* was issued in 1939). It was unfortunate that discussions of and reactions to its findings in the years following its publication were somewhat muddied by the fact that the INTO was in dispute with the Department of Education on other contentious matters, particularly the issue of salaries (a long, bitter dispute gave rise in 1946 to a protracted teachers' strike). It was therefore improbable that the vital issue of the language could have been discussed in an atmosphere of reasoned calm. Nor was it. The Minister for Education, in conflict with the INTO almost as a way of life, was in no mood to be conciliatory on a matter about which he had strong personal feelings. He simply did not wish to hear from his National School teachers that the majority of those teaching infants were "opposed to using Irish as the sole medium of instruction when English is the home language,"[32] nor was he concerned to learn that "the great bulk of evidence supports the view that a smooth and easy educative process imposing comparatively little strain on the child and making his life in school a happy one, is extremely difficult in a language other than his home language – even with the brighter pupils, and next to impossible with those of average or slow mentality."[33] Rather, in a Seanad speech in 1942 he cast serious doubts on the good faith of the INTO, and in the Dáil in 1943 he declared that Irish could not be saved "without waging a most intense war against English, and against human nature itself for the life of the language."[34] Human nature, however, was to prove characteristically recalcitrant. The INTO was not to be browbeaten by the minister, or by the Gaelic League, a branch of which had issued a pamphlet attacking the INTO in 1941. Its backbone stiffened by its experience of persistent conflict, the organization steadily proceeded with its plans and programmes, producing a booklet in March 1947 outlining a plan for education, which included in its remarks on Irish the opinion that "the general tendency is towards making Irish almost a dead language,"[35] insisting that the department, so zealous for the language, was in fact contributing to its demise through an insistence on written Irish (each child was required to sit an examination in Irish at the end of his primary course) at the expense of oral proficiency.

The simple, if tragic, fact was that with the Irish rural world in decline, and the gaelicization policy in schools in English-speaking areas a very limited success, increasingly attacked by the teachers themselves, the future for the language was bleak indeed. Furthermore, the bitter conflicts of the 1940s in which some of the revivalists were made to appear as irrational dogmatists made it all the more easy for individuals and organizations to defend in public values other than the strictly national. Even in the period when the revival policy had been prosecuted with the greatest intensity in the 1930s, values other than linguistic nationalism had almost surreptitiously been expressed in educational practice. It is a most telling fact, revealed in the INTO's report on language teaching in 1941, that in the teaching of religion "in the overwhelming majority of the schools the home language was used as the medium of instruction."[36] In other words, the religious faith of the people could not be jeopardized by any national imperative. In the period following the 1940s it became more possible to defend publicly liberal educational values as well as religious values – the respect for individual human development for example – in the face of the nationalist demand that education serve precisely defined national priorities. This change in the Irish intellectual climate was eventually in the 1960s and 1970s to allow for reassessments of educational practice.

If some revivalists thought such developments to be almost unbearable signs of national apostasy, not all supporters of language revival in the 1940s were content simply to berate their fellow-countrymen for a lack of zeal in what they considered the nation's primary enterprise. Rather, there were those who, reading the signs, even detecting a hint of ambivalence in de Valera's attitude to the educational policy, set themselves to the task of a renewal in the language movement itself. For twenty years language revival had in the main been left in the government's apparently trustworthy hands. In the 1940s individuals once again began to sense that responsibility must rest with themselves. At the same time an opinion gained in currency that the association of the language with the depopulating districts on the west coast, indeed with rural Ireland, was unhelpful. Irish was increasingly being associated with rural impoverishment and deprivation, and with a semi-artificial folk culture that many Irish people found embarrassing if not ridiculous. In Dublin young men and women began to assert their right to espouse Gaelic revival in a modern urban manner, satirizing the professional rural Gaels who vulgarized a distinguished intellectual tradition in their employment of Gaelic as a tool of advancement in the state bureaucracies. So the 1940s saw the growth of urban-based language organizations concerned with publishing books, magazines, and a newspaper.

Flann O'Brien (Brian O'Nolan) who had shown in his English-language novel *At Swim-Two-Birds* (published in 1939) that the Irish mythological past could be explored in a satiric modernist mode, published under a different pseudonym, Myles na gCopaleen, *An Béal Bocht* (The Poor Mouth) in 1941. This comprehensively satirized the literary exploitation of the western island, in a hilarious send-up of the island reminiscence, particularly in its translated form. The life evoked in this work is so awful, so miserable, so squalid, the narrator's endless naive complaint so wearisome in its blend of querulousness and bombast that his oft-repeated lament, "I do not think that my like will ever be there again!" is likely to be greeted with general relief. Later the author was to characterize his book as "an enormous jeer at the Gaelic morons with their bicycle-clips and handball medals, but in language and style . . . an ironical copy of a really fine autobiographical book."[37] What Myles na gCopaleen was satirizing therefore was not the original Irish versions of island literature. Rather it was their translation and the cultural and social assumptions that underlay the complacent regard in which such works were held by people who had neither a developed knowledge of the Irish language itself nor an understanding of the actualities of the Gaelic past they so sedulously venerated. For Brian O'Nolan (who wrote variously under the pseudonyms Myles na gCopaleen, Flann O'Brien, and others) was in no way antagonistic to the Irish language. It was its contemporary defenders he found unacceptable – the kind of "Gael" he found "the most nauseating phenomenon in Europe. I mean the baby-brained dawnburst brigade who are ignorant of everything, including the Irish language itself."[38] O'Nolan in fact believed that the continued existence of the Irish language in the country was essential for Ireland's literary and cultural future, for he believed it "supplies that unknown quantity in us that enables us to transform the English language and this seems to hold of people who know little or no Irish, like Joyce."[39] O'Nolan was later to berate the poet Patrick Kavanagh for his indifference to the state of the language:

> Any notion of reviving Irish as the universal language of the country is manifestly impossible and ridiculous but the continued awareness here of the Gaelic norm of word and thought is vital to the preservation of our peculiar and admired methods of handling English.[40]

Such a sophisticated understanding of the cultural significance of the Irish language was rare in the ranks of those who were concerned for its fortunes. In O'Nolan the language had a power-fully gifted apologist whose sensitive awareness of the future that was possible for Irish was singularly prescient. Irish would have to survive as a second language and as a vital cultural catalyst.

Other developments of the 1940s show that a new activism was stirring. A periodical *Inniu* (Today) was founded in 1943; a book club, *An Club Leabhar*, started five years later, made Irish-language literature available to a surprisingly large reader-ship (a new book was guaranteed a sale of 3,000 copies). Journals such as *Comhar* (founded in 1942) and the Gaelic League's *Feasta* (founded in 1948) offered publishing opportunities to a rising generation of poets and Irish-language short story writers. In 1943 Comhdháil Náisiúnta na Gaelige (National Gaelic Con-gress) was formed. This organization, when it became vitalized by a ginger group which had in 1935 formed an intervarsity body of students interested in Irish revival, became after 1946 one of the most inventive bodies in the language movement. It was responsible in 1953 for the establishment of Gael-Linn, which through its exploitation of modern media was one of the most successful and energetic proponents of revival in the postwar period.

The early 1940s therefore represented a watershed in the for-tunes of the Irish language. The Irish-speaking districts of rural Ireland had entered a crisis which inevitably posed a threat to the language and to the ideology which had sustained the revival policy. The National Teachers began to express open dissatis-faction with their role in the revival attempt and on its effects on school life and achievement. Finally an awareness grew among concerned individuals and in the organizations they founded that the only hope for its future was to encourage interest in the language in the towns and cities. The myth of assimilation with the Irish language as the primary element in the receptive matrix of Irish reality could be sustained no longer with any credibility as emigration flowed unabated from the countryside, through the years of "the Emergency" and in the next fifteen years.

In the future the revival of Irish was to be seen as requiring individual effort and enthusiasm; it was to become primarily an urban-based, individualistic concern, espoused by educated, socially aware men and women who would propose a vision of Gaelic tradition and life as an alternative to the prevailing liberal capitalist values that would dominate the country as Ireland became a willing recruit to the consumer society. In a sense, indeed, the crisis that overtook the language movement in the 1940s as the impetus of the official revival policy began to wane (the revivalists were right to detect in Mr. de Valera a lack of immediate zeal) and as the Gaeltacht entered on a period of almost fatal decline was paradoxically beneficial to the cause of Irish. As I have suggested earlier, the Irish Free State had set itself an impossible task when it adopted a policy of language revival without relating such a venture to any radical social and economic programme. The inevitable outcome was the failure which began to be evident in the 1940s both in the depleted population of the Gaeltacht and in the lack of major linguistic progress in the rest of the country. A change of attitude was forced upon the revivalists which in fact encouraged them to adapt their ideology, aspirations, and activities to actual social conditions in Ireland in a way that they had scarcely done before. The following decades were therefore to see a proliferation of Irish-language organizations all effectively dedicated to keeping Irish before the public mind as an essential and undeniable presence in the cultural life of the country. In so doing, revivalists abandoned in practice, if not always in theory, the unrealizable dream of a linguistic exchange in a country where no revolutionary reordering of economics, society, and consciousness made that possible. Instead they effected what was possible – the protection of Irish as an element in Irish life even when the country as a whole became almost fully absorbed by the values and social forms of the consumer society. Had the crisis for the language, related to the crisis in the countryside, not been so marked in the 1940s and early 1950s a misguided dependence on the ineffective state revival policy might well have continued for much longer than it did, so affording the language no protection when

Ireland entered on a period of rapid social and cultural change in the 1960s. As it was, the crisis of the 1940s had allowed the revivalists just enough time to prepare for the even more difficult times ahead. When these arrived at least the troops were in position.

The early 1940s were no less marked by the agitation that began to mount against the censorship policy as it had operated since 1929. Certainly there had been critical rumblings throughout the previous decade, but these had been uncoordinated and were easily set aside by the staunch defenders of the system. In 1940 Seán O'Faoláin, who had been at the heart of a brief controversy in 1936 when his novel *Bird Alone* had fallen under the Censorship Board's interdict, founded the periodical the *Bell*. From almost the first issue O'Faoláin made it his business to mount a sustained, unremitting attack on the Censorship Board. What gave his criticism its extra cutting edge (and the pro-censorship lobby was incensed by the *Bell*'s campaign) was that O'Faoláin could not be dismissed as simply another Ascendancy freethinker writing to the *Irish Times* on behalf of free thought. He accepted the need for certain standards of literary expression in any society. What he doubted was whether the Censorship Board was to any degree in touch with Irish standards and taste as they actually were. Indeed he argued, with a spikily infuriating common sense, that the fact that so many Irish writers had met with the board's disapproval displayed how remote its members were from an understanding of native taste and standards. These O'Faoláin sensed were "in the most debatable state of flux."[41] As if to provide its critics with just the ammunition they required, the board had recently banned Kate O'Brien's novel *The Land of Spices*, and in 1942 it set its face against an account of the lives of two country people in County Cork, which had been written by Eric Cross, *The Tailor and Ansty* (1942). The first work is largely set in a convent, in a manner which a reviewer in the *Irish Independent* found to be "a picture of rare fidelity and charm, with the portrait of the Reverend Mother splendidly life-like in every line." Unfortunately, he also found "one single sentence in the book so repulsive that the book should not be left where it would fall into the hands of very young people."[42] The Censorship Board agreed with him and, presumably on the basis of that one sentence, which refers to homosexual love, tried to ensure that the dangerous work would fall into nobody's hands at all.

In response to the banning of *The Tailor and Ansty* a controversy began, which culminated in a full-scale debate on censorship, following a motion critical of the Censorship Board tabled by Senator Sir John Keane, in the Seanad in November and early December of 1942. It was a curious event indeed. Europe at war and the senate of the Irish state occupying itself for four full days of debate because an author had innocently recorded the Rabelaisian directness of speech characteristic of country life almost everywhere. The debate in the Seanad made much play both with Kate O'Brien's and Eric Cross's books and with the fact that the Censorship Board had recently banned a book on the "safe period" as a means to family planning written by an English Catholic gynaecologist and published by a Catholic publisher, Sheed and Ward of London. The debate was quickly transformed into a dramatic tussle of epic proportions between Sir John Keane, the motion's proposer, and Senator Professor William Magennis, who had served on the Censorship Board since 1933 and as its chairman since February 1942. Sir John was the loser, for despite the fact that other members of the Seanad were critical of aspects of the 1929 act and of its operation, when the motion expressing criticism of the act was put, the house divided thirty-four votes against to two votes for. Professor Magennis, who spoke for four and a half hours in defence of the board and all its works, had carried the day.

The debate, however, had afforded the opportunity for substantial criticisms of censorship to be voiced in public at length and had revealed the attitude of mind – intolerant, paternalistic, and blustering – which apparently governed the board's activities. Furthermore, the Senate debate stimulated opposition to the censorship policy of a more coordinated kind than had existed hitherto. A Council of Action was formed in November 1942, which worked busily in preparing a memorandum critical of current practice and making suggestions for improvements. By 1945 the government accepted that some changes were necessary and brought in a bill which allowed for the establishment of an Appeal Board (one of the ideas proposed by the Council of Action). The act became law in 1946. If the supporters of a rigorous censorship policy thought the new act would quiet criticism, they were to be disappointed. For the liberal reformers, having scented blood, were quite unprepared to rest from their efforts. In a Seanad debate on the 1945 bill Professor Magennis, stung into an unguarded taunt in the course of a heated exchange, had asked, "Is Ireland to be Irish or is it to be subjugated again by a foreign printing press by means of a spiritual defeat?"[43] Since the new Censorship Board in the postwar period continued to ban almost wholesale the works of most serious modern Irish, English, American, and European authors (in 1954 the record for books banned in any one year was established at 1,034) it seemed clear that the new body, even with its appeal machinery, was involved in an effort to insulate the country from the rest of the world rather than in an attempt to protect readers from the grosser forms of pornography. From the 1940s onwards the Censorship Board was forced to conduct its business in the face of a persistent, well-directed criticism from a small group of liberals, writers, and polemicists, aided by the support of the *Irish Times*, that the entire policy was rooted in an effort to employ the act as a weapon of cultural protectionism.

III

The critics of the censorship policy in the 1940s were in fact, it can be argued, the vanguard of the intellectual and cultural changes that were to take place in Ireland over the next thirty years. For it became an aspect of their critique of censorship that not only was it a manifestly absurd policy but that Ireland, in crisis as the flight from the land accelerated, could not adapt to save itself if it did not open windows to influences from abroad. They reckoned that Ireland would have to abandon its obsessive absorption with its own past and its own diminished cultural forms and adapt to the world about it, openly accepting what energy and diversity it could find within itself, if it was to survive as a modern nation. Censorship was a dangerously inhibiting check on such necessary adaptation. Their attacks on censorship were therefore only a part of a larger ideological conflict in the country that in the 1940s was manifested most obviously on this issue, but which was to be expressed increasingly in various social and cultural debates in subsequent decades.

It was Seán O'Faoláin in his remarkable periodical the *Bell* (founded in 1940 and edited by O'Faoláin until 1946) who defined the nature of the conflict with the greatest precision.

O'Faoláin understood that the crisis in the countryside must involve major social and ideological changes in the country as a whole. He sensed a "new jostling spirit" in "the wholesale exodus from the countryside" and that "men are leaving home who were content enough to stay hitherto."[44] He argued that Ireland was "feeling the full force of the cold blast of social change."[45] He did not nevertheless simply bewail the collapse of rural Ireland that he believed was at hand, if it had not already begun:

> Is this wholesale flight from the fields the sign of an embryonic, intelligent ambition among our country folk? It is, no doubt, for the moment mainly a physical dissatisfaction: no more. It is just as likely to be inspired by the meretricious appeal of the streets – glorified by the movies, which have now penetrated to the smallest villages – as inspired by healthy ambition. Yet the seed of ambition is there, too; and that seed is dynamite. The results will show themselves slowly enough, but the comparison with other countries suggests that they will ultimately, if not altogether in our time, alter the whole appearance and conditions of Irish society.[46]

O'Faoláin here senses that the processes at work in the Irish countryside will slowly but irresistibly draw Ireland into the modernized industrial world. The social changes and the intellectual and cultural adaptations required will be enormous. He reckoned that Ireland was ill-prepared to meet the challenges that these would involve.

> We may not go the whole of that road, but in as far as we are on the road one may say that the old patriarchal, rural Ireland is slowly beginning to disintegrate. And it is disintegrating just at the moment when the classes who, as I have said, normally provide the intellect – the initiative, the direction, and the revolutionary ideas to meet revolutionary changes – can do nothing better than wail for the past, like John Ball, dig their heads in the sand and try by repression to hold back the tide. One comes thereby back again to the final conclusion that the really terrible threat to Ireland is an intellectual one. We are not really wide-awake at all, not keeping pace at all with the irresistible movement of life.[47]

O'Faoláin tried in his journal to help his readers keep pace with that movement in two ways: he sought through attacking censorship and the attitudes it represented and through frequent editorials in which he attended to international political and diplomatic developments to open Ireland's windows to the world beyond its shores, the world in which its postwar future would lie; second, he sought to open his countrymen's eyes to the actual conditions of their own country. In this latter enterprise he was governed by the historical awareness which had fired his study of Daniel O'Connell in *King of the Beggars*. Ireland was not a great restored nation, but a "country at the beginning of its creative history, and at the end of its revolutionary history."[48] He believed that the period since independence had seen a kind of *putsch* which had brought an intellectually and culturally impoverished middle class into power. This ruling elite had inured itself against an awareness of the dismal facts of Ireland's social reality as a nation but newly formed in the nineteenth century and as yet lacking in many of the appurtenances of civilization, in dreams of the Gaelic past, the noble peasant, the seamless garment of Irish history and culture. With fine indifference to the fluttering in the dovecotes, O'Faoláin launched attack after attack on these romantic conceptions in the name of a pragmatic realism. The Gaelic revival had become mere jobbery, the enthusiasts for the language "vivisectionists" who had actually "done irreparable harm to the language." The vision of the heroic virtue of the west was mere escapism.

> If there once was an old association of the Peasant with Liberty it is all over. The romantic illusion, fostered by the Celtic Twilight, that the West of Ireland, with its red petticoats and bawneens, is for some reason more Irish than Guinness' Brewery or Dwyers' Sunbeam-Wolsey factory, has no longer any basis whatever.[49]

Ireland's cultural grandeur, whatever the truth of former times, was now merely a myth that gave comfort to an insecure, uprooted middle class which had cashed in on the revolution and had instinctively resisted change ever since.

In opposition to romantic conceptions of Ireland, O'Faoláin employed his journal to open as many windows as possible, so that a full and varied picture of modern Ireland might be developed. He thought it unlikely that the new Ireland that had emerged since the democratic triumphs of O'Connell in the nineteenth century would show any very complex forms of life, since it was, he understood, as yet only at the beginning of its history, but what variety and complexity there was he was keen to discover. He believed that even the diminished social life of a real Ireland was of much greater interest to writer and citizens alike than the simplistic unrealities propounded in the ruling ideology and esteemed by the ruling elite.

In his journal O'Faoláin reasserted the doctrines that had been the staple of editorials in the *Irish Statesman* twenty years earlier. Ireland was not a cultural unity but a synthesis, even a mosaic, a hybrid society that had developed following the English conquest. Bluntly stated, the truth was not that Ireland had assimilated all the stranger brought but "the sum of our local story is that long before 1900 we had become part and parcel of the general world-process – with a distinct English pigmentation."[50] The implications of this truth were clear to O'Faoláin. Irish people should be "honest and realistic and admit that our object is not unilingualism, but that we should speak, according to our moods and needs, both Gaelic and English."[51] They should also admit and celebrate indeed the fact that "Irishmen writing in English have won distinctiveness for an Irish literature which stands apart from, and even challenges, the achievements of contemporary writers elsewhere."[52] In asserting that Anglo-Irish literature was an indigenous literature (note that he calls such writing "Irish") O'Faoláin, as Russell had before him, was engaging in cultural warfare against a dominant ideology that he thought simplified Irish reality to the point of dangerous fantasy.

What made O'Faoláin's reiteration of the *Statesman*'s doctrines more persuasive than they had been in the earlier periodical was the fact that the *Bell* was willing to present documentary evidence to justify its assertions. In Russell's *Statesman* the debate as to the exact nature of Irish reality had often been conducted on a theoretical, even sometimes a mystical, level. The *Bell* set itself the task of a documentary, empirical exploration of Irish social life from which a portrait of national diversity would emerge. So writers from a variety of backgrounds were invited to present their viewpoints on the contemporary scene.[53] These were presented in a symposium in the journal in September 1941 when the Gaelic, classical, Norman, Anglo-Irish, and English strands were represented by individual contributors. Contributions from the six counties of Northern Ireland were particularly welcomed as they gave a sense of that province's distinctive industrial life. A series of articles dealt with the experience of differing Irish personalities, the film censor, the editor of the *Irish Times*, an entrepreneur, the Protestant archbishop of Dublin, a director of the Abbey Theatre. All kinds of hidden Irelands were briefly brought into the light – Elizabeth Bowen remembered her girlhood dancing classes in Dublin; a day in the life of a Dublin mechanic was evoked, as was the daily experience of a bank official, a jockey, a music teacher. Life cutting turf on the bog was investigated, as were the desperate conditions in Irish prisons and in the slums. Irish restaurants, galleries, architecture, furniture, whiskey, street ballads, journalism, crime were all explored in an effort to see Ireland steadily and whole, stripped of the romantic cloaks of misconception. The picture that does emerge is of an Ireland of some social if not cultural diversity (it is noticeable that O'Faoláin sought diversity in professions and trades) which could not easily be contained within the dominant ideological framework. It was an Ireland where creative effort was restricted by poverty (a depressing series was devoted to "Other People's Incomes") and a lack of an inspiring communal vision. But there were signs of individual life. Not the least of these was the fact that the periodical attracted a generation of young Irish writers and critics to its pages. A section of what was to become Brendan Behan's *Borstal Boy* was published in the *Bell*. Conor Cruise O'Brien, writing as Donat O'Donnell, began his career as a literary critic in its columns, as did Vivian Mercier. From the North came poems from John Hewitt and W. R. Rodgers.

It is difficult to assess that precisely was the *Bell*'s impact on Irish society. The periodical was published each month in an edition of 3,000 copies. Probably about 1,000 of these went overseas. O'Faoláin himself, noting that "in Ireland there is only this one secular magazine,"[54] reckoned that each edition was seen by about 30,000 people. Certainly this was a small enough number, but Vivian Mercier, writing in the *Bell* itself, was at pains to point out that it managed to keep its audience, and this fact rather contradicted the rarely uninterrupted pessimism of its editorials. Mercier sensed too that the periodical's main readership was the small-town intellectual, hungry for mental stimulus, and undoubtedly it was with such that it must have had its greatest influence. Dermot Foley remembered[55] how in Ennis, County Clare, he awaited each edition with excitement, discovering to his surprise that there were other readers in the town and that an O'Faoláin editorial, on the Gaelic revival for instance, could rouse considerable controversy and debate. Furthermore, the

Bell's sympathetically critical interest in the amateur theatre movement brought it to the attention of many people who, keen only to find their own activities reported on, might not otherwise have seen the periodical at all.

It is, of course, even more difficult to assess how the *Bell* affected the intellectual and cultural life of the country. What one can do, however, is determine what were its distinctive contributions to that life. Among these were, first, the simple fact that hitherto unsayable things got said. Irish follies which in many instances derived from the excesses of ideology, were ridiculed in the *Mise Eire* (I am Ireland) column in ways which, together with Brian O'Nolan's humorous column "Cruiskeen Lawn" in the *Irish Times* in the same period, brought back a real bite to published Irish satire that even *Dublin Opinion* had not managed in the earlier years of independence. Second, and more important, the sociological investigative thrust of the periodical's concerns brought a much-needed revival of humanism and rationality to the discussions of Irish identity that had preoccupied intellectual life since the foundation of the state. This point needs some brief elaboration.

A principal effect of the efforts to define Irish identity in terms of local attributes, such as religion, language, and culture, in the first two decades of independence had tended to present the Irish manifestations of those things as in some way isolated and distinct from their expressions elsewhere, particularly in Britain and on the continent of Europe. Furthermore, the absence from Irish cultural life of much sustained critical reflection on the actualities of daily experience in literature (such works as attempted this were more often than not banned), documentary film, art, and drama had left most Irish people dependent throughout the period on journalism for social self-examination. Regrettably, almost all Irish journalism in the period had contented itself with the reportage of events and the propagandist reiteration of the familiar terms of Irish political and cultural debate until these categories became mere counters and slogans often remote from any actualities. Irish journalism therefore comfortably reinforced the prevailing sense that Ireland, marked, as the nationalists constantly stressed, by distinctive religious, social, and linguistic forms, was somehow different from the rest of the world. It did not challenge Irishmen and women to reflect seriously on their own reality. It allowed, by contrast, an absorption with abstractions such as Sovereignty, the Faith, Republicanism, the Language. Had it so challenged, that sense of Irish uniqueness so necessary to the unthinking acceptance of the dominant nationalist ideology would have been disturbed. For an empirical examination of Irish social life would have revealed as well as things unique to the country the degree to which Irish life was influenced by the world around it.

O'Faoláin and his contributors, through attending in an empirical, investigative manner to Irish realities, opened windows in the *Bell* to show how much Irish life was not some absolute state of national being but an expression of humanity's life in a particular place, bound up with European history, geography, economics, and social forces of all kinds. The *Bell* was therefore a vital organ of empirical, humanistic self-consciousness at a moment when the new state was entering on a period of profound challenge. As such, it probably helped to make more generally available ideals of rational reflection and social analysis without which the country could not have responded to the postwar crisis as capably as it did. For prior to the period of the *Bell* only in certain sections of the state's civil service[56] had principles of scientific investigation and level-headed statistical assessment commanded much respect. Perhaps the *Bell* helped to prepare the ground in the wider community for a period when social analysis was to become a crucial partner in a process of modernization with economic development. Be that as it may, an American critic has supplied a just assessment of the *Bell*'s remarkable contribution in the 1940s. O'Faoláin had in his articles and editorials produced

> . . . the fullest analytic description of contemporary Ireland, and of its strengths, faults and derivations ever given. More than anything else these writings, close in manner and approach to the best eighteenth century pamphleteering justify his title as first Irish man of letters.[57]

There were further signs during the war years that ideas and influences that were to become commonplace in the postwar period were already at work. Three examples must suffice. In 1942 Professor Patrick Abercrombie, professor of town planning in the University of London, published the Dublin Town Plan. Town planning as a concept had been introduced to Ireland earlier in the century when Lord and Lady Aberdeen in 1911 invited Patrick Geddes to present a Town Planning Exhibition in Dublin. In 1922 Professor Abercrombie's plan entitled "Dublin of the Future" had been published, but since that date, despite the reconstruction following the Civil War and the creation of new areas of housing in suburbs to the north of the river Liffey, little systematic thought had been given to urban development in the country's capital. Certainly none of Abercrombie's major proposals (a new cathedral, a national theatre, a Bourse) had been implemented. In the new Abercrombie proposals concepts such as the "greenbelt," "ribbon building," "satellite towns," and "urban sprawl" were offered to the city administration as categories suitable for understanding their own experience and for guiding future policy. Abercrombie even advised Dubliners to ponder the garden city: "A town should be an urban pattern set on a background of green." The appearance of such a document was a sign that Irish administrators realized that much of the Irish future would be urban and that the towns and cities would be forced to renewal and redevelopment (Cork and Limerick cities both retained planning advisers from the late 1930s onward). And contemporary social facts suggested that new thinking on Irish urban life was timely indeed. In 1938 a survey of the tenements of Dublin found 60 percent (6,554 out of 11,039) of tenements and cottages unfit for human habitation. In these 64,940 persons were forced by economic circumstance to make their homes. For those families who had been rehoused in the building programmes of the 1930s, problems remained. As a commentator noted in 1945:

The new settlements in Crumlin and Drimnagh are without any of the essential social amenities. There are no parks, no playing

fields, no town halls. No schools were provided at first. . . .
There are no factories, no technical schools, no secondary
schools, no football grounds. . . . A fine police barracks has been
provided to control the unruly crowds of workless adolescents.[58]

In the future administrators could not say that they had not been
warned nor that they had no idea that a better way might exist.

In the visual arts the early 1940s represented a crucial turning
point. The self-conscious nativism of the early years of independence had diminished and Irish art was at its most representative
in the staid academicism of the annual Royal Hibernian Academy
exhibition. But throughout the 1930s, despite the unsympathetic
climate, a number of painters had resolutely persisted in taking
account of modern European art. In the 1940s it became clear
that their influence as artists and teachers had had effect. In 1943
it was possible to found the Irish Exhibition of Living Art. Among
its founders were Mainie Jellett, Evie Hone (the stained glass artist
and member of a renowned artistic family), Louis le Brocquy, and
Norah McGuinness. Within a few years, energetically guided by
Norah McGuinness, the event became "the arbiter of artists with
an interest in international developments and new ideas."[59] These
exhibitions brought to the attention of an Irish public the fact
that there were Irish painters whose work reflected the artistic
concerns of the Continent. Following the inauguration of the
Living Art Exhibition it was no longer possible to pretend that
Irish art and Modernism were entirely antithetical. The exhibition
of the work of Irish artists together with that by English and
European painters, revealed how Irish art had in fact responded
to the Modern movement, for all the antagonism of the local
critical climate. In addition, exhibitions were mounted in Dublin
in the early 1940s of Modernist art that explicitly announced the
validity of Modernism. Herbert Read, who had brought surrealism to London in 1936, defended in the *Bell* a Subjective
Art Exhibition held in Dublin in January 1944, where the paintings exhibited caused a deal of controversy. In August 1944 a
Loan Exhibition of Modern Continental Painting opened to a

contemptuous review by the poet Patrick Kavanagh in the *Irish Times*. "It would have been better," a writer in the *Bell* opined without apology in the heated debate on the value of Modernism that immediately arose, to have nailed "him down rigidly to his absurdities on the subject of modern painting."[60] The same writer also sensed "there is now in Ireland a public of connoisseurs in embryo."[61] In the future that embryo would grow as modern Irish painting and sculpture entered on a period of vital diversity and experiment.

A regular audience for symphonic music also began to establish itself in Dublin during "the Emergency." Since independence musical life in Dublin had languished. In the 1920s only the energy of Colonel Fritz Brase, a German conductor who at the government's request established the Free State Army Bands, and with an enthusiasm beyond the call of duty, brought life to the Dublin Philharmonic Society, for a few years giving Dubliners a chance to hear orchestral music, saved the city from complete mediocrity in musical matters. The 1930s had been almost without musical interest.[62] Much had been made in newspaper and periodical of the distinctive tradition of Irish folk music and a wearisome debate had been conducted (akin to that which so characterized literary discussion in the decade) on the question of whether Irish music would develop through the country's exposure to the art music of Europe or solely through the absorption of the native folk idiom.[63] While efforts were made in the schools to stimulate the latter process and Irish traditional music began to be afforded a new and welcome respect, the opportunity for Irish people to acquaint themselves with the idioms of contemporary art music simply did not exist. It was scarcely possible, indeed, for the interested Irish person to hear the familiar favourites of the classical repertoire. So, as in much of intellectual life in the 1930s, the debate about music was conducted in a curiously scholastic context without much of the thing itself to give substance to the arguments. It was radio that gave what substance there was. From its inception in 1926 the Irish radio station had realized that classical music as well as folk music on record and in performance could play an important part in programming. A station orchestra from humble beginnings (four musicians in 1926) grew to number twenty-four members in 1936, twenty-eight in 1937, and forty in 1942.[64] In 1938 and 1939 the Radio Eireann orchestra had given a series of public concerts in Dublin with guest conductors and soloists; they had not achieved any great popularity. In 1939 Mr. Paddy Little was appointed Minister for Posts and Telegraphs (it was his ministry that was responsible for broadcasting), and because of his own enthusiasm for music he was prepared in 1941, despite the lack of real success two years earlier, to sanction a new series of public concerts by the station orchestra. The season was to be one of eleven concerts at fortnightly intervals before and after Christmas. The orchestra this time played to capacity audiences. Indeed the Mansion House (with seating for around 800) proved too small to meet public demand, and in 1943 the concerts (which were an annual event until 1947) were transferred to the Capitol Theatre (with seating for about 1,800). Joseph O'Neill has suggested that Dublin's cinema-minded audiences had become aware through Hollywood films of the existence of the world's great orchestras and that by the early 1940s "symphonic music had lost its terrors."[65] Be that as it may, it was these concerts that for the first time in independent Ireland created a regular audience for orchestral music and introduced in public performance the idioms of recent symphonic work by Sibelius and the experiments of Debussy, de Falla, and Stravinsky.

So Ireland, as the countryside began that depopulation which was to provoke radical reassessments of official economic policy in the late 1950s, was disturbed by acrimonious controversies over language revival, education, and censorship as new conditions began to transform the social basis on which these had rested. The watershed in Irish social life was accompanied by novelties in the intellectual and cultural life of the country – the magisterial denunciation of rural life in the work of Patrick Kavanagh, the re-emergence of associations dedicated to the protection of the Irish language, the humanism and practical internationalism of the *Bell*, the bitterly satiric voices raised against myopic ideological dogma, the hints that Irish life was opening once again, despite the apparent hermeticism of the war years, to ideas and influences from abroad that would bear on its future life as a largely urbanized society concerned to define itself not predominantly in terms of its local past but in relation as well to the economic, social, and political developments of contemporary European history.

CHAPTER 7

Stagnation and Crisis

I

"We emerge," wrote Seán O'Faoláin in the *Bell* in July 1945, "a little dulled, bewildered, deflated. There is a great leeway to make up, many lessons to be learned, problems to be solved which, in those six years of silence, we did not even allow ourselves to state."[1] Independent Ireland had survived politically, but the years of the war had seen the stirrings of changes that in the following thirty years were to alter the shape of Irish society in significant ways. Predominant among these was the widespread rejection of rural life that in the immediate postwar period quickened into what almost amounted to an Irish exodus. So the Commission on Emigration reported in 1956 that a situation had arisen in which the province of Leinster was almost as populous as Munster and Connacht combined and noted that nine counties, most of them essentially rural counties of the northwest and along the western seaboard, accounted for three-quarters of the aggregate decline in the twenty counties in the state in which population reduction had occurred between 1946 and 1951. The result of this postwar emigration was to shift the balance of population somewhat between the towns and the countryside.

In 1951 41.44 percent of the population lived in cities and towns, with over one-fifth of the population of the twenty-six counties living in Dublin and its immediate neighbour, Dun Laoghaire. This change in the Irish social profile was due less to the growth of the towns and cities than to rural depopulation. There was nonetheless some internal migration, almost entirely to Dublin. In 1951 about one-third of the population of County Dublin had been born outside the county. The population of Dublin, which in 1936 had been 472,935, by 1951 had risen to 575,988, and by 1961 it would rise to 595,288. Dun Laoghaire, a town immediately adjacent to Dublin, in 1936 boasted a population of 39,785; by 1951 that figure had risen to 58,485, and by 1961 68,101 persons were recorded as residing in that area. So the process had begun which by the 1970s was to make Dublin and its environs the most populous part of the country with a population of over a million.

The problems faced by the Irish state in the postwar period were at root economic. The crisis in the countryside which was inexorably altering the balance of Irish society posed a challenge to the Irish state of a fundamental kind. Would an increasingly urban society be able to sustain itself as an economic unit in the modern world, and could any new policy check the flow of emigration from the countryside?

Initially the postwar period had been marked by economic growth, which resulted both from increased consumer spending at home as the austerities of the war years declined and from a rise in exports to Britain. The state involved itself in the building of schools, houses, roads, airports, and harbours.[2] But the 1950s were troubled by crises in the balance of payments, in 1951 and 1955, owing to fluctuations in the conditions of external trade which, together with the continuing exodus of emigration, were widely felt to reflect an Irish stagnation that was increasingly unacceptable. In 1957 there were 78,000 unemployed in a year when emigration was responsible for a net loss of population of 54,000. The 1950s, therefore, saw a good deal of Irish heart-searching and concern about the future. A common note in the literature of the period was a sense of the country lying in the stagnant sidestreams of history. Patrick Kavanagh in his periodical *Kavanagh's Weekly* (which he edited with his brother in 1952 for several iconoclastic months) denounced the tired mediocrity that Ireland exhibited at every hand: "From ... Independence Day there has been a decline in vitality."[3] "There is no central passion,"[4] he declared, in a society where "all this is horrid when you believe in People as distinct from the Nation, when you believe that Pat and Micky and Tom on the edge of the bog have potential as great or as little as a group of people everywhere."[5] The young Ulster poet John Montague in his sequence poem of 1953, "The Sheltered Edge," portrayed Ireland enduring a protracted post-revolutionary fatigue, creative nerve quite atrophied. His images embody what was in fact a fairly widespread sense of cultural and social despair.

> Standing at the window, I watch the wild green leaves
> Lurch back against the wall, all the branches of the appletree
> Stretch tight before the wind, the rain lash
> The evening long against the stubborn buildings
> Raised by man, the blackened rubbish dumps,
> The half-built flats, the oozing grey cement
> Of hasty walls, the white-faced children
> Deprived of sun, scurrying with sharp laughter
> From point to point of shelter,
> And arched over all, the indifferent deadening rain.[6]

In evoking such enervation, individual and social, and in detecting in 1951 an "almost palpable air of distrust and ineffectuality,"[7] Montague anticipated what the secretary of the Department of Finance was to assert seven years later in a report of 1958:

> After thirty-five years of native government people are asking whether we can achieve an acceptable degree of economic progress. The common talk among parents in the towns, as well as in rural Ireland, is of their children having to emigrate as soon as their education is completed in order to secure a reasonable standard of living.[8]

The author of that report, which was to prove a powerful stimulus to new thinking on Ireland's economic future in a way which was to prove highly regenerative, was a T. K. Whitaker. He had been forced by the dismal circumstances of the 1950s to a radical reconsideration of his economic philosophy, which to that date had been highly antagonistic to large-scale state involvement in the planning and financing of economic development. Whitaker once told the Irish journalist Tim Pat Coogan that his new outlook had been provoked by a cartoon on the cover of the humorous magazine *Dublin Opinion*. The cartoon, encapsulating the public mood, showed Ireland "as a downhearted Kathleen ni Houlihan asking a fortune-teller, 'Have I a future?'"[9] Whitaker (a civil servant in the Department of Finance) set himself to the task of providing that future.

The change of direction in the economic affairs of the state, which dates from the presentation of this report and the accession of Seán Lemass to the position of Taoiseach upon the retirement of de Valera from parliamentary politics (he was elevated to the presidency in 1959), was to have a profound effect on Irish society in the next decades. An Ireland that had espoused nationalism for a quarter of a century and employed manifold tariffs in the interests of native industry was to open its economy to as much foreign investment as could be attracted by governmental inducement. Furthermore, an Ireland that had sought to define its identity since independence principally in terms of social patterns rooted in the country's past was to seek to adapt itself to the prevailing capitalist values of the developed world. Within three years of this economic *volte face* Ireland had made a first application for membership of the EEC. In 1965 an Anglo-Irish Free Trade Agreement was arrived at with Great Britain and duly entered upon. Each signalled Ireland's willingness to participate fully in the postwar European economy. Economic growth was to become the new national imperative, in place of the language and the protection of native values and traditions. The 1960s and 1970s were therefore to be decades of rapid social and economic change, which stimulated much debate and controversy in the

country. Indeed, those two decades of Irish intellectual and cultural life were notable, as we shall see, for reassessments and
revisionism, for artistic and literary efforts to adapt to change,
and for an increased public involvement in an informed Irish
self-awareness.

The features of modern Irish social and cultural history that
allowed Ireland to make this major ideological shift without
undue strain merit some study. Primary among them was the
long-term effect of the neutrality policy of 1939–45. Prior to
that period the twenty-six-county state had sought to justify its
separatist ambitions by highlighting aspects of Irish social and
cultural life which could be identified as traditional and uniquely
pertaining to the national being. It had done this almost in
defiance of the facts that Ireland was a society which had largely
become modernized in the late nineteenth and early twentieth
centuries and that it had become highly anglicized, open as it
was to English mass communications. The period of neutrality
between 1939 and 1945 came precisely and most fortuitously at
the moment when even those regions that had most profoundly
seemed to embody the ancient Gaelic civilization that justified
separatist ambition were entering on a crisis. From about 1940
onward, as we have seen, thousands of young men and women
voted with their feet against the conviction that they were
uniquely favoured in their western fastness, immune from a
modern world closely identified with anglicization and England
itself. The effects of this crisis on national *amour propre* were
severe. As Liam de Paor cogently stated it:

> The failure marked by this emigration was a profound one; for
> the very people who flocked from the country in such numbers
> were the sons and daughters of those who had fought a revolu-
> tionary war (although not to the finish) in the early part of the
> century, and on whose behalf the revolutionary war had been
> fought. Their going made nonsense of the official ideology of
> the twenty-six-county State, of what was taught in the schools
> and preached from pulpits and platforms.[10]

We have discussed earlier too how such material transformations of the Irish social structure were accompanied by signs of change in the intellectual and cultural life of the country; the *Bell* was highlighted as a striking example of these. It is unlikely, however, that merely intellectual changes would have enabled Ireland to make the ideological adaptations that in face of the generally perceived crisis of the 1950s did take place with so little disturbance. The emotional experience of neutrality was probably the crucial element in the process. Neutrality and the experience of the war years had mobilized Irish public opinion for the first time to consider the twenty-six-county state as the primary unit of national loyalty. The twenty-six counties had become an entity in a new way in those years, one that its citizens had been prepared to defend in arms.[11] The period 1939–45 had given Irish men and women to understand that it was possible for the twenty-six counties of Ireland to be a nation-state without the distinguishing marks of language and a hermetically sealed national culture. In such knowledge was the ground prepared for a determined impulse to adapt to developments in the contemporary world to take root and flourish. Before the period of "the Emergency" such large-scale adaptations as were to follow would perhaps have been almost impossible because they would have generally been thought to involve a dilution or contamination of the national being so necessary to the ideal of a separate political existence. After the war such fears were substantially reduced. The state was real and had proved its reality in the most tangible way. Citizens had been prepared to bear arms on its behalf.

Other factors expedited the transition. Among these were the existence of a disciplined and competent civil service that had since 1922 maintained standards of public probity unusual in newly independent states; the existence of carefully controlled financial institutions; and experience in the semi-state bodies of the central involvement of the state in activities of an entrepreneurial kind. All these factors, together with the fact that the state since 1922 had achieved political stability, created a context in which modernization was possible. Perhaps too just as important were the realities of the social climate. Since independence despite all the efforts of the Irish Irelanders, Gaelic revivalists, and apostles of a distinctive Irish way of life, the twenty-six counties had remained in many aspects a social province of the United Kingdom. This was as true in the 1950s as it had been in the 1920s. English newspapers and books which had not met with the censors' disapproval circulated freely; the BBC was audible throughout much of the country. Domestic architecture, home furnishings, styles of dress were all influenced by English tastes. Success in England, whether on the boards of a West End theatre or on the pitches of the English First Division, was almost unconsciously esteemed above success in Dublin. Ireland as a social province of the United Kingdom had had ample opportunity to absorb the values of the capitalist mixed economy on the neighbouring island. Furthermore, since the 1930s most Irish emigration had been in quest of the employment that the British economy offered to unskilled labourers, to men prepared to work on the roads and on building sites. Modern transportation was inevitably bringing the two countries closer together. That Ireland in the late 1950s was prepared to adapt its own economy to the prevailing economic values of the world in which it found itself surprises little when one considers how this modern Irish diaspora had demonstrated that the Irish economy and the British were intertwined, whatever the distress such a recognition forced upon the economic nationalist.

It must also be recognized that the full-scale emigration of the 1950s, while posing a severe ideological challenge to the independent Irish state, actually reduced the dimensions of the practical problems it faced. Had the crisis of the countryside been followed by massive internal emigration to Irish cities the state would have been confronted by possibly insoluble problems. As it was, the drain of population from the Irish countryside and from the small towns of the rural districts to the suburbs of British cities and the Irish districts of London meant that internal emigration was of manageable proportions. The process of urbanization that Ireland's decision to adapt to the prevailing economic climate in Western Europe inevitably involved was therefore initiated without internal social tensions of a kind which might have overwhelmed the state.

The quality of social life in Dublin in the 1950s and early 1960s is highly germane in this regard. As we noted, in 1951 almost one-third of the population of the city had been born outside the city's county bounds. By the beginning of the next decade the city had swollen appreciably, much of the population rise attributable to the influx of country people, particularly young women. Most of those who came to the city were able to find employment (had the numbers been greater, as they might have been, the presence of large numbers of the unemployed young would have placed intolerable strains on the city). They were therefore able to find work in a city which was fairly close to home. The trains and buses at weekends were packed, throughout the 1950s, with new urban dwellers returning to maintain contacts with their roots in the countryside. The pains of urbanization then were less acute in Ireland than in most other European countries, where simple distance made such relatively comfortable migrations impossible. The process of change was thereby rendered the more acceptable in Ireland, the alienation and loneliness that characterizes life in most modern cities effectively reduced. One could always escape for a weekend at home.

Those migrants to the city who chose to marry and raise families in Dublin felt the pressures of urban life most keenly. The novelist Edna O'Brien could bring her country girls to Dublin (in *The Country Girls*, 1960, and *The Lonely Girl*, 1962) and allow them a brief idyll of youthful discovery followed by disillusionment before sending them on to the more exotic attractions of London, but the young woman or man from a rural background who sought to establish a family in the city was confronted there by adjustment to the novel ways of modern urban family life. For by the 1950s, despite the slow rate of economic growth in the country as a whole, Dublin had been transformed from the elegant, colourful, and decaying colonial centre of English rule in Ireland into a modern if rather dull administrative and commercial capital. Where pre-Treaty Dublin, the Dublin of Joyce in *Dubliners* and *Ulysses*, was severely inhibited by a stultifying lack of economic and social opportunity for most of its citizens, the new Dublin, while scarcely the scene of major redevelopment or an economic boom, had become socially and economically more complex, less marked by its earlier preponderance of the labouring poor. As A. J. Humphreys noted in his study *New Dubliners: Urbanization and the Irish Family* (1966), even by 1946 the signs were evident that the new Dublin, with its decline of the class of general labourers and the growth of skilled workers and especially of the white-collars, had become "a modern, industrialized community."[12] In 1946, Humphreys records, the new Dublin enabled 21.1 percent of its population to engage in work in the worlds of commerce and finance, 12 percent in administration and defence, 8.9 percent in the professions, and 13.7 percent in personal services, while 32.2 percent were occupied by non-agricultural production.[13] The figures suggest the occupational diversity of the modern city.

Adaptation to this world, often in the new estates of semi-detached and terraced dwellings that had been constructed to meet the demand for housing in the 1930s, 1940s, and 1950s in areas of the city such as Crumlin, Whitehall, Cabra, Inchicore, Raheny, and Artane, meant adaptation to the world of the nuclear family. The Irish immigrants from the countryside or small town, with their firmly established distinctive mode of family life and social organization, encountered in Dublin precisely the same pressures as urban dwellers elsewhere, and, as Humphreys discovered, they reacted in the same ways. A radical disjunction, familiar from contemporary sociological analysis, between the male world of work and the female world of homemaking and child care, produced in the new Dubliners just the same role changes as had occurred elsewhere. As Humphreys summarizes it (his research was done between 1949 and 1951):

> ... the traditional balance between the sexes characteristic of the rural family is upset in the city. The greater share of direct

domestic responsibility and labour falls upon the wife rather than the husband, and generally upon the women rather than the men. At the same time, a marked decline takes place in parental power and in the power of the aged in general.[14]

What surprisingly did not occur in Dublin was that swift secularization which has frequently been identified with the growth of urban life elsewhere. Humphreys in his studies discovered that ideologically no essential changes in an individual's world-view took place in the move to the city. Contact with new ideas, he reported, "as well as engagement in a rationally organized economy, has not brought about any profound transformation in the ideology of New Dubliners which remains substantially the same as the countryman's."[15] This meant that while an urban dweller from almost any part of the industrial world would have recognized much as familiar in the Dublin that had developed since independence (once he or she had recovered from surprise at the vast numbers of cyclists who thronged the streets in the 1950s), he or she would have been struck nevertheless by the degree to which Catholic belief and practice still dominated daily life. The sense of the crucial role of the family in society survived the transition from country to city, even as the new urban ways transformed that family life in striking ways. Perhaps, indeed, the very fact that the family was undergoing transformation in the new economic and social circumstances of the city heightened the individual's commitment to those familialist values to which the church encouraged loyalty. So the New Dubliners were encouraged to ignore how much their new situation challenged the very basis of those values which had found their more appropriate setting in the countryside from which they had come. This ideological continuity with the rural past in modern Dublin undoubtedly made the process of urbanization less painful than it might have been, accounting as it does for the fact that in the Dublin of the 1950s and 1960s cross-culturally, the urban family and familial kinship and neighborhood groupings were "undoubtedly among the very strongest in solidarity and power to be found in urban communities in Western societies."[16]

The church had swiftly grasped the fact that in the postwar period it would be forced to respond to Irish urbanization. From the late 1940s onwards it set in motion a major church-building programme in Dublin city, under the direction of its strong-minded, socially aware archbishop, John Charles McQuaid. From the late 1950s date many of the vast churches in the new suburbs of the city that in their confident grandeur and echoes of Byzantine style dominate their neighbourhoods in a way which to many Dubliners seemed peculiarly apt in a diocese ruled by their esteemed and redoubtable archbishop. Often, indeed, the move to the city brought the country man and woman closer to the actual bricks and mortar of the church than they had been in the countryside. Between 1940 and 1965 thirty-four churches were built in Dublin and twenty-six new parishes were formed.[17]

The 1950s were remarkable for urban churchgoing. Churches in suburb and city centre often allowed for the celebration of six masses on a Sunday to accommodate the vast numbers who flocked to fulfil their religious obligations, and daily masses were required to meet the demands of the faithful. As in the post-Famine period, the church had met the challenge of the Irish rural world with major building programmes, so in the 1950s in similar fashion she prepared herself in Dublin for the demands of Irish urban growth.

The state was somewhat less assured in its adaptive efforts in the 1950s. Until the final two years of the decade, when T. K. Whitaker and Seán Lemass decisively set Ireland on a new course, the postwar period was one of hesitancy and uncertainty. In political terms this uncertainty was reflected in a new electoral volatility in the country. Following a period of twenty-five years in which there had been only one governmental change, there were four changes of government between 1948 and 1957 (Fianna Fáil surrendered power to coalition governments for two periods, 1948–51 and 1954–57). Ideologically the fires of economic nationalism and the quest for cultural self-sufficiency were waning, but as yet they had not been replaced by a coherent set of new values. The handling of social policy in the postwar period serves as a crucial indicator of the state's lack of ideological assurance. In 1947, responding to postwar impatience at deficient social services, it might seek to reform the health services in a manner that brought the state itself more noticeably to the fore in the provision of welfare. In so doing, Ireland might have appeared to be modelling itself on contemporary Britain, resolutely preparing to challenge the church's teachings on the dangers of state power and on the social dimension of the national life, which was reiterated so forcefully in the years following the war and in the early 1950s. But the events of 1951, when a controversial scheme was proposed by the Minister for Health (Noel Browne) in the coalition government (the coalition comprised all the parties in the Dáil other than Fianna Fáil) that had wrested power from de Valera's party in 1948, show that such an ideological conflict, even if embarked upon vigorously, would scarcely be fought to the finish. The church, determined to maintain its role and influence, was adamant that its teaching on social matters should not be set aside nor should an individual's right to act, his conscience properly informed by the church, be abrogated by any state bureaucracy in a welfare state. Browne's scheme[18] was an attempt to provide a free health scheme to pregnant mothers and to ensure proper postnatal care of mothers and children. Browne, a young radical whose party, Clann na Poblachta, was the most socially progressive in the Dáil, was perhaps unwise in proposing that the scheme would operate without a means test. Such a proposal could be met with well-reasoned objections that perhaps disguised professional self-interest of one kind or another. But the death knell of the scheme was sounded when the hierarchy let it be known through a committee established to investigate the matter and through a letter to the Taoiseach that it took the gravest exception to Browne's scheme, finding it contrary to Catholic social teaching.

The interparty government was quite unprepared to back its young firebrand Minister for Health against the hierarchy. Some of his government colleagues had been unpersuaded of Noel

Browne's wisdom on some points of his scheme, others found it distasteful, and others had always thought Browne altogether too volatile and deficient in that measured pragmatism esteemed by the political mind. It was unlikely that they would have backed him wholeheartedly, even against the Irish Medical Association, which perhaps had been his initial target when he proposed the scheme. The government certainly did not care to back him in open struggle with the hierarchy, a struggle he himself had unabashedly made public. So the government withdrew the scheme and informed the hierarchy of its intention to do so amid many widespread political expressions of loyalty to the church, which even included one from Browne himself. Browne's declaration after his resignation that he accepted the hierarchy's views on the matter, whether the fruit of conviction or expediency, did nothing to help his subsequent political fortunes. A storm of controversy ensued in which the issue of church-state relations was discussed exhaustively in periodicals and in the daily press.

What emerged from this protracted debate, the first of its kind in the history of the state, was that the church authorities were absorbed by the dangers they sensed in increased state power; indeed, the social distresses that had occasioned the debate in the first place were rather lost sight of in much ideological dogmatism. It was accordingly borne in on legislators that an Ireland that might wish to adapt to its difficult circumstances by increased state welfare services would have to reckon with episcopal opposition to the presumed ideological and social dangers of welfarism. "The Welfare State is almost upon us," warned Dr. Cornelius Lucey, Coadjutor-Bishop of Cork. "Now, under one pretext, now under another, the various departments of State are becoming father and mother to us all."[19] So the state in the 1950s, in the midst of an ideological as well as a social and economic crisis, was forced to proceed with great caution when it sought to employ increased welfare as an adaptive stratagem. Caution and hesitant uncertainty were often indistinguishable.

In the field of foreign policy, in the postwar period the state also exhibited a lack of assured conviction.[20] On the one hand

Ireland seemed anxious to emerge from the political isolation of wartime neutrality to play a part in the developing international bodies of the postwar period. The country benefited in the years immediately after the war from the European Recovery Fund, which allowed the state among other things to improve housing and to organize the country's transport system under central government control. Ireland involved itself in the Council of Europe and in 1955 was admitted to the United Nations. De Valera had stated his agreement with the UN Charter in 1946, but the Soviet Union had prevented Irish entry for almost a decade. Following entry, for a few brief years, the country played a role which anticipated the intermediary position between the great power blocs that some Third World countries occupied in the United Nations in the 1960s. In 1961 Ireland became a member of UNESCO. Some of this diplomatic activity, however, was less directed towards full participation in international affairs than towards the solution of the Irish problem of partition. Ostensibly because of the partition issue Ireland refused to join NATO in 1949, and in the same year the country was declared a republic outside the British Commonwealth of Nations (the repeal of the External Relations Act in 1948 had broken the Irish link with the Commonwealth).

The decision to move to the status of a republic outside the Commonwealth shows how much Irish external relations were still dominated by the country's relationship with Britain, persistently soured as it was by the partition of the island, for which Britain was held wholly responsible. The decisions on NATO and the republic were of course taken by the interparty government, not by Fianna Fáil under de Valera, who had guided Irish foreign policy for many years. But these two acts of foreign policy were not in essential conflict with the general direction that de Valera had taken. Indeed, the nature of the coalition that comprised the interparty government of 1948–51 meant that de Valera's long-term republican policy was prosecuted with a directness and haste he would not have wished. Seán MacBride, leader of Clann na Poblachta, with his past association with the IRA and his resolute republicanism, was in all probability the man who pressed the issue. J. A. Costello, the Taoiseach and a leader of Fine Gael (which in its earlier form as Cumann na nGaedheal had advertised itself as the Commonwealth party), believed that the declaration of the republic might take the issue of republicanism and the gun out of Irish politics. In this hope he was to be singularly disappointed.

The IRA, attracting recruits as the interparty government's antipartition diplomatic campaign showed no signs of success, began a campaign of antipartition violence in the 1950s directed against Northern Ireland. For the republic of twenty-six counties was hardly the republic of separatist dreams. Its declaration was unlikely to have satisfied that minority in the country which since 1922 had refused to countenance any constitutional arrangement other than a thirty-two-county republic, pure and undefiled, nor those who, prepared to work within the existing system, were nevertheless in essential sympathy with that undying aspiration. As the state, in seeking to reform the social services, was constantly in mind of the hierarchy's pronounced views on social organization and policy, so the state tentatively breaking out of the political isolationism and neutrality of the war years was required to exercise a caution it did not necessarily find burdensome, even when it was inhibiting, on matters which might relate to national sovereignty. As in church-state relations, caution and uncertainty had a tendency to appear under the same guise.

So the state, as a social and economic crisis developed all about it in the 1950s, seemed to lack the self-assurance and ideological conviction necessary to meet it. But the social changes that were in part responsible for the general crisis were in fact preparing the ground for the new seeds that, planted at the end of the decade, would produce a rich harvest of economic regeneration and social and cultural change in the 1960s and 1970s. The society was becoming increasingly urban, though not because of emigration, at a pace which could prove politically destructive. The modern communications, which had in part been responsible for the rejection of traditional satisfactions in the countryside and small towns, were bringing Ireland into contact, in the imagery of the cinema and mass circulation periodicals, with the social forms of advanced capitalist consumer societies, thereby raising Irish expectations and creating demand for a new economic order.

II

There were various signs that a new Ireland, an Ireland less concerned with its own national identity, less antagonistic to outside influence, less obsessively absorbed by its own problems to the exclusion of wider issues, was, however embryonically, in the making. The *Bell* and the *Dublin Magazine* were joined by new literary periodicals. In these a younger generation than that associated with the older journals began to publish their work, though they also availed themselves of the opportunities afforded them by their seniors. *Irish Writing* (edited by David Marcus and Terence Smith from 1946 to 1954 and by Seán J. White from 1954 to 1957), *Poetry Ireland* (edited by David Marcus as a separate periodical from 1948 to 1952 and subsequently as a supplement of *Irish Writing*) and *Envoy* (edited by John Ryan and Valentin Iremonger) all gave such new writers as Pearse Hutchinson, Patrick Galvin, Basil Payne, Thomas Kinsella, Benedict Kiely, James Plunkett, and John Montague greater opportunities to see their work in print in Ireland than had existed for writers since the first decades of the century. What was notable about each of these journals was their determination to put literature first, not to be sidetracked by arguments for or against nationalism or the Irish tradition. A foreword to an issue of *Envoy* in 1950 caught the mood: "The younger poets . . . take their nationality more for granted,"[21] while Robert Greacen in *Irish Writing* set the tone for many Irish writers of his generation: "If they set store on any one quality it is on personal integrity. Write about what you feel and think and know as honestly as you can and with as little jargon as possible."[22] He sensed that "the new Irish writers, for their part, seek neither to decry nor accept harp or sickle or ammer; they are not sufficiently naive to be able to work to any ingle symbol."[23]

The poetic mentor of many of the new young poets was Auden, heir cultural hero James Joyce. Indeed *Envoy* was the first Irish eriodical to attempt a full-scale critical response to Joyce's work ince the *Irish Statesman* ceased publication. The journal's critical steem of Joyce, expressed in a special issue, was related to its ather self-conscious Europeanism. Its first editorial had hoped he journal would serve "abroad as envoy of Irish writing and at ome as envoy of the best in international writing." The latter ntention was expressed by the publication of work by Nathalie arraute, a first publication in English of extracts from Chekhov's "Sakhalin Island" and essays on English, European, and American writers. *Irish Writing* also brought European writing to the ttention of Irish readers. A piece by Jean-Paul Sartre was ncluded in Issue three in 1947, and extracts from Beckett's ficion appeared in later numbers. Also, *Irish Writing* began to ublish essays by non-Irish critics of Irish writing, alerting their rish readers to the fact that the literature in English of their ecent past was beginning to generate wide international critical ttention. Among those who contributed to a special W. B. Yeats dition in 1955 were Donald Davie (at the beginning of his oetic and academic career in Trinity College, Dublin), Peter Jre, Hugh Kenner, Peter Allt, and two Irish critics who had no eason then or later to feel diffident in such company, Vivian Mercier and Denis Donoghue. In October 1951 a correspondent n *Hibernia* noted the numbers of American students who had een coming to Dublin to study Joyce and Yeats in recent years.

A new iconoclasm was in the air, distinct from the satiric, ntagonistic bitterness that had characterized the work of an arlier generation of writers. "We must look outward again or lie, if only of boredom," wrote the poet and critic Anthony Cronin in the *Bell* in 1953. Instead of assaulting the society they ound so inhibiting, young writers simply got on with their work, tating what they thought to be obvious when occasion called or statement. So John Montague in 1951 could reflect with commendable detachment, "Ireland is at present in the awkward semi-stage between provincialism and urbanization, and the writing that will best serve should deal with the problems of the individual against this uneasy semi-urban setting."[24] So Denis Donoghue could blandly inform the readers of *Studies* in 1955, writing on "The Future of Irish Music," "It is quite possible that Irish music may have no further existence" and "there is in Ireland today no composer whose works an intelligent European must know."[25]. And a young Trinity College-educated historian F. S. L. Lyons, reviewing a book by two fellow academics from University College, Dublin, on such a contentious issue as the Great Famine, could almost surreptitiously introduce a new concept to discussion in Ireland, "historical revision."[26] The *Bell*, even under the editorship of the socialist Peadar O'Donnell, lost much of its interest in aspects of Irish social life, and in its last years (it closed in 1954) was heavily literary in content, in a way it had not been in the 1940s. The poet Austin Clarke began publishing poetry again after a silence that had lasted since 1938 when in *Night and Morning* he had wrestled with the Catholic moral conscience with an anguish reminiscent of Joyce's Stephen Dedalus. His new work had moved beyond the Manichean bitterness of that personal, haunted volume. In its place came a humanistic critique of Irish society in a satiric verse which suggested mordant assumption that the clerical excesses of modern Ireland were hopelessly inauthentic expressions of the native sensibility. Clarke's satire of the 1950s was vigorously sane, the persona adopted that of a man who has transcended parochial absurdities in a broad, humanistic vision of Irish identity and who find aberrations from this tiresome and infuriating. A sceptical, radical mind found expression in a body of verse that a younger generation in the 1960s was to find invigorating. In the 1950s too the poet Patrick Kavanagh abandoned the crude, boisterous satire bred of anger and frustration, which he had produced in the late 1940s and early 1950s, for a lyrical celebration of everyday Irish experience that has served for many Irish men and women since as a metaphor of the surest kind of liberation, a liberation of the irit. In 1953 Alan Simpson, a young, dedicated theatre director, unded, with Carolyn Swift, an experimental theatre in tiny emises in Dublin, the Pike Theatre Club, where in 1954 endan Behan's *The Quare Fellow* first came to life and in 1956 muel Beckett's *Waiting for Godot* had its Irish première and cond English-language production. The Pike was in fact only e, if perhaps the most celebrated, because of its association th Behan's famous play about prison life and with Beckett's st major theatrical success, of various small theatres and theatre oups that sprang up in Dublin in the 1940s and 1950s as ung actors, directors, and designers brought a new generation's ergy and enthusiasm to the theatrical life of the city.

It was one such actor, Cyril Cusack, who achieved the *succès scandale* of the 1950s when in 1955 he took the Gaiety Theatre r a three-week presentation of Sean O'Casey's anticlerical play, *he Bishop's Bonfire*. The play opened amid much anticipatory tagonism, and on the first night the capacity audience seemed sured of a riot in the best traditions of Irish theatre as well as dramatic performance. The play ran for five weeks rather than e three Cusack had planned. Cusack had approached the pro- uction of this play with high seriousness (he had even sought lvice on the script from a London prelate)[27] and had no wish become involved in what almost amounted to a theatrical test se. But the fact that the play, certainly one of O'Casey's least ccessful, was produced in Dublin at all was a blow struck for tistic freedom. That such a blow was all too necessary was ade evident three years later, when a Dublin tourist organization oposed to mount a Dublin International Theatre Festival (the st such festival had taken place in 1957) which would include oductions of O'Casey's *The Drums of Father Ned* and three ime plays by Beckett, as well as a dramatic realization of Joyce's *Ilysses*, entitled *Bloomsday*. When it became evident that the Arch- ishop of Dublin, John Charles McQuaid, was opposed to the roduction of the O'Casey play and of *Bloomsday* (he had been ked, unwisely, to open the festival with a votive mass) and when owerful representatives of public opinion, including Dublin trade unions, supported his view, the organizers withdrew the play (they were bound by their constitution to avoid controversy) and eventually cancelled the festival for that year.

Furthermore, in 1957 Alan Simpson had been arrested and charged with "presenting for gain an indecent and profane performance"[28] – the play in question being Tennessee Williams' *The Rose Tattoo*. Simpson, charged on a summary warrant normally used only to arrest armed criminals and members of the IRA, refused to give an undertaking that he would withdraw the play and stood trial. Released on bail, he decided the play should continue, and before the next performance the entire cast was advised by the police that by appearing in such a play they ran the risk of arrest. After a year of complicated legal proceedings Simpson was cleared in a Dublin district court of the charge against him. This outcome to an unfortunate incident compacted of elements of farce and great personal anxiety for Simpson was something of a turning point in Irish theatrical life. For had the judgment gone against Simpson, subsequent directors and theatre managements would have been forced to exercise an inhibiting caution in all doubtful cases. As it was, the judgment meant that adventurous experiments could be embarked upon in the assurance that the police would be less inclined to proceed against a play even when they received complaints from the public or from the various self-appointed watch committees that sought to protect the Irish moral environment from theatrical pollution. The court's judgment gave encouragement to all those who might have lacked Simpson's cool resolution, making more clear the way for less courageous spirits.

For the Gaelic revivalist, the 1950s also brought novelty of an encouraging kind. Certainly the fortunes of the language in general continued their protracted decline. In 1951, instead of 704 primary National Schools teaching through Irish the number had dropped to 523, and the next decade was to see an even sharper reduction. Emigration was working its constant attrition on the Irish-speaking and partly Irish-speaking areas. But the response of the revivalist that we detected at its inception in the early

940s, which involved the recognition that the state could not
e depended upon to revive Irish, that the arena of the future
truggles for the language must be the anglicized towns and cities,
nd that individual effort could not be postponed quickened into
igorous life in the 1950s. By 1963 an American commentator
ould count "a minimum of sixteen major national organizations
ounded since 1940 for the promotion of particular aspects of
he revival."[29] One of the most energetic and inventive of these
as Gael-Linn, which, founded in 1953, set itself with a will to
he business of fund-raising. It involved itself, for example, in the
roduction of two films, *Saoirse?* (Freedom?) and *Mise Eire* (I
m Ireland) which were immensely popular. The music for these
as composed by Seán Ó Riada, a composer whose work was to
ecome widely acclaimed in the 1960s. And Brendan Behan's
ork *An Giall* (which in English became *The Hostage*) was
ritten on a commission from Gael-Linn.

The revivalist could also take heart, even in the desperate cir-
umstances of the 1950s, in the fact that modern Irish writing
as shakily finding its feet. In 1945 Seán Ó hÉigeartaigh had
ounded a small publishing house, Sáirséal agus Dill, which
mong other things published the work of the novelist and short
tory writer Máirtín Ó Cadhain and of the poet Seán Ó Ríordáin.
he publication of such writers and of the poetry of Máirtín Ó
Direáin allowed the critic David Marcus to write in 1955:

> During the last ten years or so Gaelic writing in Ireland has moved
> into a new era. There has been an eager and widening awareness
> among the reading public and an atmosphere of excitement in
> the writing itself – two factors which, in supplementing each
> other, have generated continuous growth; and among the new
> writers which this activity has produced are many whose freshness
> and modernity might be said to have given Irish literature in
> Gaelic something it never had at any previous stage of its long
> development – an *avant garde* movement.[30]

Máirtín Ó Cadhain's novel *Cré na Cille* (The Graveyard Earth)
eemed to its readers then and since particularly a work of that

avant garde, as it made them believe that, in Seán Ó Tuama
words, the Irish language could be forged into "a flexible an
compelling instrument of modern thought and feeling."[31]

In the visual arts, too, the evidence mounted that the era c
nationalistic isolation was coming to an end. Numbers of younge
painters in the postwar period began to build on the work of th
Living Art Exhibition, on the foundations provided by Evi
Hone, Mainie Jellett, and earlier innovatory spirits. By 1955
future director of the National Gallery, James White, could writ
of the new "mature young painters of Ireland" and could com
pare the present most favourably with the past:

> Twenty-five years ago, a handful of painters and sculptors lived
> a somewhat remote life from the people of the country and
> were understood by a minority. Today hardly a week passes
> without a couple of exhibitions by individual artists. Three
> major group shows are held in Dublin and as many as ten
> group shows are held in cities and towns outside the capital.
> The work of our principal contemporary artists has been
> shown in North and South America, in Canada, France, Italy,
> Germany, Norway, Sweden, Finland, Belgium and Holland.
> Artists like Scott, Dillon, Hanlon, O'Neill, Middleton . . . are
> known and regarded with interest in countries where art is a
> tradition as old as memory. The main reason is that they use
> an international idiom or style deriving from the Paris School.
> This style is applied to the interpretation of Irish subject
> matter.[32]

Irish artists were able to exhibit abroad in part because the officia
mind had paid some attention to a remarkably gloomy repor
presented to the government in 1949. The *Report on The Art
in Ireland* by Professor Thomas Bodkin, former director o
the National Gallery of Ireland, then professor of fine arts and
director of the Barber Institute of Fine Arts in the University o
Birmingham, stated bleakly that

> . . . measures which might have been taken effectively in 1922
> to foster the Fine Arts and rehabilitate the art institutions of

the country are no longer likely to prove sufficient. In the intervening twenty-seven years the resources of such institutions and the status and power of those who administer them, have been steadily curtailed rather than augmented. We have not merely failed to go forward in policies concerning the Arts, we have in fact regressed, to arrive, many years ago, at a condition of apathy about them in which it had become justifiable to say of Ireland that no other country in Western Europe cared less, or gave less, for the cultivation of the Arts.[33]

Bodkin in his report cast a cold eye on the museums and galleries which the British had established in the country and lamented their decay and disorganization. He observed how little Irish industry exhibited any sense of aesthetic values, berated the universities for their philistinism, and reflected sadly that for many years after independence "no financial provision whatever was made for the development of cultural relations between Ireland and other countries."[34] Bodkin noted that a partial remedy to this latter deficiency had been instituted in June 1947, when a grant-in-aid of £10,000 was voted for expenditure by the Minister for External Affairs and a committee named the Advisory Committee on Cultural Relations proposed to advise him. Bodkin suggested that an immediate activity for the new committee was the encouragement of exhibitions by Irish artists abroad. Of the many proposals in the Bodkin Report, this was one of the very few that were implemented. Bodkin's report, however, stirred the state into some small concern for the arts, which was expressed in the establishment of an Arts Council in 1951. The creation of this body, while scarcely an imaginative, energetic response to the criticisms of the Bodkin Report, was at least a measure of recognition that the state must act as a patron of the arts in a modern society, even though the patronage in fact provided was for some time to prove considerably less than adequate.

In 1955 James White had expressed his concern about "the absence of criticism and informed writing on the visual arts"[35] in Ireland. In the 1950s that void in Irish intellectual life had begun, however minimally, to be filled. The periodical *Envoy*, for

example, was the first of the essentially literary publications (i
proclaimed itself *A Review of Literature and Art*) to attempt a
assessment of the visual arts in the post-independence period. I
did this in a manner which for the first time recognized tha
painting and sculpture in Ireland were not simply adjuncts to
literary movements. Rather, they were an artistic activity in thei
own right. Critical essays were therefore published with accom
panying reproductions, on the work of Louis le Brocquy, Coli
Middleton, Nano Reid, Thurloe Connolly, George Campbell
Daniel O'Neill, and Hilary Heron, on religious art in Ireland an
on artistic Modernism, alongside the assessments of Irish literary
figures. The public at large in the post-war period was mad
aware of these inroads of artistic Modernism by the occasiona
building commissioned by official bodies that displayed know
ledge of developments in European architecture. In 1943 the
new airport building at Collinstown airport, serving Dublin, ha
been designed in the Modernist idiom by Desmond FitzGerald
In 1953 the architectural firm Michael Scott and Partners, which
was to be responsible for much new building in the 1960s
designed the central bus station in Dublin in the Modernist mode
a sign of things to come. Private housing in limited areas o
Dublin's suburbs had since the late 1930s reflected the func
tionalist ideas of contemporary European and British architecture
The late 1940s saw a good deal of private development in this
idiom in the city, which in the 1960s and 1970s was to become
the characteristic mode of the commercial redevelopment o
Dublin, as it had been in postwar London.

In the 1950s opposition to censorship, that bulwark against
external contamination, entered on a decisive phase. The Act o
1946, with its appeal machinery, had by no means satisfied the
growing body of opinion in the country that thought the policy
inappropriate both in its form and execution. Indeed, the operation of the censorship policy under the new legislation had
proved, as we saw, even more restrictive than the old, measured
simply in terms of books banned. Perhaps the Censorship Board,
reacting to the increasingly vociferous criticisms of its activities,

intensified its cultural and moral crusade. In so doing, it was acting in unconscious concert with other conservative institutions and organizations who seemed to sense that changes were afoot which must be resisted. The Archbishop of Dublin, for instance, in 1944 forbade attendance at Trinity College by Catholic students, replacing the church's strongly worded advice by fiat. In 1956 the National Council of the church made the Dublin diocesan regulations on this issue applicable throughout the country. Individual Catholics, however, chose to ignore him, and it became clear that lay Catholic opinion was no longer so quiescent before episcopal admonition on social and cultural matters as it once had been. The Catholic periodical *Hibernia*, for example, when it cleared its mind of the heat generated by the Cold War, published thoughtful essays by Catholic laymen on constitutional issues, Northern Ireland, and the social and cultural life of the country that, coloured by a devout religious loyalty, were nevertheless in tone and content remote from the simplicities of episcopal denunciation and proscription. In 1958, for example, a young journalist Desmond Fennell addressed himself, shortly after the Simpson case had been settled in court, to a sensitive Catholic response to the moral issues raised by Tennessee Williams's play *Cat on a Hot Tin Roof*, which had recently caused such controversy in Liverpool that its transfer to Dublin had been cancelled. Fennell admitted to having seen the play in Düsseldorf (where it had also met with opposition, as it had even in New York). He concluded that "the ultimate moral question is paradoxically an aesthetic one, 'Is this art?'" The answer in Williams' case was clearly positive. The "play's uniting theme is the saving power of love."[36]

In 1956 the Irish Association of Civil Liberties (which had been founded in 1948), following several years of vigorous newspaper assault on the operations of the Censorship Board, organized a petition requesting the Taoiseach, J. A. Costello (an interparty government was once more in power) to establish a commission to investigate the board's operations. A large meeting was held in the Mansion House in Dublin to publicize the censorship controversy. Instead of acceding to the petitioners' demands, the Minister for Justice, who was responsible for the board, filled two vacancies that arose in 1956 by the appointment of two individuals known for views likely to commend them to the board's critics. Disagreement between the three earlier appointees and the two new members quickly developed. In 1957 the division between them became so unbridgeable that the three former members resigned from the board. The Fianna Fáil Minister for Justice (for an election had reversed the political position once more) quickly appointed a new board comprising the two recent recruits with three other individuals who proved to be altogether more open-minded than members of the board had been in the past. No longer did the Censorship Board see itself as waging a war against an alien campaign of cultural and moral contamination but operated as a body "making it difficult for the average person to read books which were pornographic and had no literary merit."[37]

It would be wrong, it must be stressed, to make too much of these signs of a changing intellectual and cultural climate. For most people in Ireland in the postwar period, the amateur dramatic movement, which burgeoned in the 1950s in festivals and competitions, was their only point of contact with artistic activity of any kind. For many, literature, art, intellectual endeavour, or architectural innovation would have seemed luxurious irrelevancies set against the daily struggle for survival in years of economic despair. The efforts of state and of individuals to brighten up the general deprivation of life in the country through festivals of one kind or another (these were also designed to attract tourists to Ireland) could not really achieve much against such a bleak background. An Tostal, for instance, a spring festival organized by the Tourist Board for the first time in April 1953, like the Tailteann of an earlier decade, never quite established itself as its organizers had hoped, though the Dublin International Theatre Festival, which derived from it, survived the debacle of 1958 to flourish in the 1960s in a happier climate. That, on the evening of the first Tostal, police had to break up with baton charges a crowd of riotous young men in O'Connell Street in Dublin did not augur well for its future.

Perhaps indeed a truer impression of the times emerges when one reflects, not on the various signs abroad of cultural change, but on the frustrated, unhappy histories of three of the country's most gifted writers, who scarcely found the attractions of an insecure, bohemian existence in the pubs of Dublin in the 1950s adequate compensation for lack of public appreciation of their real artistic ambitions and of financial support.[38] Indeed, each of the careers of Patrick Kavanagh, Brian O'Nolan, and Brendan Behan shows the terrible marks of years of public indifference or misunderstanding. The only future that seemed open to the Irish writer in the late 1940s and early 1950s was penury in his own country or an appeal to the wider public gallery through eccentricity, showmanship, and bravado that would distract both public and writer from the serious business of his art. The effects of this dismal quandary were all too apparent in various ways on what one critic has called this "doom and drink-sodden triumvirate."[39]

Reading the poet Anthony Cronin's memoir *Dead as Doornails* (1976), in which the period and the lives of these three writers are memorably recalled, a sense develops that they were the "tragic generation" of modern Irish letters, despite John Ryan's more benign recollection that "the windows had been flung open and intellectually speaking, people were breathing again."[40] The changes in the intellectual and cultural life of the country that I have detected were not such as to clear the air of a cultural provincialism all these artists in their different ways found intolerable. Nor indeed, in a period when the empty country cottage and the boarded-up suburban house in Dublin or Cork were the visible signs of the heavy toll of emigration, could they, unless they could be accompanied by major economic improvements, do much to hold young Irish men and women from the emigrant ships. For it is the emigrant, so poignantly evoked in Brendan Kennelly's poem "Westland Row" (the name, then, of a Dublin railway station for the boat to Britain), who seems finally the

most truly representative figure in what for many were very dismal
times indeed:

> Brown bag bulging with faded nothings;
> A ticket for three pounds one and six
> To Euston, London via Holyhead.
> Young faces limp, misunderstanding
> What the first gay promptings meant—
> A pass into a brilliant wilderness,
> A capital of hopeless promise.
> Well, mount the steps: lug the bag:
> Take your place. And out of all the crowd,
> Watch the girl in the wrinkled coat,
>   Her face half-grey.
>   Her first time.[41]

PART III

1959–79

CHAPTER 8

Economic Revival

In 1957 a sympathetic and informed Irish-American scholar, John V. Kelleher, who had long interested himself in Irish literary, cultural and political affairs, published a bleakly pessimistic assessment of Ireland's contemporary standing in *Foreign Affairs* (the American journal of international relations). There he pondered the possibility that the Irish nation, beset by manifold problems and lacking regenerative energy, might vanish from history through "an implosion upon a central vacuity."[1] The fact that this unhappy, if original, fate was avoided is usually credited by historians, and by those who participated in the economic revival of the early 1960s, to the adventurous policies suggested by T. K. Whitaker, ably and energetically prosecuted by the Fianna Fáil Taoiseach Seán Lemass, who succeeded de Valera in 1959. Indeed the period from 1958, when the government White Paper *Economic Development* appeared, for which Whitaker was responsible, to 1963, when the First Programme for Economic Expansion was succeeded by the Second, soon became almost legendary years in Irish self-understanding. Irish men and women believe now, as they believed then, that those five years represented a major turning-point in Irish fortunes. In the collective memory,

1958–63 is seen as the period when a new Ireland began to come to life. The Irish associate the successes of those years with a renewed national self-confidence that helped the country to survive future vicissitudes.

Whitaker's recipe for economic revival was, as Oliver Mac-Donagh succinctly designated it, "latter-day orthodoxy, a body of Keynesian solutions."[2] These included a much greater involvement by the state in investment in productive industry than had been thought wise in more prudent years, the employment of increased Central Bank power to direct investment by the commercial banks, and encouragement of foreign investment by packages of attractive incentives.

The First Programme envisaged a growth rate for Ireland of 2 percent per annum. Between 1959 and 1963 the annual growth rate achieved was in fact a very encouraging 4 percent. In 1962 therefore a commentator could report that between 1958 and 1961 the GNP had increased by 15.5 percent, volume of production by 28.5 percent, total imports by 30.25 percent, car registrations by 29.5 percent, and the volume of personal expenditure by 11.5 percent.[3] Between 1957 and 1962, another commentator noted in 1965, the number of people "engaged in the production of transportable goods alone, rose from just under 150,000 to just over 170,000, an increase of 13 percent."[4] The fact that analysts began so soon to remark on the economic changes that were occurring (and those are only two examples of many assessments that appeared as the 1960s progressed) suggests how deeply a sense of a new age had entered the Irish collective mind. The state policy, which in the 1960s was to attract over 350 new foreign-owned companies to Ireland and to allow an economic growth "faster and more sustained than in any previous period in Irish history",[5] was recognized as a policy which would in a short space of time change the face of the country itself. Seán Lemass wrote in 1962 in the *Spectator* of the new Ireland which under his direction was preparing to play a part in "a unified Europe;" this, he hoped, would resolve the local issue of partition in a wider, continental harmony. Others agreed with him. Denis Meehan, professor of ancient classics at Maynooth, in 1960 had already sensed the new era as it dawned:

> In purely physical terms the population cannot dwindle any further; the bottom of the curve must come somewhere; there is literally nowhere to fall from. On the contrary some sort of minor boom may ensue in the economic field: American and West German industrialists will be attracted in by the cheapness and geographical convenience of Ireland as a distribution centre; such young people as are in the country will find pretty gainful employment by staying at home.[6]

And by 1965 a young historian, David Thornley, could risk publishing his pamphlet "Ireland: The End of an Era?" where he suggested:

> We are for the first time at the threshold of a delayed peaceful social revolution. It would be foolhardy to go on to predict its course. Its seems certain that our island will become affected increasingly by the spread of European social and philosophical ideas, strongly tinged with Catholicism. It is reasonably certain that many of the issues of education and social welfare will slowly be transplanted from the field of emotional controversy to that of economic efficiency, and that a great deal more money will be spent on both. It does seem certain that the depopulation of the countryside will continue and perhaps accelerate, and that our social habits and our politics will take on a flavour that is ever more urban, and, as a consequence, ever more cosmopolitan. And this in turn will sound the death knell of the attempt to preserve any kind of indigenous Gaelic folk culture in these islands.[7]

Thornley, as this quotation demonstrates, clearly recognized that the ideological change of direction initiated by the economic decisions of the late 1950s would have profound effects on Irish social and cultural life. The fact was that "the economic nationalism of Sinn Féin" was "dead as the policy of the state."[8] This would alter the face and mind of the nation since it sounded a death knell for a traditional Ireland, already dying on its feet.

What surprised Thornley was how easily the transition from one ideological ideal to another had been managed. "What is remarkable," he wrote, "almost to the point of incredibility is the passiveness with which this change has been accepted inside a single generation."[9] In fact enthusiastic approval of the new order of things might more accurately have described the public response to the economic revival. Donald S. Corkery, an American journalist who published an account of the new Ireland in 1968, wrote in that volume of the manifest psychological changes he had recently noticed in a country that in the past had been characterized by a deep-seated inferiority complex. The new policies had acted, he sensed, as a "powerful tonic, almost a magic elixir:"

> Returning to Ireland in early 1963 it was impossible not to feel the atmosphere change or notice the many signs of modernization. There was an unaccustomed briskness about the way Dubliners moved and a freshness of complexion which I had not seen before. Even the grumbles were indicative. There were too many Germans and other foreigners moving into the country to suit some people; there were complaints about all the money being spent on jet airliners and luxury hotels; and it was annoying that the upsurge in car ownership meant that the Irish would now have to take examinations for driving licenses.[10]

Thornley's near incredulity at Ireland's rapid transition from a society ostensibly dedicated to economic nationalism and its social and cultural concomitants, to a society prepared to abandon much of its past in the interests of swift growth in the context of the modern British and Western European economies has been shared by other historians and commentators. Some of them have sought the explanation in a conjunction of factors: the introduction of television to the state in 1962 (although British television had been received on the east coast of Ireland for some years prior to this date); the modernizing impulses in Catholicism abroad which followed in the wake of the Second Vatican Council and the effects of these in Ireland; the fact that the late 1950s saw the emergence into positions of power and influence of men who had been born since independence; and the quickening pace of interest in social and cultural developments in the outside world of the kind that we have noted were evident even in the 1940s and '50s. Others, while ready to accept that each of these factors may have had a part to play, nevertheless felt that something more profound was at work. Some, most notably the historians Oliver MacDonagh and John Whyte, had recourse to a general theory of Irish historiography which proposed that Ireland since the Famine had been marked by a "series of sudden transformations at intervals of roughly a generation."[11]

David Thornley, in his pamphlet of 1965, struck by the changes he saw in process about him, hinted at an even more ambitious explanatory thesis. The new era of economic vitality was quite simply the inauguration of "delayed peaceful social revolution." This consummation devoutly to be wished had been, Thornley suggested, "held back by the civil war, Sinn Féin, and by the unsophistication of our social philosophy."[12] Such a view therefore denied to the first decades of independence the historical significance that many had given them (Thornley asserted that "the pace of changes between 1922 and 1945 had been positively and negatively exaggerated in romantic history".[13]) It dismissed, with an iconoclasm entirely characteristic of the 1960s, the period since independence as simply years of misguided postponement of the necessary Irish social revolution that had been in the making before the Civil War and the establishment of the Free State. For decades, that revolution had been thwarted as a conservative social order had been buttressed by essentialist ideology.

In an earlier chapter I outlined the features of Irish social life and intellectual and cultural development which I believe allowed the ideological and material changes of the late 1950s and early 1960s to proceed without undue conflict. Nothing I said there accounted, however, for the remarkable enthusiasm with which the new tasks were embarked upon. Thornley suggests that this enthusiasm was the product of an authentically Irish Catholic nationalist aspiration to social and economic improvement and modernization, at last allowed free, almost explosive, expression in the 1960s as "traditional" Ireland and its constraining ideologies swiftly became defunct.

There were those who, realizing that the collapse of traditional Ireland and its "corresponding ideologies of illusion"[14] might not have been followed by a ready and bold adoption of new aspirations, sought an explanation for the remarkable transition in the early 1960s in terms of the individual genius and vision of Seán Lemass. The Irish journalist and commentator John Healy, for example, in his columns in the *Irish Times* ("Backbencher" and its successor "Sounding Off") contributed much to the growth of a Lemass legend which proposed Lemass as almost sole architect of the new Ireland. The historian Joseph Lee in a Thomas Davis lecture on RTE radio put an academic imprimatur on such a view when he introduced a series of broadcast lectures on change in modern Irish society with a near-hagiographic celebration of Lemass's contribution to the modernization of the state. Lee highlighted Lemass's dedication to efficiency, his desire to remould the Irish Republic into a streamlined, functional, corporate state which would allow decisions to be taken with a managerial dispatch. Lee celebrated Lemass' antagonism to mediocrity in the public and private domain that sheltered behind notions of hierarchical tradition, his passionately pragmatic belief that in "a small society with no inherent momentum of its own and with a heritage of stagnation, it was men that mattered. The initiative, or lack of it, of a handful of individuals could make or mar important institutions for a generation."[15] And in Lemass, Lee believed, Ireland had had an individual of quite remarkable vision at the helm; for "only a conquistador of the spirit"[16] could have hoped in the stagnant conditions of mid-century Ireland to make clear the way for the modern Irish version of the merchant adventurer.

Perhaps Lemass's most vital contribution to economic revival and the psychological breakthrough of the early 1960s was his capacity to distinguish modernization from anglicization. As Lee astutely noted, when Lemass disclosed that "the historical task of this generation is to secure the economic foundation of independence,"[17] he was arousing his people to a new mission which he believed could do more to achieve the country's most profound aspirations – genuine political independence and unity between North and South – than the previous decades of economic isolation and cultural self-regard. Lemass succeeded therefore in linking an achievable economic resurgence within the economic orbit of the United Kingdom, and eventually within Europe, to Irish patriotic instincts and hopes (it was to release less noble instincts too, as we shall see in Chapter twelve). It was indeed a bold stroke of a kind which must go a fair distance toward justifying Lee's concluding assessment: "It was to be the historical achievement of Seán Lemass to lay the foundation of a new Ireland perhaps destined to endure as long as its immediate predecessor."[18]

So in Lemass the age had its man who called a new breed of Irish entrepreneur and manager into the centre of the Irish stage – those new rich Irishmen who, in the playwright Hugh Leonard's witty phrase, upon finding that "they could not now get through the eye of a needle began to manufacture bigger needles with wider eyes."[19] What Professor David C. McClelland termed the almost inexplicable "mental virus"[20] which seems necessary if a society is to modernize, was certainly abroad in the social atmosphere of the 1960s in Ireland, infecting individuals in many different spheres.

One of the most crucial of those was the educational. Indeed the fact that as economic improvement became evident, and as Ireland set its sights on membership of the European Economic Community, a concurrent sense developed that educational reforms were long overdue was a sign that the new impulse at work in Irish society was a desire for genuine social modernization. For a conviction grew that only by giving educational opportunities to the mass of Ireland's young could the economic potential of the state be realized. It became a matter for serious concern that without major reforms Ireland would be left hopelessly behind as the pace of economic and educational change quickened in the United Kingdom and in continental Europe, following the policy decisions there of the immediate postwar period.

Since independence the Irish educational system had changed but little if one excepts the major effort to gaelicize schools in hopes of linguistic revival. The general profile of the educational system bequeathed by the departing colonial power remained, even as late as the early 1960s, essentially unchanged. A system of church-controlled, state-supported National Schools offered basic education to the mass of the population (the School Attendance Act of 1926 made school attendance obligatory between the ages of six and fourteen). Secondary schools, also largely in the control of the various churches, often managed and staffed by religious, offered further education to fee-paying pupils, while a small state-supported vocational sector provided technical education for pupils who, for one reason or another, sought further training but could not gain or did not seek entry to the more academically oriented, more expensive, secondary schools.

If in the first forty years of independence, however, little in the nature of educational restructuring had been attempted, the state, through the Department of Education, had made strenuous efforts to ensure that uniformity of curricula and standards was achieved and maintained. This rigour was most profoundly expressed in the control of the National Schools. As a result, the educational system, where it was encountered by almost the whole of the population, was notable for its austere authoritarianism, the pupils held to a sharply defined curriculum leading to a primary certificate, the teachers themselves held vice-like within the control of the department by a salary rating system (abandoned in 1959) based on the findings of an inspectorate which in the circumstances was invariably viewed by the teachers as the enemy's chief representative. At the heart of the system was the National School teacher; for many pupils he or she was the only teacher they ever encountered. Rigidly controlled by the Department of Education, these teachers were often themselves, by reason of background and social experience, the stern agents of authoritarian social, cultural, and religious control. As Charles

McCarthy outlined it, a source of that ubiquitous Irish authoritarianism which marked Irish life in many of its aspects in the modern period was to be found in the carefully regulated relationship between church, state, and National Teacher:

> These young men and women were drawn from the most academically able in the country, but, certainly in the case of the men, from a remarkably limited social group. It appears to me that they came primarily from small farmers and small shopkeepers in the south and west, and in many cases had themselves left home as early as thirteen or fourteen years of age, attending first the preparatory colleges (which now fortunately have been disestablished) and also the diocesan colleges, all residential in character. From there they went to a residential training college which was conducted on remarkably authoritarian lines.[21]

For forty years therefore the National School seemed a representative Irish institution in the new state, a peculiarly resonant symbol of a society where authoritarian control enforced ideals of nationalism, religion, and language. In literature and in reminiscence, such schools figured largely as centres of austerity and rigour, marking for life generations of Irishmen and women. What they did not do was create genuine equality of opportunity, a fact which became clear in the 1960s.

In 1962 the government appointed a commission to investigate the conditions of Irish education. The commission's report was published in 1966 under the title *Investment in Education*. In preparing this report, a small group of statisticians and economists, with the help of an inspector of secondary schools, made the first full-scale, scientific investigation of the Irish educational system. Their work was supported by the Department of Education and by the Organization for Economic Cooperation and Development (OECD). The historian F. S. L. Lyons remarked upon the "peculiarly apt symbolism" in the fact that the report was in part financed by the OECD, since he saw the report as an expression of the changing ideological and psychological climate of the 1960s, when Irishmen with increasing frequency tended "to measure their achievements by the standards of western Europe."[22]

The tone, concerns, and recommendations of *Investment in Education* certainly reflected a radical ideological departure in Irish educational thinking.[23] From the introduction onwards, a novelty of approach was apparent as the commission recorded how throughout its work its members had tried "to keep before our minds at all times the character and purpose of education and that the term 'educational system' has little meaning if it is considered apart from the human needs which it is there to serve." The key words here were "human needs," and the report, declaring itself "essentially fact-finding and analytic in character,"[24] showed by cool, systematic, scientific investigation that the Irish school system could by no means be said to serve human needs as it ought. So instead of an Irish educational document reflecting on national identity, on the revival of Irish, and on cultural imperatives of one kind or another, *Investment in Education* dissected the social facts of Irish education, to reveal the class and geographical components of the system, setting out its human deficiencies for all to see.

Many of these were devastatingly depressing. Despite the investment in school building that had taken place in the postwar period, much of the educational plant was in dire condition. Less than half of all schools had piped drinking water and modern sanitation. And for all the traditional rigour of the National Schools, many pupils were leaving them without the basic qualification of a primary certificate. In the year 1962–63 it was found that an estimated 17,500 completed full-time education when they left the National Schools (in 1961–62 the report reckoned about 54,500 in all left National Schools, some for further education; the figures for 1962–63 would have been close to this). Of these, 26 percent of boys had a primary certificate, 7 percent of boys had failed the relevant tests, 10 percent of boys had been absent, and for 57 percent of boys there was no trace or record of them having completed school through taking the examination. In the case of girls leaving school, 30 percent passed the certificate tests, 10 percent failed, 11 percent were absent, and of 49 percent there was no trace or record. In all 11,000 of those leaving National School in the academic year 1962–63 left without a certificate either because they had failed the test or because they had left before reaching or completing the sixth standard, when all pupils were required to be entered on the examination lists. "The annual emergence," commented the report with a reserve that suggests irony, "of a large number of young people who apparently have not reached what is commonly considered a minimum level of education, can hardly be viewed with equanimity."[25]

Almost as damning were the report's findings with regard to entry to secondary school and university, which showed that participation in post-primary education was marked by striking differences between counties and a clear association between class and educational advancement which became "the more marked the higher the age group and the higher the level."[26] It seemed clear from the report that despite its vigorous instinct for centralization and control, the Department of Education was presiding over a school system shaped by forces other than educational. The availability of secondary schooling, for example, was sometimes as much a matter of local religious history as it was of central educational planning. *Investment in Education* therefore revealed two areas where major changes were required: primary education, where so many were failing to receive even a required minimum of education, and secondary education, which was inaccessible to far too many and availed of by far too few.

Partly in the cool revelatory light of the *Investment in Education* report (the report was published when pressures for change had already begun to mount), the impulse to reform the Irish educational system took hold in the 1960s, and led to rapid changes. The opening of secondary education to the majority of young people following decisions taken by the government in 1966 was perhaps the most dramatic of these. The Second Programme for Economic Expansion had proposed that the minimum school-leaving age should be raised from fourteen to fifteen by 1970. Consequent upon such a decision was a reordering of the relationship between the National Schools and the secondary schools. Since it would have been unreasonable simply to protract attendance at National Schools, the proposal implied that all pupils should have some experience of secondary education Accordingly, in 1967 Donough O'Malley, the Minister for Education, announced a new dispensation in Irish education which would abolish fees in the vocational sector and provide supplementary grants to such secondary schools as chose to waive their charges to pupils. The plan also provided for free transport to and from school for pupils who lived more than three miles from the nearest secondary school. The effects of these arrangements were swiftly evident. In 1967–68, 118,807 pupils were enrolled in 595 schools. In 1968–69 this figure had risen to 133,591 in 598 schools. By 1973–74, when a rising population of school-going children was putting pressure on a secondary school system that had been opened to the majority, 554 secondary schools enrolled 167,309 pupils. The figures in relation to the school bus service show that good use was being made of this simple but socially innovatory service. In 1968, 31,350 pupils availed themselves of the service. By 1973 this figure had risen to 61,533.[27]

There were other innovations at the secondary level. State-supported comprehensive schools were instituted in 1963. By 1974–75 there were thirty of these, in areas where privately owned secondary facilities were inadequate. Secondary schooling in Ireland had traditionally been segregated by gender. The opposite was true of the new comprehensive schools: of the thirty schools of this kind built by 1976, twenty-six were for boys and girls, three for boys alone, and one for girls alone. In that year there were 13,162 pupils attending comprehensive schools. The vocational sector also felt the reforming and innovatory pressures of the period. Schemes were devised that would allow cooperation between vocational schools and secondary schools; the Intermediate Certificate examination introduced in 1963, which was common to secondary and vocational schools, brought the vocational sector into a closer relationship with the rest of the educational system. After 1975 no new comprehensive schools were established but the introduction of the concept of the community school (the first opened in 1972) was an equally innovatory replacement. These schools involved vocational educational committees working in cooperation with religious orders or diocesan authorities and the Department of Education in the provision of a broad range of secondary educational opportunities, often in areas where new city housing schemes catered for a burgeoning population.

From the early 1960s, therefore, Irish secondary education became an integral part of a system of mass education. A writer in 1970, reflecting on Ireland's position in a world educational crisis, remarked, "Education is the most rapidly and inexorably expanding business in the country."[28] That expansion did not take place without considerable debate and conflict. An increased state role in the funding of secondary education necessarily involved much discussion about management and control. Perhaps indeed so much time and energy were expended on issues of this kind that strictly educational matters were somewhat neglected. It is notable, therefore, that in the twenty years in which the social revolution of the largely free availability of secondary education took place did not see any radical appraisals or reorderings of the academic content of secondary education. Individual subject curricula were reformed and reorganized, but overall, secondary education remained geared towards the attainment of a Leaving Certificate largely based on strictly academic assumptions, with vocational subjects enjoying less social esteem than traditional arts and sciences.

It may be that the most profound and direct effect of the educational decisions of the 1960s with regard to secondary schooling (I shall be suggesting some less direct cultural effects in later chapters) was the manner in which it enforced a major reorganization of primary education in the National Schools. Since most pupils might be expected to leave National School for a secondary school, it was clear that pupils would choose to transfer at an earlier age than fourteen, when in the past the Primary Certificate was taken. In 1967 this examination was abolished. Such a drastic redirection of the traditional aims of the National School must undoubtedly have stimulated the reappraisals that resulted in the radical new Primary School Curriculum of 1971. That the kinds of contentious issue that occupied all those involved with secondary education in the period were somewhat less pressing during the 1960s in the primary sector, where matters such as control and state and church responsibility had been defined and understood for many years, perhaps meant that the educational content of the curriculum could receive attention. Reorganization of the management of the National Schools, giving representation on new boards of management to parents as well as to bishops' appointees and to the principal teacher, took place in 1975, after the introduction of an altogether innovatory curriculum earlier in the decade. This new curriculum had represented an infusion of novel thinking into the cultural life of the country.

The signals that changes were afoot had been evident since the early 1960s. In 1963 a school library scheme had been initiated in the National Schools and the amalgamation of schools where numbers were small had meant that funds could be made available for the provision of such things as visual aids to brighten up what until then had most usually been dismal schoolrooms indeed. In 1968 an assistant secretary in the Department of Education published an article in *Studies*[29] which revealed that he, a very crucially placed individual, was in favour of as major educational reforms in the National Schools as had occurred in the secondary sector. The article displayed a commitment to the concept of child-centred education which had taken root in the UK and in the United States.

The new Primary School Curriculum of 1971 admitted in its introduction a dependence on educational thinking abroad. The Plowden Report, published in the United Kingdom in 1967, was an obvious source for a passage such as the following:

Recent research, conducted in many countries into the learning processes and development of children has shown ... that knowledge acquired through the child's personal experience and discovery is likely to be more meaningful and purposeful to him than information acquired at second-hand.[30]

So the ideological thrust of the introduction to the curriculum was unequivocally in the direction of child-centred education. Invoking the fact of divine creation, it was affirmed that each person "is entitled to an equal chance of obtaining optimum personal fulfilment." The aims of primary education were defined as follows:

1. To enable the child to live a full life as a child.
2. To equip him to avail himself of further education so that he may go on to live a full and useful life as an adult in society.[31]

Part of that equipment, the introduction assumed, would be an understanding of Ireland's "ancient spiritual and cultural tradition", together with an appreciation of modern Ireland's "democratic institutions." But the introduction also recognized that education must be more than merely a handing on of tradition. It must prepare children to live as adults in a changing world.

The curriculum introduction had an unexceptionable Irish authority to cite in support of these new departures in the National Schools – none other than Patrick Pearse.

What the teacher should bring to Irish pupils is not a set of readymade opinions, or a stock of cut-and-dry information but an inspiration and an example; and his main qualification should be, not such an overmastering will as shall impose itself at all hazards upon all weaker wills that come under its influence, but rather so infectious an enthusiasm as shall kindle new enthusiasm.[32]

An INTO survey of 1976 demonstrated that the new curriculum had indeed generated some of that enthusiasm. Some

64.4 percent of teachers approached replied to a questionnaire that the new curriculum had "affected favourably" their job satisfaction.[33] Critics, however, pointed to lowering standards in the knowledge of the Irish language among pupils. Impressionistic evidence suggested, however, that a quite new atmosphere permeated the primary schools where the new curriculum had been imaginatively presented.[34]

At the other end of the educational scale the period brought crucial changes. Tertiary-level opportunities were created not only by an expansion of student numbers at the universities, but by the swift creation in the 1970s of nine regional technical colleges. These colleges brought to Irish tertiary-level education an increased awareness of the technological demands of a modern society and marked the beginning of a much greater emphasis in Ireland on technical education than had existed hitherto. The establishment of the National Institute of Higher Education in Limerick in the 1970s was also a sign of the state's new commitment to the creation of a technically skilled population, ready to play its part in a new industrial society, for that institute was also geared to technological education. In 1979 plans for a further National Institute of Higher Education, combining existing colleges in Dublin with new facilities, were drawn up. These institutions were subsequently granted full, independent university status as the University of Limerick and Dublin City University.

In a modernizing society, education reforms and innovations have a close companion in expanding information services. Ireland in the 1960s and 1970s was no exception. The Economic and Social Research Institute was founded in 1960 and since then has provided a steady stream of sociological and economic information to enable planning to proceed on rational lines. The Central Statistics Office has also supplied much data against which statements about the Irish economy and society could be tested. In 1968 the *Economic and Social Review* started publication, giving the opportunity for the first generation of Irish sociologists to publish scientific analyses of Irish society. The Catholic periodicals *Christus Rex*, the *Furrow*, and *Doctrine and Life* began to publish articles that attempted social investigation. Indeed in 1962, the last-named periodical published one of the first studies of the relationship of the mass media and society to appear in Ireland. From the 1960s, too, Irish investigative journalism became established in the daily newspapers. Before that date only the periodical the *Bell* had sought to bring Ireland, warts and all, to the attention of an educated, concerned readership. Since the 1960s the daily newspapers have provided a steady flow of documentary reportage that has increased the store of information in a society starved in the past of serious self-examination.

What the new sociological studies of Irish society revealed in the 1960s and '70s was that Ireland was undergoing rapid transformation. The modernizing virus was producing all kinds of symptoms which warranted close observation. The demographers could explore the changing patterns of population and fertility and the rapid urbanization of Irish society. As we saw earlier, in 1956 the population had stood at 2,898,264, but by 1961 it had fallen to 2,818,341. In 1966 the loss had almost been made good, and in 1971 the population had risen to 2,978,248 – the highest (a crucial psychological turning point) to that date in the history of the state, showing an intercensal rise of 3.27 percent. By 1979 the population had increased by a further 386,633 (though it has been suggested that the 1971 figure was an underestimation). It was noted, too, how Ireland was changing from a primarily rural, agricultural society to an industrial, urban society. In 1926 only 32.27 percent of the population had lived in towns of over 1,500 persons. By 1951 that figure had risen to 41.44 percent, by 1966 it was 49.20 percent, and in 1971 it topped the halfway mark at 52.25 percent. The growth of Dublin was most marked. By 1979 over a third of the population in the state resided in the greater Dublin area. In the intercensal period, 1971–79, the counties of Kildare, Meath, and Wicklow, where new dormitory suburbs had been built to serve the city, recorded population increases of 34.9 percent, 26.6 percent, and 26.4 percent respectively. But it was not only Dublin and its environs that increased its population in the period. Other urban centres experienced notable increases in population. For example, Galway's population rose from 27,726 in 1971 to 36,824 in 1979, a phenomenal growth of 32.8 percent in eight years. Overall the population rise recorded in the 1979 census was 13 percent, drawing from the authors of the *Preliminary Report* the coolly satisfied comment that "the accelerating rise in population in recent years restored the total state figure to about the average level which pertained during the 1891–1901 intercensal period."[35] Other early responses to the *Preliminary Report* of the 1979 census were less measured, as the figures revealed in irrefutable terms the new Ireland many had sensed developing about them. "Another Irish myth has been debunked," remarked an *Irish Times* report, in terms that were echoed frequently in public and private discussion, "for the Ireland of the 1970s contrasts sharply with the internationally popular image of a sleepy backwater on the fringe of Europe. No longer is this the rural island of the emigrants, but a fast-growing industrializing frontier on the edge of industrial Europe."[36]

The evidence for this Irish transformation had of course been available earlier, in the analyses of the structure of the workforce in the 1971 census and in the various statistics published yearly in the *Statistical Abstract of Ireland*. The 1971 census had revealed that, since the 1966 census, the number of persons at work in agriculture, forestry, or fishing had declined by 58,500 (or 7.8 percent) in the total of all other groups. The largest increases in absolute terms were in electrical and electronics workers (with 5,800), engineering and related trade workers (with 9,000), professional and technical workers (with 15,000), clerical workers (with 11,700). It is notable that the numbers of women clerical workers had risen by 18.3 percent. For women, domestic service was no longer a principal source of employment as it had been in the 1920s and '30s. And the fact of Irish urbanization indeed had been implicit in the census record of 1971, showing that the east of the country (with 409,900 gainfully employed persons) contained more than a third of those at work in the state and that just over a quarter of the recorded employed persons in the state were engaged in agricultural occupations.

Marriage and fertility patterns were also changing markedly in the period and were the object of analytic inquiry. The demographer Brendan Walsh showed in a series of papers and essays how Irish family life was altering, presumably under the impact of industrialization and urbanization. The nuclear family that Humphreys had recognized in Dublin in the 1940s was becoming a national norm. In a paper published in 1972 Walsh noted that the marriage rates had been showing an upward trend since 1951, with a dramatic acceleration since 1966.[37] His figures were startling. The marriage rate (per 1,000 unmarried adults) rose by at least 20 percent between 1966 and 1970 and by over 40 percent between 1958 and 1970. What was surprising in the Irish context, where contraception by artificial means was legally made difficult and was forbidden by the church, was that this rise in the marriage rate was attended by changes in fertility patterns. The number of first and second births to couples grew rapidly in the 1960s, "more or less in pace with the growth in the married population" but by 1970 the births of fourth or subsequent children had fallen by 20 percent from the peak such births had reached in the early 1960s. As Walsh noted, the papal encyclical of 1968, *Humanae Vitae* (which forbade artificial contraception for the Catholic faithful), did not materially affect the decline in the numbers of couples prepared to give birth to large families. In a further essay published in the *Irish Times* in 1979, Walsh concluded that "the evidence down to 1977 shows that never before in modern history has as high a proportion of our population been married, especially at the relatively young age of 20–24."[38] The conjunction of higher marriage rates with lower fertility rates still held at the end of the 1970s. Indeed, Walsh computes, on the basis of the fertility levels of 1961, that a fall in fertility of about one-third had occurred by 1977.

So in a period of major economic change and urbanization a new generation of Irishmen and women adapted to social patterns directly akin to those of populations in other industrialized countries. Early marriages and smaller planned families began to characterize Irish social life, as they did social life in most of the Western world. Ireland had joined the "age of the nuclear family."

In this context the issue of women's role in society became, as it had done in the United States in the 1960s, a matter for debate and social action. In 1970 the government established the first Commission for the Status of Women, chaired by Thekla Beere (it reported in 1972). In the same year the Irish Women's Liberation Movement held its first meeting, marking the beginning of a wave of feminist activism in Ireland that over the following decades would insistently add the concept of gender to the political and cultural life of the country.

In this rapidly urbanizing and industrializing society consumerist values made swift advances. A feature of the nuclear family, as noted by many sociologists, was the manner in which parental authority was lessened. Parents, themselves finding many of their social relations outside the kinship framework in professional, sporting, and cultural organizations, surrendered much of the responsibility for their offspring's education to the school system. A lengthy schooling protracted youth well into late adolescence, and a new social group was created, composed of young adults who had largely escaped parental direction but had not yet entered the workforce. In Ireland, as elsewhere in the postwar period, this resulted in the development of a constituency of young people in which consumerism was encouraged in magazines, television advertisements, and the faddishness of the popular music industry. By the early 1980s, when over 50 percent of the population was under thirty years of age, this market was significant indeed. The parents of these young people were no less, if perhaps differently, affected by the values of the consumer society in those years. Ostentatious consumption in a society enjoying a rapid rise in its standard of living marked the late 1960s and '70s in Ireland. Motor-cars, houses, and foreign holidays became major preoccupations if not passions. In 1978, for example, as the *Irish Independent* reported, half of all new houses in Dublin were detached houses, built for the upper end of the market. Restaurants charging extraordinarily inflated prices sprang up in the countryside as well as in the cities to cater for a new rich clientele and for the expense account executive whose tax liabilities could be self-indulgently eaten away. Supermarkets and the shopping precinct replaced many small shops and the wine bar and the off-licence catered for a middle class whose drinking habits had been influenced by package holidays and images of the good life nightly presented on the national television channels.

Television was without doubt a major instrument in Ireland's conversion to consumerism. RTE, the national station, was opened in 1962. A survey conducted in 1967 showed that about 80 percent of urban households owned television sets but, as the political scientist Basil Chubb stated, set ownership was "far from evenly spread,"[39] and in parts of rural Ireland the percentage fell as low as 25 percent. Since 1967 the number of television sets in rural households rose steadily. By 1980 there were few parts of the country where television was not a part of a majority of the people's daily lives. In 1978, 83 percent of all homes had a television (92 percent in the Dublin area; 54 percent in Connacht).[40] Much of the material broadcast on RTE was of British and American origin. The advertisements were sometimes British-made on behalf of British products, while Irish-made advertisements on behalf of Irish goods and services, where a company could afford it, were created for an audience accustomed to British advertising techniques. One effect therefore of extended viewing of the national television channels (a second channel began broadcasting in 1978) was a sense of Ireland firmly within the British commercial sphere of influence.

The countryside as well as the towns and cities were profoundly altered over the course of twenty years. For those who survived the crisis in rural Ireland which became acute in the immediate postwar period, the 1960s and '70s were years of challenge and opportunity. The countryside, like the cities, became considerably modernized. Since Ireland's entry to the EEC in 1973, parts of the farming community benefited markedly from the Common Agricultural Policy and some of agricultural Ireland knew a prosperity it had not experienced in modern times. For others the challenge of the new era was overwhelming. But for those farmers in possession of viable holdings and already alerted to the possibility of organized efficient farm production through farmers' organizations such as Macra na Feirme and the powerful lobbying body, the National Farmers' Association, the 1970s were years of profit and change. Indeed a primary symbol of Ireland in the 1970s might well be the new bungalow (rarely well adapted to its environment) with its central heating and modern furnishings which throughout much of the country replaced the old farmhouse or cottage as farmers reaped the benefit of their new circumstances.

The attitudes and values of urban consumerism and the social forms of the nuclear family penetrated the countryside as prosperity increased and television, the motor-car, and secondary-level schooling altered the patterns of daily life. Such of the customary social relations of the countryside as had survived into recent times almost disappeared, declining under the impact of mechanization.[41] Indeed, this latter process had taken a heavy toll even in the previous decade. Between 1951 and 1961, for example, the number of tractors in the country increased by 350 percent while the number of horses declined by 50 percent. Large class differences between farmers who could afford the investment in mechanical equipment and those who could not began to emerge. In the 1970s new industries were located in rural areas, and as poorer farmers forsook the land for the factory floor, a managerial (and often foreign) class became a novel presence, further complicating the social mixture of country districts. Indeed, if the Shannon Electrification Scheme of the 1920s was perhaps the most socially revolutionary venture of an unadventurous decade, the creation of a new town in Shannon, begun in 1958, the first such in the history of the state, was a similar manifestation of faith in Irish social revolution in this period. The town, with its new schools, sports grounds, community halls, swimming pool, shopping centre, clubs and associations, and streets of suburban-style housing depending in part for its existence on the nearby inter-

ational airport as a tourist stopping point, and on light industries
hat were attracted to the area from the United States, Canada,
nd the EEC countries by favourable tax conditions and grants,
vas another primary symbol of the new Ireland of the 1970s.

That Ireland did not come into being without painful birth
angs. Economists may have taken comfort in the received wis-
lom that a rising tide raises all boats and may have seen confir-
nation of this complacent conviction in the fact that visible signs
of desperate poverty – barefooted children in the city streets, for
xample – became much rarer. But the fact that economic waters
lo not rise with the predictability of the daily coastal tides meant
hat there were, as well as boom years such as 1977 and 1978,
eriods of sharp austerity (following the oil crisis of 1974–75 for
xample) even as the economic conditions of the country
mproved in general in the 1960s and '70s. Furthermore, both
nodernization of the countryside and economic growth in the
owns and cities had their victims as well as their beneficiaries.
n the countryside small farmers were informed in 1974, in the
arm Modernization Scheme instituted by the Department of
Lands, that their farms were "transitional," in other words, non-
commercial in size, and that they should seek early retirement. In
nany regions where a declining population had already resulted in
evere social distress and a lack of confidence in the future, such
lraconian attempts by a central government agency to reform
rish agriculture to align it with EEC practice sounded like a
leath knell of a way of life. An anthropologist who was engaged
n fieldwork in a parish in Country Kerry when this plan was
announced wrote of the devastating effect such policies were
laving in already depressed areas (Ballybran is a pseudonym):

> Throughout the long and discouraging winter, Ballybran
> farmers gathered in clusters at the pub or each other's homes
> to listen to radio or public television reports decry and deride
> the "backwardness" and "conservatism" of the western coastal
> farmers, who were characterized as living like parasites off
> welfare handouts, grants and subsidies, who were opposed to
> progress, and who hung greedily and tenaciously onto their

unproductive and miserable farms. The spectre of forced and early retirement hovered over the nightly pub sessions in Bally-bran, and a puritanical gloom settled like a mist into each man's pint of bitter porter. "Well, lads, 'tis we're finished up now for sure" was a commonly heard refrain. The local residents read about their lives and livelihoods discussed in national papers as so much debris and dead weight.[42]

So a way of life that had once been extolled as the authenti base upon which the nation securely rested was no longer con sidered viable in Ireland in her new age. It was not, howevel that urban life was proving by contrast wholly successful Undoubtedly in the 1960s and '70s many experienced living standards higher than any they had known in the past, but poo housing conditions, in bleak, ill-planned areas of the major citie were settings for vandalism, drug abuse, petty crime, and lives c quiet desperation in the way of city life in much of the developec world. Despite the economic improvements of the period, pov erty, particularly in the inflation-dogged 1970s, scarred the live of many Irish men and women in years when social progress, the outcome of increased opportunities in a modernizing society was assumed to be a primary contemporary fact. There were ne full-scale studies of poverty in Ireland at that time, but sucl analyses as existed suggested that in the 1970s at least a quarte of the population and perhaps nearer a third lived below a "pov erty line" estimated on the basis of social security levels o payment.[43] In March 1979 a huge protest march in Dublin by PAYE workers, angered by perceived inequities in the tax system which seemed grossly to benefit farmers and the self-employed expressed volatile public discontent.

The oddly ambiguous quality of life in the Republic of Irelanc at the end of two transitional decades in the country's twentieth century history was acutely detected by two journalists who attempted to assess the condition of the nation. James Downey assistant editor of the *Irish Times*, in a review of the year in 1978 remarked on the socially disruptive features of Ireland's new affluence:

The social scientists of the sixties could foresee these things, but they could not foresee that our transition to affluence would be so speedy and disruptive, that a new class system would be developed – and stratified – so soon, that our old easy-going, tolerant, egalitarian ways would be discarded with our poverty, that the "haves" of our society – professional people included – would fight for an even better position by a ruthless use of the methods practised so successfully by the skilled working class, or that the voice of social conscience would be fainter in the seventies.[44]

But even Downey in this bleak report could not but admit that Irish society in the 1970s was "alive, vivid and thrusting." For Kevin O'Connor, writing in the early days of 1980, the vibrant energy of that new Irish society, for all its ruthlessness and indifference to much social injustice, was the dominant impression of the times. It was an energy

... fuelled by the folk memory of a race almost extinguished. A hunger for things ... the thrust of that age is energetic, affluent, declamatory. The 1980s in Ireland congeal the homogeneity of those who were born poor with those who were not.[45]

And Dublin for O'Connor, "a capital with its courtiers, multinationals, new-rich boors, careerists," and enjoying a flowering of the arts, was Elizabethan in atmosphere and expectation, the heart of a nation at the beginning of its life. That ebullient, vigorous, modernizing society in quest of affluence and success, where real opportunities existed for the adventurous and energetic, a society disinclined to view poverty as anything but self-inflicted, brash, ostentatious, and not a little callous, was of course a far cry from the Ireland dreamed of at independence and sought throughout the austere years of Eamon de Valera's stern premiership. The ideological reverberations of this obvious fact stimulated much of the debate and discussion which marked the intellectual and cultural life of the country in the period, and to this we must now turn.

CHAPTER 9

Decades of Debate

I

"Our country is in a highly mobile phase at present," wrote E. F. O'Doherty, professor of psychology at University College, Dublin, in 1963. "In fact we are going through a deep and far-reaching cultural revolution."[1] That revolution, O'Doherty sensed, was the concomitant of the ideological and social revolution he saw in progress about him. He warned (his article appeared in the Jesuit periodical *Studies*):

> One cannot radically change the material culture and hope to preserve all the rest intact. Yet this is our dilemma. We have set in train certain great and far-reaching processes within the material culture which inevitably will have great and far-reaching effects in other dimensions of the culture, have already had such effects. But while we are anxious to achieve the desirable changes in the material culture, we are reluctant to accept the other changes they inevitably bring with them.[2]

The dilemma so precisely defined in this essay, written almost at the beginning of two decades of rapid economic and social change, was at the centre of much heart-searching throughout the period. A society that had sought its rationale in a separatism justified by national distinctiveness had decided to open itself to the forces of the international marketplace, to seek economic growth as the primary national goal, and to enter fully into the economic and political life of the industrially developed states of Western Europe. Not unnaturally, the social and cultural effects of such an ideological *volte face* were the substance of much concerned, even heated, discussion. An equally comprehensible feature of debate were the frequent considerations of national identity in circumstances, where many of the traditional essentialist definitions – language, tradition, culture and distinctive ideology – were widely felt to fly in the face of social reality, no longer commanding anything much more than sentimental respect.

The language question remained as one of the most contentious of Irish issues, that contention undoubtedly charged by the increasingly perilous position of the language itself. In 1966 there were less than 70,000 native speakers in the state. An essay suggested that by 1975 the number may well have sunk as low as 32,000, recognizing that "it is perfectly clear that if present demographic and linguistic trends are not reversed the Gaeltacht as a distinct linguistic community will not survive the century."[3] The economic revival in the west of the country in the 1970s reflected, for example, in the rapid rise in the population of Galway, reinforced the tendency of Gaelic-speaking and partly Gaelic-speaking districts to abandon the Irish language for English, the language of tourism and of the multinational corporations and foreign companies that had located factories west of the Shannon in the period.

Government policy in relation to the language in the same period was marked by apparent ambivalence. There were serious efforts to face up to the linguistic crisis in the country. A government commission was appointed and reported in 1963. A White Paper followed in 1965. Each of these admitted with a realism almost unprecedented in official circles how much remained to be done. Indeed, the commission report unambiguously faced up to the crisis of the Gaeltacht which might prove fatal to the language as a whole:

> Irish is . . . driven more and more into the position of being a kind of private language needed only in conversation with acquaintances – for everything outside this limited circle the Gaeltacht man must turn to English . . . if the Gaeltacht is allowed to disappear, the will to preserve and spread the Irish language as a spoken tongue elsewhere will probably vanish with it.[4]

In 1961 a new government advisory body, Comhairle na Gaeilge, was established with thirty-seven members. In 1975 Gaeltarra Éireann – a semi-state body formed in 1958 to aid Irish revival – was reconstituted as Bord na Gaeilge, to become the main agent of government linguistic policy. In 1972 a Gaeltacht radio service was initiated, Raidió na Gaeltachta, which by the end of the decade broadcast in Irish for about twenty-five hours a week. But crucial government decisions seemed to many revivalists to undermine with one governmental hand what was being attempted with the other. The Irish-speaking colleges, which prepared students for careers as National School teachers, were phased out in the 1960s. In 1961 the main opposition party, Fine Gael, included in its election manifesto a proposal to abolish compulsory Irish in the schools and in 1966 published a policy document which stated the party's aim as language "preservation" by "realistic" means, making clear that it would remove linguistic compulsion if it gained power. For the first time a major Irish political party had clearly chosen to espouse "preservation" rather than revival, and in the nationally resonant year of the fiftieth anniversary of the Easter Rising. When Fine Gael came to power in coalition with the Labour Party in 1973, one of the earliest government decisions was to remove the requirement that pupils should pass in Irish in order to merit the secondary school Leaving Certificate. The necessity for a pass in Leaving Certificate Irish for entry to the Civil Service was also abandoned. To many these decisions seemed to sound the death knell for the language.

According to Gearóid Ó Tuathaigh, they "removed the last vestige of state policy on the language."[5]

Throughout the 1960s and '70s Irish revivalists viewed all Irish governments with the profoundest suspicion. Writing in 1967, a reporter on Irish-language matters noted in an American periodical how even in the commemorative year of 1966,

> . . . many who still proclaim allegiance to the ideals of the 1916 leaders played down the vital importance which almost all of these men attached to the task of reviving the native language. The economic gospel seemed to have ousted the social and cultural ideals.[6]

During the 1916 observance, indeed, a group of radical revivalists named Misneach (Courage), which numbered among its founders the novelist Máirtín Ó Tuairisc, felt compelled to mount a week-long hunger strike in Belfast and Dublin to remind Irish men and women of past idealism. Supporters of language revival frequently felt driven to similar straits in defiance of a state whose intentions they no longer trusted. Individuals withheld radio and television licence fees in protest at the linguistic policy and performance of the national broadcasting service. Others fought running battles with state bureaucracies over such matters as the availability of Irish-language versions of official documents; and in the late 1960s young radical voices began to be raised in the Gaeltacht itself demanding civil rights for Irish-speaking Irish citizens.

In 1969 Nollaig Ó Gadhra identified the "three main areas in which Irish speakers feel they suffer discrimination in the Republic:"

> The lack of employment in Gaeltacht areas; the failure to provide adequate programmes in Irish on radio and television; and [the strong suspicion that] the language is gradually being "phased out" in the training colleges, universities and even in the secondary and primary schools.[7]

The 1970s were, as we saw, to add fuel to the fires of the suspicion that educational policy was shifting away from language revival as one of its principal aims. In the 1970s not only was the government decision to abandon compulsion in linguistic education at the secondary level seen as a body blow to revivalist hopes, but the methods of teaching Irish in the National Schools continued to draw criticism from the teachers themselves. In 1971 the INTO commented unfavourably on the Irish-language programme for the English-speaking areas of the country outlined in the new curriculum. It was, in their view, "an overloaded, unrealistic programme" and the curriculum's recommendations on the subject contravened "the philosophic and psychological principles enunciated" in the curriculum's introductory statements.[8] In 1976 the INTO survey on the effects of the new curriculum found that knowledge of Irish was suffering in the new context. While the report did not make clear whether the INTO was antagonistic to the programme because it contravened the principles of the new curriculum or because it was responsible for declining linguistic standards, the fact that the teaching of Irish in the primary schools was a matter for contention could give the revivalist no grounds for optimism.[9]

The 1970s saw no improvement, from the revivalists' viewpoint, in Irish television broadcasting. The national television service from its inception operated under the terms of an act passed in 1960. The act charged a broadcasting authority with the responsibility for broadcasting within the state. One of the sections of the act explicitly directed the authority to "bear constantly in mind the national aims of restoring the Irish language and preserving and developing the national culture." In addition, the authority, the act directs, shall "endeavour to promote these aims." In published statements the authority proclaimed its serious commitment to these responsibilities. However, performance seemed scarcely to reflect the idealism of proclaimed intention. Individual, popular programmes in Irish, and programmes designed to improve knowledge of the language, such as the Buntus Cainte programmes of the late 1960s in which basic Irish was taught through broadcasts, records, and booklets or the bilingual programme *Trom agus Eadrom*, seemed isolated acknowledgments of linguistic responsibility in a sea of home-produced and imported English-language material. In one year, for example, from October 1975 to September 1976 Irish-language television programming amounted to a mere 131 hours, representing only 10 percent of total home production. Of this, fifty-eight hours were taken up by news broadcasts. There was only one hour of Irish-language feature material and, extraordinarily, only three hours of children's television in Irish.[10] Certainly, the fact that Irish television depended on advertising revenue determined that most of its broadcasting be in English. Few companies were willing to advertise during programmes which much of the population could not easily comprehend. And the directors of programmes were also attentive to ratings, and therefore to public opinion, in a country where at least three British television channels were available to inhabitants on the east coast and in other areas as well. Public opinion would not readily have accepted a major introduction of Irish-language material into the daily schedules.[11]

It was indeed with Irish public opinion, with the attitudes of the people, that the Irish revivalists were forced to contend. In the White Paper of 1965, which followed from the final report of the Commission on the Restoration of the Irish Language, it was evident that the government recognized this fact. The White Paper proposed as government policy for the next decade a number of vaguely defined objectives ("extending the use of Irish as a living language, oral and written," for example) but accepted, in a crucial sentence, that "competent knowledge of English will be needed even in a predominantly Irish-speaking Ireland." Bilingualism, not linguistic exchange, became the new aspiration. Nor, apparently, should that desideratum be too strenuously pursued. While ready to agree with the commissioner's general sentiments, the White Paper showed that the government was less prepared to move swiftly to adopt its recommendation on the gaelicization of a variety of Irish institutions. Phrases and terms such as "will recommend," "will encourage," "desirable," and "target" suggested a governmental caution and ambiguity almost amounting to equivocation, caught as it was between a set of proposals based on little statistical and empirical research and its own sense of public opinion.

The precise components of public opinion on the issue were made known ten years later, when a major survey of Irish-language issues resulted in a remarkably interesting report. In 1970 the Minister for Finance, who also held responsibility for the Gaeltacht, established a Committee on Irish Language Attitudes Research, charged to determine the attitudes of the Irish public to Irish, and to its restoration "as a general means of communication in a significant range of language functions." The committee's findings after several years of intensive research, conducted on a rigorously controlled basis, justified the caution of the 1965 White Paper. A high proportion of the population was found to be convinced that Irish was important to "national or ethnic identity, or as a symbol of cultural distinctiveness."[12] Linked to this were beliefs about "the intrinsic cultural importance of the language."[13] "Irish," the report recorded, "when interpreted in this sense has favourable support from about two-thirds of the adult population of the state."[14] It also revealed that over two-thirds of the national population believed that "all children should be required to learn Irish as a subject in both primary and post-primary schools," although "between 60–75 percent of the population are dissatisfied with the teaching of Irish in the educational system."[15] This dissatisfaction was probably rooted in the fact that school Irish did not often enable individuals to use the language in adult life. The committee, conscious of the gaps that can exist between attitudes and practice, also presented evidence on language usage. They found that in the non-Gaeltacht areas only about 15 percent of the population "use Irish at work, at home, and with friends, and only about 4 percent of the population appear to use it very frequently and intensively."[16] This small number of persons was from a total of about 79 percent of the population who were found to have competence varying from minimal to high in spoken Irish, with only about 21 percent of the population having no such competence whatsoever. Perhaps he social experience reflected in these figures accounted for other ttitudinal factors that the committee identified. Among these vere the fact that half to three-quarters of the population believed

1. Gaeltacht areas are dying out.
2. That if this happens the language itself will die out.
3. That being in the EEC will hasten the loss.
4. That unless something really serious is done it will disappear in a generation or two.[17]

n a further factor identified by the researchers 70 percent of the opulation was found to be highly supportive of government ction on behalf of the Gaeltacht. But it also found that "instrunental rewards or sanctions for learning the language – such as ranting entry to promotions within the public service – is [*sic*] ot generally supported."[18]

How right the government was to move cautiously in the conext of Irish public opinion was made clear by the report's sketch of the "average Irish individual's" attitude to Irish:

The average individual . . . feels rather strongly that the Irish language is necessary to our ethnic and cultural integrity, and supports the efforts to ensure the transmission of the language. At the same time, under present policies and progress, he is not really convinced that we can ensure its transmission. He has rather negative views about the way Irish has been taught in school and has a rather low or "lukewarm" *personal* commitment to its use, although in this latter case, the average person has not sufficient ability in the language to converse freely in it. On the other hand, he strongly supports nearly all Government efforts to help the Gaeltacht, but at the same time feels that the language is not very suitable for modern business life.[19]

In the course of a series of complex and detailed analyses of a vide range of data, the report tried to explain how such an pparently "schizophrenic" set of attitudes was possible in socioinguistic terms. In so doing, it created a profile of the Irish inguistic situation not totally depressing to those earnest for the urvival of the Irish language. It was clear that a majority of Irish people were strongly supportive of the use of Irish in symbolic contexts, on public occasions for example, happy that the language should play a socially integrative role through official usage. Evidence showed that commitment to the language outside the Gaeltacht, and the willingness to use it, tended to rise with the level of educational attainment. Consequently, individuals who used Irish were more often than not likely to be in influential positions in society. The fact that an interest in the language and in using it could be seen to coexist with middle- and upper-middle-class success would perhaps help to lessen the traditional identification of Irish with poverty and backwardness.[20] The report also recorded that although only a very small proportion of the adult population used Irish at all regularly outside the diminishing Gaeltacht, about 27 percent of the adult population had "spoken Irish at least occasionally with some set of intimates for a considerable period of time at some stage in their life" and "just over 14 percent of the adult population have used it intensively at some stage and for a considerable period during their life cycle."[21] It seemed that people came in and out of Irish usage at various stages in their lives and "the rather high proportion dropping at some point"[22] was balanced by a roughly equivalent population who "come in" for the first time. A particularly hopeful fact was that of this latter group "about one-third . . . have come into this category at a very late stage when they have had no conversational Irish in their family or school background experiences." Another hopeful sign was evidence that suggested "some limited evidence of a revival of interest in Irish culture among seventeen-to-nineteen-year-olds."[23]

Among young people, increasingly a distinctive social group in Ireland, as in other modernized urban societies, the 1960s and '70s saw a remarkable flowering of interest in Irish traditional music. This inescapably brought them into contact with the Irish language and did much to generate affection and real regard for the national tongue. Organizations and individuals – the Gaelic League with its annual festivals; Comhaltas Ceoltóirí Eireann, founded in 1951 to foster love of traditional music;

collectors, recorders, and broadcasters like Seamus Ennis, Seán
Mac Reamoinn, Proinsias Ó Conluain, and Brendan Breathnach
- all found themselves suddenly in the limelight of a popular
movement that far exceeded anything they might have expected
when in the 1950s they began to explore the repository of Irish
folk music. As Brendan Breathnach astutely recognized, this
movement had had little to do with nationalist ideology but
was rather a local expression of developments in youth culture
throughout the industrialized world. It was not

> the effect of any national reawakening, as was the founding of
> the Feis Ceoil and the pipers' clubs at the close of the last
> century. It was a popular change among the youth, having its
> origin in New York, and after the usual time-lag, taken up in
> Dublin and elsewhere in Ireland.[24]

So a festival known as the Fleadh Ceoil held each summer,
usually in a western town, became the mecca for upward of
100,000 people, most of them young, gathered to listen to traditional musicians who in the past had been ignored outside their
own domestic circles and small gatherings of enthusiasts. The
music of the traditional group The Chieftains, which started life
under the direction of the enormously respected composer Seán
Ó Riada (who in the 1960s became more and more preoccupied
by the musical potential of the Irish tradition), created a market
for recordings of Irish traditional music both in Ireland and
abroad, while young musicians formed such popular groups as
Planxty and the Bothy Band to explore the vitality of the native
folk tradition. One singer and broadcaster, reflecting in 1979 on
the good health that traditional music currently enjoyed, wrote
that "the island of Ireland today is vibrant with reels, jigs, horn-
pipes, slow airs and songs. This surge of traditional Irish music
over the last twenty-five years is something of a phenomenon,
something that approaches a social revolution."[25]

It must be stressed, however, that this development was simply
an aspect of the more general social changes that were in progress
in the period. The demographic, economic, and educational

developments we have discussed above had created a new social group with the leisure and freedom from responsibility to follow interests and inclinations. That among these was Irish traditional music undoubtedly was of advantage to the Irish language, for the language has commended itself through the medium of music to many who might, as a result of unhappy school experience, have had little enthusiasm for it. But the identification of Irish music and the language with leisure activities in a consumer society was scarcely what the Gaelic League in its heyday had hoped for. Nor was it what the small number of dedicated parents in Dublin, who sent their children (about 20,000 pupils in both National and secondary schools were educated through Irish) to the small minority of Irish-speaking National Schools that existed in the city, hoped for. But perhaps that and its association with Gaelic games, (which enjoyed a vibrant popularity even in Dublin in the 1970s, where Gaelic football received mass urban support for the first time),[26] together with its roles as symbolic expression of ethnic distinctiveness, and as cultural catalyst for individual writers, were almost all that could be hoped for the language in the period. With the Gaeltacht in peril it seemed terribly insufficient.

Such indeed was the anguished conviction of some social commentators who contributed to the debates about the language in the period. The new Ireland, vigorously in pursuit of economic development, had set in motion, such critics argued, a process which would destroy the core of nationality, the spiritual heart of the nation, the Irish language itself. Signs of contemporary cultural dislocation and disturbance were isolated as symptoms of a disease contracted as a result of the abandonment of Irish. Writers, among them the poet and playwright Seán Ó Tuama, the archaeologist and historian Liam de Paor, Seán de Fréine, author of *The Great Silence* (1965) – a powerful adumbration of the assumed social and cultural effects of Ireland's linguistic crisis – and the Irish scholar and former president of the Royal Irish Academy, David Greene, all detected in Irish culture an imitative insecurity and mediocrity in the face of British and North American culture that was the direct result of language loss. Political independence had not brought intellectual independence:

> There is very little sign yet of the new or creative Irish milieu that Douglas Hyde and his followers envisaged. . . . One has only to think for a very brief moment of the various aspects of Irish life today to realize that, as a people, we have few ideas of our own, that our model, in most cases, is still the English (or sometimes American) model. In business, science, engineering, architecture, medicine, industry, law, home-making, agriculture, education, politics and administration – from economic planning to PAYE, from town-planning to traffic laws – the bulk of our thinking is derivative.[27]

But it was a poet who by his words and actions expressed most powerfully this sense of cultural betrayal implicit in Ireland's new social and economic order. In 1975, when he published a collection entitled *A Farewell to English*, the poet Michael Hartnett declared that henceforth he would publish only in Irish (though he subsequently returned to English). In the title poem he wrote:

> Gaelic is the conscience of our leaders,
> the memory of a mother-rape they will
> not face, the heap of bloody rags they see
> and scream at in their boardrooms of mock oak.
> They push us towards the world of total work
> our politicians with their seedy minds
> and dubious labels, Communist or
> Capitalist, none wanting freedom –
> only power. All that reminds us
> we are human and therefore not a herd
> must be concealed or killed or slowly left
> to die, or microfilmed to waste no space.
> For Gaelic is our final sign that
> we are human, therefore not a herd.[28]

II

In part five of his poem "A Farewell to English," Michael Hartnett identified the poet's art with an act of rebellion.

> Poets with progress
> make no peace or pact:
> the act of poetry
> is a rebel act.[29]

The late 1960s and '70s in Ireland were disturbed by those who believed that the gun was altogether a mightier instrument of rebellion than the poet's pen. The anti-partition campaign of violence, which fully took hold in 1972 and which continued until 1996, posed a severe ideological challenge to the new Irish order that had developed since Lemass came to power.

Since 1922 Irish unity had been a declared aim of all electorally significant parties. The 1937 Constitution, which defined the national territory as the whole island of Ireland, distinguished the jurisdiction of the existing state from the territory of the nation, "pending the reintegration of the national territory." In so doing, the Constitution reflected the widespread belief in the major political parties and in the country at large that the constitutional arrangements of 1921/2 had left much unfinished business to future generations. Crucial amid such business was the political reunification of the nation. The Fianna Fáil party had always asserted that reunification and the revival of the Irish language were its principal national aims, and no party could have hoped to achieve parliamentary success which did not at least pay lip service to the ideal of a thirty-two-county republican Ireland.

It was, as I suggested, Seán Lemass who managed in the 1960s to wed a commitment to economic renewal to the aspiration for unity. Hitherto no ideas on how partition might be ended likely to gain wide support for their evident feasibility and practicality had even been placed convincingly before the Irish people.

emass gave Irish men and women to understand that work for onomic renewal was the best way to serve the national aim and e most practical form of nationalism, for it would make the outhern state attractive to the Northern unionist population hich had in the past had ample reason to reject incorporation to a state which could not even maintain its own population. the 1960s, when so much of the ideology that had sustained e state since independence was in crisis, as the social base altered radical ways, it was vital that at least one element of the ideo-gical complex of earlier decades retained its credibility, even if now took an almost exclusively economic form. And national-m can, through its power to command effort and commitment, : a powerful aid to modernization.[30] It was possible to see Irish volvement with the UK in the Free Trade Agreement, the ommitment to the Common Market, and the decision to attract oreign investment, as serving a primary national aim, defined by e founding fathers of the state. That for a few brief years the olicy appeared to enjoy success was gratifying indeed (there had een few successes since 1922). In 1965 Lemass visited the Prime Iinister of Northern Ireland, Terence O'Neill, at Stormont. In ne brief moment decades of public mistrust were apparently set ide as the two parts of Ireland seemed set fair for a period of conomic cooperation that might have broken down the barriers nutual suspicion had erected. In the years 1965–68 newspaper rticles, essays, and books frequently spoke of the new atmosphere oroad, of the "binding up of the ancient wound."[31] It was not o be.

The protest and violence that broke out in Northern Ireland 1 1968, which developed into the horrendous civil strife in the 970s and a guerrilla campaign against the British state in North-rn Ireland led by the Provisional IRA, was rooted in the six-ounty statelet of Northern Ireland itself. It is vital to stress this ict. The violence erupted when it did as a consequence of the ynamics of that region and society. It was not the result of a ampaign originating in the Southern state, although it eventually athered part of its support there. Few people in the Republic

indeed could have viewed the upsurge of violence in the Nor■
in the early 1970s with anything other than alarm. Not only w■
the Northern crisis likely to export its violence into the Republi■
but the experience of the Northern Catholic nationalist minori■
was bound to challenge the Lemass approach to reunificatio■
thereby threatening political stability. While the Northern mi■
ority was content to remain in a Northern Ireland under t■
ultimate jurisdiction of the British government, pending t■
reunification of the national territory, economic life could b■
pursued in the South in the happy assurance that it could co■
tribute to the realization of a noble, long-term aim. When t■
Northern minority gave notice that it found conditions in t■
Northern semi-state no longer tolerable, the possibility arose th■
the Republic might have to choose between the commitment t■
the ending of partition that underlay its traditional nationali■
ideology, and its more recent ideological commitment to th■
primacy of economic values, which since 1959 had been astute■
linked to that long-term ambition.

It was clear throughout the 1970s that the majority of the popu■
lation of the Republic did not wish the Northern crisis and th■
avowed republican nationalism of the state's traditional ideolog■
to interfere with the economic progress of the country along th■
path signposted by Lemass in 1959. Lemass retired in 1966 an■
in 1970 his successor, the Fianna Fáil Taoiseach Jack Lynch, w■
able to dismiss two powerful, able ministers, Charles Haughey an■
Neil Blaney, from his cabinet on the suspicion of conspiring ■
import arms for use by nationalists in Northern Ireland and su■
vive not only their departure from office, but the subsequent tri■
and acquittal in court of Charles Haughey on a charge of conspirin■
illegally to import arms (an event subsequently referred to as "th■
Arms Trial"). Less that two years later, when the Northern con■
flict was at its height, only six months after British Army para■
troopers had shot dead thirteen civilians on "Bloody Sunday" i■
Derry, the population of the Republic voted in a referendum by ■
margin of more than five to one to enter the EEC simultaneous■
with the UK. Following entry, both the Fianna Fáil governmen■

and the coalition government (comprising Fine Gael and the minority partner, the Labour Party) which came to power in 1973 and held office for four years with Liam T. Cosgrave as Taoiseach, participated fully in EEC affairs despite the fact that Britain and Ireland were ostensibly in serious dispute over the territory of the six Northern counties. The contrast with earlier years when Ireland had refused to join NATO because of partition and had used the Council of Europe as an arena for the airing of national grievances was stark indeed. The Republic certainly arraigned the UK before the European Court of Human Rights in Strasbourg for breaches of human rights in the operation of internment without trial in Northern Ireland, but declined to press the national question vigorously, willingly accepting the ill-fated Sunningdale Agreement of 1973 which sought a settlement largely within the six-county context. (The Agreement involved a power-sharing executive in a devolved administration in Belfast and a Council of Ireland to reflect an all-Ireland dimension, all of which collapsed in June 1974, after near-rebellion among the unionist population of Northern Ireland.)

The Northern conflict therefore did not stimulate major ideological redirection in the Republic. Thoughout a decade of violence and political vacuum in the six counties, the Southern state maintained its commitment to economic and social progress, apparently ignoring when it could the commotion at its doorstep. It was not of course that the Republic simply averted its gaze from the Northern struggle, lured by the dazzle of consumerism and material wellbeing. Decades of experience of independence in the Irish Free State and in the Republic of Ireland had given a reality to the state of a very substantial kind indeed. The great mass of the citizens of the Republic knew only loyalty to that state, its courts, armed forces, and administration. The challenge posed by the Northern Catholic minority's sharp disaffection from the political existence of Northern Ireland (which became clearer as the decade proceeded, especially after the collapse of the Sunningdale Agreement) with its implication that a new political order must be achieved on the island as a whole, was inevitably met by the inertia of a people disinclined to consider the radical restructuring of the state to which they gave their whole loyalty. For the possibilities of a new, united Ireland were insubstantial when set against the reality of a state that had known, in its several forms, more than fifty years of independent existence. Despite this fact, however, it was as a possible national apostasy that the Northern issue was often raised in the flood of debate, discussion, and heart-searching that the Northern conflict stimulated. Was it the case, such discussion often pondered, that Ireland at the greatest moment of challenge had cast away her birthright of pure, undefiled nationalist republicanism for a mess of pottage? Was it the case that when the issue of reunification became for once a real one, the Republic preferred to look the other way and to proceed with business as usual – in the EEC, in trade with the UK, welcoming British tourists, refusing to confront the British government in too direct a fashion, adopting at moments an unworthy ambivalence of word and action in relation to conflicting ideological imperatives?[32]

In the babble of voices raised to discuss Irish identity in the 1970s, earnest to discuss how and to what degree Ireland should assert her traditional nationalism and republicanism, none perhaps managed to reach such a wide audience as that of the writer, playwright, historian, diplomat, and politician Conor Cruise O'Brien. Most of this discussion, which absorbed a good deal of Irish intellectual life in the decade, took place in learned periodicals, in small magazines, and in the features and letter columns of the *Irish Times* and the *Irish Press*. Cruise O'Brien, partly because of his position as Minister for Posts and Telegraphs in the coalition government, partly because of his international reputation, and partly because of the suave almost pedantic pleasure he took in arousing controversy, managed to bring the debate about Irish nationalism out of the domain of intellectual discussion and into the arena of public controversy.

Cruise O'Brien's central thesis, propounded in newspaper articles, journal essays, public lectures, television appearances, and in his book *States of Ireland* (1972), was that Ireland's ideological ambivalence on the issue of partition was altogether too danger-ous a self-indulgence for the citizens of the Republic in a period when a full-scale Irish civil war threatened. Ireland, he argued, faced by the ideological challenge of the Northern conflict, should abandon an ambivalence that gave heart and encouragement to men of violence for a frank recognition that the republican nation-alism of the first decades of independence was based on a seriously deficient analysis of the Irish problem and an all too literary view of history.

The chief deficiency in republican nationalist orthodoxy,[33] in Cruise O'Brien's view, was that it failed to take sufficient account of the depth and nature of Northern unionist antagonism to any threat of incorporation by their Southern neighbours. Orthodox republican nationalism had always asserted that partition was an unnatural British imposition on a nation which God and history had intended to be one. The division of the country perhaps represented differences within the nation, but if the British pres-ence was removed, these differences would swiftly and easily be resolved. Until that happy date Northern unionists, however, would continue to support the link with Britain because it guaran-teed them certain privileges as against the nationalists in the six counties (the name Northern Ireland was strictly eschewed) which they would not enjoy in a united country. When Britain finally decided to quit the country, unionists would quickly come to their senses and make the best settlement possible with their fellow countrymen. To confirm the republican in this latter con-viction, ideologues had frequently invoked the years leading to the 1798 Rebellion when "staunch Presbyterians" had joined together to form the United Irishmen to rise in rebellion against the British crown.[34] Such people had once recognized their obli-gation to play a part in the history of the Irish nation, and their descendants would do so again. The Northern unionists were at present rendered incapable of recognizing that their own best interests lay in unity with their fellow Irishmen and women, because the British presence gave them a permanent guarantee that their position was unassailable. Most Irish people since 1922 had been content to see diplomatic persuasion as the most appropriate weapon to employ against the British to compel them to leave Ireland, thereby allowing the unionists the opportunity to come to their senses. A small minority had consistently reckoned that military force applied against the British occupation of Ireland would hasten the process wonderfully. Cruise O'Brien forcefully argued throughout the 1970s that neither activity was likely to prove successful. The Northern unionists, he insisted, would, in circumstances of either diplomatic or military defeat of what they regarded as their essential interests, be unlikely to "come to their senses" in precisely the manner envisaged in the republican nationalist faith. They could pose a fearsome threat to the stability of the island as a whole.

Accordingly, one of Cruise O'Brien's concerns throughout the decade was to administer what he believed were the sharp doses of realism necessary to cure the chronic low-level fantasy induced by nationalist ideology. In this respect he echoed earlier men of letters, George Russell and Seán O'Faoláin, who had challenged ideological dogma in similar fashion. They too had directed Irish attention to aspects of Irish reality which could not be contained within the framework of the dominant ideology. Russell denied the simplicities of the Irish Irelanders through an appeal to the cultural vitality of Anglo-Ireland. O'Faoláin denied the continuity of Irish nationalist history through a sustained reflection on the meaning of Daniel O'Connell's career and the tradition he established. Both of them in the *Irish Statesman* and the *Bell* had, respectively, tried to challenge nationalist complacency about the six counties by allowing Northern news and opinion space in their columns. Cruise O'Brien was better placed to argue his case than his predecessors and was rewarded with more success. Not only did he hold public office, with all the opportunities that gave him for public statement, but he was able to propound this thesis in a period when television reportage was providing the population of the Republic with a greater sense of the political realities of Northern Ireland than they had hitherto possessed. Cruise O'Brien could argue that Northern unionists were unlikely to agree to reunification with ready gratitude upon Britain's departure, while the Reverend Ian Paisley, almost nightly on the nation's television screens, provided compelling evidence of the substance of Cruise O'Brien's thesis. Russell and O'Faoláin had challenged the impalpabilities of ideology with impalpable arguments about culture. They had, it is true, tried to create a sense of the distinctiveness of the Northern counties and of the reality of the Southern state in their journalism, but this had neither the force nor the mass audience of the television image. Cruise O'Brien, as the poet Seamus Heaney remarked, was therefore instrumental in the 1970s in creating "some kind of clarity in Southerners' thinking about the Protestant community in the North. And it is not enough for people to simply say 'Ah, they're all Irishmen,' when some Northerners actually spit at the word Irishmen. There is in O'Brien a kind of obstinate insistence on facing up to this kind of reality, which I think is his contribution."[35] And the response of many in the Republic was akin to that of W. B. Yeats when he remarked to Lady Gregory (as she records in her *Journal*) of the inhabitants of the North and of their politics, "I have always been of the opinion that if such disagreeable neighbours shut the door, it is better to turn the key in it before they change their mind."

The historian John A. Murphy provided a very just assessment of this aspect of Cruise O'Brien's contribution to Irish debate in the period:

From the outbreak of the Northern troubles up to 1972 when he published *States of Ireland* or perhaps up to 1973 when he took up political office, Dr. Cruise O'Brien with characteristic pungency and courage, masterfully exposed the woolliness of Southern attitudes towards Northern Ireland and in particular the ambivalence of Southern thinking – or more accurately, feeling – about the Provisional IRA. Because he compelled people to make uncomfortable reappraisals of emotions cosily and lazily cherished, he incurred considerable personal and political hostility. He performed, then, a very great public service which will one day be appreciated as such.[36]

Cruise O'Brien combined his assault on the simplicities of traditional positions on Northern Ireland with a critique of republican nationalist historiography. Like O'Faoláin before him he was dubious of that ideology's vision of an indestructible, historic, predestinate nation that had achieved its apotheosis in the 1916 Rising. O'Faoláin in the *Bell* had been the first to mount a sustained critique of this conception, but concurrent with the celebrations of the anniversary year of 1966, and in subsequent years of reassessments, revisionist essays began to appear fairly frequently in Irish periodicals, newspapers, and scholarly journals. A sense that the social reality of contemporary Ireland scarcely reflected the aspirations of the revolutionary martyrs of 1916 provoked "articles of a speculative kind concerned with the question of how Ireland would have developed without 1916 and whether, considering everything, the rising comes out as a positive good."[37] The veneration accorded Patrick Pearse, whose memorials in the first four decades of independence amounted almost to a cult and whose memory had been kept fresh in the National Schools, began to be questioned openly. In 1972 *Studies* published an extended essay by the Reverend Professor Francis Shaw, SJ (until his death in December 1970 professor of early and medieval Irish at University College, Dublin), entitled "The Canon of Irish History – A Challenge." The article had been prepared in 1966 but was withheld by the editor, who recognized that it challenged the interpretation of Irish history which had justified the revolutionary violence of 1916, celebrated in that year. Shaw found that interpretation neither "Christian" nor "truly patriotic." He focussed his attack on Pearse, the Pearse cult, and "a canon of history which has come into being, has been carefully fostered and was newly consecrated in the massive state-inspired and state-assisted Commemoration in 1966."[38]

Shaw in his essay criticized both Pearse's political philosophy and his actions. He argued that Pearse had anathematized the majority of the Irish people as national apostates in a most arrogant and intolerant fashion, banishing them from the canon of Irish history. Pearse had established a heretical pseudo-religious nationalist creed in his identification of revolutionary self-sacrifice with Christ's crucifixion, as he had created a gospel of hate. He had been all too ready to transform the Gaelic League, with its broad-minded social vision, into a revolutionary political vanguard, thereby, in Shaw's view, sacrificing its cultural life on the altar of the "terrible beauty" of 1916. Finally, he argued, – as his essay reveals the core of his true feelings – Pearse had had little understanding of the historical Irish nation. His proclamation of "seven centuries of solid and unbroken military resistance," the "accepted backdrop to the drama of Irish history"[39] was a terrible perversion of the "Irish national consciousness," which "was more subtle, more spiritual and, I am glad to say, more peaceful."[40]

Shaw quite clearly had a sense of Irish history which would allow a greater role for the Catholic church and the orthodox piety and obedience of the faithful over the centuries than "the canon" would allow. His revisionism had, therefore, a polemical, tendentious air which reduced its force. Implicit throughout, however, was a humane repugnance for the fact that canonical historical understanding in Ireland should have cast aside as irrelevant to the nation's story so many Irishmen and women and should have elevated to sacred heights only those few who rose in violence against the oppressor. That history in Ireland should be simply a narrative of sacred, repeated events culminating in the violence of the Rising was for Shaw a travesty of historical imagining.

> The canon of history of which I speak stamps the generation of 1916 as nationally degenerate, a generation in need of redemption by the shedding of blood. It honours one group of Irishmen by denying honour to others whose merit is not less. In effect it teaches that only the Fenians and the separatists had the good of their country at heart, that all others were either deluded or in one degree or another sold out to the enemy. This canon moulds the broad course of Irish history to a narrow pre-conceived pattern; it tells a story which is false and without foundation.[41]

Conor Cruise O'Brien's assault on official republican nationalist history in the 1970s was essentially similar to that of Shaw
though executed with more subtlety and literary skill. Perhaps
beneath its subtlety, it too was tendentious for after 1973, as a
member of the Labour Party in coalition with Fine Gael, he had
immediate reasons to direct Irish historical consciousness away
from the orthodox doctrines of republicanism which were most
particularly the ideological inheritance of Fianna Fáil. Be that as
it may, Cruise O'Brien, like Shaw, distinguished history proper
from the essentially "literary current in Irish history"[42] which is
suffused with romanticism, an altogether dangerous infection in
the body politic. It was such a literary version of Irish history
that generated the 1916 Rising (Cruise O'Brien made much of
the way in which in the period leading to the Rising literature
and life intertwined), and it continued to inspire desperate deeds.
He wrote:

> To minds that are possessed by that idea of sacrifice it is irrel-
> evant to prove that a campaign like the current IRA campaign,
> for example, cannot possibly accomplish any desirable political
> objective. That can be demonstrated, it can be quite logically
> and clearly demonstrated, but it doesn't matter. The objective
> is to become part of "history" in the abstract or mythological
> sense, to achieve immortality by getting oneself killed for Ire-
> land's sake. That the actual people of Ireland, in their over-
> whelming humdrum majority, want no such sacrifice is also
> irrelevant, having no other effect than to cause the people in
> question to disappear from "Irish history" which in every gener-
> ation consists of the doings and sayings of the martyrs.[43]

As a government minister Cruise O'Brien set his face against
all those aspects of Irish popular culture which carried an infection
that presented itself as "unhealthy intersection" between literature and politics. The patriotic ballad, the commemorative
speech, the public veneration of the nationalist dead all seemed
to fall under his increasingly severe interdict. As a result, even
those who were willing to grant the substance of his views on the

Northern question found it impossible to stomach his iconoclastic handling of national sentiment. John A. Murphy was representative of a good deal of opinion when, having praised Cruise O'Brien for his stand on Northern Ireland, he continued in his article of 1977:

> He concentrates his attack on the excesses of nationalism and the ambivalences indubitably inherent in Irish nationalist attitudes but in so doing he indicts the whole nationalist population and especially anyone who articulates a unity aspiration. His attack on nationalism is a stalking-horse for an assault on nationality itself.[44]

Murphy sensed that the resentment Cruise O'Brien aroused "may have been linked with an intuitive popular feeling that he had begun to challenge the basis of Irish nationality itself."[45] There were those too who felt his sympathy for the Northern unionist position (later expressed in his support of the United Kingdom Unionist Party), which may have had its sources in a wish to protect stability on the island as a whole, was a betrayal of the nationalist minority in the North.

What was intellectually depressing about the revisionism propounded by Conor Cruise O'Brien in the 1970s was its unhistorical quality. What Cruise O'Brien believed was a false view of history, dangerous insomuch as it stimulated a current campaign of violence the only outcome of which would be civil war he challenged by speculation of a curiously unhistorical kind. Implicit throughout Cruise O'Briens's writings in the 1970s was the suggestion that Ireland would have achieved as much as it had, had the Easter Rising of 1916 not taken place, had that "unhealthy intersection" between literature and politics not been fabricated. A mind capable of severity and stringency on other matters became markedly self-indulgent on this issue. The reasons why, in the context of the imperial maladministration of nineteenth-century Ireland, a myth of the indestructibility of the Irish nation, of the seamless garment of Irish historical continuity had developed, why indeed nationalist historiography had become dominated by a sense of the repetitive successes and failures of the patriotic struggle, were almost entirely ignored. The fact that these developments had causes of quite specific kinds[46] and could not simply be talked or legislated away was not sufficiently implicit in his words or actions.

Writing in 1971, Liam de Paor reflected on the "new period of Irish history" that he sensed beginning about him – "a time of troubles because it is a time of accelerated change. The myths with which – whether we accepted them or not – we have lived for many decades have suddenly ceased to have the appearance of life and are assuming the faded look of old photographs."[47] One such myth, he felt, was the tradition "that took its form from nationalism, and was expressed in a cycle of hope, failure, apathy and renewed hope, or to put it another way, of illusion, disillusion, cynicism and renewed illusion." This was a dialectic which was suited "to a history of the dispossessed."[48] The "touch of affluence" that the 1960s had brought, de Paor asserted, "had broken the chain" – Ireland was in need of a new historical myth. As new social and economic circumstances began to loosen the hold of old ideologies on the minds of Irish people, readily accepting the new national imperative of economic growth, Cruise O'Brien's persistent debunking of the old historical myth was scarcely what was needed. Indeed, it may have been his paradoxical fate to have protracted the life of a geriatric ideology somewhat beyond its natural span, so objectionable did many find his attacks upon a respected ancestor. He perhaps helped keep its faded photograph in the frame. Happily some of what was needed in a changing Ireland was in fact beginning to be provided.

From the late 1930s onward the writing of history in Ireland had undergone a quiet revolution.[49] From that period, building on the work of a very few predecessors, Irish historians set themselves the task of exploring their country's past without palpable design upon their readers. In 1938, as we saw, the scholarly journal *Irish Historical Studies* was first published, and over forty years, guided by its editors, it offered a focus for careful, scientific historical research. One of its editors, Professor T. W. Moody, in a valedictory lecture in 1977 at Trinity College, Dublin, spoke of the role history should play in Irish life. It should be, he stated, "a continuing, probing critical search for truth about the past."[50] The degree to which this history should be distinguished from the "canon" of Irish history extirpated by Professor Shaw in his *Studies* article is evident when Moody isolates the notion of myth as "received views" which must give way before "the knowledge that the historian seeks to extract by the application of scientific methods to his studies."[51] When that occurs, such myths as the predestinate nation must evaporate since they are "incompatible with the history of social living in the modern Ireland." Moody in this lecture is certainly naive about the cultural and political neutrality of such "scientific" inquiry in every circumstance, but the note he strikes does reflect the patient, sane balance that characterized the historiographical revolution in Ireland. By the late 1960s and the early 1970s that revolution had laid sufficient groundwork for the publication of a number of synthetic studies of modern Irish history to become possible. Such works as Louis Cullen's *Life in Ireland* (1968) and *An Economic History of Ireland Since 1660* (1972) and F. S. L. Lyons's *Ireland Since the Famine* (1971) represented cultural developments in Ireland of a more crucial kind than all the raised voices debating national identity in that decade. So too was the fact that younger historians in the Irish universities could produce in the Gill paperback *History of Ireland* series, notable for its analytic vigour, a series of short introductions to various periods. Finally, Irish history in the period determined that it had come of age when, under the aegis of the Royal Irish Academy and directed at the outset by Professors T. W. Moody, F. X. Martin and F. J. Byrne, Irish historians embarked upon a nine-volume history of the country. To date seven volumes and a number of compilations of historical statistics have appeared.

This historiographical revolution, a major fact of modern Irish intellectual and cultural history, began to bear its fruit in Irish schools[52] and in the Irish mass media. Initially, a sense grew among Irish history teachers throughout the 1960s that history teaching required renovation. The Department of Education proved receptive to new thought, and the Secondary School Curriculum in History was revised in the 1960s to emphasize social and cultural aspects of the country's past. Such an emphasis replaced the approach which for forty years had been represented by an influential school textbook by Mary Hayden and George A. Moonan, *A Short History of the Irish People*, which was written "from a frankly national standpoint" and had organized its chronicle-like narrative around an understanding of the birth, growth, and maturity of a historic Irish nation. Irish publishers produced new textbooks, and these offered to pupils in Irish schools a sense of the complex social and cultural make-up of their country in its European context. The new history reached wider audiences, too, through radio and television broadcasts. The Thomas Davis Lecture series on the national radio service (the first was broadcast in 1953) regularly presented Irish historians' new findings on the distant and recent past. In 1974, RTE broadcast a series of television lectures entitled *A Question of Identity* which addressed itself to the historical strands which comprise the Irish nation. And in 1977 the major six-part RTE television series *The Heritage of Ireland* presented a vision of the country as a complicated mosaic of cultures and social forces, utterly remote from the simplicities of earlier, more ideologically committed, versions of the national story.

The 1970s, when secondary school education became the norm, was the period when the historiographic revolution (referred to in public debate as "revisionism") began to make itself felt in the schools. In the 1980s and '90s many young people educated in this period became opinion-formers in Ireland, at a time when the Irish state began a full-scale attempt to resolve the Northern question. The subtle nationalism the political class and the mass media brought to this task may have been due in part to the historiographical revolution and the dissemination of its approach in the secondary schools, as well as in the universities in the 1970s. That it had real purchase on the Irish *mentalité* was certainly evidenced in the degree to which the question of "revisionism" became, as we shall see, hotly debated in the 1990s, when voices were raised to protest that it was in fact a reactionary phenomenon, inhibiting radical change and sustaining the status quo.

III

For the church, too, in Ireland the 1960s and '70s were years of debate and adaptation. From the late 1950s onward it was recognized that the social and economic changes afoot in the country would present great challenges to the faith of the people and to the church herself. In such intellectual Catholic periodicals as the *Furrow* (which began publication in 1950), *Doctrine and Life* (which began publication in 1951), and *Christus Rex* (a periodical which had started life in 1947 and then interested itself in social matters from a Catholic point of view), articles appeared which, partly in the wake of the changes in Catholicism abroad, and partly in response to the evident changes in Irish society, began to express concern at the intellectual poverty of modern Irish Catholicism. In 1957 Father Denis Meehan, professor of divinity and classics at St Patrick's College, Maynooth, asked in an article entitled "An Essay in Self-Criticism," "Has the Irish influence in the English-speaking Church been anti-intellectual, or at best unintellectual?"[53] In 1959 an essay in *Doctrine and Life* stated the matter more directly:

> Too many people in Ireland today are trying to make do with a peasant religion when they are no longer peasants any more. We are a growing and developing middle-class nation, acquiring a middle-class culture and we must have a religion to fit our needs.[54]

This was a theme that was to recur in the intellectual Catholic periodicals as the 1960s progressed, particularly after the Second Vatican Council. It was argued in various critical articles that Irish Catholicism had played a crucial role in the past as an element in Irish national identity, but that this could change dramatically in the new Ireland that was developing, with serious effects on the religious life of the people. A writer in the *Furrow* in 1962 struck the note:

> As a nation we must take the whole question of education much more seriously than has been the case up to date. The challenge of the Common Market and the need for secular education if we are to survive as a nation is awakening our people to the need for more schools, better schools, and better trained teachers, but there is an equal need to face up to the challenge of the growth of contemporary paganism to our Christian heritage.[55]

It was feared by a number of thoughtful clergy and laity that the traditionally unintellectual faith of the Irish would be incapable of withstanding full exposure to the ideas, culture, and secularism of contemporary Europe. This small but developing Catholic intelligentsia realized that the expedients of the past employed to protect the faithful from the incursions of dangerous thought – censorship and authoritarian control – would be inadequate dykes against the incoming tide and that they had in fact been responsible for the intellectual deficiencies of Irish Catholicism which made the faithful so vulnerable in their new circumstances. In 1959 Father Peter Connolly, professor of English at St. Patrick's College, Maynooth, published a critique of the censorship policy in Ireland. An eminently balanced discussion of a Catholic view of censorship, his essay reflects the author's impatience with the local interpretation of Catholic teaching on the matter and his hope that a Catholic intelligentsia might emerge able to respond critically to the challenges and insights of modern Irish and European literature:

> A society should not be bereft of the salutary criticism of some of its own most passionately aware members, and the reaction to many of the literary bans is harmful – a cynicism about the Act and contempt for Censorship in general. The novels and the new ideas will seep through in any case but into a negative atmosphere in which the sense of intellectual adventure has gone stale and embittered. This is an aspect of the common

good which we might reconsider at greater length particularly if the problem of an intellectual Catholic elite is one which faces us in Ireland today.[56]

Father Connolly's contribution to this problem was to publish critical essays on banned books and films which took them seriously as works of art. He was joined in this enterprise by Reverend John C. Kelly, SJ, spiritual director at Belvedere College, Dublin, who wrote film criticism for the *Furrow* and in 1961 contributed an essay entitled "The Modern Novels and Christian Values" to *Doctrine and Life*. In this essay Father Kelly argued that the Christian has much to learn from the modern novel and, piquant irony indeed, employed the work of James Joyce – an ex-pupil of Belvedere College who had epitomized for many the diabolism of corrupt literature – as grist to his critical mill.

In 1964 Father Connolly put on record his views on the ways to combat censorship in Ireland:

> The real aim of whatever articles I published . . . was to bypass the kind of anti-censorship wars which . . . in my opinion, are wholly outmoded. Carried on valiantly by the *Bell* writers in the forties those wars had pushed "liberal" littérateurs and conservative Irish readers farther and farther apart and pinned them down on extreme wings. It was time to try something else. This formula was to offer positive appreciations of contemporary films and books which would simply ignore polemics about our censorship. It would demonstrate to Irish readers that in face of modern novels or films of whatever kind it was not necessary to bury one's head in the sand or, on the other hand, to sacrifice one jot of moral principle . . . we hoped for a gradual growth of the climate of opinion which would make a juvenile standard of censorship – though not all censorship – untenable.[57]

Michael Adams has suggested that Father Connolly's article in *Christus Rex* did "much to clarify the ideas of Catholics on the censorship question."[58] Certainly within five years the Minister for Justice was able to liberalize the workings of the law in relation to the censorship of films without much controversy, and in 1967 the same minister, Brian Lenihan, introduced a bill in the Dáil which would allow the removal of a ban from a book after a period of twenty years. During the Dáil debate this period was reduced to twelve years. As Adams reports, "In one grand gesture over 5,000 titles were released from limbo." Many of these were the works by Irish writers which had so offended against earlier conceptions of the moral order, and from that date they became freely available in Irish bookshops and libraries. So ended a sorry chapter in modern Irish cultural history.

Priests like Fathers Connolly and Kelly hoped that a Catholic elite would emerge, able, as Ireland became open to all the currents of modern culture, to respond with an informed critical discrimination to the major works of modern literature. To an extent their hopes were realized. Since the 1960s a generation of young Irish scholars and critics in the universities (many with a Catholic social formation) began to produce a criticism of modern literature. In 1966 the periodical *University Review* (which had been founded in 1954 as the official organ of the Graduates' Association of the National University of Ireland and had published since then occasional essays by Irish academic critics on Irish writing) published a special Yeats edition, marking a milestone in the development of a modern critical literature on Irish writing in English emanating from the universities.

Like the historiographical revolution, this quiet change in intellectual life in Ireland was a work of consolidation on the foundations built by a few pioneers. Among these were such scholars of an earlier generation as Professors Roger McHugh, Lorna Reynolds, A. N. Jeffares, and Vivian Mercier, who had addressed themselves to the study of Anglo-Irish literature when the subject had not attracted the attention of the world in the way it has since done. The recognition that Irish writing in English was a field worthy of serious study was firmly established in the Irish universities. Young scholars and critics began the work of assessing their country's recent literary past, concerned to see the Literary Revival of the nineteenth and twentieth centuries, and the literature of the independent state, in the contexts of modern etters and of Irish social and cultural history. Modern English, American, and Anglo-Irish literature began to be taught in each of the university departments of English and from the early 1970s figured in the curriculum in English in the secondary schools (a revision of the Leaving Certificate English syllabus in the secondary curriculum in the 1990s allowed for the comparative study of texts in their cultural settings, as well as for the study of film). The Association of Teachers of English with its periodical *ATE* was vigorous in its encouragement of an informed critical awareness among its members, drawing on the teaching profession itself and on the universities for essays and articles and for lectures at its annual conference. The *Irish University Review* regularly published critical essays and findings on Irish literature in English. Irish publishers began to publish works of criticism and scholarship on Irish literature in both English and Irish and were active in the production of anthologies and guides for the secondary schools. It became difficult therefore to pass through an Irish education without some experience of modern writing. Signs of interest were evident: the university departments of English attracted numerous well-qualified applicants; small journals and the newspaper literary pages reflected a wider and more informed knowledge of modern writing than in the days when the *Irish Statesman*, the *Bell* and *Envoy* tried to remind the public of the very existence of such works; radio and television programmes regularly dealt with literary matters in discussion, features, and dramatic adaptations of modern Irish writing. What all this activity meant was that a wider segment of educated opinion in the country was informed about current literature than could have been the case in the past, when censorship was rigorously in force and when universities and schools were antagonistic to the study of twentieth-century writing.

The main thrust of specifically Catholic thinking since the early 1960s had not, however, been literary, though the emergence of a generation of Irish critics and of teachers in the mainly Catholic secondary schools keen to assess and present modern literature could not be gainsaid.[59] Nor indeed was it theological. Much of the intellectual energy of lay and clerical minds in the 1960s and '70s was absorbed primarily by the sociology of religion. The recognition that Ireland was entering a phase of rapid urbanization and modernization spurred Catholic intellectuals to reflect on how religion fares in modern societies and on how Irish Catholicism should adapt to its new environment. To attempt adaptation without knowledge would, it was realized, risk shipwreck. Writing in 1964 in the *Furrow*, John A. Dowling warned of the

> . . . ignorance, not only of the facts of Irish religious life, beliefs and sociological change-factors, but of the extent to which these are important and discoverable by modern scientific methods. We have for so long assumed that sociology is a philosophical discipline – merely using experimental data, open to all who are trained to observe – that the absolute intellectual dishonesty of basing judgements on "self-evident" opinions and "principles" escapes us in practice.[60]

It was in fact from the early 1960s that a marked change became evident in the intellectual Catholic periodicals towards an altogether more empirically based sociological concern than had existed hitherto. The problem, defined by David Thornley in 1966 in *Doctrine and Life*, "that religion is both a constant, inasmuch as it is an aspect of habit, and a variable, inasmuch as it is responsive to changing social and intellectual circumstances"[61] became a principal focus of attention in *Christus Rex* (which in 1972 became *Social Studies*) and in other periodicals. Monsignor Jeremiah Newman (who was consecrated Bishop of Limerick in 1974) was perhaps the best known of the clergy who in the period confronted the sociological implications of secularization that seemed to attend urbanization almost everywhere in Europe. In 1971 in an article in *Christus Rex*, he outlined what he thought were the challenges Ireland faced:

> . . . it would be realized that the Common Market countries contain at heart the greatest and most engulfing urban agglomeration that exists in the modern world. Ireland's entry into the

Common Market would bring us face to face with this colossus and its way of life.[62]

Monsignor Newman argued in this essay that the greatest challenge of the decade would be in "the sociocultural sphere" to

. . . construct a new culture in a new context, a culture that will at once be new and relevant in that context and at the same time preserve the best of the old. It means a culture that will be considerably industrial yet without losing what is of lasting value in our rural social fabric. It means a culture that will be considerably international yet without parting with what is of value in our national heritage. It means a culture that will be considerably secular yet without losing our religious persuasions. Our beliefs, it is true, will be less structurally supported, less sociologically conditioned, but they will also be more personal. Our religious vocations will be less institutionally funnelled, less conditioned by employment possibilities, but they will be all the more consciously elected for that.[63]

The sociological investigations of the 1970s tended to confirm Bishop Newman's prognostications. Increased secular opportunities in all probability accounted for the decline in vocations that was noted by researchers. As early as 1966 David Thornley had calculated that however much the Irish church had anticipated urbanization through the establishment of new city parishes and a church-building programme, the demographic developments of modern Ireland were already placing enormous strains on an overburdened clergy. He noted that in 1966 with "4,028 secular and 1,912 regular priests the ratio of clergy to population was 1:707 as compared to a ratio of 1:830 in France,"[64] which bespoke a fairly satisfactory state of affairs. But, he argued, "in certain areas of Ireland there are actually too few priests."[65] The diocese of Dublin appeared peculiarly bereft of the ministrations of the priesthood where the ratio was 1:1,340. So the swift development of Dublin was bound to place serious strains on the church's manpower. Thornley estimated that a decree of one of the Maynooth Synods, which bound every parish priest or his curates to visit each family in his parish once a year, might involve a scrupulous observer of ecclesiastical directives in one of the large Dublin parishes in 2,000 visits a year.

Two studies[66] carried out by the Irish Episcopal Commission for Research and Development in the 1970s clearly showed that in the new Ireland of diverse economic opportunities for young men and women the church's manpower problems could not easily be met. Between 1966 and 1974 vocations to the priesthood and religious life declined from 1,409 in 1966 to 547 in 1974. While the greatest reductions had occurred in vocations to communities of nuns and brothers (declining between 1966 and 1978 by 70 percent and 83 percent respectively), recruits to the diocesan priesthood had also dropped by 31 percent. Between 1975 and 1979, however, vocations to the secular priesthood rose slightly. A new feature in Irish social life was the small, but in the Irish context scarcely insignificant, number of priests seeking laicization. In both 1966 and 1967 only one diocesan priest was laicized. In 1971 there were ten such and in 1975 twenty, though by 1978 the figure had dropped to nine. Research among secondary school-leavers in 1969[67] found that a surprising 80 percent had considered the religious life, but that 54 percent had decided against it, while 20 percent had postponed the decision. The reasons these school-leavers gave for their rejection of a religious life were the severity of the oath of celibacy and the distractions of the secular, consumer society. The figure of 80 percent had dropped to 46 percent, or by almost a half in 1974.[68] A sociologist writing in 1979 reckoned that if the trends of the 1970s continued, and he saw no reason why they should not do so, "the number of those in the priesthood and religious life in Ireland will decrease by a third, to less than 20,000 in the next twenty-five years."[69] The dramatic decline in vocations to the religious orders was reflected in the decreasing involvement of such persons in the Irish educational system, which in the 1970s allowed for a much higher lay profile in the pedagogical sphere. By 1979 only 2,300 out of 10,830 secondary teachers were religious, in schools owned in many cases by the religious orders themselves. There were only 370 priests and brothers still teaching in the National Schools.[70]

Research also confirmed that religious belief, particularly among the well-educated young, had begun to be experienced less as an all-embracing reality within which life must be ordered and as an immutable aspect of Irish national identity than as a personal expression of individual commitments and values. The four-volume "Survey of Religious Practice, Attitudes and Belief" found in 1973–74 that although 90 percent of the Catholic population still attended mass at least once a week, 25 percent of single men and women in the 18–30 age-group had forsaken this religious obligation altogether, while 30 percent of those aged 21–25 had done so. Research among university students in Dublin in 1976 also tended to suggest that the younger generation of Irish men and women had much less homogeneous attitudes to their faith than had often been assumed of Irish people in the past. A sociologist summarizing his findings in this research concluded that "the Christian orientation which emerged . . . is essentially an inner-worldly humanistic perspective."[71] A striking fact was that "one in every seven respondents who was brought up as a Roman Catholic no longer regards himself/herself as such."[72] The strong humanitarian orientation of Irish students' religious faith prompted the writer to question:

Is this evidence that Catholicism among students is losing its supernatural referent and becoming a secularized civil ethic? In other words, although the majority of Catholic students still see themselves primarily as Christians, is this becoming compartmentalized into a religious belief and practice which does not permeate the rest of their daily lives?[73]

Evidence that such was the case was provided by the attitudes of university students to the moral teaching of the church on sexual ethics. Less than one in five of all the respondents to the questionnaire in the 1976 survey believed sex before marriage to be always wrong (44 percent of Catholics seeing exceptions to the general rule) while 58 percent of the Catholic students questioned on the matter thought contraception morally accept-able.[74] In this respect Irish students were merely reflecting in an extreme form the attitudes of Irish Catholics in general in the period. For despite the Irish hierarchy's affirmation of the papal encyclical *Humanae Vitae* (1968), the Survey of 1973–74 cited above had found that 28 percent of Catholics saw contraception as "generally wrong but permissible in certain circumstances." More critically, in the age-group most likely to be most con-cerned by the church's proscription of artificial contraceptives, those of 18–30 years of age, 49 percent of men and 45 percent of women thought it not only morally acceptable but sometimes a responsibility.

Such figures clearly suggested that Bishop Newman's prophecy that Irish society would be "considerably secular" in the future was soundly based. A major proportion of the younger generation was prepared in the 1970s to base its moral perception on things other than the church's official teachings. It is true that Catholics in Ireland were aware that the hierarchies of other countries applied the papal teachings on artificial contraception with less rigour than they were applied in Ireland, but attitudes were also being formed throughout the 1970s by secular, liberal views of individual morality.

In fact much of the pressure for change of the law forbidding the importation of contraceptives came from a small but vocal minority of women who espoused the doctrines of the women's liberation movement (founded, as we saw, in 1970). The Com-mission on the Status of Women had given Irish feminists much ammunition since it revealed how little Ireland had adapted its legal system to accommodate the rising expectations of women in employment and in the home. Since 1972, therefore, the issue of women's rights was consistently debated as women served notice through various action groups that legal restrictions on their freedom of action would no longer be tolerated.[75] Church teaching, with its emphasis on the virtue of motherhood, had been buttressed by the constitutional affirmation of 1937 that "by her life within the home, woman gives to the State a support without which the common good cannot be achieved." Legal force to such pious expression had been effected by a marriage bar in the Civil Service and in local authorities and health boards, which meant that upon marriage a woman resigned from her post. In 1977 the Employment Equality Act made such restrictions on married women in employment illegal. This act represented a major victory by the women's movement in a continuing struggle that challenged the social and religious values traditionally propounded by church and state.

The right of married couples to plan their families by whatever methods they choose was established in a constitutional test case taken by a mother, a Mrs. Mary Magee, in 1972 to the Supreme Court. In 1973 four of the five judges found the constitution's clause protecting privacy infringed by that section of the law which prohibited the importation of contraceptives even for private use by married persons. More dramatically than any other event in the 1970s, this legal case (in which Mrs. Magee was supported by the Irish Family Planning Association) demonstrated that the state would be required to adapt to a changing society where conflicting values were reflected in differing attitudes on moral and social issues. Following the Supreme Court's judgment, a period of intense debate ensued in which the contraception issue became a wearisome, occasionally near-surreal, topic of newspaper letter, article, and report. There were those demanding complete freedom from any legal proscription on contraceptives and those, the indefatigable correspondent Miss Mary Kennedy of the Irish Family League at their head, who appeared to hope an absolute ban could be enforced despite the court's judgment. The fear that contraceptive legislation would be followed by demands for an abolition of the constitutional proscription on divorce was often expressed, and it was argued that abortion would be a subsequent issue on the liberal agenda. And certainly such fears were not groundless. Following the enactment of a Fianna Fáil bill in July 1979, after years of protracted political pusillanimity, which allowed for the sale of contraceptives to married persons in chemists' shops on prescription, vigorous demands that the state should recognize the increasingly alarming facts of Irish marital breakdown began to be heard. But the fact that several thousand young women from Ireland each year sought abortions in the United Kingdom did not at that time produce any significant vocal support for a change in the law in that regard.[76]

The hierarchy responded to the new social context in which it found itself in two ways. First, faced by the particular legal quandary of the Magee case, it cautiously let it be known in 1976 that the state was not bound to enforce "the principles peculiar to our faith" on "people who do not adhere to that faith." The way was cleared thereby for the state to enact legislation which would allow those married persons who claimed the right to use contraceptives to do so, so that the Supreme Court's constitutional judgment could be respected. But the hierarchy had prepared for this legal outcome by issuing in 1975 its pastoral letter *Human Life is Sacred*, which argued strenuously against what it termed "the contraceptive mentality" that "contradicts the Christian understanding of family life"[77] and is a product of modern idolatry in which "money, alcohol, drugs and sex are being given a place and a status in modern secular society which is not too different from the place occupied by the gods of money, wine and sex in pagan times."[78] The Fianna Fáil government act of 1979, which regularized the legal position on contraception, bringing it in line with the Magee judgment, showed, undoubtedly, that the government had taken due account of such ecclesiastical opinion.

Second and more generally, the hierarchy and the church as a whole throughout the 1970s committed itself to religious renewal in the country. The religious curriculum in National Schools was radically revised to bring it in line with the assumptions and methods of the new curriculum introduced by the Department of Education in 1971. Bible study was encouraged at the personal and parish level, as was greater participation by congregations in the liturgical life of the church, expressed since the Second Vatican Council in the vernacular languages. Individual bishops and clergy gave enthusiastic support to a lively charismatic movement.[79]

Hierarchical commitment to religious renewal, grounded as it was in the sociological evidence of the 1970s that Catholic Ireland was scarcely immune to the secularizing tendencies of modern industrial society, was of course reflected most dramatically in the statements issued in preparation for a papal visit of 1979, and possibly in the papal pronouncements themselves. In both these Ireland was called upon to remain steadfast to the old faith, loyal to the Holy See and papal teaching. The traditional means of grace were commended to the people, the lapsed and careless were recalled to their obligations, the historical destiny of the Irish as a Christian and missionary people was reaffirmed, the young were especially challenged to the life of faith, and the evils of secularism and materialism were roundly condemned. Throughout the papal visit itself a sense that the church saw Ireland at a crossroads gave to the occasion an aura of remarkable historical significance. An almost evangelical awareness that for Ireland the hour of decision had struck dominated the few days at the end of September 1979 when Ireland welcomed a Pope for the first time.

If the hierarchy's response to the rapid changes of the 1970s in Ireland was a major commitment to renewal in the hope that Ireland in the 1980s would remain a devoutly Catholic nation, there were those who doubted whether such was possible or even desirable. Voices were raised to question if the Christian message was not devalued by too close an association with any political or social order. It was suggested that the challenge of the modern secular world, increasingly an influence on Irish life, might enforce upon Christians of all denominations a new awareness of the radical nature of their faith and of the need for ecumenicism. The concept of pluralism was introduced to the intellectual Catholic periodicals and recommended as an appropriate mode of thought for understanding the role of church and state in a modern society. For the Christian, a pluralist society was invoked as an opportunity for both witness and humility:

Christians will have to develop more fully the ability to live in tolerance and respect for people who do not share their beliefs. They must not experience these others as a threat to the Christian faith, but as an invitation to dialogue.[80]

Expressed in religious terms, pluralism in Ireland would mean that no longer would religious and national identity coalesce as directly as they had done in the past and that no church could lay claim to be the church of "the people." New political and legal structures would be required to express such pluralist possibilities.

Churchmen who argued in this fashion were of course a very tiny minority,[81] but they were nevertheless expressing in religious terms ideas that had achieved some currency since the 1960s in cultural and political matters as well. As early as 1964 Garret FitzGerald, later to become Ireland's Minister for Foreign Affairs in the coalition government of the 1970s and subsequently leader of Fine Gael and Taoiseach, had made a plea (in terms that would have warmed George Russell's heart) for a recognition that "Irish people today are not the inheritors of a single, clear-cut traditional national philosophy that could serve as a touchstone by which to judge proposals affecting the future of our society." Rather, Ireland was formed by the influence of "a number of . . . streams of thought, all of which have some place in our minds but have not been sorted out nor fused into a coherent and internally consistent philosophy."[82] In the 1970s others dwelled on this theme, and FitzGerald himself published perhaps the most detailed study of its implications for any future unified Irish state in his book *Towards a New Ireland* (1972). Politicians, since the outbreak of violence in Northern Ireland in 1969, had made regular obeisance to the concept of the diversity of cultural and religious traditions on the island, and in 1972 a referendum was held, largely in response to the Northern crisis, which allowed for the painless removal from the Irish Constitution of the clause which spoke of the special position of the Catholic church as "the guardian of the Faith professed by the great majority of the citizens." The citizens of the Republic were perfectly willing to allow such a formal, if vague, expression of the association between national identity and Catholicism quietly to be forgotten.

In the 1970s the introduction of the concept of "pluralism" to Irish intellectual debate would certainly have seemed like a vindication to an earlier solitary thinker like George Russell, who, as we saw, had defended cultural diversity, as a national resource. And although the concept had not yet had the chance to "strike deep roots" in Irish awareness,[83] there were certainly signs in the wind that an essentialist, exclusive conception of Irish identity (Catholic and Gaelic) that had absorbed the twenty-six county state for the first half century of its existence, was weakening its hold on social life and practice. In 1970 the hierarchy relaxed its ban on the attendance of the Catholic faithful at Trinity College, Dublin (in the past a symbol of *ancien régime* Ascendancy Protestantism), allowing the college thereafter to play a central role in the higher education of the nation's young in a way that would have been unthinkable in an earlier generation (the Anglican college chapel there in time became a centre of ecumenical worship). And, at secondary level, Catholics and Protestants were mixing as they had not done before in modern times. The reduction in the Protestant population to about 4 percent (the product of low birth rates, emigration and the Catholic Church's insistence that the offspring of mixed marriages must be raised as Catholics), meant that Protestant schools had places to spare. Catholic parents, especially in Dublin, were only too ready to avail themselves of such opportunities for their children. By the late 1970s 20 percent of pupils in what had become effectively religiously mixed schools were Catholic. As the sociologist Kurt Bowen, who reported on this development, observed:

> Without discounting the class-based attraction of Protestant schools, which has always existed, I would argue that the recent growth in the number of Catholic applicants reflected their desire for a more secular education than that available in their own schools. With their diminished emphasis on denominational instruction and their religious mixture among teachers

and pupils, Protestant secondary schools went a long way to meet this demand.[84]

Bowen also noted how in the 1970s the social isolation of Protestants was giving way, in both urban and rural settings, to co-operative activity in a wide variety of civil institutions, which had once been "almost exclusively Catholic in make-up." He noted that "there seemed to be emerging among both Catholics and Protestants a new secular conviction that religious affiliation should not be a consideration in recreational and special interest activities not directly connected to their parish churches."[85] A further sign of a society attempting to find a way to deal with difference was the emergence of an appreciable demand for multi-denominational primary education, with pilot projects inaugurated in the Dublin area at Marley Grange and Dalkey.

Yet even in the 1970s when these developments were taking place, no new conception of Irish identity was articulated to take account of difference with quite the same persuasive power with which the ideal of a nation free, Gaelic and Catholic had reinforced a dominant homogeneity since 1922. Cultural production in the period, to which we shall turn our attention in the next chapter, suggested a time of transition when no new image of Ireland as other than an economy seeking to modernize itself had achieved definitive form.

CHAPTER 10

Culture and a Changing Society

The debate, controversy, and social analysis that marked intel-lectual life in the Irish Republic in the 1960s and '70s were rooted, as we saw, in a sense that Ireland was undergoing a period of rapid change set in motion by the economic decisions of the late 1950s (a similar sense was to re-emerge in the 1990s, when once again an economic crisis was followed by a period of econ-omic resurgence). It was widely sensed in the 1960s and '70s that the country was altering in radical ways (the degree of change achieved and the degree still necessary were constant topics of conversation, newspaper article, seminar, and conference), and the question as to how much Ireland's traditional identity could be retained in the new circumstances was a major preoccupation of social commentators. The belief that the country was under-going a fundamental transition was given sustenance by the fact that writers and artists, those antennae sensitive to social and cultural change, experienced a period when their relationship with Irish society underwent striking alteration.

It will have been clear from much that has engaged our atten-tion so far that the Irish artists and writers who in the early decades of independence chose to remain in Ireland had two roles available to them. They could furnish the new order with an art, which, whether in its self-conscious nativism or idyllic celebration of the rural folk tradition, would nourish the dominant essentialist ideology of the state; or, disgusted with the unreality of such programmatic artistic endeavours, they might seek to define artistic identity in terms of opposition and dissent. Both choices, however different they were in experience, had in common the fact that the artistic life involved some measurable relationship with society which either welcomed or rejected the artifacts that individuals produced. For the minor writers and artists, content to exploit conventional literary and artistic properties that did not disturb a conservative public taste, Irish society had offered a snugly comfortable provincial milieu where a complacent regionalism could be critically hailed as a national mode. For the writer prepared to employ literature and the profession of letters as weapons of dissent, social obloquy – expressed most often in the crude decisions of the Censorship Board of Publications – involved him or her, until at least the 1940s, in a certain heroism. And writers and artists under pressure can at least persuade themselves that their works count for something.

The economic and social changes of the 1960s and '70s interfered with both kinds of relationship. Obviously for the writer or artist who felt that his or her work bore intimately on traditional Irish ways of life that in indirect ways justified the existence of a separatist Irish state and which that state through its linguistic policy and cultural bias was directly committed to fostering, the period was necessarily dispiriting. It would be difficult to imagine an art that could easily be identified with the central concerns of a society energetically dedicated to economic growth; and many writers and artists, not only those who chose, or would have chosen to celebrate the old order, lamented that social change had dealt a fatal blow to a traditional Ireland that enshrined many irreplaceable values. A writer in *Christus Rex* in 1968 identified that Ireland, as he warned of the assaults it would endure when the country became more prosperous and industrialized. It was things like wedding-sets in country kitchens, of the high-spirited straw-boys at Kerry wren-dances, of the disturbing and primal response to the throb of the West Limerick tambourine. . . . I think of the domestic excitement and the subsequent festivities associated with the annual visit of the priest for the station with everybody sticking to varnish everywhere: of the ritualistic holy-water blessing of the stock on May eve; of the colourful folk-tales once told over rural fires. I think of the thrust and parry of local country conversation, the appreciation of local characters, the haggling over buying and selling and all that makes a happy arabesque in country life. . . . For me, culture means the full, variegated, multi-coloured fabric that is indigenous Irish life.[1]

As the kinds of changes we have discussed earlier took hold of Irish society in the 1960s and '70s, it became less and less possible for writers and artists to celebrate such things as "indigenous Irish life" without evasion or sentimentality. Rather, the new Irish reality was ambiguous, transitional, increasingly urban or suburban, disturbingly at variance with the cultural aspirations of the revolutionaries who had given birth to the state. And if the new Ireland made a naïve, conventional folk art impossible, it also put paid to the artist as cultural hero. For instead of a climate of opinion which allowed the artist to project himself (as Seán O'Faoláin had done, almost as a one-man opposition party in a monolithic state), the new Ireland of debate and controversy made more commonplace the kinds of critique writers almost alone had attempted in earlier years. Furthermore, the increasingly secular, modernized Irish society no longer so readily seemed to provide the dissenting artist with those manifestations of Irish purity, puritanism, and repression that had provided the angry novelist and playwright with distinctive material for the inconoclastic realism which had once found a curious readership abroad. As Irish life seemed to become more and more like urban and suburban life everywhere else in the developed world, both the pressures on artists and the uniqueness of their subject matter lessened in ways which rendered their role more complex.

Certainly the 1960s and '70s saw changes which writers and artists in Ireland could not but welcome. Among such changes were the recognition that the state must patronize the arts (however niggardly that patronage in fact was) and that literature in English (as well as in Irish) by Irish men and women is an indigenous Irish literature, worthy of support. This latter acknowledgement had been made public in the government White Paper on the Irish language in 1965 when it was stated that "competent knowledge of English will be needed even in a predominantly Irish-speaking Ireland" because English provides access to "the large body of Irish literature written in English and to the prose, poetry, songs and speeches in which Irish national aspirations have to a large extent been expressed."[2] In 1968 the then Minister for Finance, Charles Haughey, announced that he was considering a major reorganization of the Arts Council. Although the Arts Council was not in fact restructured until 1973, it was in 1969 that the same minister was responsible for the enactment of legislation that permitted writers and artists to avoid paying income tax on royalties earned from their creative work. The Arts Council between 1951 and 1973 had concerned itself largely with the performing and plastic arts, but after the legislation of 1973 (which permitted the council to establish a number of sub-committees and to appoint new officers), literature attracted greater financial support. In 1975 the council provided bursaries for the first time to four writers,[3] apportioning £7,500 between them, and in 1978 seven writers were awarded bursaries from a total of £20,000. When, however, it is realized that of an overall budget of £1.5 million for the arts in 1978 only £43,853 was spent on literature, it can be seen that the Irish state's support for its writers remained at a fairly minimal level. Nevertheless, support of any kind made a welcome change from earlier years when literature was scarcely acknowledged. In 1977 the Arts Council in an imaginative enterprise began a programme to allow writers to visit secondary, vocational, and comprehensive schools in counties Clare, Limerick, and North Tipperary. The following year the plan was extended, in cooperation with the Arts Council of Northern Ireland, to cover schools in the island as a whole. Over 140 writers in Irish and English declared their willingness, in the *Directory of Writers, 1978/9*, to pay school visits to read from their work and to discuss it with pupils. Again this was a highly welcome development of a kind that could not have taken place in earlier years, when a wrong-headed censorship made most writers highly suspect in the eyes of those charged with the education of the young.

Other changes improved the lot of the Irish writer. In part supported by Arts Council subvention and very much the result of energetic commitment by individuals, a small Irish publishing industry established itself. Liam Miller, who founded the Dolmen Press in 1951, showed the way and in his high standards of design and production, together with his commitment to Irish poets such as Austin Clarke, John Montague, and Thomas Kinsella, revived a tradition that had died with the closure of the Maunsel and Roberts publishing house in 1926 (Austin Clarke had published with Maunsel). In the 1960s and '70s Miller was joined by such individuals as Peter Fallon (whose Gallery Press became the foremost publisher of poetry in the country), Michael Smith and John F. Deane. Publication of fiction and criticism was also being undertaken by a variety of new and established imprints which in the early 1970s began to make their way in the world of letters. CLÉ, the Irish Publishers' Association, in 1979 numbered sixty members (including members from Northern Ireland), and the activities of Irish publishers were reported on in a lively monthly periodical, *Books Ireland*. Amazingly, Peter Fallon showed that an Irish publisher can stay in business while principally publishing poetry. In the 1970s he published over seventy volumes of poems, plays and stories. Perhaps equally remarkable were the exploits of Philip McDermott and David Marcus of Poolbeg Press, who demonstrated that there was a market for Irish fiction, particularly for collections of short stories. It was also David Marcus, as literary editor of the daily newspaper the *Irish Press*, who in 1968 began to edit the weekly page of new Irish writing in that broadsheet which, since that date, gave many new, as well as established, writers an opportunity to present their work to an Irish readership. All this activity meant that for the first time since the heyday of the Literary Revival, an Irish writer had a choice of whether to seek publication in Ireland or abroad, though severe problems in the international distribution of poetry and fiction remained if he or she chose an Irish imprint.

Not only had a burgeoning publishing industry provided opportunities to Irish writers which even ten years earlier had not existed, but events like the Yeats International Summer School, mounted in Sligo each summer since 1960, the Listowel Writers Week, held each summer in County Kerry, and the Merriman Summer School held each August in County Clare and dedicated to the Gaelic literary and cultural tradition, all allowed writers the opportunity to read their works in public and gave literature a publicity, even if of a superficial kind, not enjoyed in the immediate past. Furthermore, as we noted earlier, contemporary literature played its part in schoolroom and university, and current Irish writers had their work represented in school anthologies and discussed in the academic journals. There were also more bookshops in the country. Indeed, many medium-sized towns now boasted a bookshop in which works by Irish authors received well-advertised shelf space.[4] Small literary magazines, often the work of groups of young people, sprang up and lived for a few editions as in other parts of the English-speaking world, indicating that a good deal of literary ambition existed.

Nevertheless, for the writer the period was essentially problematic. The public roles which had stimulated the most serious writers in the post revolutionary period, compact of isolation or exile and heroic dissent, seemed no longer appropriate or indeed possible. Nor was a public art of any kind (whether critical or celebratory), for the writer most often experienced a sense of dissociation from the ways in which society presently defined itself. His or her own private obsessions and the social world he or she inhabited were oddly at variance, and no ideology or coherently enabling Irish literary tradition offered modes of thought and feeling to bridge the gap. And he or she could neither achieve the sane sceptical balance of Austin Clarke's mature social analysis nor the sense of individual liberation in a provincial society which was the essence of Patrick Kavanagh's late achievement. Accordingly the predominant poetic form in the 1960s and '70s was the lyric of personal, often painful, psychic exploration, in which the poet sought significance in immediacy of the self rather than in mediated political and historical experience or in any kind of coherent philosophy. The poet Thomas Kinsella, writing in 1966, defined the mood which he thought was general in postwar Europe:

> The most sensitive individuals have been shaken loose from society into disorder, conscious of a numbness and dullness in themselves, a pain of dislocation and loss. . . . Everywhere in modern writing the stress is on personal visions of the world. . . . The detailed exploration of private miseries is an expedition into the interior to find out what may guide us in the future. It is out of ourselves and our wills that the chaos comes, and out of ourselves that some order must be constructed.[5]

Private life was the primary concern of novelists in the period too. Following the decades when Irish novelists felt themselves peculiarly bound to employ the novel and the short story as the tools of surgical analysis of an apparently diseased Irish reality, and when that reality provided them with a ready if narrowly intense subject matter, the 1960s and '70s, with their more liberal and even indifferent climate and their more varied social scene, allowed novelists to reflect on individual human experience rather than on the distinctive oddities of Irish life. While their new circumstances necessarily reduced their sense of immediate social significance, the retreat to privacy in Irish fiction, in which the local environment could be taken for granted (inasmuch as recent social changes had reduced its uniqueness), bore fruit in work of a more variegated emotional and psychic weather than was the case in earlier years. That familiar figure of twentieth-century Irish fiction, the adolescent young man discovering the all-encompassing nets of religion, nation, and family and seeking to escape the oppressive constraints of Irish society still appeared, but with less frequency. Other, more interesting characters now peopled the pages of current Irish fiction. And in these pages, as the critic Maurice Harmon remarked, "the emphasis [was] not so much on the nature of the environment as on the private graph of feeling within the individual person."[6]

The Irish dramatist in an even more obvious fashion than the poet or novelist benefited from the improved economic climate. The new Abbey Theatre in Dublin, which was completed in 1966, was fairly well supported by state funds and from 1971 onward a revivified Gate Theatre also attracted state support.[7] Theatres like the Focus and the theatre associated with the Dublin Project Arts Centre could also depend on public support, as could the annual Dublin Theatre Festival. The 1970s were notable therefore as the period when Irish theatre attracted a greater degree of public financial support than it had ever done before.

Like the poet and novelist, Irish dramatists found the new context both an opportunity and a challenge. Granted indirect support for creative work in a way that was unthinkable until then, they nevertheless felt their role to be much less clear than it had been in the past. Indeed the 1940s and '50s in Ireland had been years when Irish drama, despite some signs of life, had been conventional to a degree that even the realistic novel and short story had not been. In those years various Irish dramatists had satisfied a public taste at the Abbey Theatre for kitchen comedies and well-made plays of small-town Irish life. One critic designated those decades as the period when "formula triumphed over talent,"[8] and the playwright Hugh Leonard in a caustic phrase dismissed them as the era of "parish-pump Ibsenism" when "Irish theatre . . . concerned itself with Irishmen first and men later."[9] What characterized many of these plays was an underlying complacency shared by playwrights and audience alike that the society depicted, despite the frequent grotesqueries of action they presented, was fundamentally sound. By the late 1960s and '70s it was obvious that such conventional drama, with its complacent message for a complacent audience was, not before time, entirely moribund.

In its place came an effort on the part of such dramatists as Brian Friel, Thomas Murphy, and Thomas Kilroy to discover new themes and to exploit new theatrical techniques. Christopher Murray in his thoughtful essay, "Irish Drama in Transition 1966–1978," identified four aspects in which drama in this period in Ireland broke new ground: sexual themes were treated with explicit frankness; religion was explored "radically, as a metaphysical rather than as a socially conservative question";[10] an embryonic working-class theatre brought political commitment on to the Irish stage; and the explosive issue of Irish republicanism and the Northern conflict charged some Irish plays with immediate and painful contemporaneity. Dramatists were attentive to the development of modern European and American theatre in their efforts to renew Irish drama. A "rather restless search after innovation"[11] in fact characterized theatrical life, particularly in the 1970s.

Painters and sculptors enjoyed a new if often superficial regard amid the comparative affluence of the period. The work of the Irish Living Art Exhibitions from the 1940s onward had created a small body of private patrons, willing to collect Irish paintings in the modern mode. The Exhibitions displayed the work of Irish artists alongside that of their European contemporaries, thereby playing a critical educational role. The fruits of this were that when a new affluent middle class, in the 1960s and '70s, chose to express its social dominance and self-esteem through the purchase and possession of art works, the modern idiom in which most Irish artists to one degree or another wished to work had become widely acceptable (in a way which was not the case with literature and drama) and had indeed been touched by the gloss of fashion. Commercial art galleries were established in city and suburb; exhibition openings were attended by politicians and a public anxious for cultural respectability, and amid much crass commercialism, individuals and institutions (among them the Arts Council, Trinity College, Dublin, the banks, and the cigarette manufacturers, P. J. Carroll Ltd.) assembled carefully selected collections of contemporary Irish painting. For the individual artists, this new public awareness of their activities meant that, although it remained desperately hard to make any kind of decent living solely through painting or sculpting in Ireland,[12] at least there was the chance that their work would be purchased and might indeed be exhibited in Ireland.

What the collections of Irish paintings in the period revealed was that since the 1930s, and particularly since the early 1940s, Irish art had been notable for a range, diversity, and energy that became fully clear only when such collections were assembled and when art critics and historians began the novel and difficult task of assessment and explanation.[13] This work of assembly and of criticism of recent or current art (which we detected in embryo in the periodical *Envoy*) established the general, historical outlines of a flourishing modern Irish art in which many individual artists who began work in the 1930s and '40s were joined in the late 1960s and '70s by a further generation of younger painters and sculptors. But no clear-cut school or national mode emerged despite the efforts of some critics to discern such.

Most of this new work, however, did not make an impact beyond Irish shores. For modern art in Ireland lacked both critical mass and the kind of institutional presence that would have allowed Irish painters and sculptors to have seen their work exhibited as of right alongside that of their international contemporaries in the galleries of London, Paris and New York. The Hugh Lane Municipal Gallery of Modern Art in Dublin largely rested on the laurels it had gained with the Lane bequest and lacked the will to raise the profile of Irish modern art beyond Irish shores. It was the *Rosc* (Irish for "the poetry of vision") exhibitions in Dublin which by the end of the period had begun to place art in Ireland on the kind of international stage Irish literature in English had enjoyed since the era of Joyce and Yeats (in the 1960s and '70s the flood of Joyce and Yeats criticism, particularly in North America, was in full spate). For these exhibitions managed to attract international publicity and attention

o the practice of art in Ireland in a way that had scarcely occurred
efore in the century.

Initially the *Rosc* exhibitions – brainchild of the architect
Michael Scott – did not include modern Irish artists, but the
presentation of the work of internationally renowned artists
alongside artifacts from Irish antiquity was enormously inspiring
or many younger artists in the country and exciting for visiting
critics and viewers alike. The first *Rosc* exhibition, which ran from
October 1967 until January 1968 in a large space in the Royal
Dublin Society in Ballsbridge in Dublin and in the National
Museum, attracted large numbers of visitors to see work by "the
most famous living artists of the time."[14] A second *Rosc* was
mounted in 1971 to critical acclaim as a rhythm of about four-
yearly events was set in motion. In 1980 Irish artists took a
substantial place for the first time in the exhibition of that year,
which meant that their work came to the attention of international critics who visited Dublin for the Congress of the International Association of Art Critics meeting in Dublin at the time
of the exhibition.

The changed relationship of Irish writers and artists with their
society which we have been examining, did therefore seem to
suggest that real social changes were afoot in the country. No
longer did artists and writers find themselves able or willing to
work in anything like a distinctive national mode, nor did they
feel themselves able to mount a social criticism of a society with
clearly defined targets for attack.

Paradoxically, this disinclination on the part of artists and
writers to fulfil clearly defined social and national roles coexisted
with demands that they do so. As Irish people began to sense
their changing circumstances, and as the Northern crisis challenged much that they had taken for granted about the national
life, it was the artist and particularly the writer who was often
expected to provide some kind of guidance as to the way forward.
Writers were therefore asked to reflect quite specifically on their
intuitive sense of the substance of Irish identity and on how that
bore on the struggle in the North. But with very few exceptions,

most writers were wholly resistant to the demand that they
provide anything like answers to the kinds of questions which
were (as we saw) debated so strenuously. Rather, they resolutely
continued to explore the private worlds of their own obsessions,
regarding their work in the context of modern literature as a
whole, and at most offered experimental works (the sequence of
poems of John Montague and Thomas Kinsella, *The Rough Field*
and *Nightwalker*; the experimental novels of Francis Stuart, *Memorial* and *A Hole in the Head*, the plays of Brian Friel, are all
examples) which suggested the complex, variegated, transitional
nature of Irish experience.

So if, as Thomas Kilroy remarked, Irish writing had as a recurrent theme "not so much the experience of participating in
modern life as the anguished process of adapting to it, given a
quite dissimilar and distant starting-point,"[15] it was only inasmuch
as private life was marked by that anguish. And in admitting this
theme to their work, most writers had little desire to attempt any
new full-scale restatement of Irish national life which would relate
private experience to public definitions of identity, despite hopes
that they would do so. In fact some of them vigorously rejected
that possibility. "Let us be rid at last," wrote the poet Eavan
Boland, for example,

> . . . of any longing for cultural unity, in a country whose most
> precious contribution may be precisely its insight into the
> anguish of disunity; let us be rid of any longing for imaginative
> collective dignity in a land whose final and only dignity is indi-
> viduality.
>
> For there is, and at last I recognize it, no unity whatsoever
> in this culture of ours. And even more important, I recognize
> that there is no need whatsoever for such unity. If we search
> for it we will, at a critical moment, be mutilating with fantasy
> once again the very force we should be liberating with reality.'[16]

II

If therefore Irish writers and artists fought shy of attempting any too explicit exploration of the theme of national identity in the 1960s and '70s, a concern with the relationship of the arts and the social order by contrast characterized much literary and cultural discussion. Indeed, from the 1960s onwards critics frequently pondered whether or not current writing and art reflected the changing, increasingly urban facts of Irish experience and if any traditional or novel form of national identity could be discerned as a unifying influence on the variegated artistic productions of the period. The critic Seamus Deane (who provided some of the most stimulating analyses of the relationship of literature and society in this period)[17] cast a cold eye on these possibly self-indulgent and certainly repetitive cultural dialectics. He did so in terms which might easily have been extended to include all the kinds of issues – social, political, and religious – that we touched on in the preceding chapter, as well as those that have concerned us in this one. Reflecting on a series of articles in two issues of a recently founded critical periodical, in which a succession of young critics and scholars had addressed themselves to the problem of tradition and identity in Irish literature, Deane felt himself driven to a reductive questioning of such preoccupations. Perhaps they were merely a reactionary response (though sometimes couched in the rhetoric of radicalism) to the all too real social and ideological difficulties which arose when an oversimplified anachronistic conception of Irish identity and history was found no longer to fit experience in an Ireland confronted by the Northern crisis and by "the problem of adjusting a hard-won, single-minded version of Irish identity to the complex realities of modern Europe."[18] They may have been over-literary forms of consolation, evasions, refusals to face Ireland's actual problems and revolutionary needs. "We may," suggested Deane, "be defending a new status quo in the delusion that we are radically revising an old tradition."[19] Debates about literary and artistic culture could be, he argued, forms of nostalgia for a period when it seemed literature and art had explicit roles in defining Irish identity itself or in heroically resisting suppression, before rapid social change forced writers and artists to the periphery of society.

Perhaps, however, as Deane himself allowed, the matter was not so depressingly simple. For it is possible to read such discussions about Irish identity, conducted in literary and artistic terms, as merely particular expressions of a more general intellectual current that only began to flow with any real vigour in Ireland in the 1970s. This I take to be a steadily increasing urge toward an informed Irish self-understanding, a critical concern for origins and for contemporary fact and a desire to comprehend and accept modern Ireland in its fullness which marked Irish intellectual life in the latter four decades of the century. It was in the 1960s and '70s, as we noted, that the historiographical revolution, begun in the 1930s, bore its real harvest. Economic and social history began to be added to constitutional and political history as foci of historical concern. In social anthropology and social geography, the pioneering work of Arensberg and Kimball was being followed by further studies of Irish social patterns. The artistic and literary traditions attracted increasing numbers of Irish historians and critics. The study of religion admitted sociology as a tool and the literary imagination as a guide. At a popular level, books and pamphlets about Irish craftwork, folklore, music, design, architecture, shop fronts, town planning, and natural history raised Irish self-awareness to an informed level it had not possessed in the early decades of independence. In a country that remained small and intimate in scale, there was a new openness to the inheritance of the past which had rejected much of the prejudice and many of the entrenched attitudes so characteristic of earlier decades. A healthy eclecticism was characteristic of the contemporary cultural scene, and a youthful enthusiasm remained a principal feature of the social atmosphere in a country that still reckoned itself one of the ex-colonial nations at the beginning of its life. With a confidence bred of twenty years of economic improvement, large numbers of young people were expectant o worthwhile future and dismissive of the ideological constraints that in more hesitant years had inhibited cultural and social experiment.

So, when Seamus Deane wrote in 1979 that "there is no emergent, systematic and organic reformulation either of Irish tradition, Irish dilemmas, or Irish problems,"[20] he was underestimating, I think, the significance of much activity in various humanistic fields of study in the 1960s and '70s. The body of work which would in the 1980s and '90s allow the concept of Irish Studies to gain national and international academic credibility was beginning to be published (by the 1990s the literature on Ireland's cultural and historical inheritance had increased exponentially). This was characterized by a new sense of proportion, bred of an awareness of historical and archaeological time, a sense of duration (this has been especially true of the human geographers) and by comparative perspectives and a disinclination to adapt findings to any immediate national imperative.

The change in consciousness of Irish identity that such work represented gave expression indeed to a kind of practical pluralism, in which a deepening knowledge of the country's diverse and complex past and present could act as a sustaining resource amid the challenges that lay ahead.

PART IV

1980–2002

CHAPTER 11

The Uncertain 1980s

I

In 1977 Fianna Fáil came to power when the electorate dismissed a coalition government that had in the last stages of its
administration become increasingly unpopular. Jack Lynch, the
leader of the party, formed his government with a majority that
exceeded any he might have expected. Lynch's electoral success
was undoubtedly in part caused by the widespread dislike several
of Liam Cosgrave's ministers (Cosgrave, as we saw, was Taoiseach
in the Fine Gael/Labour coalition government) had managed to
draw upon themselves during his government's term of office. It
was also a vote of public approval for the highly ambitious economic programme that Fianna Fáil had proposed for the nation
in the hustings. Such immediate matters as the removal of rates
on domestic dwellings and the abolition of road tax for private
cars were the irresistible leader items of an economic package
that would, it was hoped, through creating demand by tax cuts
and investing foreign borrowings in profitable enterprises, lead
to full employment and economic boom. A key and, as it turned
out, crippling element in the plan that was detailed in the government's White Paper of 1977, *National Development, 1977–1980*,

was heavy dependence on foreign borrowing. An Irish economist reflected in 1984 on this huge governmental wager with the economic well-being of the country at stake:

> It was a brave strategy but a risky one. It gambled on continued growth in the rest of the world; and it gambled on Irish workers being willing to accept lower wage increases than our competitor countries, so that we could increase our share of growing world trade. Regrettably, both bets lost. In particular, the second oil crisis of 1979 plunged the Western World into the worst recession since before the Second World War. Our exports faltered but imports, fuelled by foreign borrowing, continued to grow.[1]

By 1980 the effects of this lost economic wager were beginning to make themselves felt. As the decade proceeded, the economic recession grew into a full-blown crisis.

Indicators of how this economic crisis gathered and deepened in the early 1980s were readily available and made grim reading as they reflected even grimmer realities. Between 1979 and 1981 unemployment rose by 77 percent and, at 160,000 people in the latter year, seemed already dangerously high.[2] By December 1984, however, it would reach 208,000 which represented 16.4 percent of the workforce (well ahead of the overall EEC figure of 10.3 percent).[3] What was almost as disturbing was that roughly one-quarter of those in employment were public servants and therefore not directly involved in the creation of wealth (public service employment rose by 13 percent between 1977 and 1981). And almost a third of the unemployed were under twenty-five years of age.

These figures would have been alarming enough, given the youthful nature of Ireland's demographic profile. But when set beside the galloping increases that had occurred since 1979 in the Republic's foreign indebtedness, a sense of the perilous economic position in which the state found itself was overwhelming.

As recently as 1974, Ireland had been a creditor nation. In 1977 net foreign debt (when external reserves had been

ducted) stood at only £78 million. In 1978 that figure rose to
97 million, and in 1979 it exceeded £1,000 million. At the
d of 1983 it had reached the frightening figure of £6,703
illion. In fact, the state's foreign debts doubled between 1980
d 1981 and doubled once more between 1981 and 1983, and
uch of the money made available by this borrowing went to
nd current spending, little finding its way into profitable and
nployment-generating enterprises. Furthermore, since 1979 –
hen the Republic of Ireland chose to enter the European monet-
y system, despite Britain's refusal to do so, thereby breaking
e historic link with sterling – the Irish punt had declined against
erling and, more strikingly, against the dollar, keeping import
sts high.

The social results of this depressing economic picture were not
r to seek. An EEC report revealed that in the Ireland of 1983
e million people were dependent to some extent on social
elfare payments, and for 700,000 people they represented the
ain source of income. With emigration to the UK – the tra-
tional "safety valve" for Ireland in the twentieth century –
ndesirable because of the severely depressed British economy,
d unemployment and the social deprivation these social welfare
atistics highlighted so prevalent, it is not surprising that the
epublic suffered a disturbing rise in criminality. Dublin in par-
cular in the early 1980s experienced an epidemic of petty lar-
ny, housebreaking and street "muggings" which persuaded
any citizens to remain in the suburbs in the evenings for fear
walking the city-centre thoroughfares. And parts of the city of
imerick, which suffered much following the closure of the Fer-
nka mechanical engineering plant in 1977, at times resembled
e "no go" areas of the troubled ghettos of Northern Ireland.
he startling statistic that in some Dublin suburbs the crime rate
d been rising by more than 50 percent a year[4] was symptomatic
the systemic malaise that afflicted Irish society in the 1980s.
too was the steady increase in drug abuse among the young,
e extent of which is revealed in the following grim statistics.
Dublin the main drug advisory centre was at the Jervis Street

Hospital. In 1979 the number of patients attending this centr
was 415. By 1982 the figure had risen to 1,307, of whom 85
were new patients; in 1983 it reached 1,515 of whom 841 wer
new patients. Such figures of course related only to those seekin
treatment and at one particular hospital. Crime statistics agai
fill out the picture. In 1965 only two people were charged i
the state with drug offences. In 1970, seventy-one people wer
charged. In 1983 this figure had reached 1,822.[5]

Through the 1970s, although in an increasing population th
marriage rate declined somewhat, the numbers of young wome
embarking upon matrimony rose. After 1980 a decline was note
in the proportion of women aged between twenty and twenty
four years who were married. And the number of births, whic
had been climbing steadily in the previous decade, fell from 74,38
in 1980 to 66,802 in 1983. Demographers suggested that it woul
not be rash to attribute these fluctuations to the direct effects o
the recession. In the prevailing economic climate it seemed tha
marriages were being postponed and families restricted.[6]

If the recession touched people's lives in this most person
way it also affected general public perceptions of the conditio
of the country. In the early 1980s a sense developed among soci
commentators and analysts that the end of the 1970s was th
end of an era in Ireland, and this view may have reflected a
emerging public consensus. It was felt that the period inaugurate
by Seán Lemass in the late 1950s had somehow drawn to a clos
the energies released then, finally exhausted, the modes of actio
stimulated by these no longer effective. Desmond Fennell's *T*
State of the Nation: Ireland Since the Sixties, published in 198
caught, in its depressed insistence on the need for national reas
sessment of the previous two decades, something of this ne
mood. Fennell characterized the state of the national psyche
a punch-drunk confusion:

> As we passed through the recessions of the '70s and early '80s,
> with the government borrowing wildly to keep the party going
> somehow, while unemployment grew weekly and the North
> rumbled on, people seemed dazed, like sleep-walkers, and were

afraid to think. Chatter about unemployment, wages and prices, the bankruptcy of the public finances, political scandals, divorce and abortion, and Northern violence filled the air.[7]

For Fennell the underlying Irish problem was the lack of a satisfactory, workable self-image after the economic and social change of the 1960s and '70s had destroyed the once serviceable version of the national identity of Ireland as Gaelic, Catholic, and republican.

In 1982 the Institute of Public Administration devoted an issue of its quarterly periodical *Administration* to a collection of articles considering the Irish experience of government since 1957. This work was subsequently reissued in volume form under the title *Unequal Achievement: The Irish Experience, 1957–82*. The editor in his preface precisely expressed the sense of an era concluded and of a new, more difficult period waiting in the wings:

> The Irish economy is in recession. Unemployment is rising and the social problems which follow from economic stagnation are growing. Despondency seems to be on the increase, as though the intractability of our problems had at last sapped our will to solve them. It is difficult to avoid recalling the grim fifties, the last severe economic depression.[8]

Other contributors shared their editor's impression that a failure of nerve and will was putting the country at risk. The historian Joseph Lee noted that "the ship of state seems to have begun to drift increasingly out of control, in rather rudderless fashion in recent years,"[9] while two sociologists, David B. Rottman and Philip J. O'Connell, observed:

> It is striking that today, in contrast to the late 1950s, there is no confidence in Ireland's ability to control its future. No new organisations are being proposed to assist in the task of national development and the experts can only warn of the limits to what state policy can achieve.[10]

Another contributor, Thomas J. Barrington, saw national shipwreck ahead: "We have chosen to drift steadily towards disaster,"[11] while Tom Garvin reflected on an "exhaustion of political ideas."[12]

Contributory to, and perhaps in part expressive of, the despondency of this volume was its analytic awareness of the ways in which the social progress Ireland had enjoyed in the previous two decades had created new problems without always solving the old ones. Swift changes in the class composition of the Irish workforce, identified by Rottman and O'Connell, had, since they were incomplete, left behind a residue of marginal people stranded in the course of industrial development. Such people, small farmers and unskilled labourers, comprised a social group for whom the "only European parallels ... [were] in Greece, Portugal and Spain."[13] Furthermore, the educational revolution of the late 1960s and '70s had in fact produced a remarkably well-qualified population of young people. Between 1964 and 1979 there had been a two-thirds increase in participation rates in tertiary-level education.[14] But research made clear that it had been the upper middle and middle class who had chiefly benefited from the vastly increased public expenditure on secondary- and tertiary-level education (between 1970 and 1979 expenditure on education as a whole increased by 100 percent in real terms).[15] As Rottman and O'Connell reported, "middle-class dominance is strongly evident at the Leaving Certificate standard and in the late 1970s nearly three-quarters of children of members of the major professions entered a third-level institution, in contrast to less than 4 per cent of the children of unskilled workers."[16] And in 1984 an Economic and Social Research Institute study showed that, in Dublin, movement from the working class to the professional class was twice as less likely than in England and Wales.[17] Its findings tended to confirm Rottman's and O'Connell's observation that "the educational system today is a barrier to social mobility."[18]

From 1979 to the mid-1980s persistent political instability meant that various administrations found it remarkably difficult to respond appropriately to the rapidly worsening economic and social problems of the country. In 1979 Charles Haughey, who had spent almost a decade in the political wilderness after his acquittal in the Arms Trial, made a successful bid for the leadership of Fianna Fáil. In the period since his electoral triumph of 1977 Jack Lynch had found his majority something of a handicap for it apparently allowed his party the opportunity to change the leadership without unduly damaging political consequences. In fact the acrimony which Haughey's 1979 victory set loose meant that the party would not thereafter achieve an overall majority in a general election, and that disappointed and dissident elements would break away to form a new party, the Progressive Democrats (founded in November 1985).

In his first period in power, Haughey, who brought with him a reputation for decisive political action, seemed strangely immobilized by the tensions within the party. In June 1981, following a general election, he surrendered power to a coalition of Fine Gael and Labour (which depended on the support of a number of independents) led by Garret FitzGerald. FitzGerald's tenure of office was short. Exuding fiscal rectitude, he determined to rescue the public finances but was unable to retain the parliamentary support of crucial independents. His government's budget of early 1982, with its wide-ranging assault upon the national debt, included putting VAT on clothing and footwear. This was to apply even to children's shoes, on the almost Swiftian and certainly very unpopular grounds that since women with small feet could buy children's shoes and so avoid tax, children's shoes must in equity be taxed.

The election of February 1982 produced no majority, though Haughey managed to assemble sufficient parliamentary votes, including that of a crucial independent, to form a government. It was a less than secure arrangement which lasted only to the end of a year in which Haughey's administration was bedevilled by a series of accidents and scandals. These did much damage to the reputation Haughey had retained throughout the 1970s for adroit and commanding leadership. Following a further general election, Fine Gael and Labour entered upon a new coalition in December 1982 which again brought FitzGerald to power.

Although this government managed to hold office until January 1987, its freedom of action in tackling the economic crisis was hampered by divisions between its Fine Gael and Labour members, and its stability, too, frequently appeared in doubt.

Indeed, the problem of how effectively to redress the country's economic difficulties in a context of electoral uncertainty dogged all the governments that had exercised power since 1979. The need to maintain public popularity in a period of political instability scarcely allowed for the application of painful remedies. FitzGerald's government's budget in early 1982 was one such effort to restore the public finances to some order, but it foundered on the rock of political misjudgment. During Haughey's administrations, policy followed an erratic course based, as it seemed to be, on an optimistic faith in an inevitable economic resurgence, punctured by bouts of fiscal realism. Towards the end of his second term of office, Haughey, through his government's economic policy document *The Way Forward*, seemed at last to have seriously reckoned with the inevitability of a protracted period of austerity. That plan, however, was shelved on Fitz-Gerald's return to power, though the strict budgets which followed did not contradict its basic conclusions, and in a national plan of 1984 the coalition government outlined a strategy for an economic recovery based on the assumption that public spending could not be sustained at then current levels.

In a society in which so large a proportion of the population was young and in which that population was increasing (one study suggested that between 1979 and 1989 the population of the Republic might increase by half a million)[19], the stresses on the educational system were severe. Both Fianna Fáil and the coalition, in its second term of office, sought to confront the challenge of educational needs and priorities. In December 1980 Fianna Fáil issued a White Paper on educational development. Such a document had long been awaited; in the end it seemed an inadequately considered one, swiftly produced to redeem an electoral pledge. The Minister for Education's foreword, in the guise of open-mindedness, appeared apologetically aware that in many areas the White Paper could not form the basis of administrative action; he insisted that "it is nowise intended that the proposals of this White Paper be regarded as rigid or inflexible."[20] On key issues – the difficulties encountered by pupils transferring from child-centred primary schools to subject-orientated secondary schools, the necessity for curricular expansion in the secondary schools, and the need for reorganization of the universities – the White Paper only could refer to the work of existing committees (which would report in due time), propose new committees, or await new legislation (in fact it took until the late 1990s for a new Universities Act to give independent university status to the constituent colleges of the National University of Ireland at Dublin, Cork, Galway and Maynooth, and a broad revision of the secondary curriculum and examination system remains to be effected). Inasmuch as it expressed any real educational philosophy, it was one in which technology was regarded as a social panacea without which an economy cannot thrive (and it was technology rather than scientific research and development that was emphasized). The context of education was conceived of primarily as the economy, the arts being associated with leisure. There was no apparent awareness that technological innovation can depend on the creative energy of society in general and on a culture in which respect for the achievements of science as an intellectual avocation is encouraged.

The coalition's response to the educational demands of the 1980s, documented in the Minister for Education's *Programme for Action in Education 1984–87*, was similarly lacking in philosophic resource. Indeed, it was expressly stated therein that it would be inappropriate to formulate any philosophy of education in the context of the programme. The pragmatic, cost-accounting approach to educational needs was matched in this document by the same simplistic view of the relationship between technology and the economy that had characterized Fianna Fáil's 1980 White Paper. If in the 1960s the *Investment in Education* report was representative of an era in which the immensity of the tasks at hand had provoked enthusiastic optimism, in the 1980s the

Programme for Education may well have represented in its depressingly cost-conscious way an era of retrenchment and reduced vision. Yet the need to tackle educational deficiencies was acknowledged, as was the awareness that the future would depend more on technological skills in a young workforce than on the traditional sector of agriculture and related activities.

II

While the various governments that held power until 1987 seemed almost mesmerized into legislative inactivity by the magnitude of the social and economic challenges they faced, one problem, that of Northern Ireland, forced itself upon their attention in irresistible ways. Inactivity was not an option. A problem that throughout the 1970s seemed as if it could be contained and perhaps resolved, largely within the framework of the six counties of Northern Ireland, no longer appeared so. For the electoral successes of Sinn Féin (the party which provided direct political support for the Provisional IRA guerrilla campaign against the British administration of Northern Ireland) in Northern Ireland itself gave sharp notice that the Northern Catholic nationalist minority there was in a deeply alienated mood, disinclined after a decade of political disillusionment to give permanent, unquestioned support to moderate constitutional politicians whose moderation had won few tangible concessions and had brought no obvious benefits to their constituents.

It was not only changes in the political climate in the North which stimulated a quickening involvement in the problem in the Republic. The accession to the office of Taoiseach of Charles Haughey was sufficient for that. Throughout the 1970s Fianna Fáil under Jack Lynch had maintained a bipartisan approach with the opposition and the coalition government. This had broadly sought to encourage a power-sharing devolved administration in Northern Ireland, with some links of association with the Irish parliament, and had resolutely attempted to avoid embroiling the

Southern state in anything which might import violence to its territory. Haughey partly came to power in Fianna Fáil because an influential section of the party believed that a stronger, more full-blooded expression of the traditional republican nationalist stance on partition was essential. Enough others in the party were sufficiently unhappy with Ireland's economic performance after Lynch returned to power in 1977 to allow Haughey his chance in office, remembering his successful period as Minister for Finance in the 1960s.

Haughey lost little time in making clear that the days of comfortable bipartisanship were over. In February 1980, at his first party conference as leader, he put it on record that in his view Northern Ireland had failed as a political entity. He declared it as his policy that he would seek to resolve the problem in direct talks with the British government. The issue would be shifted from the Northern-Irish context to a British-Irish one. Accordingly, Haughey met the British Prime Minister, Margaret Thatcher, in London in May 1980 and at Dublin Castle on 8 December of the same year. This second meeting, which the British Foreign Secretary, the Chancellor, and the Secretary of State for Northern Ireland also attended, was interpreted by Haughey immediately afterward as having historic significance. In press conferences he gave the impression that British and Irish relations had been placed on a new footing in which the future of Northern Ireland would be resolved between himself and Mrs. Thatcher. Much was made of a phrase in the official communiqué "the totality of relationships within these islands" and of the agreement that joint studies would be commissioned "covering a range of issues including possible new institutional structures, citizenship rights, security matters, economic cooperation and measures to encourage mutual understanding." Haughey encouraged a sense that the end of partition was in sight. That this would be a distant prospect became clear when the joint studies were published. But this was scarcely the point. Haughey, by apparently making progress on the issue of partition, made it imperative that a successor should be seen to act with similar conviction and historic authority. In a matter so fraught with dangers and pitfalls this was the thorny legacy which Garret Fitz-Gerald inherited on coming to power in 1981.

Furthermore, when FitzGerald took office in June 1981 events in the North had taken a threatening turn. A hunger strike to achieve political status for republican prisoners in the H-block cells at Long Kesh (the Maze Prison) was taking place when Haughey met the British Prime Minister in Dublin. By the time FitzGerald became Taoiseach, a second hunger strike had been undertaken which would sacrifice ten martyrs before it was called off, giving to the Provisional IRA both in the North and the South a moral legitimacy in many people's minds it had never hitherto enjoyed. That Mrs. Thatcher failed to perceive this outcome, in obdurate resistance to the strikers' demand for political status in prison, or in perceiving it did not give it sufficient weight, was a significant misjudgment on her part. For her intractable stand against the hunger strikers' demands was precisely the stuff of which Irish martyrs are bred, linking Bobby Sands (the first to die) and his nine companions to Pearse, Emmet, and Tone. Their sacrifice gave the "armed struggle" a dignity and a purchase on Irish feeling which meant that Sinn Féin as the mouthpiece for the IRA would have to be accommodated in any future settlement, an outcome just as likely to unsettle governments in the Republic as in Britain.

During the months of the second hunger strike, in the midst of which FitzGerald came to power, more popular demonstrations of support for the republican cause were mounted in the Republic than at any time since the aftermath of "Bloody Sunday" in 1972. Black flags were displayed in most towns and villages, marches and protest meetings held. These expressions of solidarity with the republican hunger strikers culminated in a mass demonstration to the British embassy in Dublin on 18 July at which serious rioting took place. FitzGerald could have scarcely experienced less auspicious circumstances in which to grapple with the Northern Irish question. His nationalist credentials implicitly and explicitly cast in doubt by his Fianna Fáil adversary, with Northern violence threatening to spill over onto the capital's streets, and Provisional Sinn Féin apparently ready to seek electoral support in the Dáil, it was obviously necessary to take action. Its mode was altogether less obvious.

FitzGerald's response was to propose a referendum to change the 1937 Constitution so as to make it more acceptable to Northern Protestants, thereby removing the basis of unionist argument that the Republic was a sectarian, irredentist state. Articles 2 and 3, which laid claim to the whole island of Ireland as the national territory and asserted the *de jure* right of the twenty-six-county state's government to rule the six counties of Northern Ireland, would be deleted if the referendum were carried. FitzGerald indicated his intention to mount a "constitutional crusade" to influence Irish public opinion to this end. His approach to the Northern question therefore was radically different from that of Haughey, for it clearly placed much greater importance on the susceptibilities and political significance of the unionist population of Northern Ireland. This became even clearer after a meeting with Mrs. Thatcher in November 1981, when FitzGerald agreed in a joint communiqué that "any change in the constitutional status of Northern Ireland would require the consent of a majority of the people of Northern Ireland." Predictably, Haughey was contemptuous of FitzGerald's mooted crusade and indignant that FitzGerald had interrupted the process he claimed to have inaugurated himself with his meeting with the British Prime Minister in London almost a year earlier. Electoral exigencies did not allow FitzGerald much time to prosecute his crusade with any vigour, for in the new year Haughey had returned as Taoiseach.

And it was to be a period of icy British-Irish relations. Haughey denounced the British Secretary of State for Northern Ireland's attempts to create a legislative assembly with devolved powers in the province before he had embarked upon the task. He did not too strenuously dissent from his Minister for Defence's claim, after the sinking of an Argentinian battle-cruiser by British forces in the South Atlantic Falklands/Malvinas war, that Britain had become the aggressor, ordering Ireland's derogation from EEC sanctions against Argentina's breach of international law. These acts served notice that the "special relationship" Haughey had made much of in his first term of office was definitively at an end. Ireland had a profound quarrel with Britain – partition – and until Britain moved to end that injustice, relations between the two sovereign governments would constantly be soured.

Events north of the border in the first half of the 1980s threatened to transform the Northern problem into an all-Ireland one, making it more a source of Irish instability than a cause of a British-Irish disagreement, as Haughey saw it. The effect on Northern nationalist opinion of the hunger strikes made it possible for the Provisional IRA and Sinn Féin to embark on a radical new direction. Traditional Sinn Féin policy had been almost always to hold itself apart from the electoral process in the North and South. During the hunger strikes Bobby Sands had stood for election to the Westminster parliament in a by-election and was successful. Two H-block prisoners were elected to the Dáil in the general election of that summer (one of them, Kieran Doherty, dying, as a result of his hunger strike, shortly thereafter). Initially, Sinn Féin justified this departure from a traditional policy in terms of the extraordinary circumstances in which it found itself. But involvement in H-block committees (groups which espoused the prisoners' cause) introduced its leaders to the possibility of really popular political activism, and a more general electoral support. Consequently, at a meeting in Dublin in October 1981, the traditional policy was abandoned for a pragmatic, flexible exploitation of the democratic system. Local elections would be contested in the North and the seats, if won, occupied. Seats in the Dáil, Westminster and Stormont would be contested but not occupied. In a chillingly memorable sentence, Danny Morrison, national publicity director for Sinn Féin, gave succinct expression to the new policy: "Will anyone here object if, with a ballot paper in this hand and an Armalite in this hand, we take power in Ireland?"

The political party likely to be most immediately affected by this strategic shift was the Social Democratic and Labour Party (SDLP), which represented the non-violent constitutional nationalist position in Northern Ireland. That party had throughout the 1970s enjoyed the support of the Southern political establishment, and it was assumed that it would play a crucial role in any resolution of the Northern Irish problem. Were it to be replaced, or seriously undermined by Sinn Féin's elected representatives, any Dublin government would find its negotiating position *vis-à-vis* the British government rendered very uncertain. For what case could it put as a democratic government, a partner of Britain in the EEC, while an armed struggle continued with the electoral support of a substantial section of the nationalist population in the North against the British governance of Northern Ireland? Furthermore, such a state of affairs, in which an Irish government might find itself unable to act with real authority, could allow undemocratic forces in the South to claim that they were acting where the government would not. And electoral success for Sinn Féin in Northern Ireland might encourage that party to activism among the socially alienated, young unemployed in the Republic itself, thereby threatening political stability there. In the British general election of June 1983 Sinn Féin proved that such fears were not groundless as their candidates took 13.4 percent of the vote to the SDLP's 17.9 percent, with Gerry Adams the high-profile victor in West Belfast.

Earlier in the year, in anticipation of such an electoral threat, the leader of the SDLP and the leaders of three of the Republic's political parties (Fine Gael, Labour and Fianna Fáil) reached an agreement on a proposal largely emanating from John Hume of the SDLP that an all-Irish forum be established. This body would, after extensive consultation, set out the basis of the constitutionalist position on the problem of Northern Ireland, recommending ways in which the conflict might be peacefully resolved in some new Irish political order. The intention was to impress upon the British government the dangers of an inaction which would leave the political arena open for a nascent, politically active Sinn Féin in Northern Ireland and to outline various parameters within which joint Irish and British ameliorative action might be taken.

The performance of Sinn Féin in elections to a new and short-lived Northern Ireland Assembly in October 1982, when the party had won five seats in the bitter aftermath of the hunger strikes of the year before, had been the danger signal, alerting politicians throughout nationalist Ireland. And they responded with considerable seriousness of purpose and sustained intellectual determination. Initially, doubt had existed whether Fianna Fáil under Haughey would agree to participate in an all-Irish forum, since it was not clear that Hume and the other party leaders unambiguously held that a unitary Irish state and the ending of partition were immediate desiderata; but Fianna Fáil decided to involve itself in the proceedings, perhaps fearing its position might go by default. In the event that was scarcely the problem.

The New Ireland Forum met for the first time on 30 May 1983. Unionist parties, although invited, refused to attend, though some unionists made individual representations. Sinn Féin was not invited. The Forum reported eleven months later, during which time twenty-eight private sessions and thirteen public sessions were held, at which the various party members heard oral, and studied written submissions (these totalled 348). There were also fifty-six meetings of a steering committee comprising the chairman and the party leaders. The published results of this intense activity were at once challenging, generous in spirit, but practically limited.

The challenge of the *Forum Report* lay in its unblinking recognition of the desperate, tragic nature of the Northern Irish conflict and of its potential for even more widespread violence. The report listed the statistics of conflict with compassionate urgency. The violent deaths of 2,300 men, women, and children in fifteen years were reflected upon:

These deaths in an area with a population of 1½ million are equivalent in proportionate terms to the killing of approximately

84,000 in Britain, 83,000 in France or 350,000 in the United States of America. In addition over 24,000 have been injured or maimed. Thousands are suffering from psychological stress because of the fear and tension generated by murder, bombing, intimidation and the impact of security measures. During the past fifteen years, there have been over 43,000 recorded separate incidents of shootings, bombings and arson. In the North the prison population has risen from 686 in 1967 to about 2,500 in 1983 and now represents the highest number of prisoners per head of population in Western Europe. The lives of tens of thousands have been deeply affected. The effect on society has been shattering. There is hardly a family that has not been touched to some degree by death, injury or intimidation.[21]

After a decade in which the Republic had tended to hope the Northern-Irish problem could be isolated by a mental quarantine, such a passage in an official document represented a courageous recognition of the human dimension of the problem that confronted the Irish government and its people.

The *New Ireland Forum Report* revealed a generosity of spirit too in its sincere efforts to comprehend the Northern unionist *mentalité* and acceptance that "nationalists must . . . acknowledge that unionists, sharing the same island, have the same basic concerns about stability and security as nationalists. The major difference between the two traditions lies in their perceptions of how their interests would be affected by various political arrangements. These perceptions have been largely formed by different historical experiences and communal values."[22] Such a formulation, particularly in that final sentence, for the first time gave official, diplomatic expression to a view of Irish history that diverged from republican nationalist orthodoxy, in which unionist instransigence was always regarded as the misguided result of British manipulation or as a self-interested desire to maintain sectarian ascendancy. The creation of a positive vision of an Ireland in which unionists might feel more at home was identified in the report as a central aim for constitutional nationalists. The statement "Society in Ireland as a whole comprises a wider diversity of cultural and political traditions than exists in the South, and the constitution and laws of a new Ireland must accommodate these social and political realities"[23] is one that Æ of the *Irish Statesman* might have penned.

The *Forum Report* envisaged three constitutional frameworks within which a settlement might be achieved: a unitary state, a federal constitutional state and a joint authority, without dealing with the fundamental problem: that without unionist consent none of these options could be set in place.

Immediately after the report's publication, disagreements developed between Haughey and FitzGerald on the status the document afforded to the federal constitutional state and to joint authority. Haughey was insistent that these would not resolve the Northern Ireland conflict and that the report opted only for a unitary state. It was not at all clear in his utterances why a federal state could not be a united state and why such would be a failure in Ireland. What was clear was that the spectacle of Haughey and FitzGerald squabbling in public on the differing interpretations reduced the report's impact, suggesting that the consensus achieved was largely cosmetic.

These disagreements swiftly seemed to become academic, however, when in November 1984, after a meeting with FitzGerald, Mrs. Thatcher bluntly stated that none of the three options would be acceptable to the British government: they were "Out, out, out," as she stated at a televised press conference, which was read in Ireland as a studied insult to the Irish Taoiseach. (Her attitudes to Irish perspectives had scarcely been softened by the IRA's attempt to assassinate her and her cabinet in the Brighton bombing in October.) It was a measure of FitzGerald's maturity as a statesman at a fraught time that he swallowed his pride at this rebuff and continued the work of persuasion (ably assisted by officials in the Department of Foreign Affairs) that doing nothing would exacerbate the problem of Northern Ireland. The *Forum Report* had fortunately envisaged British opposition and had stated that the Forum would consider other proposals if those on the table proved unacceptable.

By June 1985, at a meeting in Milan, Mrs. Thatcher accepted that something must be done and an intensive period of negotiation ensued which bore fruit in the Anglo-Irish Agreement, signed at Hillsborough Castle, near Belfast on 15 November 1985. This gave the Irish government a consultative role in various aspects of the governance of Northern Ireland, with an Irish secretariat in Belfast. This concession to Irish interests was balanced by a clear statement, accepted by both the Irish and British governments, that no change in the status of Northern Ireland could take place without the consent of a majority of the population there and that at present no such majority existed. Crucially for the Irish government, Britain declared that it would not stand in the way of a United Ireland if in the future a majority in the North desired such an outcome. Britain thereby signalled publicly for the first time that it was essentially neutral in the Irish quarrel, a change in policy which could be built on over time.

The Anglo-Irish Agreement was only a shadow of joint authority as envisaged in the *Forum Report*. It was reckoned something altogether too substantial by unionist opinion in the North. The Unionists felt betrayed by Mrs. Thatcher who, they claimed with good reason, had not kept them abreast of where the negotiations were leading. And whatever the constitutional assurances the Agreement contained, a Southern Irish secretariat in Belfast looked like the thin end of a very green wedge which would prise the North apart from the United Kingdom. Protest was unanimous, bringing all sectors of the unionist community together in a mass demonstration at Belfast's City Hall. Loyalist violence now had a sharp ideological edge in the context of such perceived betrayal. It was not clear that the RUC and British Army could maintain order, especially as IRA violence continued unabated, culminating in the horror of the Remembrance Day massacre in Enniskillen in November 1987, when a memorial service at the Cenotaph there was bombed. An agreement which had been designed to bring about peace and stability and to strengthen the centre ground in Northern Ireland (the SDLP benefited electorally from it) looked as if it had also deepened antagonisms. For to almost all unionists it was anathema. Haughey had rejected it immediately on behalf of Fianna Fáil, and Sinn Féin was adamantly opposed, in public, to the Agreement's position on consent. Yet Sinn Féin was, under the direction of its president, Gerry Adams, in the process of altering its strategy. In November 1986 the party agreed (with a rump departing in protest) that henceforth it would take any seats it won in elections to the Dáil.

In this challenging context, John Hume, the leader of the SDLP, in 1988 began secret talks with Mr. Gerry Adams, the President of Sinn Féin, to see whether the new British position, implicit in its acceptance of the Anglo-Irish Agreement, could wean the Provisional IRA away from the path of violence it had travelled so far along since the early 1970s (the discovery in late 1987 that the IRA was importing substantial armaments from Libya made clear the level of military threat the movement posed).[24] Contacts between the parties were intensified and became public, to the great consternation of unionists, who felt increasingly isolated. However, the fact that Sinn Féin was willing to engage in such dialogue perhaps indicated that its commitment to a long war was weakening and that it knew it could not overtake the SDLP electorally while supporting the IRA's armed campaign. Sinn Féin had endured much opprobrium after the Enniskillen massacre in 1987. The military future, furthermore, seemed to involve a bloody stalemate. So although nothing came of these talks in the 1980s, they helped to prepare the way for the radical departures of the 1990s.

III

The *New Ireland Forum Report* had acknowledged in a rather half-hearted way the settled Northern Protestant perception that law in the Republic of Ireland was unduly affected by Roman Catholic social policy. It accepted without analysis unionist fears that "their civil and religious liberties . . . would not survive in a

United Ireland in which Roman Catholicism would be the religion of the majority of the population."[25] Developments in church-state relations in the Republic in the 1980s could not have been adduced to put their minds at rest.

In 1980 and 1981 a number of Catholic pressure groups – some new, others semi-secret societies with histories of private influence on Irish public affairs – gave support to a campaign that sought an amendment to the Irish Constitution that would make it impossible for an Irish legislature governing under that Constitution ever to pass laws permitting abortion in any circumstances. Unquestionably, many of the people who involved themselves in some of these organizations, the Society for the Protection of the Unborn Child (SPUC) and the Pro-Life Amendment Campaign (PLAC) for example, were moved by a genuine abhorrence for the way in which abortion had become, as they saw it, all too readily available in other jurisdictions and were concerned that Ireland as a Christian nation should bear witness to its respect for the sanctity of human life. The fact, however, that it was wholly improbable in the foreseeable future that any political party would attempt to make abortion legal in Ireland gave many Irish people reason to suspect the good faith of at least some of the campaigners.

In the aftermath of the papal visit of 1979, when the Irish people had been challenged by supreme authority to uphold traditional values, conservative-minded individuals had decided that it was an opportune moment to check the erosion of such values (which in their view had been enforced by legislative change in the 1970s) by a show of carefully marshalled popular force. However the plan went badly wrong. For instead of a moral majority calmly affirming its respect for life to the discomfiture of a small group of shallow progressives, the amendment campaign, although ultimately successful in constitutional terms (by a two-to-one majority in a referendum in which only 50 percent of the electorate chose to vote), stimulated an intense, very bitterly conducted debate (some reckoned a kind of moral "civil war"). In this debate it was revealed that a significant proportion of the

Irish population was not prepared to support the sort of moral absolutism that the amendment proposed.

The divisions unleashed by the amendment campaign intensified until a direct church-state conflict arose. It was Haughey who, two days before his second administration fell, introduced the wording for the amendment: "The state acknowledges the right of the unborn, and with due regard to the equal right to life of the mother, guarantees in its laws to respect, and as far as practicable, by its laws to protect and vindicate that right." On his accession to office, FitzGerald, informed by his Attorney General that this wording was dangerously deficient and might paradoxically expedite the introduction of legislation permitting abortion, presented his own government's version: "that nothing in [the] Constitution shall be invoked to invalidate any provision of a law on the grounds that it prohibits abortion." The major Irish Protestant churches, which had all registered their disapproval of the decision to amend the Constitution and of the Fianna Fáil wording, made clear that they found the new wording less objectionable. The Catholic hierarchy, however, gave formal support to the Fianna Fáil formulation, while recognizing that the faithful had the right to exercise their informed consciences on the matter. The nation was therefore afforded the unedifying opportunity to observe Fianna Fáil, with the support of the Catholic bishops, arrayed on the issue against a coalition government that had made belated and ineffective attempts to take account both of its own doubts and of the vigorously expressed views of the Protestant churches. Tragically, what had too readily, even opportunistically, been seized upon by the leaders of Fianna Fáil and Fine Gael as a political asset in an electorally unstable context (for what party could allow another to go to the polls clad in the armour of moral righteousness while remaining defenceless itself?) had opened a wound in the Irish body politic which had in recent times seemed entirely healed. That the Church of Ireland primate, Dr. John Armstrong, felt called to protest "This is the Mother and Child Act all over"[26] suggests how painfully deep such wounds cut, indicating the inter-confessional tensions the debate provoked. And the manner in which the Catholic church's teaching on a moral and social issue received majority constitutional support even when Protestants protested vigorously, seemed once again to prove to Northern Protestants that a political accommodation with their neighbours in the twenty-six-county state would be risky. The amendment was carried by 66.9 percent to 33.1 percent, on 7 September 1983, with consequences few then really foresaw.

On 9 February 1984 a group of Catholic bishops appeared in a public session at the New Ireland Forum to receive questions and present the hierarchy's views on various matters. On this occasion the bishops, through the eloquent, evidently sincere person of Bishop Cahal Daly, wished it to be made clear that "we have not sought and we do not seek a Catholic State for a Catholic people."[27] It was also stated that in any new Irish political arrangements which might encompass the whole island:

> What we do here and now declare, and declare with emphasis, is that we would raise our voices to resist any constitutional proposals which might infringe or might imperil the civil and religious rights and liberties cherished by Northern Protestants.[28]

Even with the clamour of the amendment debate still ringing in many people's ears, to have said that these words struck a hollow note would have been unfair to the future Cardinal, who delivered them with evident conviction. But other less eirenic episcopal utterances which followed tended to vitiate the significance of the bishop's words. Questioned specifically on the issue of divorce – constitutionally forbidden in the Republic and a civil right if not exactly cherished by Northern Protestants one they individually and through their representative church bodies recognized as a necessary legal remedy for flawed social realities – the bishops at the Forum took refuge in unhelpful generalities. Nor indeed could they respond in any convincing way to the question as to why Protestants and other non-Catholics should not be afforded in the existing Republic the same civil rights the bishops would be earnest to protect were Northern Protestants to join in the future with their neighbours in forming a new Irish state.

The actual position of the Catholic hierarchy on this question became clearer. They would not grant that divorce *was* a civil right. However in view of a rising rate of marriage breakdowns (about 70,000 persons in the state were enduring such breakdowns without recourse to divorce legislation) the church increasingly granted marriage annulments. In 1985 Garret FitzGerald declared himself in favour of removing the constitutional ban on divorce. In the knowledge that the Catholic church could not approve such a change, he outlined in April 1986 what divorce, Irish-style, would involve (a decree granted after five years' separation, with provision for dependent spouses and children) and pressed ahead with a referendum in June, buoyed up by opinion poll evidence that he could carry the day. It was a bold, not to say foolhardy, step, given that significant figures in his own party were dead set against divorce in Ireland and that the Fianna Fáil opposition would do nothing officially to help and would privately work to frustrate FitzGerald at any price, thereby keeping the conservative sections of the electorate happy. In such circumstances the Catholic hierarchy did not have to oppose FitzGerald too vigorously in public but could depend on lay ginger groups (Opus Dei, the Knights of Columbanus, Family Solidarity) and local parish communication to carry the message that Ireland should reject the proposed constitutional amendment. When anti-divorce groups managed to associate divorce with loss of property rights, especially for married women on farms, in rural Ireland, FitzGerald's proposal was fatally torpedoed. The referendum was defeated in June by a majority of almost two-to-one. The Protestant Bishop of Cork drew a salutary lesson, commenting in July 1986: "The glorious vision of the New Ireland Forum has been set aside. . . ." Bishop Samuel Poyntz asserted: "Many will interpret the 1986 referendum result as sending out a signal that we are not prepared to accept as of now the price of unity by consent."[29] He did however prophesy, accurately as it turned out, that within ten years Ireland would have accepted divorce.

So the 1980s saw an amendment to the Republic's Constitution that could be interpreted as augmenting its confessional aspects and the defeat of a referendum which would have reduced them. One further event can be adduced to show how the 1937 Constitution, while reflecting liberal democratic ideals in many of its articles, also obliged citizens to live in a state marked by religious confessionalism. In rejecting an appeal from the High Court by a plaintiff (Mr., later Senator, David Norris) seeking a declaration that two acts inherited by Ireland from the period of British rule which made homosexual acts and conduct illegal were unconstitutional, a Supreme Court judge made specific reference to the confessional preamble of the Constitution itself. In his judgment, delivered on 22 April 1983, Supreme Court Justice T. F. O'Higgins made quite clear that the preamble in which, as he stated, the Constitution "proudly asserts the existence of God in the most Holy Trinity and recites the People of Ireland as humbly acknowledging their obligation to 'Our Divine Lord Jesus Christ'" formed a key element in his deliberations that led to his rejection, together with two of his fellow judges, of the plaintiff's case. His argument was that a constitution framed in the spirit of the preamble could not conceivably render inoperative laws "which had existed for hundreds of years prohibiting unnatural sexual conduct which Christian teaching holds to be gravely sinful."[30]

The successful campaign to amend the Irish Constitution to prevent any possibility that abortion would be legalized in Ireland, the dismissal of the Norris case and the defeat of the divorce referendum certainly gave comfort to conservative-minded people who regarded such things as welcome blows on behalf of traditional religious values in an ongoing battle against liberalizing and secularizing tendencies. Some Catholic commentators were not so sure. They inclined to look at more general trends of the 1980s. What they found was that, despite these compelling indications of the social influence of a conservative

Catholicism still vigorously at work in the country, the process of secularization, observed in the 1960s and '70s, was continuing into the 1980s. Considering all the surveys to hand of religious attitudes and beliefs in Ireland, the sociologist Liam Ryan concluded in 1983: "A picture emerges of a people largely believing in God and in the Church, but in possession of a belief which has little impact, not just on the wider world of business and politics, but also in many areas of private morality."[31] Encouraged by the fact that the decline in religious belief and practice had been "minimal, compared to Europe as a whole," the author of this report was nevertheless disturbed to note that "those who are less active religiously, whether in belief or in practice, come predominantly from three groups: the young, the urban, and skilled or semiskilled workers."[32] It was such evidences of religious decline that allowed a journalist (Peadar Kirby) in 1984 to publish a book entitled *Is Irish Catholicism Dying?* without appearing wholly alarmist.[33]

It must be said, however, that the influence of Catholic Ireland was not directed solely on behalf of conservative forces in the late 1980s. For in that decade there was a discernible if not especially dramatic shift to the political left both at the hierarchical and parish levels. The bishops' pastoral letter of 1977, *The Work of Justice*, while scarcely a radical document, did raise the issue of Irish poverty in a compassionate way. And in 1983 the National Conference of Priests of Ireland chose unemployment as the theme of its annual meeting, concluding, as Peadar Kirby has remarked, with what amounts to "a new breakthrough for a document coming from Church leaders in that it sought to identify with the unemployed whom it called 'the new oppressed' rather than just offering to help them."[34]

A specific catalyst to this new social awareness in Irish Catholicism was the public visibility, particularly after United States policy brought the region onto the world stage, of the work of Irish missionary priests, brothers and nuns in Latin America. Since the foundation of the bishops' Lenten appeal on behalf of the developing world in 1973, through their agency Trócaire, public perception had been gradually educated to an awareness that missionary outreach involved the encouragement of social improvement as much if not more than direct evangelism. A sense of Catholicism as a socially directed, even radical, force developed. Accordingly, during President Ronald Reagan's visit to Ireland in June 1984, the considerable opposition to his South and Central American policy expressed then did not lack its share of clerical and religious voices. The Most Reverend Eamonn Casey, Bishop of Galway, the member of the hierarchy most readily associated at that time in the public mind with development issues, was noticeable by his absence when the US President received the freedom of Galway city. In the summer of 1985 Bob Geldof's marshalling of the international popular music business to present the Live Aid concert in London, on behalf of the world's hungry, was a similar phenomenon, for it seemed right that a citizen of a country that had once been a land of the hungry and dispossessed should play a key role in responding to current famine.

IV

For language revivalists the 1980s enforced a realistic, chastened sense of actualities and possibilities. A key document reflecting this mood was *The Action Plan for Irish, 1983–1986*, issued in 1983 by the state's principal body responsible for language matters, Bord na Gaeilge. This document drew attention to the stark facts of language decline ("Today, some sixty years after the foundation of the State, only 1 percent of our population can be said to be native speakers using Irish as their normal day-to-day language in Gaeltacht areas"),[35] and recognized, with a frankness not customary in such contexts, that in order to achieve the aim of a bilingual society, "it will be important to fully acknowledge that English has for long been an authentic community language in Ireland."[36] Bord na Gaeilge reckoned that its bilingual aim for society would be "nearer attainment if, by the end of the century, a situation had been reached in which one third of the people had a reasonable speaking knowledge of Irish, another third had a basic ability in the spoken language, and the remainder some basic understanding."[37] It proposed a series of short-term sensible steps that might be taken in pursuit of this scarcely immodest aspiration, while challenging the government on the seriousness of its concern for the perilous position of the language. That in the period immediately following the document's publication there was little general sense of urgency on the need to act on the board's advice cannot but have increased the pessimism which, as well as realism, characterized the mood of many committed to the wellbeing of Ireland's historic language in the 1980s. A constituent of that pessimism was a fear that late twentieth-century Ireland might witness the death of Irish, its terminal condition allowing a final brief remission in which Irish-language verse briefly flourished. Such was the view of one Irish-language poet, Máire Mhac an tSaoi:

> Irish – that is Gaelic verse is so intensively conservative that at all times it has taken a major cataclysm to cause it to change. The coming of Christianity is such a jolt. . . . To-day it is possible that yet another crisis, this time the death throes of a language, is producing another last flowering.[38]

The Indian summer of Irish verse-making was in fact a moment of profuse creativity in the history of modern Gaelic poetry in the country. Since the launching of a poetry broadsheet (*Innti*, edited by Michael Davitt) in 1970 by a group of University College, Cork undergraduate poets, Munster and its Irish-speaking areas had been the epicentre of a remarkable upsurge in the public performance and publication of Irish language verse (a publishing house, *Coiscéim*, gave this wave of younger poets the chance of volume publication). Recalling in 1996 this upsurge of poetry in Irish, the critic Alan Titley remembered that in 1984/5 "twenty-five different volumes of poetry in Irish were published",[39] and noted an anthology which "contained nearly four hundred poems from ninety-four collections by fifty-nine poets" drawn from work of a mere ten years.[40] In this "poetic plenitude and anarchy,"[41] Titley observed a fertile Irish/English bilingualism, as the younger poets in Irish simply ignored the *cordon sanitaire* between the languages some earlier revivalists had futilely sought to establish. While, in poet and critic Theo Dorgan's phrase, this "moment of reclamation" was making Irish-language poetry reasonably popular among some of the young, Irish itself however was entering "yet another spiral in its long decline."[42]

As if to acknowledge this sad fact, two works, a play produced for the first time in 1980 (*Translations* by Brian Friel, which premièred in Derry) and a volume of translations of poems in Irish from the period 1600–1900 (*An Dunaire, Poems of the Dispossessed* by Thomas Kinsella and Seán Ó Tuama) published in 1981, both made a notable impact in Ireland. The first of these, set at a moment in the nineteenth century identified by Friel as the point in the nation's history when the process of language shift was irretrievably set in motion, may indeed have touched a chord of national self-doubt and guilt. *An Dunaire* was an act of powerful repossession of something about to be lost, comparable to Daniel Corkery's rediscovery of eighteenth-century Gaelic Ireland in the 1920s in *The Hidden Ireland*.

In 1986 Bord na Gaeilge issued a further, very thoughtful, document: *The Irish Language in a Changing Society: Shaping the Future*, which sought to challenge what it saw as a laissez-faire attitude by the government to the language issue. The report accepted that the old ideological imperatives about language revival no longer had any real impact in modern Ireland and may indeed have been counter-productive anyway. It recognized that the state had moved from attempting language revival/restoration to the encouragement of bilingualism. The effort to foster bilingualism was unfocused, perhaps necessarily so since it was dependent on individual choices, ignoring the influence of social groups. It observed that new elites had developed in the country with "a strong tendency to exclude 'things Irish', or markers of a specifically Irish identity, from a place of honour."[43]

Concurrently, the report argued, Irish society in general was suffering from a vitiating identity crisis, so that

> ... while some debate has been initiated, there is not yet emerging a definite philosophy about what being Irish means in the contemporary world. On the contrary there are cross-currents, ambiguities, ambivalences and disconfirming experiences. ... This inchoate relationship to our Irishness weakens the capacity of a comparatively small society to take collective action on its problems. Instead, a fractious and individualised society, riven by inter-group conflicts and with few mobilising values for collective endeavour, exhibits a depleted potential for self-management while drifting increasingly towards a provincialised cultural dependence and assimilation.[44]

There was, accordingly, "a certain emptiness in the way Irish people now assert a sense of separate peoplehood, and a lack of consensus whether this is something worth asserting at all."[45]

The Irish Language in a Changing Society offered a realistic vision of how Irish could play a part in developing a positive sense of national identity. It recognized, however, that its vision was to some degree "subversive" in nature, since it challenged increasingly powerful interests at a time when there was "no widely shared ideological rationale for the establishment of a bilingual society." What Bord na Gaeilge proposed was radically in contrast with the ideology of earlier efforts made by apologists of the language, but like them these depended on a change of consciousness by a significant proportion of Irish people:

> In calling for a refurbishment of Irish identity we suggest that the Irish language has an integrating and stimulating role to play. This is by no means a plea for a return to the outlook of the narrow nativistic ideology of the revivalists, current in the early 20th century. Neither is it to favour Irish as opposed to English; in fact we are fortunate in having one of the major languages in the world. Rather it seeks for a sense of confidence in our uniqueness within a polyethnic Europe. A process of revitalising Irish identity could perhaps espouse a new and serious political neutrality, reflect a sophisticated distrust of modern

hidden imperialisms, show solidarity with the Third World, show a strong tendency towards humanism and egalitarianism, and in re-examining Irish history, transcend any myopic pre-occupation with the grievances of the past.[46]

The first fruits of this thinking were observable in a widespread Bord na Gaeilge advertising campaign which sought to remind the populace that Irish was "part of what we are." Its exact impact cannot be judged, but it reflected the broadly humanistic outlook of those in the Republic in the 1980s and '90s who valued the language as an element in modern Irish identity. This compared strikingly with Northern Ireland where language in the same period (Irish and Ulster/Scots) became markers of competing putative ethnicities. However the ideological alignment of Irish with Third-World anti-imperialism risked making Irish seem marginal, especially in the 1990s when the country would experience an economic resurgence that would make it one of the richest countries in Europe.

V

In the midst of the severe economic drift and the crises of the 1980s it would have been a lot to expect any government to give language preservation, or indeed any matter of cultural or artistic significance, high priority. The newly appointed Arts Council (the eighth such) in 1984 in fact found it necessary to issue a statement drawing attention to the insufficiency of funds for the huge increase over the preceding decade in the community's artistic activities (arts organizations in the country had accumulated debts of £1.5 million setting many of them at risk) and to launch a vigorous public campaign to put pressure on the government that included after 1982 a minister of state for arts and culture.

This campaign, although stimulating short-term ministerial ire did, within three years, result in the government issuing the White Paper *Access and Opportunity*, which set a target of "doubling (in real terms)"[47] provision for the arts, drawing down funds from the recently formed national lottery. When Charles Haughey returned as Taoiseach in a minority government in March 1987 he soon moved to go some way to adopting its key proposals. In November he announced that £8 million would be made available from lottery funds and in a statement of 1988 he "signalled that the arts were an integral part of future government policy."[48] A report commissioned by the Arts Council, *The Performing Arts and the Public Purse: An Economic Analysis*, authored by John O'Hagen and Christopher Duffy in 1987, had highlighted how great a proportion of its grant went to the National Theatre Company (the Abbey Theatre). This was a nettle that was not grasped as the claims of regional and community arts were increasingly pressed under these new circumstances.

It had in fact been Haughey, in the second of his 1980s administrations, who had established a body whose purpose was to honour and support the achievement of creative individuals. On the recommendation of the then director of the Arts Council, Colm O'Briain and of the Taoiseach's cultural adviser, the poet and author Anthony Cronin, Aosdána was inaugurated in 1982. This honorific body provided for a membership not exceeding 150 persons, of artists – including novelists, poets, dramatists, painters, sculptors, musicians etc. – born in Ireland or resident there for five years (the rules now allow for 200 members). The scheme also allowed for five-year annuities for artists resident in Ireland who depended solely on their creative work.

Other developments, even in the depressed conditions of the 1980s, improved the lot of creative people in Ireland and added to the country's cultural capital. In 1981 an Irish Film Board was established to seek to encourage the native Irish film industry, in its attempt to represent the Irish experience and thus escape the constraints of international stereotyping imposed by Hollywood. For a time in the 1980s it seemed just possible that a distinctive Irish film movement might emerge, since the board was able to offer development funds to film-makers (often in joint ventures with British television companies) to break new thematic ground. The critical and popular success of such films as *Angel* (1982), *Ann Devlin* (1984) and *Eat the Peach* (1986), all of which had board support, showed what might have been achieved.[49] But the abolition of the board by Charles Haughey, when he returned to power in the straitened economic circumstances of 1987, once again made film-making in Ireland predominantly dependent on international backers with their eye on the North American market. Happily, other institutional additions to cultural life were longer lasting. In 1982 a County Monaghan house that man-of-the-theatre Sir Tyrone Guthrie had left to the nation as a retreat for writers and artists, welcomed its first guests, under the joint auspices of the Irish and Northern Irish Arts Councils (with the help of the European Regional Fund). In 1983 the coalition government set a zero-rate tax on books, giving a much needed boost to Irish booksellers (who had been suffering in the recession and from the effects of a disadvantageous exchange rate of the Irish punt with sterling and the dollar) and giving impetus to an expanding Irish publishing industry. The National College of Art and Design's move to newly converted premises in Dublin also brought a sense of optimism and new life to an area of Irish higher education long associated with conflict and frustration. In 1984, Section 32 of the Finance Act allowed corporations and individuals to set sponsorship of the arts against tax. In 1984 VAT was removed from tickets for theatre and live performances and in 1985 was reduced on cinema tickets.

Artistic activity was increasing in the Irish regions (epitomized by the successes of the Druid Theatre in Galway). The Arts Council moved to encourage this development by supporting the establishment of arts centres in various parts of the country, and arts officers were appointed at regional and county level by local authorities. At a national level, in 1989 the government decided to establish an Irish Museum of Modern Art in Dublin.

Cultural production in the 1980s gave much evidence that the country was in a mood of reassessment and self-analysis. A growing consciousness that the problem of Northern Ireland would have to become a central preoccupation of the political class in Ireland, in a way it had not quite been even in the 1970s, was reflected in a number of developments in the cultural sphere. The journal the *Crane Bag* (which had been founded in 1977 by a University College, Dublin philosopher, Richard Kearney, and a Benedictine priest, Mark Patrick Hederman) in the early 1980s explored the possibility of pluralist politics in a new way. It sought to move beyond the predictable categories of national debate, sponsoring the notion of a mythical fifth province as a kind of free space in which new accommodations of the old quarrels could be imagined. Writers, artists, academics, intellectuals from the North and South, and from opposed political perspectives, twice a year were given the opportunity to consider, in themed issues, the questions the editors had posed in the journal's second issue in 1978: "Is there an alternative way in which Irish people can develop a sense of identity? Can we go beyond the idioms of religious sectarianism, nationalist self-righteousness and bourgeois preoccupation with the 'greasy till'?"[50]

Overall the journal, it must be said, risked a certain air of abstraction, but it represented a serious commitment by public intellectuals to engage with Ireland as a whole without falling into familiar polemics. Compared with the debates of the 1960s and '70s analyzed above, which were in essence ideological, individual articles in the *Crane Bag* and their cumulative impact both suggested that the Irish imbroglio could not be resolved in terms of traditional ideologies. Creative new thinking, in which ambiguity, fluidity and even the muddle of compromise, would have to replace the conflict of irreconcilable opposites. The words of a character in Brian Friel's play *Translations* (quoted indeed by one of the editors in his article "Between Conflict and Consensus" in 1985) might be said to represent the *Crane Bag*'s philosophy: "We like to think we endure around truths immemorially posited . . . [but] it can happen . . . that a civilisation can be imprisoned in a linguistic contour which no longer matches the landscape of . . . fact;" the same character also observes "confusion is not an ignoble condition." Richard Kearney insisted of the journal he and Hederman edited that it had "sought to occupy a critical position between conflict and consensus, between the clashing demands of politics and art." As such, it was not "a programme of propaganda" but at its best "a promissory note."[51]

From 1986 onwards *The Irish Review* to an extent filled the gap left by the *Crane Bag*, which ceased publication in 1985. It lacked the imaginative brio of the earlier journal, however, being largely academic in tone and content. It nevertheless sought to take the measure of contemporary Ireland, North and South. Edited from Cork, Dublin and Belfast, it included Richard Kearney in its founding editorial team. And it did, in its interdisciplinary focus, contribute to the burgeoning academic field of Irish Studies in Ireland and abroad.

The opening night of Brian Friel's *Translations* in Derry in September 1980 was not only a notable event in theatrical history but it inaugurated the work of a new cultural ginger group that was to make a considerable mark in the 1980s and '90s. The Field Day Theatre Company was the brainchild of Friel himself and the actor Stephen Rea. Their intention was to establish a Derry-based company which would present first-rate drama "in a distinctively Irish voice that would be heard throughout the country."[52] Such plays would be premièred in Derry and would then tour. They hoped that this work, emanating from a city that had suffered so grievously in "the Troubles," would make a distinct, if indirect, contribution to the rethinking that was required in the political sphere. Friel spoke in 1982 of their hopes, while ruefully acknowledging how such ambitions must appear grandiose. He hoped their activities "should lead to a cultural state, not a political state, a possibilty of a political state follows."[53] Friel admitted in an *Irish Times* interview that Field Day had appropriated the *Crane Bag*'s concept of a fifth province "as a province of mind through which we hope to devise another way of looking at Ireland, or another possible Ireland . . . one that must be articulated, spoken, written, painted, sung."[54] By 1984 Field Day had expanded its membership (its directors were Friel and Rea, Seamus Heaney, Tom Paulin, David Hammond and

Seamus Deane, all Northeners; they would be joined by the County Kilkenny-born dramatist Thomas Kilroy in 1986) and its activities included issuing pamphlets on matters as diverse as Hiberno-English and emergency legislation, which aroused considerable controversy. Further links with the *Crane Bag* were also evident, since Richard Kearney contributed to the second trio of pamphlets, and Seamus Deane, who had written for the *Crane Bag*, was both a director and a pamphleteer.

Friel may have been capable of ironic self-deprecation about the ambition of this shared enterprise, but in fact Field Day, through its theatrical interest in translation and versions, did reflect a general tendency in cultural life in the 1980s.[55] For poets and writers in the period, as if sensing that national traditions (at least those available in the Anglicized and Americanized culture of the island and in official nationalist ideologies) had exhausted themselves, or had proved inadequate to the current crises, now sought new modes of vision. In this context, the translation of poetry from the Irish became a quest for alternative perspectives, and the translation of central and eastern European verse and versions of classical drama (the *Antigone* in particular) became common. Many poets published versions of poems by the Russian poet Osip Mandelstam about whom Seamus Heaney wrote in his collection of essays *The Government of the Tongue* (1988), which also examined work by Polish and Czech poets and pondered "The Impact of Translation." In 1987 Paul Durcan published his collection of verse *Going Home to Russia*, in which the title poem introduced a sequence of verses which made Russia, even under communism, seem preferable to what modern Ireland had become.

It was Seamus Deane who most precisely identified the Field Day project with a national crisis, when in 1985 he wrote of the group's intention to compile a major anthology of Irish writing of all kinds. He judged: "the central crisis of the island has reached such an advanced stage that it would be irresponsible to avoid the opportunity to provide a sense or vision of the island's cultural integrity which would operate as a base for an enduring and enriching settlement."[56] Deane was of course referring here to the continuing conflict in the North. It was, I think, a measure of how deeply by the mid-1980s that problem had entered Southern consciousness as a primary concern that Field Day achieved such visibility in the South as well as in the North of the country, and helped to determine the terms of Southern debate. For at no time since independence had a Northern-based movement or ginger group had any real effect on intellectual and cultural life South of the border (if we exclude the historiographical revolution which in the person of Belfast-educated T. W. Moody had its Northern axis; ironically revisionism became, as we shall see, an object of critique in the 1990s). This in the longer term may come to be seen as Field Day's most remarkable achievement.

Other key literary and dramatic works of the period indicate that crisis was a prevailing Irish condition which had to be confronted. In 1983 the poet Brendan Kennelly published with a small Dublin press his long historical collage-poem *Cromwell*. It quickly became a national bestseller. An almost unremittingly dark vision of Irish history as a nightmare from which the dreamer longs to awake made it an unlikely contender for such success. Its appalled, compassionate vision of violence at the heart of human affairs nonetheless gave it grim currency in a period when almost every news broadcast from the North carried its cargo of atrocity. Kennelly caught a mood of gathering revulsion from a "war" that had gone on far too long, as he sought to escape "the terrible incestuous angers of Ireland," fearing a time when "all the living" would become "shaken ghosts/The future a prison crammed/With cowed nobodies and stammering haven't-beens."[57]

In 1984 Frank McGuinness's play *Observe the Sons of Ulster Marching Towards the Somme* was produced in Dublin by the Abbey Theatre Company. A powerful exploration of the Ulster-Protestant psyche, it dramatized the relationships among a group of Ulstermen as they were caught up in the slaughter of the Great War. A vision was unfolded of historical entrapment, akin to that in Kennelly's poem. It too was remarkable for its compassion, expressed in pity for the fate of British soldiers in that terrible war and in understanding of the effect memory of sacrifice had on the Protestant unionist mindset. The play's metaphoric implications were stark for those in the South who had not attempted such acts of empathetic imagining. They could all be prisoners of an unchanging past and future. That the play was presented at the National Theatre and drew sympathetic audiences, again suggests that the South was beginning to face up to the challenges a political settlement of the national question would involve.

Nicholas Grene, in *The Politics of Irish Drama*, has identified McGuinness's play as a key entry in a group of 1980s' dramas which adopted "the same strategy of recreating the past in order to find a means of better understanding the troubled issues of the contemporary period."[58] Another such work was Thomas Murphy's *Bailegangaire*, first produced by the Druid Theatre, Galway, in 1985, with Siobhán McKenna in the lead role. Grene rightly points out that most of the "historical" dramas of the period were primarily concerned with a colonial inheritance that had left the Northern Ireland problem to be solved by the present generation. By contrast, *Bailegangaire* addressed an even more fundamental legacy, that of "poverty and its consequences."[59] A compelling dramatization of how an archaic past impacts inevitably on a dishevelled present struggling to achieve modernity, it highlighted in particular how that patrimony bore most heavily on the country's women (the fact that McKenna was associated with the major female roles of Irish drama, Pegeen Mike and Juno, to the point where she had almost become *the* icon of traditional Irish womanhood, reinforced this in the first production). In a decade in which Ireland was asserting its full presence in the modern world in the international success of the Dublin-based rock band U2, with the "Liffey sound" taking over where the "Mersey Beat" had led the way, as Yuppie style defined suburban ambition (the Thatcherite revolution in the UK had its Irish acolytes), Murphy's play was a stark reminder that the national traumata of the past could not easily be set aside.

VI

The grinding poverty of that past, from which Ireland had apparently escaped in the 1960s and '70s, was indeed something which might have rapidly returned in the late 1980s. By 1986 the national debt stood at £22 billion, with an annual interest bill of almost £2 billion. The spectre of default and the imminent arrival of the International Monetary Fund loomed large. With 17 percent of the workforce unemployed in 1986 and emigration of the young once again "a massive indictment of economic failure,"[60] the national mood flirted with despair. In 1989 the historian Joseph Lee, in a major history of twentieth-century Ireland, was clearly affected by the sombre climate when he judged: "It is difficult to avoid the conclusion that Irish economic performance has been the least impressive in modern Europe, perhaps in all Europe, in the twentieth century."[61] He sought the explanation of that dismal state of affairs in the Irish failure since independence to deploy intellectual as well as material resources. Be that as it may, and he makes a case with fine rhetorical brio, material resources, even as he wrote, were in fact being deployed with a disciplined determination that had escaped governments since 1977.

In 1987 Charles Haughey and Fianna Fáil had been returned to power following a general election and in a short time announced a series of cuts in public expenditure that amounted to £485 million. The Minister for Finance, Ray MacSharry, was responsible for these enormous savings which seemed to bear especially hard on the health services. He would scarely have been able to carry through this draconian, but necessary, pruning of expenditure in a government that had come to power by the exercise of the casting vote of the chair in the Dáil, had he not won the support for such action of the leader of the opposition, Alan Dukes. MacSharry has generously admitted that, to some degree, Dukes put the national interest before that of his Fine Gael party in offering such support in a speech made in the western Dublin suburb of Tallaght in September 1987 (which in the same year allowed a Programme of National Recovery agreed, with the employers and trade unions, to inaugurate a period of political stability).[62] The fact that this decision became known as the "Tallaght Strategy" was not without appropriateness, for Tallaght was an area that had experienced much social deprivation since it was developed in the 1970s.

The late 1980s in Ireland were marked, therefore, by severe "fiscal rectitude" that closed hospital wards and made 20,000 public servants redundant. In the most impoverished areas of the country's cities, what began to be perceived as an underclass lived on the edge of destitution as the decade ended. The novelist Roddy Doyle's *The Commitments* (1987) made that world visible to literature, and critics began to talk of a new school of Dublin realism in Irish fiction that was taking the measure of contemporary urban alienation. In this body of work, Dermot Bolger's *The Journey Home* (1990), with its vision of an Ireland of exploitation, political corruption, drug addiction and abandoned ideals – an anti-pastoral – set a grim seal on a decade in which Ireland had seemed to lose its way. That in the midst of such deprivation Charles Haughey gave his blessing to a scheme which would allow Dublin to become an international financial centre seemed at the time a desperate throw of a gambler's dice. In April 1989 a major German bank, attracted by the tax breaks Ireland offered, opened for business in the new Irish Financial Services Centre. It was a portent of things to come.

CHAPTER 12

Revelations and Recovery

I

On 24 April 1990 the Abbey Theatre in Dublin premièred a new play by Brian Friel. Just as *Translations* in 1980 had caught a public mood in its vision of a culture negotiating transition made explicit in the linguistic shift from Irish to English, *Dancing at Lughnasa* seemed a work of special contemporary relevance. Set in 1936 in rural Donegal at harvest time, it dramatized in warmly celebratory terms the lives of five sisters, living together in the family home along with the youngest sister's seven-year-old child and their brother, Father Jack, recently returned from an African mission. Their world is on the cusp of change as the rural economy is threatened by modernization. Older forms of cultural expression are being replaced by the jazz tunes a new-fangled wireless spills into a cottage set, so often in Irish twentieth-century drama the site of an imagined pastoral. But this is no idyll for at the play's end we learn that this is the last year in which their courage and familial solidarity will keep them together.

In Act One, in a wonderful *coup de théâtre*, the five sisters are stirred into a wildly pagan dance by an Irish tune on the wireless. For a moment it is as if we are witness to the ecstasy that their narrow lives as single women (the child in the play has been born out of wedlock) in straitened circumstances has denied them. At once a carnivalesque celebration of their womanly exuberance it is also a premonitory exhibition of thwarted energies being released in a symbolic ritual. Of its effect on the eldest sister, the piously strait-laced schoolteacher and principal household support, the playwright insists she should be in the dance "almost unrecognizable" and "grotesque," as she expresses "a pattern of action which is out of character and at the same time ominous of some deep and true emotion."[1]

Friel's play, which became an instant classic of Irish theatre, seemed to serve notice that in Ireland's post-colonial experience (analogies are drawn with Father Jack's Ugandan sojourn) the energies of women could not easily be contained in conventional, patriarchal versions of the social order and that Irish society would ignore such a force at its peril. In the same year it was joined by a remarkable and equally successful work by John McGahern, a novel tellingly entitled *Amongst Women*. A mesmerizing evocation of the life of small-farm Ireland in the post-independence period, its main character is an ex-IRA activist who cannot adjust to the civilian life of the Free State and the Republic. He rules his family in the self-declared republic of the family farm as an iron-willed patriarch, driving his sons from him and deforming his daughters' lives. A widower, he has married again; with compassion and lucid accuracy the novel recounts how the balance of power in the family tilts across the fulcrum of gender as the years run on. A powerful study of the pain of love in a flawed familial world, the novel quickly took on the significance of parable and prophecy in a decade when politics and social and cultural life would be marked by major changes in Irish power relations in which gender and sexuality would play a crucial role.

In the early summer of 1989 the Taoiseach, Charles Haughey, had called a snap election on what appeared to be insufficient grounds to the electorate (an electorate, it must be noted, already infected by cynicism since Haughey had returned to power in 1987 helped by a pre-election advertising campaign which appeared to rule out the kind of health service cuts which his government almost immediately introduced). He failed again to reach an over-all majority and could hold on to power only by entering a formal coalition with the Progressive Democrats (the PDs), who num-bered among them those who had broken with Fianna Fáil because of Haughey's central role in the party. In so doing Haughey took a great political risk, not only because he was making himself dependent on erstwhile colleagues who had become opponents, but because a determination not to enter formal coalitions with other parties had always been a core value of his own. That he countenanced such an arrangement at all was probably a measure of his own addiction to power and that he effected it, a testimony to his political skills and capacity to quell, if only temporarily, dissent in the ranks. He had, however, in a move that reflected changed social realities, broken another mould in Irish politics in appointing a woman, Máire Geoghegan-Quinn, to his cabinet in 1979, the first woman to serve in such a role since 1922.

Haughey as politician was profoundly aware of the significance of image and symbol in politics. He probably relished the fact that no politician since de Valera had attracted so much adulation and execration. The adulation was based on a reputation for hyper-competence earned in a period as Minister for Finance in the 1960s, on the whiff of danger that surrounded him since his acquittal at the Arms Trial in 1970 on a charge of conspiring illegally to import arms, and on the sumptuousness of his life-style (which included a neo-classical mansion, a private island, fine horses, an art collection). An aura of invincibility, of devastat-ing charm deployed and withheld at the whim of an enigmatic but commanding personality gave him the air of one not lightly to be crossed on any matter. Familial and personal claims on various parts of the country (he was simultaneously Mayo-man and true-bred northside Dubliner), together with his reputa-tion for staunch anti-British republicanism, added mythic stature. His machismo was a given, charisma undoubted. By contrast, his enemies feared a famed temper and suspected dictatorial tendencies. Some reckoned that he was mired in financial corruption (the source of his ostentatious wealth was unknown).

Haughey's sense of style as a political weapon had made him artistic patron as well as ward boss who could intimidate with a glance. His almost seigneurial vision of his chieftainly powers (he clearly took the title Taoiseach very seriously in respect of his own person) had found expression in 1985 in the RTE/Channel Four film, subsequently released as a video cassette, *Charles Haughey's Ireland*. This included scenes in which Haughey sat at table in his island fastness off the coast of Kerry like a vacationing high king. And in 1990, when in the first half of the year Ireland held the presidency of the European Union, as German reunification was planned after the fall of the Berlin Wall, Haughey exploited his international prominence to the full. Few could have imagined then that by the end of the year a new Ireland would be inaugurated – Mary Robinson's Ireland.

Mary Robinson (née Bourke), like Haughey, was Mayo-born. There the resemblance ended. The Bourke family had a history of British colonial service and Protestant and Catholic ancestry (she herself married a Protestant whom she had met as an undergraduate in Dublin). She graduated from Trinity College, Dublin in 1967 (at a time when many Catholics still observed an episcopal ban on attendance at such a "Protestant" institution) and embarked on a career in the law which was marked by brilliant advocacy on behalf of litigants seeking redress in contentious areas of social legislation. Elected to the Seanad (Senate) by the graduates of her alma mater, she was to the fore in pressing for change in the law forbidding artificial contraception. She appeared for the plaintiff in the Mary McGee case in 1972 and for Josie Airey, who in 1978 won her case before the European Court of Human Rights, which required the Irish state to give free legal aid to citizens, including those seeking a legal separation who could not otherwise have afforded the cost of legal representation. It was she who argued the Norris case before the Irish Supreme Court and subsequently won the day for gay rights before the same Court of Human Rights in Strasbourg. She had

consistently championed women's rights while setting her feminist concern with the oppression of women in a broad context of
ethical and political awareness. She had joined the Labour Party
in the hope of election to the Dáil (electoral success in that arena
defeated her) but in 1985 she had resigned from the party in
protest at the Anglo-Irish Agreement. Where Haughey had
denounced it as a vitiation of the republican demand for a unitary
Irish state, free of any British interference, Robinson thought it
"fatally flawed" in as much as Unionists had been kept in substantial ignorance as it was being negotiated.

The presidency of Ireland, established by the 1937 Constitution, while holding certain crucial constitutional powers in the
matter of dissolving parliament and examining legislation, had
long seemed largely a ceremonial office. Its symbolic significance
was sufficient, however, for Fianna Fáil to consider it a position in
its gift as the party which thought of itself as a national movement.
When the leader of the Labour Party, Dick Spring, invited Mary
Robinson to run with his party's support for the presidency,
which would fall vacant upon the retirement of Patrick Hillery
at the end of 1990, few gave her any chance. It was assumed that
a Fianna Fáil candidate, or one approved by that party, would be
found either to stand for election or to take office as an agreed
figurehead, as they had done since 1938 when Douglas Hyde
first ascended to the presidency.

In the event Mary Robinson found herself matched against an
extremely popular Fianna Fáil minister, Brian Lenihan, and a
Fine Gael candidate, Austin Currie, who, uniquely, had served
in ministerial office North and South of the border. Robinson
ran a vigorous campaign as an independent, with the support of
both the Labour Party and the smaller Workers' Party. Travelling
extensively, she discovered a new constituency. It comprised those
who outside the main political parties constituted energies and
forces in civil society – women's groups, environmentalists, community groups, social activists of one kind or another – who in
the past had usually felt excluded from the political process. By
the autumn of 1990 what had seemed a quixotic crusade took

on an impetus of its own and it was clear that Robinson would give Lenihan a real fight. Gaffes by Lenihan himself and an attempted smear of Robinson by a Fianna Fáil colleague, who questioned her commitment to family values, were crucial in carrying the long shot of the early spring past the post at the second count in November (Lenihan topped the poll at the first count, but with insufficient votes to elect him).

Robinson's election, though it represented a surprising shock to the body politic, in as much as she had seemed successfully to challenge the comfortable order of things, was, it can be argued, a particularly graphic manifestation of a significant process that had been at work in Irish society since the 1980s. Internationally, as Linda Connolly has observed of the women's movement in general during the period, "established feminist organisations" which "cooperated and formed alliances with each other, depended on the state for resources and developed into professional organisations."[2] In Ireland the movement had travelled the same route. A pressure group that had reintroduced a women's agenda to Irish politics (before independence, Irish suffragism had been a vigorous movement) by radical action in the 1970s had by the 1990s become, in Connolly's words, "part of established interest-group politics."[3] The Council for the Status of Women, for example, founded in the fervour of feminist agitation in 1973, had by the 1990s become the highly professional and influential National Women's Council, a body that politicians opposed at their peril.

On her election Mary Robinson made a point of thanking Mna na Eireann (the Women of Ireland), "who instead of rocking the cradle rocked the system," but also made clear that she saw herself as a people's president "because [she] was elected by men and women of all parties and none, by many with great moral courage who stepped out from the faded flags of the Civil War and voted for a new Ireland."[4] The sense that she had been popularly elected gave her great strength during her presidency. She sought to enhance the powers of the office as they had hitherto been understood, by using her role as President to influence public opinion.

nd as a constitutional lawyer, she was especially equipped to
o so.

Yet it was not simply Mary Robinson's astute legal understand-
ng of the constitutional limits of her position that made the
Robinson presidency so effective an instrument for change in
reland in the 1990s. Her travels throughout the country as she
ought election had softened what before had seemed a slightly
ustere, academically reserved personality. In office she quickly
ame to symbolize at home and abroad the new kind of Irish
woman the women's movement had helped to create since the
970s – highly capable in professional life, liberal in social atti-
udes, politically adroit, even tough, but bringing to public affairs
true appreciation of how the human dimension must always be
espected. She also understood how the cultural sphere is the zone
n which politics is often conducted in modern and post-modern
ocieties.

At her inauguration, when she declared she would "rely on
ymbols," she revealed that her thinking had been influenced by
he *Crane Bag* and Field Day philosophies. She hoped that the
presidency could be a symbol of a "Fifth province – a place
within each one of us, that place that is open to the other – this
econciling and healing fifth province."[5] It was clear that she
wished to embrace the diversity of Ireland's population, both in
he South and in the North, where she continued to keep channels
open to the unionist community, whose views she felt had been
disregarded in the signing of the Anglo-Irish Agreement of 1985.

Robinson quickly expanded the social activity of the presidency,
both in her own official residence in Dublin and in her frequent
ravels throughout the country and abroad. She invited people
from all sorts of backgrounds, representing different cultural traditions and interests, to feel themselves part of her own voyage
of discovery about the potential of Irish life. Visits to meet with
women's groups, peace and community activists in Belfast had a
special symbolic import (at a second such meeting in June 1993
he shook hands with Sinn Féin's Gerry Adams). Just before, in
May 1993, she had taken the unprecedented and bold step of

meeting Queen Elizabeth II in London, signalling that a proces
of normalization of relations between two sovereign states, shar
ing responsibility for good governance in Northern Ireland, wa
well advanced. As a biographer remarks: "For an Irish audience
seeing the Irish President in Buckingham Palace was an especiall
potent symbol. In more ways than one, it broke – as Mary Robin
son said later – a psychological barrier."[6] Her sense of the Iris
nation was not bounded by the island of Ireland. From the star
of her presidency she had kept a lighted candle in a window o
her residence in the Phoenix Park in Dublin to remind the country
that Ireland had scattered its people to many parts of the world
to constitute what was increasingly termed a "diaspora." Thoug
some found this gesture almost mawkish, it undoubtedly struc
a note in the United States among the American Irish (whose
influence on Irish politics would increase throughout the decade
and in a period when issues of memory and commemoration
would enter national debate with renewed force, it had emotiona
salience for many. The economic crisis of the 1980s indeed ha
stimulated a new wave of emigration, creating a "green card"
and "illegal" generation of young, highly educated Irish migrant
to the United States who did not view their departure from
Ireland in the traditional, definitive terms of exile. In the poe
Greg Delanty's word's: "many of us learned the trick/of turning
ourselves into ourselves/free in the fe fiada [unseen] anonymity/
of America."[7] The candle in Áras an Uachtaráin (The President'
House) spoke for them as well as for many more nostalgic exile
of earlier migrations.

The election of Mary Robinson as President probably had tw
direct political effects. First, it further set in doubt Charle
Haughey's leadership of Fianna Fáil among those members o
the party who believed he had betrayed tradition and principle
in entering a coalition with the PDs. A group of disaffected and
ambitious members of his parliamentary party planned to unsea
him. They wanted a leader who could gain an overall majority
in a future election. The impetus of change gathered around th
figure of Albert Reynolds, who became Taoiseach when Haughey

was forced to resign over a wiretapping scandal in February 1992 (the actual incident, in which two journalists had their phones tapped on the instructions of the then Minister for Justice, Seán Doherty, had taken place almost ten years earlier).[8] Secondly, the Robinson triumph significantly boosted the popularity of the Labour Party and its leader Dick Spring. When in November 1992 Reynolds was forced into an election by the withdrawal from coalition of the PDs (whose departure they believed he had deliberately engineered), the success of the Labour Party in Dublin cut into Fianna Fáil's traditional support in the city. Consequently Reynolds failed to gain the overall majority he had been put in place to deliver and was forced into a further coalition, this time with the resurgent Labour Party itself which had doubled its representation in the Dáil. Dick Spring became Tánaiste (Deputy Prime Minister) and Minister for Foreign Affairs, leading a party with thirty-three parliamentary seats. Reflecting the new role which women were playing in Irish professional life in the 1990s, twenty women deputies took seats in the new Dáil.

In 2000 the sociologist Michel Peillon, reflecting generally on the Robinson presidency (Robinson left office in 1997, after deciding not to seek a second term), considered that she had achieved almost mythic status in Ireland, in a country that was, as economic well-being increased rapidly in the second half of the decade, learning to celebrate itself:

> She came to symbolize an Ireland that was confidently taking its place in the world; one that had achieved recognition. She represented an Ireland from which the gloom was seemingly lifting. And this modern Ireland did not reject the past or exclude tradition: all could celebrate this Ireland. Mary Robinson was the medium of this celebration; or rather, Ireland celebrated itself through its President.[9]

Peillon associates the Robinson presidency with a spirit which returned to Irish life in the 1990s, which had been almost completely suppressed since the early nineteenth century. It is through the carnivalesque, he argues (drawing on the work of Georg Bataille), that societies cope with the perceived "problem of 'consuming' a surfeit of resources."[10] By 2000, when he was writing after five years of explosive economic growth in Ireland, with major public events such as St. Patrick's Day "turned into ostentatious displays and dissipations of wealth and energy,"[11] his thesis seemed persuasive. However Robinson's celebratory note had first been struck in altogether more exiguous conditions than those of 2000. If in the latter years of her presidency, Robinson was afforded iconic status in an Ireland *en fête*, the real strength of her contribution to the country may have been that in a difficult time she had discovered and helped people to understand the great social capital invested in Irish civil society. It was well, it can be argued, that she had – for in the 1990s key building blocks of the Irish social order were suddenly to be revealed as fashioned from all-too-human clay. Economic success, as we shall see, undoubtedly helped the country and the body politic to weather these extraordinary revelations about the nature of power, influence and authority in Ireland; but the kind of self-confidence Robinson had engendered enabled many ordinary citizens to feel that their own participation in society was a real resource, in a decade when the foundations of the Irish social structure seemed to fracture.

II

Most crucially, the Catholic church experienced unimaginable problems in the 1990s and found its authority in Irish life undermined from within and attacked from without. For a series of controversies and major scandals meant that it scarcely ever appeared in anything other than a negative light in the Irish media, which for much of the century had been markedly respectful of ecclesiastical interests.[12]

To begin with, the issue of abortion emerged again in a way most likely to disturb the church's equanimity. The 1983 amend ent to forbid abortion had seemed definitively to rule out the ossibility of legal abortion in Ireland. The impetus for this mendment had come from lay Catholics, but the hierarchy, in aking its preference clear on the form of words to be put before e people at the very least had suggested it was happy to have e running made for its views by the lay activists. In conse- uence they could not escape the irritation, impatience and out- ght obloquy which was directed towards the amendment's spon- rs, when after nine years its effects were made manifest in lation to one tragic case.

In February 1992 the news broke that the Attorney General, arry Whelehan, had sought and been granted an interim injunc- on, citing the 1983 amendment, to restrain a fourteen-year-old regnant victim of rape from travelling to the UK for an abortion. he girl and her family had already made the journey to England hen the judgment was handed down. The country was appalled y this horrific turn of events. Emily O'Reilly comments in her ook on the tactics of those who had masterminded the 1983 mendment that the public should not have been as surprised as was. Cases taken since 1983 had shown that the courts were bliged to interpret the amendment in a severe way (forbidding bortion information, for example).[13] But few had imagined such n acute dilemma. It got much worse. The girl (who, evidence uggested, had threatened suicide) and her parents returned from ngland and awaited the further judgment of the High Court, hich confirmed the injunction in terms that effectively made iss X (as she was known to protect her identity) a prisoner of he state. It appeared that the irresolvable conundrum at the heart f Article 40.3.3 of the Constitution – "with due regard to the qual right to life of mother and child" – would be "solved" by lways giving the child's right to life precedence. The High ourt's judgment was appealed to the Supreme Court and to eneral astonishment that court, by a majority of four-to-one, oncluded that a threat to the life of an expectant mother (includ- ng the possibility that she might commit suicide) was grounds or an abortion and that such persons could travel abroad for the

termination. However only those whose lives were at risk could
be permitted to travel for that purpose. (For Miss X and her
family their terrible ordeal had something of a conclusion when,
reportedly, she had a miscarriage.)

Accordingly, three challenging prospects opened up for the
Irish state and its people. Abortions when a mother's life was at
risk might legally be performed by Irish doctors, though it was
unlikely many would choose to do so; conversely many of the
5,000 and more women who travelled to England each year for
abortions might find themselves restrained by court orders; and
the government might have to produce a new amendment to
deal with this confusing situation.

All this was bad enough, but when it became known that a
vote in favour of the 1991 Maastricht Treaty (the blueprint for
European economic and monetary union), which was to be put
before the electorate in a referendum later in 1992, was in jeopardy because of a protocol the pro-Life movement had insisted
be placed in the Treaty in support of what was now shown to be a
dangerously ambiguous article in the Constitution, then patience
wore very thin. Voices which in the past could not have been
raised in support of abortion in even the most limited of circumstances, now made themselves heard. The behaviour of the hierarchy, and of what were perceived as the machinations of its lay
shock troops, could now be openly criticized. In the event the
referendum on Maastricht was passed by a considerable majority
with another referendum promised to protect Irish women's right
to travel and to acquire information on abortion. That referendum took place in November of the same year (concurrently
with the general election). Although two significant rights had
been affirmed, it left what was called the "substantive issue" of
abortion still defined by the Supreme Court judgment. Pro-
choice and anti-abortion groups had both, for radically different
reasons, opposed the proposal to deal with this issue, which would
have allowed an abortion when the mother's life was threatened
but would have ruled out the possibility of, or determination to
commit suicide as constituting such a threat.[14] Tellingly, in the

summer of 1992, a bill making its way through the Dáil to liberalize the contraceptive laws, in response to the AIDS crisis,
was passed without much contention.

There is no doubt that the Catholic church's position as moral
arbiter in Irish society was weakened by this crisis. Consequently
it began to seem possible that moral life could be governed by
principles other than those of a church which claimed sole right
properly to inform the consciences of its members. An individualistic morality, which took cognizance of specific circumstances,
began to replace obedience to authority and its absolutes even
among devout believers (in the matter of contraception it was
obvious that many of the faithful had for years simply disregarded
church teaching in that area of their lives), especially as revelations
began to emerge that distinguished churchmen scarcely practised
what they preached.

This was brought home with stunning force in May 1992 when
the popular and high-profile Bishop of Galway, Eamonn Casey,
suddenly resigned and left the country. It had come out that he
had had an affair in the early 1970s with an American woman,
Annie Murphy, who had borne his child. A picture emerged of
a man who had apparently spurned both his former lover and
son and had enjoyed the fruits of his episcopal office without
much attention to his obligations as a father. The sense of betrayal
among many devout Catholics was palpable, as was, by contrast,
a relish for the scandalous, especially among those who had borne
in the past the brunt of church disapproval for their less than
perfect marital circumstances. The sight of Annie Murphy being
interviewed on prime-time national television was a watershed in
Ireland. In retrospect, in the light of subsequent, quite terrible
revelations concerning churchmen and women, Casey's behaviour seems possibly less egregious than it did at the time. But
in 1992 it certainly undermined ecclesiastical credibility.

That credibility was profoundly challenged as the decade wore
on: a spate of clerical child abuse and other sexual scandals set
the church in the dock of public opinion in a way that would
have been unimaginable in the recent past. One of the most

disturbing and momentous of these scandals involved a member of the Norbertine Order, a Father Brendan Smyth.[15] In March 1991 he was interviewed by the police in Belfast and charged with the sexual abuse of minors. Released on bail, he fled to his home abbey, in County Cavan, across the Irish border, where for almost three years he had avoided the efforts of the Northern Ireland authorities to have him extradited to appear before their courts. In January 1994 he finally surrendered himself to Northern justice and in June of the same year he pleaded guilty to seventeen charges, dating back to the 1960s. He was gaoled in Northern Ireland and on his release stood trial in Dublin. He died following a heart attack a month into his second gaol term, in 1997. An Ulster Television documentary broadcast in October 1994 by the *Counterpoint* programme brought deeply troubling aspects of the affair to wide public attention (UTV is readily available in much of the Republic). It was argued that not only had Catholic church authorities long known about their paedophile priest, but that they had sought to deal with the problem he presented by moving him from post to post in the hope that he might desist from his activities. The possibility that he might have been turned over to the civil authorities had not, it seemed, entered into their calculations, which appeared to be related more to guarding the Church's good name than to protecting children.

The *Counterpoint* programme and the subsequent book by its researcher, Chris Moore, certainly damaged the reputation of the Catholic church in Ireland. Moore's judgment in his book that "to the bitter end, all those in authority in the Catholic church whom I approached singularly refused to be held accountable for Fr Smyth"[16] was especially damning. Ironically it was the civil authority in the Republic that first felt the heavy aftershock of this seismic event in Irish ecclesiastical history.

The *Counterpoint* programme claimed that "extradition warrants issued by the RUC in the last week of April 1993 had been sent to the Republic but never acted upon."[17] This meant that seven months had passed between the date on which these were sent and the date on which Smyth voluntarily left the Irish jurisdiction. It would eventually become known that this circumstance had arisen simply because of decisions taken within the busy office of the Attorney General in Dublin in respect of the prioritization of work to be done there. In the autumn of 1994, however, it created the context in which a considerable political crisis unfolded.

The Taoiseach, Albert Reynolds, wanted to appoint the Attorney General, Harry Whelehan, to the presidency of the High Court. His coalition partners in the Labour Party were not enthusiastic about this. Dick Spring and his Labour ministerial colleagues were intent that the Attorney General should explain to the cabinet in person and to their full satisfaction how the Smyth matter had been handled in his office and how what had come to seem like an undue delay in executing the extradition warrants, had occurred. When Whelehan was nonetheless appointed president of the High Court without the agreement of Spring and his Labour ministerial colleagues (they had left the cabinet meeting in protest at Reynolds' intention to proceed with that appointment), then the stability of the coalition government was in obvious jeopardy. By mid-November, after much high drama in the Dáil generated both by the Smyth affair and Whelehan's appointment, Spring and the other Labour ministers resigned from government. Since he could no longer depend on a parliamentary majority to sustain him in office, Reynolds, with a good grace, bowed to the inevitable. He resigned as Taoiseach and as leader of Fianna Fáil. Subsequently Labour entered a new coalition with Fine Gael and Democratic Left (a recently-formed party). This coalition (dubbed "The Rainbow coalition") summoned enough votes in the Dáil to elect John Bruton, leader of Fine Gael, as Taoiseach; the Rainbow coalition would hold power until the summer of 1997. That the charging of a single member of the regular clergy in Belfast in 1991 should have set off a chain of events which brought down an Irish government in 1994 was the stuff of awful fantasy made real. In the aftermath of the crisis Albert Reynolds had the look of a man struck by lightning, unsure if he had lived to tell the tale or not.

The effects of all of this on Harry Whelehan, who resigned after only six days in office, could only be imagined.

For many in holy orders the fact that the Catholic church in Ireland had become the focus for child abuse scandals was a terrible ordeal. In 1995, in the Catholic periodical the *Furrow*, which in the 1990s addressed the subject in a number of anguished articles, Father Enda McDonagh, professor of moral theology at St. Patrick's College, Maynooth, acknowledged that "the pain lines of the Brendan Smyth affair run their savage way throughout the island of Ireland"[18] and reflected that "a sense of darkness, of winter darkness, of the darkness of death has surrounded recent revelations."[19] He bravely recalled Christians' complicity with the Jewish Holocaust of the 1940s in a way that allowed profoundly troubling analogies to seem possible. In the light of subsequent revelations on the national television station, RTE, in a three-part documentary entitled *States of Fear* (transmitted in April and May 1999), about the conditions that had prevailed until quite recent years in Irish industrial schools and reformatories run by religious orders, this did not seem to be an over-reaction. For these institutions, to which orphaned and unwanted children were dispatched and many young people were incarcerated for crimes and misdemeanours, were revealed in some instances to have been places of virtual slavery, of vicious cruelty and sexual depredation. And it was clear that the state had not taken its supervisory responsibilities seriously. In May 1999, Taoiseach Bertie Ahern responded to public outrage over the revelations by issuing a formal government apology on behalf of the state and its citizens to the victims of this system and a commission was established to investigate the matter (which has not yet finally reported). Writing of the appalled reaction of the Irish public to these exposures of a dark stain on the nation's twentieth-century life, the journalist and social commentator Mary Kenny observed:

> The scale of the cruelty seemed so systematic that it was as though it was inherent in our history: not only were the religious

who ran these institutions accused before the bar of history, so was the Irish state, which utterly failed to take responsibility for those in its care. So, indeed, were the complacent middle classes, who used these reformatories as a source for servants, and so was the media, which remained indifferent to the punitive regimes around them.[20]

So devastating were the traumata undergone by the church in the 1990s, as "a veritable avalanche of clerical scandals" poured "into the Irish public arena," that Kenny could conclude in 2000: "the very concept of 'Catholic Ireland' was by the end of the century, gone."[21] In this she was echoing what some members of the clergy were admitting in private. In a public letter to the papal nuncio, published in 1995 in the *Furrow*, the correspondent reported how "three times in past months different priest friends have said to me that they now see their function as making sure that the Irish Catholic church gets a decent burial."[22] Tom Inglis, in his book *Moral Monopoly: The Rise and Fall of the Catholic Church in Modern Ireland*, assessed the position of the church in more measured terms: "Suddenly, the Church has lost its sacredness and has become another interest group in civil society which is open to the same inspection as any other."[23]

What Mary Kenny's dramatic death notice reflected was not that Ireland had ceased to be a religious country (the fact, for example, that about a million people turned out to pay their respects to the relics of St. Thérèse of Lisieux, when they were toured through the country in the summer of 2001 bespeaks vibrant popular piety), but that the conservative social construction of people, nation and state was no longer as securely in place as it had been for much of the century (Inglis offers an extended analysis in these terms).[24] Individual Catholics were disregarding aspects of church teaching they found onerous or disagreeable, while a process of secularization was making life outside the social direction of the church available to many. In 1996 one analyst observed that "the fact that women are becoming more and more alienated from Catholic teaching on the family and on sexuality is bound to have huge consequences for the whole fabric of Irish society."[25] She also noted that the figures for those who claim they never attend religious services "is getting closer to the European average and would seem to indicate that Irish people's religious practice is converging towards that of other European countries."[26] In 2001 another analyst found it striking that "Irish weekly church-attending under twenty-five-year-olds are now a minority of their age group."[27] A national survey in 1998 had found weekly attendance at mass stood at 48 percent of Catholics in urban areas, though 77 percent of Catholics in rural areas maintained the practice of weekly mass-going. The overall figure of 60 percent represented a steep decline from the 91 percent of Catholics as weekly mass-goers in 1973.[28]

Perhaps even more seriously for the future of the church, vocations to the religious life fell away drastically. As recorded by Inglis, between 1966 and 1995 "the number of priests, nuns and brothers decreased by over one-third (35 percent) and in the same period "the number of vocations dropped from 1,409 in a year to 111, a decrease of 92 percent."[29] Although the decline among the secular clergy was much less marked than the among the regular, a crisis in religious life that had been in the making since the 1960s now seemed irreversible. Inglis paints a picture of a geriatric institution sapped of new blood.

At the political level this climate was reflected in legal changes. In 1993 the Fianna Fáil Minister for Justice was able to put a bill through the houses of the Oireachtas to decriminalize homosexual relations between consenting adults (the state in fact was required to do this on foot of the victory David Norris had won before the European Court of Human Rights). It met with surprisingly little dissent, despite the fact that the age of consent was set at seventeen. In 1995 a referendum to change the Constitution to allow divorce under fairly strict conditions was narrowly carried (50.3 percent in favour, 49.7 percent against), despite the fact that the same groups who had fought against change in 1986 had returned to the fray.

The social climate of 1990s' Ireland suggested, moreover, that the moral policing in sexual matters the church had enforced in the early decades of independence had almost completely broken down. In 1997 Garret FitzGerald challenged the nation by claiming that recent statistics showed that "for many people the institution of marriage has simply lost much of its significance ... [there is] a widespread dissociation of marriage and childbirth."[30] Michael O'Connell, analyzing the matter further, acknowledged the salience of FitzGerald's conclusion, observing that "the trend towards the unlocking of parenthood and marital status was a broad European one. However, in Ireland the change was taking place far more quickly than elsewhere – at an electrifying pace sociologically speaking."[31] O'Connell concludes:

> The trend overall in Ireland is one where people feel less obliged to get married, are marrying later, no longer rigorously associated marriage and parenthood, or for that matter see marriage as a strict condition for having a sex life. And they are less willing simply to endure a married relationship that no longer meets their experience.[32]

The fact was that many young women in the 1990s thought that a career was at least as important as marriage. The nuclear family as a social norm, established, as we saw in the postwar period, was losing its attraction, especially for young women. The statistics reflected a changed workforce. In 1976 there were 212,000 women in that workforce. By 1996 the figure stood at 488,000,[33] though much of the work undertaken by women was part-time. The suburban Irish family with the mother and children at home and the father at work was increasingly a thing of the past. High house prices and other costs often made it necessary for both partners to work outside the home – especially in the cities. And society became more tolerant of the arrangements people made to cope with marital breakdown. This was highlighted by the fact that Taoiseach Bertie Ahern, who had assumed the leadership of Fianna Fáil when Albert Reynolds resigned in 1994, and had taken power in 1997 in coalition with the PDs, was in a second relationship, although he had not divorced his wife. His partner Celia Larkin accompanied him at state and civic occasions, to little adverse comment.

III

If the church was assailed by manifold problems and shamed by a flood of discreditable revelations in the 1990s, the state and the Irish political class were far from immune from the unmasking mood that gripped the media and public alike in an extraordinary decade.

In May 1991 a British television station broadcast a documentary on suspected corruption in the Irish beef trade. The allegations of irregularities in a beef empire, Goodman International, were so grave and were made so publicly that Haughey's government, pressed by Desmond O'Malley of the Progressive Democrats, was forced to set up a tribunal of enquiry on the matter headed by the President of the High Court, Mr. Justice Liam Hamilton. No one in 1991 could have foreseen that the 1990s was to be a decade of tribunals, some of which would complete their investigations into various forms of alleged Irish corruption before the decade's end, others which are still sitting at the time of writing. In the event Mr. Justice Hamilton's tribunal delivered its report in July 1994, making public once more the scarcely surprising fact: tax evasion and other scams had been operated in the industry. The political ramifications of this matter were considerable. In 1992 the Taoiseach Albert Reynolds had employed the privilege of the tribunal to challenge Desmond O'Malley's evidence to it. Shortly thereafter, his government, as we saw, fell, when O'Malley withdrew the PDs from the governing coalition (though Reynolds was probably happy enough to see the end of what he had hoped would be the "temporary little arrangement" of the coalition with the PDs that Haughey had bequeathed to him). When the enquiry's report appeared in the summer of 1994, the distrust of Reynolds' new coalition partners in the Labour Party was aroused since they believed he precipitately announced that he had been vindicated by the tribunal, before they had had a chance to consider the implications of what Mr. Justice Hamilton had found. In the autumn the distrust occasioned among his coalition partners by this incident was intensified by the Whelehan affair which broke the Labour/Fianna Fáil coalition, brought down Reynolds's government, effectively ending his political career.

For all its dramatic political consequences, the legal cases it generated and its considerable constitutional implications,[34] the beef tribunal and subsequent report did not catch the public imagination or generate righteous indignation in the way later enquiries did. Of these the McCracken Tribunal and the interlinked Moriarty Tribunal were epic, even tragic public dramas, substantially damaging as they did the reputation of Charles J. Haughey.

Like the Father Smyth affair, this controversy began with a police matter. In February 1992 Ben Dunne of the Dunnes Stores chain was charged in Florida (after a night of wild partying), with the possession of an illegal drug (he was fined and required to attend a London clinic to help him with his drug problem). So affronted was his sister Margaret Heffernan, at the image of the family firm being besmirched that legal conflict erupted in the family. She commissioned a study of Dunne's conduct of its financial affairs. Documents existed dealing with large unexplained payments to politicians. The details leaked out. In 1997 the Taoiseach John Bruton established the McCracken Tribunal to examine these payments. It reported in seven months. Among its principal findings were that Ben Dunne had paid substantial sums to Charles Haughey. It was also revealed that Haughey seemed perfectly at ease with having a prominent businessman gift him large sums of money (indeed he seemed to believe it was his due). In its investigations, the enquiry had opened a trail which eventually led to the Cayman Islands and the role of a company there, Ansbacher (Cayman) Ltd., which had been providing a safe haven for the offshore funds of a wealthy Irish elite. Haughey's personal accountant, Desmond Traynor, had, until his death, been the linchpin of an ingenious arrangement that could only credibly have been devised to expedite tax evasion (though not all who availed of its services necessarily evaded tax). This scheme effectively involved a coded "mirror" account operated by Traynor within a Dublin private bank which allowed interest-bearing deposits to be technically "offshore," but available for clients' use.

When Charles Haughey appeared before Mr. Justice McCracken, he claimed lack of knowledge of his own financial affairs, saying that he had left such matters to Traynor so that he could devote himself to public life without the distraction of money worries. McCracken found many of his claims "unacceptable and untrue." And: "By allowing himself to be put in a position of dependency, Mr. Charles Haughey failed in his obligations to his constituents and to the citizens of [the] state. . . ." A recent account of Haughey's career concludes of the McCracken Tribunal's findings: "The publication in full of Haughey's initial [evasive] response to McCracken, coupled with a retraction and a grovelling apology in which he effectively accepted that he had lied, reduced his reputation to tatters."[35]

In October 1997 the Moriarty Tribunal was established to investigate matters further (although it was held up by various legal challenges and got down to its real work only on 28 January 1999). For a fascinated public the wait was strikingly worthwhile. At last the mystery of Charles Haughey's millions began spectacularly to unravel. Instead of the great financial acumen that his supporters attributed to him, Haughey was revealed as a man who had in the 1970s and '80s lived wildly beyond his means and had become hugely indebted to a strangely supine creditor, the Allied Irish Banks, and subsequently had depended on such businessmen as could be persuaded to bankroll his ostentatiously lavish way of life.

Sadly, for one who had aspired to greatness and an honoured place in Irish history, Haughey's performance at the Moriarty Tribunal became the stuff of comedy. As the details of his extravagance emerged and the extent of his dependency was etched in the public mind, he began to seem tragic too. In poor health, he seemed like a victim of hubris, instead of the commanding political presence he had been at the height of his powers, as the highly effective Minister for Finance he had been in the 1960s and as the decisive Taoiseach of the late 1980s.

Haughey was not alone in his vicissitudes. Indeed he seems only to have been at the apex of a sector of society that, with a fine abandon, had indulged itself since the economically resurgent 1960s. A Department of Industry and Commerce enquiry into the Ansbacher account, published in July 2002, presented a case that it was a "deliberately complex . . . sham trust structure" made use of by pillars of the community. It reckoned that there was evidence that it "facilitated widespread tax evasion" (although the Inspectors who carried out the investigations cautioned: "a finding that any particular individual is a client of Ansbacher is not a finding that that person evaded tax"). Furthermore, in October 1997 the Minister for Foreign Affairs, Ray Burke, was forced to resign amid rumours about his role in alleged planning scandals in north county Dublin. A tribunal under the chairmanship of Mr. Justice Feargus Flood began its hearings in 1997 to examine the planning history of land there. In 1998 its remit was extended bringing Burke to its attention. At its hearings dramatic allegations and denials emerged about considerable alleged payments by developers to Burke. A key witness at the tribunal, James Gogarty during his evidence also made serious allegations against George Redmond, retired assistant city and county manager in Dublin, who had been involved in planning matters for three decades. When Redmond was arrested at Dublin airport in February 1999, returning from abroad with a substantial sum in his possession, questions about his role in planning increased. Subsequently allegations were reported that he had about twenty accounts under his control. It was also reported that there was "evidence that about a million pounds had passed through those accounts over the previous twenty years."[36]

The picture of suspicious payments that the Flood Tribunal helped to create lacked the high drama of Haughey's downfall.

It suggested, however, that a culture of tax evasion had been tolerated among Ireland's elite for many years, inducing individuals to believe that they were immune to serious penalty. (Though the tribunals gave the Revenue a lot to investigate.) That leniency for tax defaulters could indeed await those prepared to keep their heads down, had in fact been encouraged by action of the state itself. A tax amnesty had been granted in 1988 accompanied by dire warnings of future proceedings against defaulters. In the financially straitened conditions of that year, to wide astonishment, it was revealed that the amnesty had amassed a very welcome £500 million for the state coffers. In 1993 the exercise was repeated with even better terms on offer. The message it inevitably sent to evaders and to compliant taxpayers alike was that cynical pragmatism dictated government policy. Probably, criminally acquired assets were "laundered" on both occasions. The state brought in about £200 million from the second amnesty with over £1.3 billion written off.[37]

Writing in September 1999, as the decade of tribunals drew to a close, the *Irish Times* columnist and author Fintan O'Toole gave this stark estimate of a malaise at the apex of Irish society: "We have to adjust our understanding of contemporary Ireland to take account of two startling facts. One is that, at least from the early 1980s onwards, a large swathe of Ireland's ruling elite silently withdrew its allegiance from the state. The other is that organized crime in Ireland, which we used to imagine as the preserve of shifty working-class men . . . is also carried out by respectable, beautifully tailored members of the upper-middle class."[38] O'Toole might have noted that some of those in the upper echelons of society who could be judged as having failed in their duties as citizens were often the loudest in their proclaimed nationalism (Haughey, for instance, published his collected speeches as *The Spirit of the Nation* in 1986). Yet other things in the period suggested that white-collar crime pervaded more widely than among an elite golden circle, or in the upper-middle class. Many ordinary people had lodged money in banks, employing, often on the banks' advice, bogus foreign addresses to evade tax in a symbolic act of exile from a country whose services they were willing to exploit, but whose state they were determined to cheat. A black economy burgeoned in which almost everyone seemed to be involved in one way or another. Where conscience pricked, the very high levels of personal taxation, especially of PAYE workers, in the 1970s and '80s, were adduced in exculpation.

Church, people, nation, through much of the twentieth century in Ireland, had shared a consensus on basic aspects of sexual morality, on marriage and on family life and values, which they were happy for the state to uphold by law. For many however – especially since the 1960s when a thwarted, energetic materialism had been released and given respectability as economic nationalism which could result in Irish unity – commercial life was conducted with little or no sense of civic duty and compliance. Tax law in particular was regarded by many as less a matter of ethical responsibility than an evil to be evaded if at all possible. The tribunals of the 1990s merely made manifest flagrant examples where the state was treated as an inconvenience to be circumvented. That the state itself in the period seemed capable of moral uncertainty did not induce much confidence even in those who wished to give Caesar his due.

This disturbing fact was made grimly evident in the revelation in 1994 that the Blood Transfusion Service Board (BTSB) had unknowingly given a contaminated blood product to patients in the late 1970s which meant that at least 55,000 women would require tests to establish whether or not they had been infected with the hepatitis C virus, thereby exposing them to a potentially fatal illness. Quite soon over 1,000 women were found to have been affected by the virus. A tribunal of enquiry, which reported in March 1997, confirmed what had been slowly forced into the public domain since 1994: that in a state institution professional error had meant that women treated for rhesus negative blood had been infected with a dangerous disease.

Shocking as that was, the state's self-protective attitude as it sought to avoid liability was a signal affront to the public's sense of how their democratic state should behave. Compensation was offered in terms which would have avoided the acceptance of liability and any further legal action by victims. It was made clear by the state that anyone who took a case to the courts would be met by the state's obdurate determination to avoid liability. A dying woman, a Mrs. Brigid McCole, bravely persisted in seeking a court judgment in the matter, only to have the state appear to oppose the speedy hearing of her case in what seemed a cruel fashion. At the last moment the BTSB did admit liability and offered compensation, which Mrs. McCole accepted. She died on 2 October 1996, a few days before her case had been scheduled to take place. A separate scandal involving blood products (hepatitis C- and HIV-infected product had unknowingly been given to haemophiliacs in the 1980s) further rocked the public's confidence in the medical services. In 2002 the Lindsay Tribunal report on the matter criticised the BTSB but did not apportion any individual blame.

IV

It is difficult at this date to assess the effects on Irish society of the scandals and revelations involving both church and state in the 1990s. There was undoubtedly some reduction in faith in institutions, an increase in cynicism about public life, and a gathering determination that some of those most grievously involved should be held to account (the tribunals were themselves an indicator that the public at least wanted to know what had been going on). What perhaps can be said, as we suggested above, is that Irish society was able to deal with revelations which might otherwise have caused a major breakdown in national self-belief because of two things. Mary Robinson's releasing in the early 1990s of the energies of civil society (which her successor Mary McAleese continued to endorse) meant that many people were prepared and enabled to derive a sense of personal and social dignity from a wide variety of their activities in the public sphere, despite the failings of politicians. And good citizenship was uncoupled to a degree from the practice of religion, so a crisis in the church's moral authority did not mean society lacked moral guidance and a sense of its autonomous worth. Secondly, from the mid 1990s the country enjoyed a remarkable economic boom which enormously increased national self-confidence at a time when revelations of political and economic malfeasance might otherwise have alienated the public from the freedoms of the neo-liberal, and increasingly global, marketplace. In the boom years the alleged misdoings of some of the few who found themselves before the tribunals paled before a success story that drew the attention of the world.

Some simple statistics reveal the scale of this economic explosion. Ireland's growth rate averaged around 7 percent for the decade and around 9 percent for the second five years of the decade. In 1999 unemployment stood at 2 percent (virtually full employment). Consumption rose remarkably. In 1995 the Irish consumer spent £23 billion on goods and services, in 1999, £34 billion, and in 2000 the figure almost reached an extraordinary £40 billion.[39] What a London-based economist in 1994 had dubbed "the Celtic Tiger" was taking to its new-found wealth with enthusiasm. And those who had benefited from the boom could take satisfaction from an OECD report that in 1999 had found "the Irish economy has notched up five straight years of stunning economic performance. No other OECD member country has been able to match its outcomes in a variety of dimensions."[40] In 2000 Raymond MacSharry and Padraic White (both of whom could rightly feel proud of Ireland's achievement, MacSharry as former Minister for Finance, White as former director of the Industrial Development Authority, responsible for attracting foreign direct investment) concluded of "the most far-reaching transformation of the economy since the foundation of the state":

. . . under virtually every indicator, greater economic progress was made since 1987 than in any comparable period over the previous sixty-four years. Rising real incomes have ensured that living standards have converged on the European average, virtual full employment has been reached and the tide of emigration has been reversed. Workers are now returning to take up employment at home, rather than leaving to try and find work abroad.[41]

Economists and social commentators have adduced a variety of reasons for the Irish economic miracle of the 1990s. A blend of factors, some fortuitous, some planned, is identified in accounts to date.[42] Crucial were the protracted boom of the 1990s in the United States and the strategies adopted by the Irish state to make Ireland attractive to foreign direct investment in the era of the knowledge economy. The fiscal rectitude of the Haughey/MacSharry period, together with a sustained neo-liberal commitment to reduce capital and personal taxation (for which the Progressive Democrats and Charlie McCreevy, Fianna Fáil's Minister for Finance in Bertie Ahern's government, were the most vigorous advocates) was accompanied throughout the decade by the institution of social partnership with the trade unions, established by Haughey in 1987. These agreements, which effectively brought the unions close to the heart of government, secured industrial peace as Ireland prepared for and adapted to the European Single Market, completed in 1992. International capital was attracted to Ireland, especially in the information technology sector, by a well-educated, English-language-speaking workforce in a country where an infrastructure inferior in European terms was being significantly improved by a major injection of structural funds from the European Union. A low level of corporation tax undercut the competition in the investment stakes (much to the chagrin of Ireland's European partners).

MacSharry and White were right to set the successes of the 1990s in a historical context. For twice in the twentieth century the economic basis of independence had seemed fundamentally in question – in the late 1950s and in the late 1980s. The scale of Ireland's success as the century ended can most obviously be measured in demographic terms. When Ireland had seemed to be dying on its economic feet in the 1950s, its population was at its lowest recorded level (the nadir was reached in the 1961 census at 2,818,341). The preliminary report of the 2002 census revealed that the country's population stood at 3,917,377 and had risen by 8 percent since 1996. With an annual increase of 1.3 percent, Ireland was doing well in European terms. When one considers that in the 1950s a country with a population of under three million was incapable of generating sufficient employ-ment to stem the flood of emigration that had drained Ireland since at least the 1840s, then the achievement of the 1990s comes into striking focus. For by the end of the decade a shortage of labour was what seemed to threaten the opening up of a vista of endless growth. Married women, who had in the past been forced out of the labour market, were encouraged by tax reform to join the workforce.

The statistics of consumption reflected the booming economy of the second five years of the decade, reaching, as we noted, the figure of £40 billion spent on goods and services in 2000. By 1999/2000 urban families spent an average of 612 euro per week, with Dublin families spending an average of 684 euro (the average gross weekly income in Dublin stood at 842 euro). Over 90 percent of households owned a washing machine and almost 90 percent a fixed telephone. In 1987 only 5.3 percent of house-holds had a microwave oven; in 1999/2000 71.5 percent did so. Almost 50 percent of households owned two or more television sets and 85 percent of homes could boast a video player; whilst almost a third of householders possessed a dishwasher.[43] Mobile phone use became commonplace, expanding from 25,000 units in 1990 to 1,408,000 in 1999.[44] The new car in the driveway became a symbol of suburban affluence (the sale of luxury cars per year almost trebled between 1993 and 1997, and rose from 1,606 in 1987 to 5,789 in 1997[45]).

That Ireland was becoming more and more of a suburban and commuter society (or what Mary Corcoran has dubbed, in a telling term, an "ex-urbanisation" society)[46] was made clear in the preliminary report of the 2002 census. The population of

Dublin city and Dublin County as a whole grew by 6.1 percent between 1996 and 2002 but the city population increased by only 2.7 percent. It was in the outlying suburbs that major growth took place. The Esker area of the west Dublin suburb of Lucan almost trebled its population between 1996 and 2002. And in the province of Leinster, with Dublin as the lodestar, the population exceeded two million. Accordingly many commuter towns within a range of fifty or so miles of the capital saw large increases in population, when rocketing house prices in Dublin put a home beyond the reach of many first-time buyers (and even of those couples where both were in paid employment) as Dubliners and migrants who sought work in the city bought and rented properties far from their places of employment. Long-settled suburbs of Dublin actually saw their populations fall as offspring spread their wings for the green-field sites, where new housing estates mushroomed. County Meath's population rose by 22.1 percent, while that of County Kildare rose by 21.5 percent. The town of Ratoath in County Meath increased its population by 82.3 percent in a six-year period. In the west of Ireland Galway city increased its population by 14.9 percent as its suburbs burgeoned. Throughout the countryside bungalow blight intensified.

The majority of this development was a response only to market forces and reflected little spatial planning. Inadequacies in the transport network swiftly became all too obvious, with traffic gridlock in the cities and overcrowding in trains and buses. Mary Corcoran has described the new Dublin of ex-urbanized citizens:

> The ex-urbanised city now climbs to the foothills of the Dublin mountains and sweeps down to the seaside towns of north Wicklow, also extending northward and westward beyond the city's boundaries. On the perimeter of the city, industrial estates, business parks and, most recently, shopping malls have sprung up, all of which are linked through a series of ring roads and motorways.[47]

Corcoran sees the shopping malls, to which access is almost entirely by car, in this new Irish environment as centrally involved in the construction of novel forms of consciousness – uprooted, and displaced, inhabiting a globalized system of distribution in a globalized economy. In the mall, private space masquerades as public space and makes consumption seem communal as "citizenship is being defined as the capacity to participate in the new means of consumption."[48]

Consumption of a specific kind began to pose a real problem in a decade of high disposable incomes. Alcohol abuse became a significant problem of affluence. Between 1989 and 2001 Ireland's alcohol consumption per capita increased by 40 percent.[49] Young people were especially vulnerable to clever advertising campaigns that made drinking a part of youth culture in a way it had not been before. In January 2003 a joint committee of the houses of the Oireachtas heard that the incidence of intoxication among teenagers had increased by 370 percent since 1996.[50] Huge theme-bars aimed directly at the youth market opened in the cities, replacing more traditional public houses where a diverse clientele had traditionally mixed. Opening hours were extended in the hope that drunkenness would decrease as drinking became a more relaxed social activity. Instead, public disorder in the early hours of the morning in cities and even in small towns became a serious problem.

Drug abuse remained to scar inner city communities and to add to the muggings and larcenies that swelled the crime statistics (though following the shooting dead of the crusading crime correspondent Veronica Guerin in 1996, the Criminal Assets Bureau had significant successes in breaking up organized crime). Suicide, particularly among young men, rose alarmingly. The gap between the poorest and richest in society palpably widened, even if the majority had grown richer in the boom.[51]

As a newly rich nation in the 1990s, Ireland found itself, to its considerable surprise, the object of immigration, a situation for which it had scarcely prepared itself. Ireland for so long had been a country of emigration that immigration had never registered as a potential problem in public debate. In the period 1996 to 2002, 153,067 persons moved to the state, an average of

25,511 annually. The economy by the end of the decade, as we saw, was beginning to be troubled by labour shortages, so many of these new residents quickly found employment. However, the position of those who came to Ireland as refugees, seeking political asylum, was altogether more problematic (from a low figure of thirty-nine persons applying for refugee status in 1992 those seeking such status rose to 7,724 in 1999).[52] Forbidden to work, subsisting on small state handouts, often forced to wait years before their cases could be heard, asylum-seekers in the 1990s faced hostility in the popular press as they were branded as "fake" applicants, driven from such places as Somalia, the former Yugoslavia, the Democratic Republic of Congo, Nigeria, Libya, and Algeria only by economic ambition.

What cannot be gainsaid about the Ireland of the 1990s, however, is that a sense of success, nationally and internationally, gave the country a confidence that its problems could be overcome. An inveterate fatalism about the nation's role in the world was replaced by a spirit of enterprise and expectation. There was little debate about adopting the euro in 1999 (the actual currency to become legal tender on 1 January 2002) as the appropriate currency for an economy which was a European success story. The achievements of an indigenous IT company like Iona Technologies; the sheer effrontery of Michael O'Leary's Ryanair in successfully undercutting major airlines; the renovation of Croke Park, in Dublin (the headquarters of the Gaelic Athletic Association) to make it a state-of-the-art stadium; the exploits of the Irish soccer team in the European and World Cups, the Tour de France beginning in Ireland in 1998; the award in 1995 of the Nobel Prize for Literature to Seamus Heaney, all represented ways in which the Irish could feel good about themselves. The country took in its stride the information that Ireland had become the world's major exporter of computer software and accepted as appropriate recognition of a new status its accession to a seat on the United Nations Security Council in 2000. All this managed to keep the national mood high even in 2001 and 2002 when economic indicators began to signal that the boom was ending.

V

The enhanced self-confidence of an economically successful state may be judged by future historians as salient among the complex of factors which enabled the Irish government in the 1990s to address the vexed issue of the status of Northern Ireland with creative, energetic flexibility.[53] Other elements in the equation that by the spring of 1998 allowed a far-reaching agreement to be reached in Belfast between the British and Irish governments on the future governance of the province, can be adduced. With the collapse of communism in Eastern Europe and the Soviet Union and the ending of the Cold War, the United States had less reason to fear offending its NATO ally, Britain, by involving itself in the Irish imbroglio. It was probably this which allowed a President of the United States, Bill Clinton, who was elected in November 1992, anxious for a foreign policy success, the chance to make resolution of conflict in Northern Ireland a policy aim. For by focusing on Ireland he could satisfy an Irish-American constituency which had long pressed for US action on Northern Ireland. Furthermore, Peter Brooke, the British Secretary of State for Northern Ireland, had publicly signalled the United Kingdom's awareness that things were stirring when, in November 1990, he had put on record that Britain had no "selfish strategic or economic interest" in Northern Ireland and would not stand in the way of a united Ireland if it was achieved by consent. Political change now brought new players onto the stage of British-Irish affairs. John Major succeeded Mrs. Thatcher as Prime Minister in November 1990. Albert Reynolds succeeded Charles Haughey as Taoiseach in February 1992, retaining power in coalition with Labour following the general election in late November of that year. Both Major and Reynolds were pragmatists anxious to be rid of the burdens of the past. Furthermore, secret contacts begun in October 1990 between the British government and Sinn Féin (which augmented communications which had been passing between them since at least the mid-

1980s), while the IRA was still engaged in bloody armed struggle, seemed to indicate that the republican movement was keen to start negotiations. It seemed also that the armed volunteers and their electorally significant political wing (Sinn Féin took 11.3 percent of the votes in the 1989 local elections in Northern Ireland, but in a context of ongoing violence lost out to the SDLP in the general election of April 1992) were anxious to end in a settlement the military conflict they knew the IRA could not win, even if it could sustain its armed campaign. In the early 1990s the scale of IRA attacks on economic targets in London, the toll of inter-community violence in Northern Ireland (when full-scale ethnic cleansing of a Balkan dimension began to seem a dread possibility, with IRA assaults on the centres of "Protestant" towns and loyalist murder gangs terrorizing Catholic areas of Belfast) and the continued opposition of all strands of Northern unionism to the Anglo-Irish Agreement with its Irish secretariat in Belfast, all meant that the Irish and British governments could not avoid the issue.

At the heart of the matter for the Irish government was how to reconfigure its historic and currently unrealizable claim on the six counties of Northern Ireland. The reunification of the national territory was indeed an imperative enshrined in Articles 2 and 3 of the 1937 Constitution. Since the Anglo-Irish Agreement, that unity, it was formally acknowledged, would require unionist consent. The problem in the 1990s, however, was how to address the issue of British sovereignty over Northern Ireland, which the Irish Constitution only accepted as a *de facto* matter, and of unionist consent, in terms which might interest the IRA sufficiently to tempt it into calling an extended ceasefire which might in time become permanent. But in tempting the IRA, the Irish government could not put the British in the position of seeming further to abandon an already alienated unionist community. Working with the British, the Irish government had to square this circle, conscious that republican nationalist orthodoxy had since before the foundation of the state viewed unionist withholding of consent to participation in an independent Irish polity as a veto on the democratic development of the country as a whole. According to that orthodoxy, it interfered with the nation's right to self-determination. This remained as the republican movement's proclaimed core value, and was not to be easily set aside.

How self-determination might be exercised in the actual conditions of the 1990s, when unionist determination to resist incorporation in an all-Ireland polity had been demonstrated in the face of twenty-five years of violence intended to expedite that incorporation, became the crux of the matter. It was central to the new discussions between John Hume and Gerry Adams which became public in April 1993, "with the expressed aim of finding a means of ending violence."[54] Hume teased out with Adams what consent might mean in a country divided about the exercise of self-determination, though Hume's attempt to nuance the key issue that they had already explored in the 1980s did not seem to produce a solution (though evidence has been adduced that Adams of Sinn Fein had as early as the mid-1980s accepted the need for a form of unionist consent, whatever was the view of the IRA then). However the Joint Declaration issued by Reynolds and Major on 15 December 1993 revealed the possibility of a way forward. The Prime Minister stated on behalf of the British government what Peter Brooke had earlier averred – "that they [had] no selfish strategic or economic interest in Northern Ireland" – and declared "that it is for the people of the island of Ireland alone, by agreement between the two parts respectively, to exercise their right of self-determination on the basis of consent, freely and concurrently given, North and South, to bring about a United Ireland, if that is their wish." The Taoiseach for his part stated that "it would be wrong to attempt to impose a united Ireland, in the absence of the freely given consent of a majority of the people of Northern Ireland", accepting that "the democratic right of self-determination by the people of Ireland as a whole must be achieved and exercised with and subject to the agreement of a majority of the people of Northern Ireland."

Arguably, all this could have been read as a sophisticated gloss on hard political realities, but it seems to have offered the republican movement sufficient grounds for believing that in negotiations fundamental change, or the creation of the conditions for change, were possible, while leaving them in a difficult position if they rejected it. The formulations of the Joint Declaration did not of course remove what they had traditionally thought of as the unionist veto to a democratic settlement of the national question, but in August 1994 the IRA called a "complete cessation" of its military campaign. And the long process of preparing for talks began with President Clinton playing a key role at crucial moments. Much suspicion was engendered among unionists and others by the words "complete cessation." They feared the IRA's decision was merely tactical and did not represent a permanent rejection of violence as a political instrument. Their suspicions, which have not been fully assuaged to this day, were given grim credibility in February 1996 when the IRA resumed its military activities with a powerful car bomb at Canary Wharf in London. A new ceasefire was announced in July 1997, shortly after Tony Blair's landslide victory for Labour in the general election of May of that year in the United Kingdom. Sinn Féin had not expected in August 1994, when the IRA called its first ceasefire, that the Irish government would have John Bruton of Fine Gael at its head as they moved towards negotiations (they suspected him of pro-unionist sympathies). The Whelehan affair had put paid to the premiership of Reynolds, with whom they had felt more secure. Blair offered a new opportunity, as did Bertie Ahern, Reynolds's successor as leader of Fianna Fáil, elected Taoiseach at the head of a new coalition with the PDs in June 1997.

What was by now dubbed "the peace process" moved on. Talks between representatives of parties that had been elected to a forum in May 1996, and the two governments, had begun in June of that year, under the chairmanship of the US Senator George Mitchell (who as President Clinton's economic envoy to Northern Ireland had won wide respect). Sinn Féin entered these talks ostensibly "to smash the union"[55] in the autumn of 1997 (the Democratic Unionist Party and the recently formed United Kingdom Unionist Party had withdrawn from the talks). The

agreement that emerged from agonizingly protracted negotiations on 10 April (Good Friday) 1998 was much less than the
end of the Union between Great Britain and Northern Ireland
for which Sinn Féin avowedly hoped. Yet it was an agreement
capable of being presented by Sinn Féin as a transitional stage in
a process which would lead inexorably to that desired end, when
national self-determination would be complete. The SDLP could
represent it as the expression of its leader John Hume's vision of
an agreed Ireland, endorsed, as it was in May 1998, in referenda
North and South of the border, effectively allowing for a self-
determination *de nos jours*, so ending the justification for violence
by any group. And the Unionists could feel secure that the union
depended not on the British government's willingness (made
dubious for many of them by the way the Anglo-Irish Agreement
had been arrived at) to maintain it, but on the settled will of a
Northern majority, as they gained a devolved administration
(albeit one in which they were obliged to share power with their
former opponents and enemies), in a period of more general
devolution in the United Kingdom as a whole. The two governments could employ it as the basis of an ongoing normalization
of relations between two sovereign powers formerly in territorial
dispute.

The broad shape of an agreement had been signalled before
the talks in the identification of three strands that reflected a
complex of relations which found a violent epicentre in Northern
Ireland: relations in Northern Ireland between two communities
with conflicting national identities and constitutional hopes;
relations between Northern Ireland and the Republic of Ireland;
and relations between Britain and the two jurisdictions on the
island of Ireland. The Good Friday Agreement put flesh on this
skeleton in providing for a 108-member elected Assembly in
Belfast, with a First and Deputy First Minister and with safeguards
to ensure cross-community support of an executive, in agreeing
to establish a North-South ministerial council, which would allow
for cooperation in twelve specific areas (from education to inland
fisheries) and a British-Irish council to tackle issues of mutual

concern. Not dissimilar in overall shape to the ill-fated Sunningdale Agreement of 1973, the Good Friday Agreement had the advantage over that earlier attempt to end direct rule from Westminster, of the participation of Sinn Féin – which could be assumed to speak for the IRA (despite that party's refusal to accept that that was its role) and that it was endorsed by referenda in both the Northern and Southern jurisdictions. A serious weakness was that a broad swathe of the unionist community represented by Dr. Ian Paisley's Democratic Unionist Party (which had not been party to the Agreement) was adamantly opposed to what it regarded as a sell-out. And even among those unionists in the Unionist Party of Northern Ireland who gave the agreement their support and were prepared to "work the institutions" it made possible, strong suspicions about republican intentions remained. The issue of the decommissioning of what was known to be the IRA's considerable arsenal – an issue which had dogged the pre-talks process – was not resolved to unionist satisfaction during the negotiations and has remained as a difficult bone of contention in the five years in which the institutions envisaged in the Agreement have failed to become securely established.

The major problem has been diminishing support for the Agreement in the unionist community in face of what is seen as the IRA's refusal to decommission (to date two symbolic acts of decommissioning have taken place in the presence of the international arms inspectors appointed to oversee this process). Sinn Féin for its part, insisting that it was not in fact the IRA that had signed up to the Agreement and therefore was not bound by its clauses to decommission, suspects that unionist demands for IRA disarmament are a disguised expression of an unwillingness to work the Agreement, with its stringent requirements for equality of status in a transitional North of Ireland polity and root-and-branch police reform.

The Northern Ireland Assembly, which came into existence in July 1998, and the cross-party Executive which it brought into being after much delay in November 1999, were suspended in

February 2000 in the face of the First Minister's threat of resignation on the lack of progress on IRA decommissioning. On foot of an IRA statement that a disarmament process would soon begin, the Unionists agreed to re-enter the Executive in May of that year. In July 2001 the Unionist First Minister, David Trimble, resigned over the IRA's failure satisfactorily to decommission and agreed to return only in October of that year. In October 2002, under a similar doubt, as once again the Unionists expressed loss of faith in the IRA's short and long-term intentions, the Assembly and Executive were suspended and Northern Ireland returned once again to direct rule from Westminster.

This punctuated and difficult process has meant that the institutions which would have most directly involved the Republic have not had very much of a chance to prove what they can do in enhancing and developing relations between the North and South of the island and between Britain and Ireland (in periods when the Northern Ireland Assembly is suspended, the strand two and three institutions function, when they do so, without Unionist participation). The existence of the North-South ministerial council and of the British-Irish council is barely noted in the media and does not register in the public mind, so much attention being directed to the stop-start process of politics in Northern Ireland.

The most conspicuous effect of the Good Friday Agreement on the political life of the Republic has in fact been the emergence of Sinn Féin as a serious electoral threat to the traditional parties. The high profile as dedicated peacemaker afforded Gerry Adams by the Irish media (Sinn Féin has been allowed unfettered access to the airwaves since January 1994) and the impressive performance of Martin McGuinness as Minister for Education in the Northern Ireland Executive have given Sinn Féin a cachet, an air of successful novelty, together with a whiff of excitement and danger, in the post-Agreement period which has made traditional politics seem jaded by comparison. Sinn Féin had its first major success when it opposed, with others, the ratification of the Nice Treaty in a referendum, which was defeated by a small majority in a low poll in 2001 (in a re-run in October 2002 the major parties, by vigorous electioneering, saw to it that many of those who had abstained in the first vote came out to vote in favour, which they duly did). In the general election of May 2002 the party took five seats in the Dáil, making it in association with the Greens and Independents a significant parliamentary presence.

The entry of Sinn Féin into democratic politics north and south of the border, which it is hoped will mean the permanent and not merely tactical eschewal of violence by the IRA, has involved pain for many. The release of paramilitary prisoners held for violent crimes in both jurisdictions caused much grief and confusion for those who had lost family and friends at their hands. For the unionist community, the replacement of the Royal Ulster Constabulary by the Police Service of Northern Ireland was felt as a body blow (many reckoned they owed their very survival to what had been a body of men and women unfairly reviled, they felt, in nationalist propaganda). For their part, the republican movement has had to abandon for the time being its core value (that British jurisdiction should end forthwith in Ireland as the Irish right of self-determination is straightforwardly vindicated) and has had to participate in institutions in a Northern Ireland Assembly that throughout the twentieth century they would have damned as illegitimate. It was not for this that their volunteers had given their lives in action or on hunger strike. In the pain, confusion, uncertainty and weary impatience, together with the determined, focused work of many, that has accompanied the Irish peace process after the initial euphoria of Good Friday 1998, it has sometimes been difficult to comprehend how great a change the country as a whole has undergone in the period since the IRA's first "cessation" in 1994. In an interview which the poet Seamus Heaney gave in 1996, during the months of renewed IRA violence, he spoke of the lightening of the spirit he had experienced in the autumn of 1994 when the IRA declared that first "cessation." Speaking of a poem he had written of that occasion, he reflected:

I wanted to capture that moment. I had the physical pleasure of that bright Sunday morning after the ceasefire. There was also the political and psychological brightness of that moment. I do believe that, whatever happens, a corner was turned historically in 1994. We've passed from the atrocious to the messy, but the messy is a perfectly okay place to live.[56]

Some events, particularly the horrendous bombing of Omagh on 15 August 1998 by dissident republicans opposed to the Good Friday Agreement, with its cruel loss of life, indicated in the period that the atrocious was never far from the mess conflict resolution can involve. But Heaney's perception seems sound. The 1994 decision was widely sensed in Ireland to open a field of possibility for the country. Heaney himself had published an article in a Dublin newspaper that bright September Sunday following the ceasefire in 1994, where he had concluded: "the cessation of violence is an opportunity to open a space – and not just in the political arena but in the first level of each person's consciousness – space where hope can grow."[57]

The same sense of liberating possibility, of hope, can be derived from the new articles in the Constitution of Ireland, which were endorsed in the referendum on the Good Friday Agreement and made applicable in December 1999. Their incorporation in the Constitution represents a fundamental shift in Ireland's legal expression of its territorial claim on the six counties of the North. That act of the people opened up the liberating possibility of a nationalism defined not by implacable territorial imperatives and irredentist demands but by respect for the democratic rights of all. Article 2 reads in its new form:

It is the entitlement and birthright of every person born in the island of Ireland, which includes its islands and seas, to be part of the Irish Nation. That is also the entitlement of all persons otherwise qualified in accordance with law to be citizens of Ireland. Furthermore, the Irish nation cherishes its special affinity with people of Irish ancestry living abroad who share its cultural identity and heritage.

The new Article 3.1 affirms:

> It is the firm will of the Irish nation, in harmony and friendship, to unite all the people who share the territory of the island of Ireland, in all the diversity of their identities and traditions, recognising that a united Ireland shall be brought about only by peaceful means with a consent of a majority of the people, democratically expressed, in both jurisdictions in the island.

CHAPTER 13

Conclusion: Culture and Memory in an International Context

I

In an astute study of the Constitution of Ireland published in 2000, Patrick Hanafin reflected on how that document had sought to enshrine in key clauses a "definitive narrative of Irish identity,"[1] which in its territorial ambitions constructed an exclusive version of Irishness. For, he argued, it "created an essentialised Irish type, a *fior Gael*, who was Catholic and nationalist, as the dominant subject of Irish law."[2] To achieve this, it had cast the Protestant and unionist community of Northern Ireland as the other, against whom the citizens of the Republic defined themselves in homogeneous terms. Yet the very act of claiming the North in Articles two and three involved contradictions, for the aspiration to a unity postponed pending the integration of the national territory, admitted difference to a text which celebrated the "people" as if they constituted an undifferentiated whole. Hanafin judges therefore, pondering the replacement of the old Articles two and three by the new: "the very fact that this sacred cow of Irish nationalist discourse was revised by the people in a referendum in the summer of 1998 is a sign of a transformed society."[3] Also in 2000, the literary critic and cultural analyst Declan Kiberd saluted this constitutional change, marking it as the evidence of a monumental shift in Irish consciousness. He wrote:

> Of all the measures written into the Belfast [Good Friday] Agreement, the most astonishing is that by which the citizens of the Republic are to remove the territorial claim on the six northern counties currently part of the United Kingdom. Every schoolchild in the Republic has been taught to see that claim as a force of nature, confirmed by the very shape of Ireland as an island. Yet over 94 percent of the southern electorate voted to rescind the claim. . . . The vote was, in fact, a recognition that any people's claims need no longer be mediated by means of the nation and that identity is rooted less in the relation between people and territory than in relations of persons to one another.[4]

Kiberd attributed this significant shift in attitudes about the national question to the South's concern for the well-being of "Unionist fellow islanders."[5] In the euphoria that followed the Good Friday Agreement, such generosity of spirit may well have played a part in encouraging the electorate to endorse change so convincingly. Hanafin's more cold-eyed analysis interpreted the vote not only as the reflection of a society that had undergone remarkable social change since 1937, which challenged the exclusivist version of Irish identity it had constructed, but a sign "that the irredentist ethos of the Constitution no longer [sat] comfortably with the current Irish societal paradigm."[6] The country, under the pressure of manifold change, was becoming detached from the version of national identity the Constitution had constructed, so it could countenance constitutional reform, in the interests of peace, as part of the transformation a remarkable decade brought.

Cultural and intellectual life in the Republic in the 1990s had in fact engaged in various ways with the issue of Irish identity, to a degree that suggests a creative struggle was indeed in progress to respond to the changes that had been set in motion in the late 1950s and which were accelerating rapidly in the last decade of the century. What kind of country was Ireland, moving as it was from economic crisis to sudden affluence in the European Union and the global economy? How should it relate to its past and commemorate that past, what is the role of woman in the national story, and what of the Irish language and the cultural traditions associated with it in a period of multiculturalism, what of the role of the plastic arts, and how could technology and science sustain the newly rich Ireland that had so amazingly come into existence? – these were some of the questions asked and answered in various ways in the 1990s and at turn of century. The intensity of the controversies they engendered indicated a society undergoing an even greater act of self-analysis about its identity and place in the world than had occurred in the 1960s and '70s.

Fintan O'Toole in his book *The Ex-Isle of Erin: Images of a Global Ireland* (1997) announced that in 1996 Ireland had come of age. For in that year, the year that marked the seventy-fifth anniversary of the signing of the Treaty which founded the state, the citizens of Ireland produced more wealth per head than those of the United Kingdom. No longer could Ireland blame residual problems on the old dependency on Britain. A suddenly wealthy country had found a new role, in a world which had seen the demise of the British Empire and the rise of a new globalized economy. A paradox ensued for O'Toole:

This is the paradox of the Republic in the aftermath of the British Empire: its national independence is underwritten by transnational corporations and by a supra-national European Union. Its sovereignty is a power that can be exercised mostly by giving it up. Its separation seventy-five years ago from one political and economic union, the United Kingdom, is justified by its membership of a bigger political and economic union, the EU. It cultural distinctiveness lies not in any inherited tradition but in the particular way that it reacts to an overload of global stimuli, taking possession of Anglo-American norms, putting its own stamp on them and exporting them back to England, America and the rest of the world.[7]

For O'Toole the key fact in this paradoxical version of separatism which fate has delivered, is that in cultural terms Ireland now inhabits a global economy. In this new order "the values, desires and dreams of people everywhere must be assimilated to international norms."[8]

So "Ireland" could be marketed as a branded cultural artefact, as the "Riverdance" phenomenon and the later "Lord of the Dance" demonstrated internationally. The first, a surprisingly convincing blend for the stage of Irish traditional dancing with North American showbusiness panache, exuberantly re-sexualizing what had, since the nineteenth century, been overlaid with an inhibiting Victorian respectability, was first presented as interval fare by RTE for the Eurovision Song contest in Ireland in 1994. The effect was electrifying in the double sense that it made what had been the preserve of cottage kitchens, parish halls and the emigrant clubs of Britain and North America, immediately exciting for a mass audience on television and that it released energies that lay untapped in a traditional Ireland that the diaspora had cast on foreign shores. It was simultaneously authentic and completely new, a moment when past and present ignited a sense of the future, in which Irish identity in process was a matter for celebration. "Lord of the Dance" by contrast, offered a brilliantly-packaged overstatement of a theme. As such, it took its place with other cultural "products" of the period. Among these were various manifestations of New Age Celticism in printed or recorded form, the boy bands which advertised fresh-faced Irish energy, and the ubiquitous Irish pubs which mushroomed in cities around the world, until in a very peculiar, putative repatriation they invaded the Dublin scene, giving to the themed establishments of the capital a further air of post-modern weightlessness. In such phenomena, Irish identity, rather than remaking itself in acts of the imagination, seemed bereft of significance, a similacrum in a world of simulacra, where meaning had been hollowed out to allow for the easy transportation and assembly of Ireland Lite.

It was this trivially post-modern country that drew from the poet Derek Mahon in a long poem set in Dublin, the satirically pained, *fin de siècle* observation:

Mostly now the famous Georgian doors
will house a junk-film outfit or an advertising agency.
the fountain's flute is silent though time spares
the old beeches with their echoes of Coole demesne;
foreign investment conspires against old decency,
computer talks to computer, machine to answering machine.[9]

II

Yet a post-modern turn in the culture was not always represented in the obviously commercial, or in the slick emptiness of the advertisers' take on identity (in the period television advertisements became marked by an ironic, knowing play on Ireland's new-found modernity, especially in sexual matters), or in the virtual reality of cyberspace. It could find expression in darker, truly ambiguous cultural productions too, which raised complex critical issues. Among these were a novel by Patrick McCabe and a trilogy of plays by Martin McDonagh. McCabe's novel *The Butcher Boy* (1992) took as its setting the kind of small provincial town in which much conventionally realist Irish fiction had allowed innocence to accede to experience as a male hero comes of age. Bleakly parasitic in post-modern fashion on this tradition, McCabe's grim text renders innocence monstrous through the casually black-comic first-person narrative of a young lad who is the unconscious victim of a society that has made him the dangerously disturbed creature he is. Victim turns predator in the book, even preying on the priest who molests him in the reform school to which he has been dispatched. McDonagh's trilogy of plays (*The Leenane Trilogy*, first produced in 1996 and 1997) feeds artistically on an even more august Irish tradition, the western plays of J. M. Synge, as well as on the staple of the Abbey Theatre's repertoire of peasant plays, which had stultified the theatre until the 1960s. Grotesquely violent, with the superficial

motivations of a TV sitcom, they were realized in the Druid
Theatre productions like *The Playboy of the Western World* as if
directed by Quentin Tarantino (Christopher Morash has pointed
out that all three plays, like *The Playboy*, involve an alleged murder
of a family member).[10]

Both these works achieved international as well as local notice.
Butcher Boy, Neil Jordan's film version of McCabe's book, was
released in 1997, while *The Leenane Trilogy* played in theatres in
London, New York and other cities to great acclaim. In Ireland
they induced a troubled response: some were exhilarated by the
iconoclastic energy they involved, others unsure what their scar-
ifying violence might portend for the society they represented in
such brutal terms. Was the success of the *Leenane Trilogy* in
particular (written by a London Irishman, who took his view of
Ireland from limited exposure to its canonical drama) symptomatic of a coarsening of taste which allowed a *nouveau riche* Irish
audience to laugh at its immediate ancestors, and international
audiences to indulge a view of the Irish as the unreconstructed
primitives of historical stereotype? Or did *Butcher Boy* (in prose
and film version) and the *Trilogy* involve penetrating interroga-
tions of the present in terms of familiar images of the past? As
Morash has written of McDonagh's work:

> The plays are, in a sense, copies that have forgotten their
> originals. . . . By creating an image that audiences are invited to
> see as "traditional", and then removing from it the last vestige
> of "traditional values", the plays stage the contradictions of a
> society that continues to nurse images of itself in which it no
> longer believes.[11]

Was modern Ireland, such works could be taken to ask, a society
bereft of values, as those which had sustained it in the past were
discarded? As the decade went on and the economic success of
the country seemed to make such grim versions of Irishness
anachronistic, critics pondered how indeed they, and works like
those of Friel and McGahern with their rural focus, could relate
to the new social conditions. Joseph Cleary, for example, reflected

that a society enamoured of its own modernity relied "heavily on invocations of the darkness of the past to validate its sense of its own enlightenment."[12] For him Cathal Black's 1996 film *Korea*, with its narrative of rural electrification hard-achieved in the 1950s, was read as expressing in this context a hesitation "between confidence and doubt, to suggest a sense of tentativeness about the course of Irish social development that will not easily resolve itself."[13] In 2002, Luke Gibbons, by contrast, considered the same film, with its Civil War flashbacks, as part of a new capacity and intent in Ireland to say things that could not be uttered in the past about the pain of Irish history. Works of recollection in a period of new wealth were aspects of "traumatic memory,"[14] which the good times had not assuaged. They were cultural versions of the tribunals of the 1990s, which made the decade an era of revelations.

A curious obsession with the past in the decade of a radical, beneficial change in Irish economic fortunes was in fact a characteristic of much cultural production in the period. And it was not only the rural, Catholic and Gaelic past that had been the stuff of so much conventional art and semi-official ideology in former days, which began to be opened up for recollective inspection in the 1990s. Rather, in the last decade of the century, as the encroaching millennium encouraged retrospection, diverse voices recalled individual experience as it had been affected by history to a degree that had scarcely occurred before. In the theatre, where in the 1980s Frank McGuinness and Tom Murphy had shown the way, this often involved dramas which depended on monologues, as personal ghosts were summoned in memory to challenge historical orthodoxies. In this respect Friel's *Dancing at Lughnasa*, in which the action all takes place in the memory of an adult narrator remembering the sexual and social complexities of his Donegal origins, set a kind of agenda for the decade, which was followed by playwrights such as Marina Carr in *The Mai* (1994) and Sebastian Barry in *The Steward of Christendom* (1995). In this latter play a Catholic chief superintendent with the pre-independence Dublin Metropolitan Police, recalls in old age his childhood and happy marriage, the death of his wife in childbirth, the death of his son in the Great War, and his relationships with his three daughters. At the heart of the drama is his paean of love and praise for the Queen, Queen Victoria, whom he had loyally served as an Irishman, until her death and history overtook him and those like him, the many who had taken the "wrong" side in the Irish twentieth century by enlisting to fight for "gallant little Belgium" in 1914. As Nicholas Grene has observed of this powerful play, Barry sought in *The Steward of Christendom* "to re-write the traditional nationalist version of Irish history as a tyrannically patriarchal colonial power oppressing a feminised Ireland from the viewpoint of a man who sees his role as a servant of protective matriarchy."[15] Barry's play was a contesting of the past, a serving notice that the past was not solely owned by those who had won power in the land. The past could be remembered and interpreted in many ways by differing individuals.

Frank McCourt's international bestselling book *Angela's Ashes* (1996), was the most popular work of recollection in the decade (more exacting works of memorialization and memoir were Seamus Deane's novel *Reading in the Dark*, Dermot Healy's *The Bend for Home*, and Nuala O'Faolain's *Are You Somebody?: The Life and Times of Nuala O'Faolain*, all of which appeared in 1996). McCourt's evocation of a grotesquely deprived, almost Dickensian, childhood in a class-ridden Limerick city (made even more grim as a place in Alan Parker's rain-washed film version) came from an emigrant Irishman, one who seemed to insist that the diaspora could strike back, that it would not be inhibited by misty-eyed sentiment about the old country or by symbolic presidential gestures. A sentimentality of its own about American opportunity, however, probably accounted for its popularity on both sides of the Atlantic. Limerick, initially affronted by a deeply unflattering version of its past, quickly saw how tourism might be boosted through opportunistic exploitation of what might otherwise have meant only notoriety.[16]

III

A preoccupation with the past and its contested meanings in drama and literature was accompanied in the 1990s by a vigorous debate about the practice of history itself as an academic discipline with national implications. In 1986 the newly founded *Irish Review* had headed its first issue with an article by the renowned Irish historian Roy Foster (then at work on the book he was to publish as *Modern Ireland* in 1988). Entitled "We Are All Revisionists Now," the article assumed that the historiographic revolution set in motion in the 1930s had been completed by younger scholars. The rousing version of Irish history as a " 'story of a people coming out of captivity' "[17] no longer had purchase in the Irish academy, whatever its popularity in Camden Town. In Irish academe "revisionism" had made "swift progress."[18] Aware that the term "revisionist" had been questioned in the press, and that historians identified by the media as such were assumed to claim for themselves an offensive impartiality about the traumata of Ireland's distressing history, Foster in 1986 had nevertheless envisaged a serene enough future for Irish historians: the old battles "are so long forgotten that those once called 'revisionists' are now being themselves revised."[19] He summed up: "In a country that has come of age, history need no longer be a matter of guarding sacred mysteries. And to say 'revisionist' should just be another way of saying 'historian'."[20]

By the early 1990s such equanimity had shown itself to be premature as the ideological foundations of history as a scientific discipline with pretensions to objectivity came under intensified, sustained attack in the Irish universities and, more generally, in cultural debate. As Foster himself advised in 2001: "The idea of 'revisionist historiography' as a conspiracy against nationalist probity . . . certainly gathered volume from the late 1980s."[21] This counterattack on the assumed pretensions and failings of revisionism reached a crescendo in 1991 with the publication, under the auspices of the Field Day Theatre Company, of a collection of essays entitled *Revising the Rising* (the book marked the seventy-fifth anniversary of the Easter Rising). Seamus Deane's essay in this volume launched an assault on the ideology ("unionist," "partitionist," "pluralist," even "British national-ist") that he took to underpin revisionism in general and, in particular, the work of Foster himself. Deane's analysis was in part echoed by some other contributors to the book in a manner that set the tone for what became in the 1990s a settled critique in which cultural theorists in the universities took as a given that historical writing was one discourse among many, which could not escape its imbrication with ideology. And historical writing that claimed to dispel the myths of the past, when not simply deluded, was as likely as not written in fully conscious or troub-lingly unconscious lack of sympathy for Irish nationalism or for the pain of Ireland's subject, colonial experience. It was deemed to represent too a form of shamefully evasive "liberal humanism," predicated on an impossible impartiality or objectivity. As such, it should be unmasked in the kind of terms Deane deployed in another intervention of 1991 which identified "revisionism" with periods of Irish history when there is

> . . . anxiety to preserve the status quo, to lower the political temperature and to offer the notion that historical processes are so complex that any attempt to achieve an overview cannot avoid the distortions and dogmatism of simple-minded orthodoxy. This is a powerful antidote against criticism and rebellion.[22]

In 1997 Deane was even more explicit, stating: "The rhetoric of revisionism obviously derives from the rhetoric of colonialism and imperialism."[23]

Some analysts of this development in the country's intellectual life read it as a regrettable reversion to a traditional nationalism among significant opinion-formers,[24] if currently expressed in the accents of fashionable theory. Others sought to contextualize the debate dialectically, allowing thereby the idea of post-revisionism to take hold.[25] It was hoped that this concept could clear a space for local, specific studies of neglected aspects of Irish history, and could proceed without necessary recourse to grand narratives of the nation or their revision. In fact local histories of individual Irish counties appeared in the 1990s and works dealing with specific issues caught the public imagination.[26] However, it was not a work of literature or drama or of historical research, but a film, which most convincingly indicates that in the 1990s history had become a highly contested matter, in which the meaning of the present was being politically addressed by many in vital ways amid Ireland's new prosperity (tax breaks were introduced for film makers in 1993 by a newly-appointed Minister for the Arts and the Film Board re-established).

When Neil Jordan's *Michael Collins* was released in November 1996, with its heroic narrative of the Rising of 1916, the War of Independence and Civil War it became an instant box-office success, both in Britain and Ireland, and the object of an intense critical debate. In 2002, Stephen Rea (a founder of the Field Day Theatre Company) who, in the film, played the part of a Dublin Castle spy, one of several who passed crucial information to Collins and his men during the War of Independence, recalled the impact of the film on the popular mind:

> Suddenly history was being discussed, suppressed stuff was coming out into the open. Kids would come up to me who had never heard of Michael Collins. This was in Ireland. They were never taught about Michael Collins. They didn't know who he was. There was a deliberate silence about that pivotal time, that whole area of history. There was a very exciting feeling in Ireland then that things were opening up and you could discuss issues again . . . the film made discussion possible and in doing that it also helped Irish society to move on.[27]

Not all who saw the film and observed its impact were as sanguine (though Rea himself entered a caveat about its portrayal of Eamon de Valera). In Britain and in Northern Ireland there were even demands that the film should be banned. Some Irish intellectuals preferred to attack the film on the grounds that they thought it likely to foment anti-British nationalism at a time when the Provisional IRA had returned to violence after the "cessation" of 1994. The historian and political commentator Ruth Dudley Edwards, for example, feared that Collins, as represented by the charismatic Liam Neeson, had become "a cult figure in fashionable Ireland" and could "become the acceptable face of Irish irredentism throughout the English-speaking world."[28] By contrast, nationalist Ireland in general tended to read the film benignly as a powerful foundational myth for the state that had emerged from a period of bloodshed and an endorsement of those who in current circumstances were seeking to shift the republican movement as Collins had done, from brutal violence to a political compromise. For in the film it is de Valera as ascetic, zealous diehard who is made to seem tragically ridiculous in face of the convincing humanity of Collins, who fights only because he has to and comes to see "we've got to learn to build with what we have."

The debate provoked in Ireland by *Michael Collins* focused in particular on one scene – that in which a police officer, drafted in from the North of the country to give some backbone to counter-insurgency, is assassinated in a booby-trapped vehicle. This was not only an anachronism (one of a number in the film), since in the War of Independence such a tactic had not been used, but it seemed a direct reference to the *modus operandi* of the Provisional IRA in modern Northern Ireland (it was greeted by cheering audiences in some cinemas in Ireland). Accordingly there were those who objected to the manipulation of history which anachronism involves, and those who rejected the claim such an historical elision seemed to imply: that the struggle of 1919–21 and the struggle in present-day Northern Ireland were one and the same. This latter point touched a raw nerve since many in the Republic had, since 1969, sought to distance themselves from Northern events by distinguishing past and present IRA violence, while a minority had regretted that the Irish state had not given open support to those whom they believed to be true inheritors of the republican flame.

In the heat of the controversy this film generated, only a few

ritics were able to address the film as text and to note its com-
lex, almost literary, layering of allusion and reference which
nade it more than simply an epic costume drama with current
olitical implications.[29] Its negotiations of gender issues, for
xample, in the context of nationalism's troping of Irish identity
s female and erotic, was not emphasized. Nor indeed was the
vay in which the film adapted a prevailing theatrical obsession
o the screen. For the film, like so many plays of the period, was
work of memory, introduced by a survivor who advises that
vhat follows is a work of creative interpretation: "Life is possible.
Ie [Collins] made it possible." That the Irish response to the
ilm so centrally engaged with the film as history (interpreting
he introduction in strictly political terms), rather than as a work
nterrogating the imaginative and psychological constituents of
epublican nationalism and the nature of memory, suggests how
irmly the historical itself remained as a crucial category of Irish
elf-understanding, even in a period of rapid social and cultural
hange.[30]

IV

Michael Collins, as Ruth Barton observed, "was made and
eceived as a national event in Ireland."[31] It made history a public
natter in the way nothing had quite done since the commemorat-
ve ceremonies that had marked fifty years since the Easter Rising
n 1966, in which the then government had played a leading
ole. And commemoration indeed was a marked feature of the
lecade. The manner in which in the 1990s the Irish government
nvolved itself in acts of commemoration indicated in fact that it
appreciated how the capacity to foretell the past remained a key
skill of governance in a period of change and crises of public
confidence in church and state. Two events at the end of the
lecade required careful planning if they were to be commemorated in a way the government could enthusiastically endorse
throughout the Northern "Troubles" official commemoration

of the Easter Rising had been fairly muted): the 150th anniversary of the Famine, in 1997 (the worst year of the Great Hunger wa 1847), and the bicentenary of the United Irish Rebellion, in 1998.

The summer of 1997 was designated by the Irish governmen as the time when Famine commemoration should climax anc conclude (time was needed to prepare for the next act of com memoration in 1998). There was something almost Canute-like about this decision, for the mid-1990s had in fact seen a remark able, apparently unquenchable flood of Irish and North American interest in the catastrophe which had overtaken the country ir the mid nineteenth century. In the past a poor Ireland in the olc country, all too conscious of its contemporary failures, and a struggling Irish-America in the New World anxious to put its past behind it if it could, had found it very difficult to confron this profoundly painful chapter of their distinct histories. Wealth and success in both constituencies seems to have allowed a hitherto unspoken misery to be admitted in all kinds of ways some deeply moving, others exploitative – even crass.[32] Writing in 1996, one commentator noted how the memory of the Famine had already stimulated in Ireland and abroad "Public and private ceremonies, remembrance and memorial services, publications, paintings and plays, television documentaries and debates, symphonies and statues, exhibitions and conferences, famine walks and wakes, even a court case"[33] as if in an outpouring of suppressed feeling. A dominant note in much of this and subsequent memorializing was an expressed determination not to have a terrible experience written out of history. ("Revisionist" historians who were reckoned to have sanitized the suffering in their conscientiously neutral tones were given a particularly hard time in debate and in the press.) All this suggested that, as nationalist Ireland was preparing for a historic settlement with the British state, it was simultaneously acknowledging to itself that the national story involved a tragic relationship with England which must be put right, once and for all. For as Luke Dodds observed in 1996:

The Famine represents one of the key determining events in the relationship between Ireland and England, a powerful, all-encompassing metaphor for loss, death and victimization. The 150th anniversary could not have been more timely. As the traditional relationship between the two countries is beginning, however haltingly, to be transformed through the peace process, the famine has re-appeared, centre stage.[34]

Yet this involved problems. Roy Foster has identified an obsession with commemoration in 1990s' Ireland, as an effect of a culture becoming absorbed by "the idea of self-validation through received memory."[35] The problem of what became known as "Faminism" was that the self-validation offered by this particular memory in Ireland was "received" only among the nationalist and republican communities North and South. Although parts of Ulster had in fact suffered significantly in the 1840s, and Protestants and Catholics had both endured starvation then, the memory of the dead had, over the intervening 150 years, become a property of nationalist feeling in which Protestants and especially unionists could not easily share. Unionists, indeed, would necessarily feel uncomfortable as defenders and supporters of a union with a Britain which had been put in the dock of public opinion to the degree that the British Prime Minister, Tony Blair, had felt moved to offer what could be read as a national apology to the Irish for what had transpired in the 1840s. It was as if unionists were being asked to feel a guilt they were signally disinclined to shoulder; they had their own more recent sufferings to remember.

At a time when the government of Ireland was actively seeking a resolution of the Northern problem, and hoped to create a climate in which Unionists there might feel reasonably secure as they negotiated in John Hume's terms "an agreed Ireland," a more inclusive set of memories was desirable. The United Irish Rebellion of 1798 was accordingly commemorated by official Ireland in 1998 in a way that emphasized how the memory of the past could be made conducive to sound democratic and inclusive politics in the present.

This was by no means a simple task. Like the Famine, the 179⁹
Rebellion, in its tale of republican endeavour brutally suppressed
could supply much grist to the mill of historical grievance. On
hundred years earlier it had been the Irish Republican Brother
hood (with its violent revolutionary tradition) which had le
the way in organizing memorial events (and by so doing ha
reinvigorated a tradition of physical force nationalism for the new
century), only to find that Catholic Ireland awaiting Home Rul
also appropriated the Rebellion for its own more pacific, Catholi
nationalist politics.³⁶ In the 1990s the political class had th
double responsibility of ensuring that the commemoration wa
not hijacked by the modern republican movement and that th
event was to be remembered in a way which could appeal t
Protestant and Catholic alike throughout Ireland.

Like the Famine, "1798" stimulated an extraordinary range c
activities, from scholarly publication to pageants and the creatio
of a heritage centre (there was even a commemorative crean
liqueur). As Ian McBride has observed:

> Few Irishmen or women can have escaped the mighty wave of
> anniversary fever which broke over the island in the spring of
> 1998. As if atoning for the failed rebellion itself the bicentenary
> was neither ill-coordinated nor localised, but a genuinely
> national phenomenon produced by years of planning and organ-
> isation.³⁷

When the Taoiseach Bertie Ahern launched his government'
commemoration programme in 1998 he made no bones abou
its purpose: "We are commemorating the most sustained effor
in Irish history to reconcile and unite what were three communi
ties with different religious beliefs and ethnic backgrounds – Prot
estants, Catholics and Dissenters."³⁸ In the year of the Goo
Friday Agreement, an inclusive interpretative agenda was bein
envisaged. Recent historical scholarship had fortunately supplie
support for this eirenic perspective on what had hitherto beer
represented as a bloody business. For a book by Kevin Whelan
The Tree of Liberty: Radicalism, Catholicism and the Constructior

f Irish Identity, and a contribution from the same hand to a
>lume of essays on 1798, *The Mighty Wave: the 1798 Rebellion
1 County Wexford* (both published in 1996, the latter edited by
)áire Keogh and Nicholas Furlong), had engaged with the
Jnited Irishmen in a way the government and official Ireland
>und ideologically persuasive.

Whelan himself was well aware that in these works he was doing
1ore than adjusting the historical record as established in the
:ademy, but intervening directly in the public sphere. His book
ad been a considered effort to reassess the nature of the back-
round to the Rebellion in County Wexford, thereby downplay-
1g what earlier historians had seen as its sectarian aspects and
mphasizing its Enlightenment, republican and democratic inspi-
1tion. In his contribution to *The Mighty Wave*, Whelan was
ninhibited in claiming a current relevance for his interpretation.
By recovering," he asserted, "the real history of the Wexford
.epublic, we can re-appropriate a profoundly democratic symbol,
nd an inspiring example of an effort to construct a representative,
:cular and pluralist politics on the island of Ireland."[39] The sec-
1rian version of 1798 should be discarded as discredited and its
1odernity, its pluralist "forward looking democratic dimen-
ion,"[40] its essential unity as to North and South (taking due
ccount of the role of Presbyterians in the Rebellion), its mobiliz-
1g of mass politics, should all be highlighted. "By relieving the
.ebellion of its oppressive weight of misinterpretation, 1798
eases to become divisive,"[41] Whelan proclaimed, and we "can
1ake it speak to the Irish people as a whole, including our dias-
•ora. We can use the 1790s as a vision and inspiration for the
990s."[42]

It was clear that the Irish government welcomed Whelan's
ersion of the 1790s, for the mission statement issued in April
997 to civil servants and diplomats by the government-
ppointed "1798 Commemoration Committee", with its base in
he Minister of State's office in the Department of the Taoiseach,
choed its terms almost exactly.[43] For such a version of a grim
•eriod in the country's history could perhaps serve the immediate

need for a national rapprochement between Protestant and Cath
olic, North and South, and would surely do no harm. In th
same spirit the government gave financial and moral support t
a plethora of events centred on Wexford, organized by Comorad
'98, established there by the county council, which presented th
progressive version of the Rebellion, as commemoration becam
celebration and then heritage, to be exploited as tourist resource

The problem was, however, that just as the revisionists ha
been accused of draining the horror from the Famine in thei
neutral tones, so the celebrants of an exemplary Wexford Republi
in the 1790s, model for a new Ireland in the 1990s, were criticise
on the grounds that they had wished, rather than convincingl
argued, away the sectarian violence the Rebellion had involve
in Wexford and in so doing they were evading both past an
present problems. It was a historian, Tom Dunne, who entere
that critique. He wrote:

> Growing up in New Ross, my early life was saturated in the
> culture of '98. This has heightened my awareness that the events
> we commemorate this year were so terrible and traumatic that
> we have never confronted them. The temptation has always
> been there – and has usually been given in to – to make a
> horrific past palatable, and this has not only robbed people of
> their history, but has made it more difficult for us as a com-
> munity to face the still lethal legacies of that time in our own
> day. Any commemoration should keep in full view the over-
> whelming fact that perhaps in excess of twenty thousand people
> died horrible deaths in the course of three hot summer weeks
> in that prosperous county.[44]

In other words 1798 should serve as a warning for 1998 and an
attempt to avert the historical gaze from its darker aspects migh
encourage a similar refusal to face unpalatable truths in the pre
sent, linked as they were to forces unleashed in the 1890s. S
Dunne felt himself bound to disagree profoundly with Whelan'
admonition that we should raise our eyes from "pikes, and deaths
murder, mayhem and martyrdom" to contemplate "the living

principles of democracy and pluralism which the United Irishmen formulated." Dunne countered:

> However universalist in origin, the principles of the United Irishmen have long become identified with one side in the Northern Ireland conflict, and no "peace process" can succeed through the rehabilitation of their rhetoric, or by constitutional arrangements alone. As the United Irishmen found, obstinate realities like sectarian conflict are not so easily overcome.[45]

So what the government genuinely intended to be a commemorative effort in which all could share, ran the risk, in Dunne's terms, of alienating unionists, just as much as the Famine memorials, by permitting nationalists to occlude the sectarian violence in their own tradition. It is striking however, that though the unionist community in Northern Ireland largely chose to ignore the 1798 commemoration, which had been envisaged in part as intimate with their presumed historical memory, cross-community acts of commemoration did take place there in 1998.

V

Other historical issues with contemporary relevance aroused heated debate in the Irish academy in the 1990s, amounting almost to the kind of "culture wars" that had disturbed universities in North America since the early 1970s. Whether Ireland was or was not a post-colonial society became a matter of contention, with historians and economists sceptical of a set of theoretical models about Ireland's alignment in the world which became normative in the field of cultural studies.[46] At a popular level the film version of Roddy Doyle's novel of north-side Dublin working-class life, *The Commitments*, had given this concept cultural kudos, when its hero announced: "The Irish are the niggers of Europe, lads ... Say it proud, I'm black and I'm proud." In 1995 a foundational form of post-colonial theory and critical practice as it related to Irish writing was given wide currency in

Declan Kiberd's bestselling and prizewinning volume of literary criticism, *Inventing Ireland*. In celebratory tones in respect of the cultural nationalist writers of the Irish literary renaissance, this volume drew on the writings of the Algerian writer Frantz Fanon, for whom the struggle to establish an independent nation state is a proper initial response to the colonial predicament. By contrast, in the most advanced versions of post-colonial analysis of Irish society[47] Ireland was in no sense a successful nation that had heroically invented itself in a colonial context, but was reckoned to be in the midst of a profound and ongoing crisis which affected and affects the colonized world as a whole under capitalism. The violence of the Northern conflict until the mid 1990s was only the most obvious manifestation of a general pathology deriving from the colonial condition the Irish people have endured for centuries. The establishment of the Free State and the Republic of Ireland were not ameliorative stages in a process of a post-colonial construction, in which, despite many difficulties and failings, substantial achievements could be attributed both to the state and to Irish society in general (an implicit assumption of this volume, in fact). They were themselves manifestations of the post-colonial, not workable attempts at state and nation-building as a society sought to deal with the problems a colonial and politically dependent past had bequeathed. And the economic miracle of the 1990s had not positioned Ireland among the first world nations of continental Europe, any more than it had raised the tiger economies of Asia to a similar status in the 1980s and early 1990s. To imagine that it had was to fall prey to the false lure of modernization theory (especially attractive, it was argued, to liberals and neo-liberals alike, anxious for differing reasons to escape the trammels of a traditional social order). Such theory lacked, as Joseph Cleary had it, "the wider historical and geographical span of modern colonial capitalism that constitutes the proper contextual frame for the study of modern Irish society."[48]

At their most self-avowedly radical, Irish theorists of post-coloniality in the 1990s allied their work with the "subaltern studies" of the Indian subcontinent and examined aspects of

Ireland's past and present – its popular nationalisms, as distinct from the state-sponsored variety – as sites of resistance to be read as paradigms of liberationist politics. An endorsement of the concept of ethnos and the ethnic community was implicit in some of such writing even as the grand narrative of traditional nationalism (which was taken to underpin the hegemony of the Irish state formation) was eschewed.

The relationship of post-colonial theory to nationalism and the degree to which it transcended or merely offered in a new guise the emotional satisfactions of Irish nationalist feeling was in fact a recurrent issue in cultural debate in the 1990s. The *Field Day Anthology of Irish Writing* (1991) was the stimulus for a good deal of often vigorous discussion. This three-volume work by various hands under the general editorship of Seamus Deane (promised as we saw in the mid-1980s), published by the Field Day Theatre Company in Derry, offered itself as an inclusive re-reading of the multiple traditions of Irish writing. Some critics were ready to complain, however, that its ostensible pluralism was undermined by the overarching assumption that all those traditions shared in the colonial predicament, in which a healthy nationalism had not yet been realized. As such, it was judged by Francis Mulhern, for example, as expressing a form of "prospective" nationalism in which Field Day "takes its distance from one after another version of cultural nationalism but holds on to the axiom that founds them all: the proposition that the sovereign cultural concern of the Irish population is its national identity. To a nationalist this is a self-evident truth."[49] Another critic censured Deane's general approach in this and other work in similar terms, in the name of a more deconstructive version of post-colonial theory: "He falters at the conceptual leap from the nation into whatever comes next,"[50] wrote Colin Graham, earnest to escape from the tired binaries of "revisionist/anti-revisonist" polemic. He offered, by contrast, as a proper object of study "the fractured range of complex cross-colonial affiliations which have existed within the British-Irish axis by acknowledging and adapting the critical methodologies which post-colonialism has employed to disintegrate and fragment the monologism of cultural affili-ation."[51] Such a project, which did not presume that a final realiz-ation of Irish identity was implicitly on the agenda, might, it could be argued, allow unionists to participate as equals in a cultural debate about the future, in a way they scarcely did in the 1990s.

Writing about these sometimes acrimonious controversies, Stephen Howe has reflected:

> The intensity of these culture wars, the unusually high profile of literary politics in Ireland and its intrinsic intertwinement with arguments over historical interpretation, national identity and politics itself in the more narrow and conventional sense, help explain the sharpness of the contestation. They help explain why, for instance, [the novelist] Colm Tóibín, can in the course of a discussion of literary history, suddenly burst out apropos of the Easter Rising and by extension of Irish nationalism gener-ally: "I loathe everything about it, every single moment of it." Such explosions of rage are lurking, barely concealed, beneath the surface of much of the writing we are examining, from all sides of the arguments.[52]

What this does not explain, however, is why, in a period when Ireland was undergoing an undeniable improvement in its econ-omic fortunes, cultural debate was so fraught. It was probably that the focus of debate was often the status of the country itself in which much emotion was invested – fragile post-colonial society in a global capitalist world or a confident nation taking its proper place among the richest countries of Europe – that sometimes gave the culture wars the quality of a stentorian dia-logue of the deaf. On the one hand it could be demonstrated that Ireland by any objective measure of incomes, life-expectancy, literacy rates, educational opportunities, housing stock, access to information, citizens' rights, was a member of the club of first world European states. Indeed in the 1990s income had "risen to the European average in terms of GDP per person, adjusted to purchasing power of currencies."[53] Those who thought such things definitive were impatient to the point of exasperation with the argument that the global economy might offer temporary relief to a post-colonial people but did not alter a fundamental condition of dependency shared with the Third World nor palliate the cultural and psychological pathologies associated with the ongoing crisis of capitalist modernity. On the other hand it was argued with ideological rigour that economic and social indicators cannot be analyzed ahistorically, but must be part of an investigation of "the *discrepant* ways in which Irish political and cultural life, which were obviously shaped and textured by European developments, were at the same time over-determined by the country's dependent socio-economic composition."[54]

Considered as a cultural phenomenon in its own right, the post-colonial turn in cultural and critical discourse in the 1990s in Ireland shared something with the developments in literature, drama and film, that we noted above. For it did allow intellectuals to say, just as novels, plays and memoirs were doing in the period, that whatever about the ambiguous present, the past had indeed been grim, even atrocious. That the Field Day Theatre Company, with its roots in Derry, was a key force in disseminating the concept of the colonial and post-colonial in Irish thought in the 1990s, may be salient. For in Northern Ireland atrocity was not a matter of a superseded history the Celtic Tiger could choose to forget,[55] but an experienced reality that not even the Good Friday Agreement had ended. So colonial and post-colonial critique served as the ghost at the feast. On the metaphoric level, in the zone of discourse, at the very least, such critique augmented the acts of memory and revelation that marked the decade in other cultural spheres. It offered too international perspectives, however arguable, on Irish experience at a time when so much attention was directed to unravelling the meanings of the Irish past.

VI

Seamus Deane in his general introduction to the *Field Day Anthology of Irish Writing* in 1991 had asserted that the work did not "propose that we have here an exemplary instance of either a 'national' or a 'colonial' literature or body of writing."[56] However it did in his view "propose that the interchange between these conceptions of writing, more violently and frequently effected in Ireland than in most European countries, demonstrates the configurations of power within a society that consistently has refused to accept their force or yield to their allure."[57] The anthology initially met with a very positive critical response, especially abroad. However feminist critics in Ireland were quick to observe with dismay that an enterprise so manifestly and ambitiously attentive to the "configurations of power within society," alert to the fact of colonization, had a glaring lacuna in its pages – the issue of women and the "colonization" of women by a patriarchal society had been ignored. Although feminist objections to the anthology were sometimes expressed in terms of the exclusion of particular current writers, and involved the observation that the editorial team (which included the present writer) was all-male, the affront was more fundamental. For the anthology which had embraced a wide variety of types of writing had ignored, they argued, the "discourse of woman" which had been a highly significant fact of political and cultural life in the Republic since the 1970s. The ensuing controversy probably marked the point where Field Day as a political and cultural force began to wane somewhat. That the feminist critique of the anthology certainly had justification was acknowledged by Deane, who moved to commission a further volume from a group of women scholars and editors, which might fully reflect women's writing and discourse (a two-volume addition edited by a team of women scholars appeared in 2002). Yet Field Day had been founded as a response to the "Troubles" in Northern Ireland and its great achievement in the 1980s had been to inject an essentially Northern sense of how the crisis there was an all-Ireland matter into the consciousness of the South. The controversy over the anthology's attitude to women was the site where tectonic plates collided: a markedly Northern view of the country's current state of national crisis met a powerful body of opinion in the South which saw the position of women in the Republic as a matter of at least equivalent political and social import.[58] In consequence, the way in which the anthology might have contributed to a re-imagining of the country as a whole regrettably got lost to a large degree in a quickly established journalistic consensus that it had committed a folly in the arena of gender politics.

The 1990s were in fact the decade in which not only did the women's movement achieve, as we saw, a kind of professional critical mass in public life up to and including the presidency, but a period in which women writers and artists noticeably flourished. In 1996 one critic could justifiably conclude that "any genuinely attentive reader of contemporary Irish poetry knows that the standard-bearers for the next century will be found equally among the women poets as among the men now coming into their stride."[59] An anthology and annotated directory of twentieth-century Irish women poets, which appeared in 1999, reflected much of this activity. It included more than a hundred poets who had been published in volume form.[60] Many were younger poets who had graduated from the poetry workshops that had been a feature of cultural activity since the 1970s throughout the country (in 1995 there were more than 600 public poetry readings in the country as a whole). In 1995 Eavan Boland's *Object Lessons – the Life of the Woman and the Poet in Our Time* (Boland had herself contributed unstintingly to the workshop movement) was published, to give the authority that an internationally acclaimed Irish woman poet could to the belief that a woman's imaginative engagement with the matter of her private and public life was wholly valid as artistic subject.

That engagement in the 1990s served notice that in a decade when Ireland was involved with acts of memory, commemoration, retrieval and revelation, the distinctive contribution of women to that process must be heard. For as Anne Fogarty has argued, the work of some of the most interesting women writers of the period in no way retreats to a subjective sphere which could be invoked by literary historians "as an absent presence that sanctions cultural debates which still remain inveterately male-centred."[61] Rather, as she argued, women's writing is "integral to the cultural history of Ireland in the 1990s,"[62] for "above all, their writing is compelling because of its desire to interrogate notions of identity, whether it be in the realm of the sexual, the national, the local, the political, or the familial."[63] And they produce work in which issues of identity surface in highly complex forms that reflect the imbrication of the private with the public in disturbing ways, both akin to and different from work produced by men in the same period. Fogarty judges:

> Their writing depicts the self not only as fissile and divided but also as defined by and entangled with historical, familial, and socio-political legacies of meaning. Moreover, the probing of identity in their writing occurs in tandem with a number of other shared thematic concerns . . . including the use of retrospection, the surprising prevalence of Oedipal plots and incest themes, the employment of the double or split self, and the scrutiny of the limits of language and of narrative.[64]

It was such work, indeed, which made lines by Eavan Boland representative of the decade, when she addressed Joyce's Anna Liffey:

> Maker of
> Places, remembrances,
> Narrate such fragments for me:
> One body. One spirit
> One place. One name.
> The city where I was born.
> The river that runs through it.
> The nation that eludes me.
> Fractions of a life
> It has taken me a lifetime
> To claim.
>
> ("Anna Liffey")[65]

VII

The national inheritance invoked here as "fractions of a life," for some poets in the 1990s still included the Irish language. Indeed as the use of Irish as a vernacular became more and more in doubt even in the Gaeltacht (a sobering report in 2003 suggested that the numbers actually using Irish on a daily basis in those districts had declined to as low as 10,000)[66] its cultural prestige remained high throughout the decade. For example, one of the most distinguished poets currently at work, Nuala Ní Dhomhaill, writes only in Irish (though her work has attracted many translators, including Michael Hartnett and Paul Muldoon, bringing it to a wide international audience). Her achievement was recognized when she succeeded John Montague as professor of poetry in a scheme sponsored in association with Irish universities by the Arts Councils of Northern Ireland and of the Republic. That hardy cultural prestige and the sense that Irish is a major "fraction" of Irish identity helped as well to sustain the popularity among a small minority of parents of schools where all instruction is through the medium of Irish. In the country at large at the beginning of the twenty-first century about 20,000 pupils attend Irish-language primary schools, about 5,000 attend such secondary schools.[67] The belief that Irish could be a "cool" acquisition for young people (as distinct from the dreary imposition many found it in the English-speaking schools) was fostered in the 1990s by an Irish-language television channel (TG4) which began broadcasting as Teilifís na Gaeilge in 1996. It broadcasts sixteen hours per day (though not entirely in Irish), with soap opera, European football and international films interspersed with more demanding fare. The effect (production values are high) is to suggest that Irish is a vital and attractive cultural asset in a country beginning to acknowledge, as immigration becomes a reality, the challenges of multi-culturalism.

In fact the term multi-culturalism became ubiquitous in journalism in Ireland in the late 1990s, replacing indeed "pluralism" as a desideratum of liberal and progressive thought and deployed as a way of referring to a condition in which new immigrant communities began to make the country more socially heterogeneous. As Ireland took its place in January 2002 as "by far the world's most globalized country,"[68] it found itself issuing more and more work permits to non-European nationals (the numbers grew from under 5,000 in 1994 to 40,000 in 2002) to sustain its high levels of growth, making it evident on a daily social basis that the country was now a significant small economy in an international system of trade, with its often desperate economic migrants. Some of these entered the country illegally, often as the victims of organized crime. In 1998 the novelist Hugo Hamilton chose the crime fiction genre (itself a burgeoning subset of Irish fiction) to explore this dark side of the new Ireland. The plot of *Bad Bastard* revolves around the smuggling of Romanians into the country by a vicious Irish criminal. In 2001 Susan Knight allowed a number of these new Irish to speak in their own voices. Her book *Where the Grass is Greener: Voices of Immigrant Women in Ireland* collected interviews with sixty-one women from thirty-one countries, many of them recent arrivals, which reflected a country uncertain of how it should respond to a sudden influx of non-nationals in its midst (recurrent themes were the difficulty newcomers experienced in breaking through a superficial friendliness to real intimacy with the Irish and the centrality of alcohol in social life).

That a globalized Ireland now felt itself to be capable of competing with the best in the international economic stakes (however it felt about itself in even the recent past) was evident in the changed attitude to research and development at government level in the 1990s. Since the foundation of the state, science had attracted very little state support. In the late 1990s, however, the recognition that in an advanced economy knowledge is a key asset took hold of the official mind and a programme was put in place to bring Ireland closer to international levels in research and development in the advanced economies of Europe and North America. In 1996 the government issued for the first time a White

Paper on Science, Technology and Innovation, making scientific innovation a national imperative. Subsequently the Higher Education Authority, responsible for university education, was charged with creating a number of centres of research excellence that would bring together in inter-disciplinary contexts the best practitioners in various fields and attract outstanding scientists from abroad. And in a national plan for 2000–2006 the government envisaged earmarking about 2.5 billion euro for research (a dramatic rise, since in the period 1994–1999 the state had spent the equivalent of a mere 500 million euro on research activities.[69]) Science Foundation Ireland was founded in 2000 to support research in biotechnology and information and communications technology.

Also in the late 1990s the role of science as an aspect of culture began to be considered in national debate. A topic that since 1922 had received almost no attention from academics and social commentators (Æ in the *Irish Statesman* in the 1920s was one of very few alert to the potential of the huge increase internationally in scientific knowledge in the early twentieth century)[70] started to surface, for example, as an aspect of Irish Studies. The *Irish Review* began to publish articles on the history of Irish science and on the significance of science as a cultural phenomenon in the country.[71] And the *Irish Times* expanded its science coverage, publishing a weekly page covering developments in Irish and international science. In this context John Wilson Foster's edited volume *Nature in Ireland: A Scientific and Cultural History* (1997) was something of a watershed. In this work he brought together twenty-six contributors with specialist knowledge, himself supplying an interwoven cultural/historical context in a broad survey of the cultural history of scientific thinking about nature in Ireland. In his introduction he characterized his book as "the first sustained traffic in Ireland between the history of the sciences and the history of culture."[72] He hoped to "re-house natural history in Irish culture from which it [had] effectively been evicted for a century or so."[73] In 1999 Nicholas Whyte in his book *Science, Colonialism and Ireland* took up the questions raised by Foster and others in the 1990s as to whether and to what degree "the Catholic church . . . discouraged science among its followers" and whether or not "the culture of Irish nationalism as it developed, being anti-modern and anti-Protestant as well as nationalist," was "responsible for the failure of the Irish state to utilise its (mainly Protestant) scientific potential after independence."[74] He concluded that the "case against either Irish nationalism or Roman Catholicism as despoilers of science remains to be proven," as did the argument tested in his book that science in Ireland should be treated as "an example of colonial science."[75] However, despite its tentative conclusions, Whyte's was a stimulating entry in an embryonic discourse of science (though a discourse notably historical in tone) in a country that in the twentieth century had emphasized literary and dramatic production as a marker of its cultural achievement and identity.

Foster in *Nature in Ireland* had noted that "science prides itself on being international in method and procedure" and that the "global span" of contemporary science's concern with environmental issues "demonstrates the growing internationalism of contemporary culture."[76] In the light of this, the emergence of science as object of cultural study and the state's commitment to raising the level of Irish research and development could be taken as counters of an internationalism of mind that co-existed with cultural introspection in Ireland at the turn of century. It was perhaps in the field of the plastic arts that an international outlook was reflected most strikingly in the cultural sphere in a decade when Irish memory, commemoration and introspection had played so central a part.

Since the publication of James Joyce's novel *Ulysses* in 1922 and the awarding of the Nobel Prize for Literature to W. B. Yeats in 1923 and to Samuel Beckett in 1969, the contribution of Irish letters to international literature could be taken for granted both in Ireland and abroad. And the fact that each of these writers had been in their different ways in the vanguard of the literary experimentalism that characterized international Modernism in the first half of the twentieth century meant that it was no matter for surprise that in the 1990s a writer like the novelist John Banville should publish finely wrought works of high artifice, owing as much to Nabokov or Borges as to any native precursor. In the field of the fine arts in independent Ireland, by contrast, it was not until the 1980s with, as we saw, *Rosc* providing the occasion, that Irish work in modern idioms began to find its place as a substantial and *recognized* contribution to international modern art. Since then, Irish artistic production has more and more reflected the "plurality of styles" of the international art world (though a fascination with landscape has remained as a kind of *leitmotif*) and has been seen to do so by international commentators. Writing in 1997 the critic Dorothy Walker noted that "the closest thing to a dominant movement in Irish art over the past twenty years was the so-called New Expressionism, which had deep roots in Germany, but made an international splash beginning in the early eighties."[77] But she also noted that conceptual art had its adherents too, with, for example, the work of James Coleman attracting international attention, while abstract work remained strong "throughout the eighties alongside the Expressionist movement."[78]

Until 1991 Ireland had had no permanent space (with the exception of Trinity College's Douglas Hyde Gallery which opened in 1978) in which twentieth-century art by Irish and international artists could be regularly exhibited. In that year the Irish Museum of Modern Art was opened in a renovated and redesigned public building – the Royal Hospital, Kilmainham (a seventeenth-century residence for retired soldiers built in emulation of the Hôtel des Invalides in Paris). In the 1990s this new facility appreciably raised the profile of modern sculpture and painting in the country, with its programme of Irish retrospectives and exhibitions by international artists and their Irish contemporaries. In 1993 Ireland was represented at the Venice Biennale after a gap of thirty years. In 1995, in what was "seen by many as a significant marker of the arrival of contemporary Irish art on the international stage,"[79] a young Irish artist, Kathy Prendergast

(born in Dublin in 1958), won the Premio Demila award at
Venice, presented to the best artist under forty years of age. Also
in the 1990s the Hugh Lane Municipal Gallery of Modern Art
in Dublin enlarged its collection through a well-informed purchasing policy, adding works by younger Irish artists to the holdings bequeathed to it by Hugh Lane himself. And outside Dublin,
galleries such as the Crawford Municipal Art Gallery in Cork
spread the message of contemporary art in international idioms
in the provinces.

It was in fact the Crawford Gallery which in 1999 held an
exhibition which suggested how a generation of Irish artists –
graduates of reinvigorated colleges of art in Dublin, Cork and
Limerick (as well as Belfast) – were making their mark in the
UK, itself in the midst of a cultural renewal associated with the
young British artists phenomenon. Writing in the volume of interviews that accompanied the exhibition, which drew on the work
of twenty artists in their thirties and forties, the gallery curator
Peter Murray noted:

> Although resident in Britain most of the artists continue their
> links with Ireland and regularly exhibit new work in Irish gal-
> leries or at the new Irish Museum of Modern Art. Their art
> practice is held in high regard in Ireland, perhaps because there
> is a perception that their work is more connected to the inter-
> national art world. Evidence of this can be found in the high
> proportion of Irish artists resident in Britain who have been
> selected in recent years to represent Ireland at the Venice Bien-
> nale, including Kathy Prendergast (1995), Jaki Irvine (1997)
> and Anne Tallentie (1999).[80]

Intriguingly, in a decade in which issues of communal memory
and national identity were the stuff of so much debate in Ireland,
many of these artists, as Murray reports, "when invited to participate . . . voiced a concern at participating" in what they feared
might be "an exhibition that would celebrate ethnicity or nationality."[81] It was not that they rejected their Irish inheritance, as
interviews with them in the exhibition handbook make clear, but

that they explored it with a keen appreciation of the fact that, as the critic Claire Schneider describes it, for "artists all around the world, national identity has become less relevant as the world becomes increasingly interconnected through mass communication and international commerce and a global art market."[82] So as the same critic observes of Kathy Prendergast's remarkable preoccupation with maps and map-making since the 1980s (a major project, *City Drawings*, has involved unannotated maps of numerous capital cities):

> No matter how precise and current, any schematic can only crudely document where a person is, politically, spiritually, and creatively. Her maps demonstrate the challenge we take on when we try to locate ourselves in space and time, and how hard it is to know who we are, regardless of the signposts in our lives. For Prendergast, identity and maps are opposite sides of the same coin. They both deal with a real world and the surreal, with facts as well as perception, and ultimately they reveal the futility of recording our constantly shifting positions.[83]

Accordingly, it might be suggested, Prendergast's art stood in the period as a kind of symbol of a time and indeed of a century in which the Irish had repeatedly attempted to map their identity, depending on the signposts the remembered past provided and on those of a national life which since the 1960s constantly pointed in the direction of change and fluid renewal in an international context.

Acknowledgements

To Peter Fallon and the Gallery Press for permission to quote lines from Michael Hartnett's "A Farewell to English" and from Derek Mahon's *The Yellow Book*; to Faber and Faber Ltd. for permission to quote from Louis MacNeice's "Neutrality" from *The Collected Poems of Louis MacNeice*; to Brendan Kennelly for permission to quote from his poem "Westland Row" and from *Cromwell*; to John Montague for permission to quote from *The Sheltered Edge*; to the Trustees of the Estate of the late Katherine B. Kavanagh, through the Jonathan Williams Literary Agency for permission to quote from Patrick Kavanagh's *The Great Hunger*; to Michael B. Yeats, Macmillan London Ltd. and Macmillan Publishing Company, for permission to reprint from *Collected Poems* by W. B. Yeats, lines from "The Statues", copyright © 1940 by Georgie Yeats, renewed 1968 by Bertha Georgie Yeats, Michael Butler Yeats, and Anne Yeats, and from "Coole Park and Ballylee, 1931" copyright © 1933 by Macmillan Publishing Company, renewed 1961 by Bertha Georgie Yeats; to Greg Delanty for permission to quote from *The Hellbox*; and to Eavan Boland for permission to quote from her poem "Anna Liffey' in her *Collected Poems*.

We have tried to trace and contact all copyright-holders before publication. If notified, the publisher will be pleased to make any necessary arrangements and alterations to subsequent editions at the earliest opportunity.

Notes and References

Chapter 1: After the Revolution

1. Patrick H. Pearse, "From a Hermitage," in *Political Writings and Speeches* (Dublin: Talbot Press, 1952), p. 180.

2. Quoted by John O'Donovan, "Trends in Agriculture," *Studies*, vol. XL, no. 160 (December 1951), p. 420.

3. Oliver MacDonagh, *Ireland* (Englewood Cliffs, N.J.: Prentice-Hall, 1968), p. 21.

4. "Ireland: Events in the Free State," *Round Table*, vol. XX, no. 77 (December 1929), p. 138. The author of the articles which appeared on Ireland in this journal throughout the 1920s was J. J. Horgan, an intelligent supporter of the new administration, whose essays are a useful source for the historian of the period.

5. The best studies of culture and society in this period are to be found in F. S. L. Lyons, *Ireland Since the Famine* (London: Collins, 1971), and *Culture and Anarchy* (Oxford: Clarendon Press, 1979). See also Malcolm Brown, *The Politics of Irish Literature* (London: George Allen and Unwin, Ltd, 1972).

6. MacDonagh, *Ireland*, p. 120.

7. Seán O'Faoláin, in his influential study *The Irish* (London: Pelican Books, 1947), popularized this thesis.

8. K. H. Connell, *Irish Peasant Society* (Oxford: Clarendon Press, 1968), pp. 114–15.

9. See Conrad M. Arensberg and S. T. Kimball, *Family and Community in Ireland* (Cambridge: Harvard University Press, 2nd ed. 1968), pp. 140–52.

10. Joseph Lee makes this argument convincingly in his *The Modernization of Irish Society, 1848–1918* (Dublin: Gill and Macmillan, 1973), pp. 1–5.

11. A richly detailed study of social and political life in County Clare in the revolutionary period is David Fitzpatrick, *Politics and Irish Life, 1913–21* (Dublin: Gill and Macmillan, 1977).

12. Arensberg and Kimball, *Family and Community*, p. 129.

13. Ibid., pp. 148–49.

14. Emmet Larkin, "The Devotional Revolution in Ireland, 1850–1875," in *The Historical Dimensions of Irish Catholicism* (New York: Arno Press, 1976), p. 645. I am indebted to this stimulating essay for the information on the devotional revolution in this period. See also John A. Murphy, "Priests and People in Modern Irish History," *Christus Rex*, vol. XXIII, no. 4 (1969), pp. 235–59.

15. See Jean Blanchard, *The Church in Contemporary Ireland* (Dublin and London: Clonmore and Reynolds and Burns, Oates and Washborne, 1963), p. 53.

16. Sir Horace Plunkett, *Ireland in the New Century* (London: John Murray, popular ed., 1905), p. 94.

17. Gerald O'Donovan, *Father Ralph* (London: Macmillan, 1913), p. 195.

18. Ibid., pp. 256–57.

19. Quoted in Herman J. Heuser, DD, *Canon Sheehan of Doneraile* (London: Longmans Green, 1907), p. 41.

20. Ibid.

21. Ibid., p. 127.

22. Ibid., p. 126.

23. *Irish Statesman*, 14 September 1929, p. 26.

24. Don Boyne, *I Remember Maynooth* (London: Longmans, Green, 1937), pp. 28–29.

25. Denis Meehan, *Window on Maynooth* (Dublin: Clonmore and Reynolds, 1949), p. 174.

26. Reported in *Catholic Bulletin*, vol. XXIII, no. 3 (March 1933), p. 241.

27. Ibid., p. 242.

28. Ibid., p. 243.

29. Full figures on Irish missionary activity in the period are cited in Desmond Fennell, *The Changing Face of Catholic Ireland* (London: Geoffrey Chapman, 1968), pp. 138–42.

30. Rev. Peter Connolly, "The Church in Ireland since the Second Vatican Council," in Patrick Rafroidi and Pierre Joanon, eds., *Ireland at the Crossroads* (Lille: Publications de l'Université de Lille III, 1978–79), p. 92.

31. *Irish Independent*, 27 June 1932.

32. *Round Table*, vol. XXII, no. 88 (September 1932), p. 767.

33. Cited by J. H. Whyte, *Church and State in Modern Ireland* (Dublin: Gill and Macmillan, 1971), p. 27.

34. Ibid., p. 34.

35. William Wilde, *Irish Popular Superstitions* (Dublin: Irish Academic Press [facsimile reprint], 1853), pp. 14–15.

36. Æ, "Rural Clubs and National Life," *Irish Statesman*, 13 September 1924, p. 6.

37. Æ, *Irish Statesman*, 12 January 1924, p. 550.

38. Sean O'Casey, *Irish Statesman*, 22 December 1923, p. 468.

39. Stephen Gwynn, *Irish Statesman*, 10 November 1923, p. 278.

40. Æ, "The Liquor Commission," *Irish Statesman*, 4 April 1925, p. 105.

41. Harold Speakman, *Here's Ireland* (London: Arrowsmith, 1926), pp. 328–29.

Chapter 2: An Irish Ireland

1. E. Rumpf and A. C. Hepburn, *Nationalism and Socialism in Twentieth-Century Ireland* (Liverpool: Liverpool University Press, 1977), p. 73. Also helpful on the kinds of support attracted by Irish political parties since independence are Maurice Manning, *Irish Political Parties* (Dublin: Gill and Macmillan, 1972), and, for a slightly later period, Michael Gallagher, *Electoral Support for Irish Political Parties, 1927–1973* (London: Sage Publications, 1976). See also Tom Garvin, "Nationalist Elites, Irish Voters and Irish Political Development," *Economic and Social Review*, vol. VIII, no. 3 (April 1977), pp. 161–86.

2. Rumpf and Hepburn, *Nationalism and Socialism*, p. 75.

3. This statement appeared as part of an advertisement in the *Irish Statesman* for 15 November 1924, under the words of the dead Arthur Griffith: "People of Ireland, hold fast to the Treaty. It is your economic need; it is your Political Salvation."

4. D. H. Akenson, *A Mirror to Kathleen's Face: Education in Independent Ireland* (Montreal and London: McGill–Queen's University Press, 1975), p. 31. I am indebted to chapter 3 of this study.

5. Eoin MacNeill, "Irish Education Policy – I," *Irish Statesman*, 17 October 1925, pp. 168–69.

6. Rev. T. Corcoran, SJ, D.Litt., "The Irish Language in the Irish Schools," *Studies*, vol. XIV, no. 53 (September 1925), p. 379.

7. Ibid.

8. Maurice O'Connell, *History of the Irish National Teachers' Organisation* (Dublin, 1968), pp. 343–44.

9. Corcoran, "The Irish Language," p. 385.

10. Ibid., p. 384.

11. Michael Tierney, "The Revival of the Irish Language," *Studies*, vol. XVI, no. 61 (March 1927), p. 1.

12. Ibid., p. 5.

13. Osborn Bergin, "The Revival of the Irish Language," *Studies*, vol. XVI, no. 61 (March 1927), pp. 19–20.

14. Douglas Hyde, "The Necessity for De-Anglicizing Ireland," delivered before the Irish National Literary Society in Dublin, 25 November 1892, in Sir Charles Gavan Duffy, KCMG, Dr. George Sigerson, and Dr. Douglas Hyde, *The Revival of Irish Literature* (London: T. Fisher-Brown, 1894), pp. 126–27.

15. D. P. Moran, *The Philosophy of Irish Ireland* (Dublin: James Duffy and M. H. Gill and Son, 1905), p. 37.

16. Ibid., p. 17.

17. Ibid., p. 70.

18. Eoin MacNeill, "Irish Education Policy," *Irish Statesman*, 17 October 1925, p. 168.

19. Seán Ó Tuama, "The Gaelic League Idea in the Future," in Seán Ó Tuama, ed., *The Gaelic League Idea* (Cork and Dublin: Mercier Press, 1972), p. 99.

20. Daniel Corkery, *Synge and Anglo-Irish Literature* (Cork: Mercier Press, 5th impression 1966), p. 15.

21. Liam de Paor, "The Twenty-Six-County State," *Irish Times*, 8 December 1977, p. 10.

22. Brian Ó Cuiv has made the point that nineteenth-century figures on the Irish language are probably underestimated, since it was not then fashionable to claim knowledge of the language. Figures in the post-independence period, when knowledge of Irish had become more fashionable, probably represent overestimation. Brian Ó Cuiv, "The Gaeltacht – Past and Present," *Irish Dialects and Irish-Speaking Districts* (Dublin: Institute for Advanced Studies, 1951), pp. 27–28.

23. Quoted in a supplement to *Fáinne an Lae* (November 1926), p. 8.

24. *Catholic Bulletin*, vol. XIV, no. 4 (24 April 1924), p. 269.

25. Daniel Corkery, "Literature and Life," *Irish Statesman*, 13 July 1929, p. 372.

26. Corkery, *Synge*, p. 24.

27. Ibid., p. 26.

28. Moran, *Philosophy of Irish Ireland*, p. 93.

29. Daniel Corkery, *The Hidden Ireland* (Dublin: Gill and Macmillan, new ed. 1967), p. 218.

30. Cited in Michael Adams, *Censorship: The Irish Experience* (Dublin: Sceptre Books, 1968). To this detailed study I am indebted in this and in subsequent chapters.

31. Richard S. Devane, SJ, "Suggested Tariff on Imported Newspapers and Magazines," *Studies*, vol. XVI, no. 64 (December 1927), p. 556.

32. Rev. M. H. MacInerny, OP, *Studies*, vol. XVI, no. 64 (December 1927), p. 556.

33. *Catholic Bulletin*, vol. XIV, no. 1 (24 January 1924), p. 6.

34. Seorsamh O'Neill, *Irish Statesman*, 2 February 1924, p. 648.

35. Lady Gregory's *Journal*, edited by Lennox Robinson, contains much amusing material on these events.

36. Cited in Adams, *Censorship*, p. 46. Gogarty was to spend considerable energy opposing literary censorship and the excesses of the Gaelic revival in subsequent years.

37. *Round Table*, vol. XX, no. 80 (September 1930), p. 834.

38. Ibid., p. 835.

39. Arland Ussher, *The Face and Mind of Ireland* (London: Victor Gollancz, 1949), p. 59.

40. Dermot Foley, "A Minstrel Boy with a Satchel of Books," *Irish University Review*, vol. IV, no. 2 (Autumn 1974), p. 210.

41. Ibid., p. 21.

Chapter 3: Images and Realities

1. Ernest Boyd, *A Literary History of Ireland* (Dublin: Allen Figgis, 3rd ed. 1968), p. 7.

2. P. S. O'Hegarty, *Irish Statesman*, 27 November 1926, p. 271.

3. Hugh Art O'Grady, *Standish James O'Grady: The Man and the Writer* (Dublin and Cork: Talbot Press, 1929), p. 67.

4. See Robert E. Kennedy, Jr., *The Irish, Emigration, Marriage and Fertility* (Berkeley and Los Angeles: University of California Press, 1973), pp. 173–205, for a detailed study of the matter.

5. For studies of Irish folk traditions and of Irish rural life, see E. Estyn Evans, *Irish Heritage: The Landscape, the People and Their Work* (Dundalk: Dundalgan Press, 1943), and *Irish Folk Ways* (London: Routledge and Kegan Paul, 1957, 7th impression 1979); Kevin Danaher, *The Year in Ireland* (Dublin and Cork: Mercier Press, 1972); and Timothy O'Neill, *Life and Tradition in Rural Ireland* (London: J. M. Dent, 1977).

6. Much interesting material on Irish social geography can be found in T. W. Freeman, *Ireland: A General and Regional Geography* (London: Methuen, 4th ed. 1969); F. H. A. Aalen, *Man and the Landscape in Ireland* (London: Academic Press, 1978); and G. F. Mitchell, *The Irish Landscape* (London: Collins, 1976). See also Estyn Evans, *The Personality of Ireland* (London: Cambridge University Press, 1973).

7. Neil Kevin, *I Remember Karrigeen* (London and Dublin: Burns Oates and Washborne, 1944), pp. viii-ix. The town remembered here is Templemore, County Tipperary. A former garrison town, it would certainly have been highly

anglicized but, as such, it merely exhibited in an extreme form a process at work through much of the country.

8. Ibid., p. 41.

9. F. R. Higgins, *The Dark Breed* (London: Macmillan, 1927), p. 66.

10. John Wilson Foster, "Certain Set Apart: The Western Island in the Irish Renaissance," *Studies*, vol. LXVI (Winter 1977), pp. 264–65.

11. Reported in *Fáinne an Lae*, November 1926, p. 7.

12. Seán O'Faoláin, *An Irish Journey* (London: Readers Union with Longmans Green, 1941), p. 136.

13. Ibid.

14. "A Holiday in Ireland," *Round Table*, vol. XIV, no. 1 (1924), p. 316.

15. R. Lloyd Praeger, *Irish Statesman*, 12 June 1926, p. 381.

16. *Irish Statesman*, 5 November 1927, p. 195.

17. For an examination of the Homeric aspects of Ó Criomhthain's work, as well as in the reminiscences of other Blasket islanders, see J. V. Luce, "Homeric Qualities in the Life and Literature of the Great Blasket Island," *Greece and Rome*, 2nd ser., vol. XVI, no. 2 (April 1969), pp. 151–68. Other works of this type were Maurice O'Sullivan's *Twenty Years A-Growing*, published in the original Irish (*Fiche Bian ag Fás*) in 1933 and in an English version translated by Moya Llewelyn Davies and George Thomson (London: Chatto & Windus) in the same year, and Peig Sayers, *An Old Woman's Reflections*, translated from the Irish by Séamus Ennis (London: Oxford University Press, 1962). In all these works Luce found an ethos that reminded him of Homer: "a simple and virile humanism, unpolished yet dignified," Luce, "Homeric Qualities," p. 164. See also J. H. Delargy, "The Gaelic Story Teller," *Proceedings of the British Academy*, vol. XXXI (1945), pp. 177–221.

18. Brian Cleeve, ed., *W. B. Yeats and the Designing of Ireland's Coinage* (Dublin: Dolmen Press, 1972), p. 10.

19. Ibid., p. 45.

20. Bruce Arnold, *A Concise History of Irish Art* (London: Thames and Hudson, rev. ed. 1977), p. 139.

21. Cited by Etienne Rynne, "The Revival of Irish Art in the Late-19th and Early-20th Century," *Topic*, 24 (Fall 1972), p. 31.

22. A useful study of the craftwork of the period and of the Celtic revival in art in general is Jeanne Sheehy, *The Rediscovery of Ireland's Past: The Celtic Revival, 1830–1930* (London: Thames and Hudson, 1980).

23. James White and Michael Wynne, *Irish Stained Glass* (Dublin: Gill and Son, The Furrow Trust, 1963), p. 15.

Chapter 4: The Fate of the Irish Left and of the Protestant Minority

1. Cited in Charles McCarthy, *Trade Unions in Ireland* (Dublin: Institute of Public Administration, 1977), p. 95. See also Arthur Mitchell, *Labour in Irish Politics, 1890–1930* (Dublin: Irish University Press, 1974).

2. Ibid., p. 96.

3. Ibid.

4. The incident is described in Patrick Buckland, *Irish Unionism I: The Anglo-Irish and the New Ireland, 1886–1922* (Dublin: Gill and Macmillan, 1973), p. 288.

5. Buckland, *Irish Unionism I*, p. 279. Buckland points out that the list, based on press reports, is not complete.

6. E. OE. Somerville and Martin Ross, *The Big House of Inver* (London: Quartet Books, 1978), p. 8.

7. Ibid., pp. 10–11.

8. Ibid., pp. 18–19.

9. Elizabeth Bowen, *Bowen's Court* (London: Longmans Green, 1942), pp. 13–14.

10. Elizabeth Bowen, *The Last September* (London: Constable, 1929), pp. 95–96.

11. Ibid., p. 44.

12. Ibid., pp. 311–12.

13. Kennedy, *The Irish*, p. 131.

14. Brian Inglis, *West Briton* (London: Faber and Faber, 1962), p. 13.

15. Ibid., p. 27.

16. These figures were reported in the *Irish Statesman*, 20 March 1926.

17. For a fuller discussion of Trinity's vicissitudes in the post-independence period, see F. S. L. Lyons, "The Minority Problem in the 26 Counties," in Francis MacManus, ed., *The Years of the Great Test* (Cork and Dublin: Mercier Press, 2nd ed. 1978), pp. 97–99.

18. Cited in L. P. Curtis, Jr., "The Anglo-Irish Predicament," *20th Century Studies*, November 1970, p. 57.

19. See Kennedy, *The Irish*, p. 128.

20. P. L. Dickinson, *The Dublin of Yesterday* (London: Methuen, 1929), pp. 2–3.

21. Ibid., p. 77.

22. Cited in Jack White, *Minority Report* (Dublin: Gill and Macmillan, 1975), p. 81.

23. Lennox Robinson, *Bryan Cooper* (London: Constable, 1931), p. 160.

24. Walter Starkie, *Irish Statesman*, 11 September 1926, p. 14.

25. Lennox Robinson, *The Big House: Four Scenes in Its Life* (London: Methuen, 1928), p. 60.

26. Ibid., p. 109.

27. Ibid., pp. 108–9.

28. *Irish Statesman*, 9 October 1926, p. 107.

29. *Irish Statesman*, 18 September 1926, p. 29.

30. *Irish Statesman*, 3 November 1923, p. 230.

31. *Irish Statesman*, 21 November 1925, p. 327.

32. Ibid.

33. Ibid.

34. *Irish Statesman*, 17 January 1925, p. 587.

35. *Irish Statesman*, 3 January 1925, p. 522.

36. Ibid., p. 523.

37. *Irish Statesman*, 5 October 1929, p. 87.

38. *Irish Statesman*, 15 December 1928, p. 290.

39. Ibid.

40. *Irish Statesman*, 7 March 1925, p. 822.

41. *Irish Statesman*, 20 June 1925, p. 461.

42. *Irish Statesman*, 16 February 1929, p. 476.

43. "The Catholic Truth Society and Emancipation," *Catholic Truth Society of Ireland Report*, 1927, p. 13.

44. A particularly critical assessment of Æ's career was supplied by Professor Michael Tierney, professor of Greek in University College, Dublin, in the Jesuit periodical *Studies* in 1937. Here he argued that Æ's mystic nationalism was antithetical to the profound Catholicism of the Irish people. See Michael Tierney, "A Prophet of Mystic Nationalism – A.E.," *Studies*, vol. XXVI, no. 104 (December 1937), pp. 568–80.

45. *Irish Statesman*, 27 November 1926, p. 269.

46. *Irish Statesman*, 29 June 1929, p. 323.

47. Cited in Donald T. Torchiana, *W. B. Yeats and Georgian Ireland* (London and Evanston: Oxford University Press and Northwestern University Press, 1966), p. 119.

48. Ronald R. Pearce, ed., *The Senate Speeches of W. B. Yeats* (London: Faber and Faber, 1961), p. 92.

49. Ibid., p. 99. For a study of Yeats's Seanad speech in its Irish context see F. S. L. Lyons, "W. B. Yeats and the Public Life of Ireland," *New Divinity*, vol. VII, no. 1 (Summer 1976), pp. 6–25. See also David Fitzpatrick, "W. B. Yeats in Seanad Eireann," in R. O'Driscoll and L. Reynolds, eds., *Yeats and the Theatre* (London: Macmillan, 1975), pp. 159–75.

50. Allan Wade, ed., *The Letters of W. B. Yeats* (London: Rupert Hart-Davis, 1954), p. 722.

51. W. B. Yeats, "Censorship in Ireland," *Manchester Guardian*, 22 September 1928. Cited in Torchiana, *W. B. Yeats*, p. 151.

52. Stephen Gwynn, *Irish Literature and Drama* (London: Thomas Nelson, 1936), p. 232.

53. Letter to Olivia Shakespear, 11 October 1928, in Wade, *Letters*, p. 747.

54. Richard Gill, *Happy Rural Seat: The English Country House and the*

Literary Imagination (New Haven and London: Yale University Press, 1972), p. 168.

55. *Irish Statesman*, 17 November 1928, p. 208.

Chapter 5: The 1930s

1. *Round Table*, vol. XXII, no. 88 (September 1932), p. 762.
2. Reported in *Round Table*, vol. XXIII, no. 92 (September 1933), p. 874.
3. Lyons, *Ireland since the Famine*, p. 614.
4. Ibid., p. 615.
5. See Louis Cullen, *An Economic History of Ireland* (London: B. T. Batsford, 1972), pp. 178–80.
6. Reported in *Round Table*, vol. XXIII, no. 92 (September 1933), p. 874.
7. *Irish Press*, 18 March 1943, p. 1.
8. O'Connell, *History of The Irish National Teachers' Organisation*, p. 366.
9. Dáil Eireann, 10 December 1935. Mr. Derrig suggested that parents were free to make representations on the matter but reckoned that they "may be misled by . . . propaganda."
10. Eamonn Ó Gallchobhair, in *Ireland Today*, vol. I, no. 4 (September 1936), p. 57.
11. John Dowling, "Surrealism", *Ireland Today*, vol. II, no. 2 (February 1937), p. 62.
12. An authorized study of the hitherto secret Catholic society, the Knights of Columbanus, admitted that by the 1950s that organization was "in virtual control" of the Censorship Board, which perhaps suggests that some Catholics were determined that the censorship should be prosecuted in the interests of a particular religious and moral creed. See Evelyn Bolster, *The Knights of Columbanus* (Dublin: Gill and Macmillan, 1979), p. 53.
13. Cited by Whyte, *Church and State*, pp. 45–46.
14. *Irish Press*, 18 March 1935, p. 2.
15. Figures from *Statistical Abstracts* for the relevant years.
16. These figures and information on Irish broadcasting are derived from Maurice Gorham, *Forty Years of Irish Broadcasting* (Dublin: Talbot Press, 1967), to which I am indebted.
17. Frank O'Connor, "The Future of Irish Literature," *Horizon*, vol. V, no. 25 (January 1942), pp. 56–57.
18. Seán O'Faoláin, *Dublin Magazine*, vol. XI, no. 2 (1936), pp. 60–61.
19. Seán O'Faoláin, *King of the Beggars* (London: Thomas Nelson, 1938), p. 368.
20. Michael Tierney, "Politics and Culture: Daniel O'Connell and the

Gaelic Past," *Studies*, vol. XXVII, no. 107 (September 1938), pp. 361–62.

21. Ibid., p. 367.

22. Seán O'Faoláin, *Ireland Today*, vol. I, no. 5 (October 1936), p. 32.

23. Seán O'Faoláin, "A Broken World," *The Finest Stories of Seán O'Faoláin* (London: Bantam Books, 1959), p. 81.

24. Seamus Deane, "Mary Lavin," in Patrick Rafroidi and Terence Brown, eds., *The Irish Short Story* (Lille: Publications de l'Université de Lille III, 1979), p. 244.

25. Whyte, *Church and State*, pp. 70–71.

26. See Maurice Manning, *The Blueshirts* (Dublin: Gill and Macmillan, 1970), p. 74. I am indebted to this study for much of the information in this section.

27. See, in particular, Basil Chubb, *The Government and Politics of Ireland* (London and New York: Oxford University Press, 1974), pp. 61–69. See also Lyons, *Ireland since the Famine*, pp. 536–50, and Whyte, *Church and State*, pp. 50–56. To each of these I am indebted.

28. Joseph Lee has suggested that the authors of what he thinks is a valuable contribution to Irish intellectual life in the period presented their findings in a manner which militated against its serious consideration. The report was 300,000 words long, so its contents were difficult to absorb. See Joseph Lee, "Aspects of Corporatist Thought in Ireland: The Commission on Vocational Organization 1939–43," in Art Cosgrove and Donal MacCartney, eds., *Studies in Irish History* (Dublin: University College, 1979), pp. 324–46.

29. Mervyn Wall, in an interview with Michael Smith, "Some Questions about the Thirties," *Lace Curtain*, no. 4 (1971), pp. 79–80.

30. Michael Tierney, "Ireland in the European Chaos," *Ireland Today*, vol. II, no. 4 (April 1937), p. 14.

Chapter 6: "The Emergency"

1. Harold Nicolson, *Diaries and Letters, 1939–1945* (London: Collins, 1967), p. 217.

2. Michael Tierney, "Ireland and the Anglo-Saxon Heresy," *Studies*, vol. XXIX, no. 1 (March 1940), p. 2.

3. "Neutrality," *The Collected Poems of Louis MacNeice*, edited by E. R. Dodds (London: Faber and Faber, 1966), pp. 202–3.

4. Nicolson, *Diaries*, p. 217.

5. Patrick Kavanagh, *Lough Derg* (London: Martin, Brian and O'Keeffe, 1978), p. 16.

6. O'Faoláin, *An Irish Journey*, p. 272.

7. Ibid., p. 273.

8. Seán O'Faoláin, "Ulster," *Bell*, vol. II, no. 4 (1941), p. 9.

9. In a correspondent's satiric letter. See "A Vatican Dispensation," *Bell*, vol. III, no. 6 (1942), p. 469.

10. Patrick Campbell, *My Life and Easy Times* (London: Anthony Blond, 1967), p. 151.

11. Peter Kavanagh, *Beyond Affection* (New York: Peter Kavanagh Hand Press, 1977), p. 57.

12. John Ryan, *Remembering How We Stood: Bohemian Dublin at the Mid-Century* (Dublin: Gill and Macmillan, 1975), p. 13.

13. John Healy, *The Death of an Irish Town* (Cork: Mercier Press, 1968), p. 23.

14. J. D. Ennis, "Where Do We Go from Here?", *Leader*, 23 November 1940, p. 998.

15. Michael Farrell, "The Country Theatre," *Bell*, vol. III, no. 5 (February 1942), pp. 387–88.

16. Ibid., p. 388.

17. Cyril Connolly, *Horizon*, vol. V, no. 25 (January 1942), p. 11.

18. In Clifford Geertz, *The Interpretation of Cultures* (London: Hutchinson, 1975), pp. 234–54.

19. Ibid., pp. 243–44.

20. See Michael D. Biddis, *The Age of the Masses: Ideas and Society in Europe since 1870* (London: Penguin Books, 1977), pp. 29–45.

21. Cited in Hugh Brody, *Inishkillane: Change and Decline in the West of Ireland* (London: Allen Lane, Penguin Press, 1973), p. 69.

22. *Commission on Emigration, 1948–1954* (Dublin: Stationery Office, 1956), p. 174.

23. Ibid., p. 182. Earlier detections of the decrepitude and dissatisfaction prevalent in rural Ireland are T. W. Freeman, "The People and the Land," *Muintir na Tire Official Handbook* (1946), pp. 97–106; H. J. Massingham, "A Countryman's Journey," *Rural Ireland* (1948) ("The urban virus infects even the peasant counties"), p. 15; Father Felim O'Brian, "Rural Depopulation," *Rural Ireland* (1949), pp. 73–99, and Stephen Rynne, "What the Farmers Are Saying," *Irish Press*, 14 October 1946. In this article Rynne, who had visited fifty-nine farms in Ireland to prepare reports on Irish farming, declared, "The country is covered with dilapidated farmsteads and strewn with antique machinery."

24. Ibid., p. 175.

25. *Leader*, 10 February 1940, p. 15.

26. Peter Gibbon, "Arensberg and Kimball Revisited," *Economy and Society*, vol. II, no. 4 (1973), p. 494. In this paper Gibbon attempts to prove that Brody's sense of novelty in Irish rural life (which was in fact shared by many contemporary commentators) is the product of a blanket acceptance of the social accuracy of Arensberg and Kimball's *Family and Community in Ireland*. Gibbon shows that in certain respects the society the anthropologists described in Clare was more affected by social change and diverse class interests

than was recognized or admitted by the anthropologists. Gibbon argues that when the deficiencies of that work are made clear, and its romantic portrait of a social order that had in fact exhibited signs of demoralization since the Famine duly corrected, then there is no need to explain the rural demoralization that was all too evident in the 1960s by such things as the sirenlike effect of modern communications luring the countryman to the pleasures of urban life. It can be explained in strictly economic terms as the long-term local effect of "the development of capitalism in agriculture" (p. 496). But it is this crude economic materialism that makes Gibbon's critique of Arensberg and Kimball altogether too partial and therefore suspect. For much of their study had been an account of rural values, beliefs, and assumptions, as well as of the social and economic structure. That they failed to provide an entirely accurate historical account of the economic basis of the society whose values they were exploring does not invalidate their account of that system of values. And it is in the realm of consciousness (of values, assumptions, and aspirations) that the changes of the early 1940s were effected, consolidating the process of emigration that the economic structure, which had obtained since the Famine, of necessity demanded. It was this shift in the consciousness of the Irish countryman that Brody sensed as a novelty in Irish rural life amounting to a watershed in the social history of the country.

27. Brody, *Inishkillane*, p. 71.

28. D. Hannan, *Rural Exodus: A Study of the Forces Influencing the Large-scale Migration of Irish Rural Youth* (London: Geoffrey Chapman, 1970), p. 94.

29. *Patrick Kavanagh: Collected Poems* (London: MacGibbon and Kee, 1968), p. 55.

30. *Leader*, 13 July 1940, p. 533.

31. O'Connell, *History of the Irish National Teachers' Organisation*, pp. 365–66.

32. Ibid., p. 369.

33. Ibid., pp. 369–70.

34. Quoted in the Dáil by General Mulcahy, 13 May 1943. See also Professor John Marcus O'Sullivan's speech, which also refers to Mr. Derrig's remarks in the Dáil on 12 May 1943.

35. O'Connell, *History of the Irish National Teachers' Organisation*, p. 379.

36. Ibid., p. 370.

37. Anne Clissmann, *Flann O'Brien: A Critical Introduction to His Writings* (Dublin: Gill and Macmillan, 1975), p. 235.

38. Ibid., p. 238.

39. Ibid.

40. *Kavanagh's Weekly*, 14 June 1952, p. 5.

41. Seán O'Faoláin, "Standards and Taste," *Bell*, vol. II, no. 3 (1941), p. 7.

42. Quoted in ibid., p. 8.

43. Senate Debates, 28 November 1945, col. 1085. Among the books Magennis stated he feared were "little books at 4d each, issued by foreign publishers . . . to teach all the secrets of sex to young children and to instruct the adult in the full technique of marital relations," Senate Debates, 20 November 1945, col. 1086.

44. Seán O'Faoláin, "New Wine in Old Bottles," *Bell*, vol. IV, no. 6 (September 1942), p. 384.

45. Ibid., p. 382.

46. Seán O'Faoláin, "Silent Ireland," *Bell*, vol. VI, no. 5 (August 1943), p. 464.

47. Ibid., p. 465.

48. O'Faoláin, "Standards and Taste," p. 6.

49. O'Faoláin, "Silent Ireland," p. 460.

50. Seán O'Faoláin, "The Stuffed-Shirts," *Bell*, vol. VI, no. 3 (June 1943), p. 183.

51. Seán O'Faoláin, "Gaelic – The Truth," *Bell*, vol. V, no. 5 (February 1943), p. 339.

52. Seán O'Faoláin, "Dare We Suppress That Irish Voice?", *Bell*, vol. III, no. 3 (December 1941), p. 169.

53. Hubert Butler has recorded that O'Faoláin was particularly generous to Anglo-Irish men and women who wished to play a role in modern Ireland: "We the remnants of the Anglo-Irish 'intelligentsia' would have been nobody's children, had *The Bell* not taken us under its wing." Hubert Butler, "*The Bell*: An Anglo-Irish View," *Irish University Review*, vol. VI, no. 1 (Spring 1976), pp. 66–67.

54. Seán O'Faoláin, "On Editing a Magazine," *Bell*, vol. IX, no. 2 (November 1944), p. 96.

55. See Dermot Foley, "Monotonously Rings the Little Bell," *Irish University Review*, vol. VI, no. 1 (Spring 1976), pp. 54–62.

56. For an excellent and detailed study of a crucial civil service department in the first four decades of independence, see Ronan Fanning, *The Irish Department of Finance, 1922–58* (Dublin: Institute of Public Administration, 1978). This reveals the degree to which senior officials in this department for almost forty years combined conservative monetary policies with the highest degree of probity and financial acumen. See also Leon O'Broin, "Joseph Brennan, Civil Servant Extraordinary," *Studies*, vol. LXVI, no. 261 (Spring 1977), pp. 25–37.

57. John V. Kelleher, *Atlantic*, CXCIX (May 1957), p. 68.

58. T. W. T. Dillon, "Slum Clearance: Past and Present," *Studies*, vol. XXXIV, no. 133 (March 1945), p. 19.

59. Anne O. Crookshank, *Irish Art from 1600 to the Present Day* (Dublin: Department of Foreign Affairs, 1979), p. 64.

60. Charles Sidney, "Art Criticism in Dublin," *Bell*, vol. IX, no. 2 (November 1944), p. 109.

61. Ibid., p. 110.

62. For information on musical life in Dublin in the first two decades of independence, see Joseph O'Neill, "Music in Dublin," in Aloys Fleischmann, ed., *Music in Ireland* (Cork and Oxford: Cork University Press and B. H. Blackwell, 1952), pp. 251–62, and James M. Doyle, "Music in the Army," ibid., pp. 65–69.

63. For a succinct statement of the view that an Irish art music must develop from the indigenous folk music of the country, see Seán Neeson, "When Gaelic Tunes Are Whistled in the Streets," *Irish Press*, 12 April 1935. For an equally succinct statement of the view that Ireland must learn the international idioms of European art music, see Aloys Fleischmann, "Ars Nova: Irish Music in the Shaping," *Ireland Today*, vol. I, no. 2 (July 1936), pp. 41–48. For a stern Irish Ireland view of the issue, see Joseph Hanley, *The National Ideal* (London: Sands, 1932), pp. 152–60.

64. See Séamus Ó Braonáin, "Music in the Broadcasting Service," in Fleischmann, *Music in Ireland*, pp. 197–203.

65. O'Neill, "Music in Dublin," p. 258.

Chapter 7: Stagnation and Crisis

1. Seán O'Faoláin, "The Price of Peace," *Bell*, vol. X, no. 4 (July 1945), p. 288.

2. See F. S. L. Lyons, "The Years of Readjustment," in Kevin B. Nowlan and T. Desmond Williams, eds., *Ireland in the War Years and After, 1939–51* (Dublin: Gill and Macmillan, 1969), pp. 67–79.

3. *Kavanagh's Weekly: A Journal of Literature and Politics*, vol. I, no. 1 (12 April 1952), p. 1.

4. Ibid.

5. *Kavanagh's Weekly*, vol. I, no. 12 (28 June 1952), p. 3.

6. John Montague, *Poisoned Lands and Other Poems* (London: MacGibbon and Kee, 1961), p. 32.

7. John Montague, "The Young Writer," *Bell*, vol. XVII, no. 7 (October 1951), p. 11.

8. Cited in Brendan M. Walsh, "Economic Growth and Development, 1945–70," in J. J. Lee, ed., *Ireland, 1945–70* (Dublin: Gill and Macmillan, 1979), p. 29.

9. Tim Pat Coogan, *The Irish: A Personal View* (London: Phaidon, 1975), p. 43.

10. Liam de Paor, "Ireland's Identities," *Crane Bag*, vol. III, no. 1 (1979), p. 25.

11. What R. Emerson calls "the terminal community" was defined by the experience of neutrality. The terminal community is "the largest community that, when the chips are down, effectively commands men's loyalty,

overriding the claims both of the lesser communities within it and those that cut across it or potentially enfold it within a still greater society." R. Emerson, *From Empire to Nation*, pp. 95–96, cited by Geertz, *The Interpretation of Cultures*, p. 257.

12. Alexander J. Humphreys, *New Dubliners: Urbanization and the Irish Family* (London: Routledge and Kegan Paul, 1966), p. 62.

13. Ibid., p. 61.

14. Ibid., p. 236.

15. Ibid., p. 232.

16. Ibid., p. 250.

17. See Roland Burke Savage, "The Church in Dublin, 1940–1965," *Studies*, vol. LIV (Winter 1965), p. 306.

18. The fullest available study of the scheme, the political controversy it occasioned, and the debates which ensued is in Whyte, *Church and State*, pp. 196–272.

19. Cited in Whyte, *Church and State*, p. 271.

20. Studies of Irish foreign policy in the period are Nicolas Mansergh, "Irish Foreign Policy, 1945–51," in Nowland and Williams, *Ireland in the War Years and After*, pp. 134–46; T. D. Williams, "Irish Foreign Policy, 1949–69," in Lee, *Ireland, 1945–70*, pp. 136–51. See also Patrick Keatinge, *A Place among the Nations: Issues of Irish Foreign Policy* (Dublin: Institute of Public Administration, 1978).

21. "Foreword," *Envoy*, vol. III, no. 9 (1950), p. 6.

22. *Irish Writing*, no. 3 (November 1947), pp. 90–91.

23. Ibid., p. 90.

24. "The Young Writer," *Bell*, vol. XVII, no. 7 (October 1951), p. 7.

25. Denis Donoghue, "The Future of Irish Music," *Studies*, vol. XLIV (Spring 1955), p. 109.

26. F. S. L. Lyons, "Second Thoughts on the Famine," *Irish Writing*, no. 37 (Autumn 1957), p. 57.

27. See Saros Cowasjee, *Sean O'Casey: The Man behind the Plays* (London and Edinburgh: Oliver and Boyd, 2nd ed. 1965), pp. 225–28.

28. Alan Simpson, *Beckett and Behan and a Theatre in Dublin* (London: Routledge and Kegan Paul, 1962), p. 148. In this volume Simpson provides a remarkably balanced account of the entire affair.

29. Cited by Gearóid Ó Tauthaigh in J. J. Lee, ed., *Ireland, 1945–70* (Dublin: Gill and Macmillan, 1979), p. 114. The figures for the National Schools are cited in Lyons, *Ireland since the Famine*, p. 820.

30. David Marcus, "Seán Ó Ríordáin: Modern Gaelic Poet," *Irish Writing*, no. 32 (Autumn 1955), p. 44.

31. Seán Ó Tuama, "The Other Tradition: Some Highlights of Modern Fiction in Irish," in Patrick Rafroidi and Maurice Harmon, eds., *The Irish Novel in Our Time* (Lille: Publications de l'Université de Lille III, 1975–76), p. 44.

32. James White, "The Visual Arts in Ireland," *Studies*, vol. XLIV (Spring 1955), pp. 107–8.

33. Thomas Bodkin, *Report on the Arts in Ireland* (Dublin: Stationery Office, 1949), p. 9.

34. Ibid., p. 49.

35. White, "The Visual Arts in Ireland," p. 101.

36. Desmond Fennell, "The 'Cat on a Hot Tin Roof,'" *Hibernia*, August 1958, p. 8.

37. Adams, *Censorship*, p. 122.

38. See John Ryan, *Remembering How We Stood: Bohemian Dublin at the Mid-Century* (Dublin: Gill and Macmillan, 1975).

39. Declan Kiberd, "Writers in Quarantine? The Case for Irish Studies," *Crane Bag*, vol. III, no. 1 (1979), p. 20.

40. Ryan, *Remembering How We Stood*, p. xiii.

41. Brendan Kennelly, *Collection One* (Dublin: Allen Figgis, 1966), p. 2.

Chapter 8: Economic Revival

1. John V. Kelleher, "Ireland . . . and Where Does She Stand?" *Foreign Affairs*, no. 3 (1957), p. 495.

2. MacDonagh, *Ireland*, p. 131.

3. James Halloran, "The New Society: Community and Social Change," *Doctrine and Life*, vol. XII, no. 7 (1962), p. 374.

4. David Thornley, "Ireland: The End of an Era?" *Tuairim Pamphlet* 12 (January 1965), p. 12.

5. Brendan M. Walsh, "Economic Growth and Development, 1945–1970," in Lee, *Ireland, 1945–70*, p. 33.

6. Denis Meehan, "Views about the Irish," *Furrow*, vol. XI, no. 8 (August 1960), p. 506.

7. Thornley, "Ireland: The End of an Era?" p. 16.

8. Ibid., p. 10.

9. Ibid.

10. Donald S. Corkery, *The Irish* (London: Eyre and Spottiswoode, 1968), p. 30.

11. Whyte, *Church and State*, p. 361. See also MacDonagh, *Ireland*, p. 132.

12. Thornley, "Ireland: The End of an Era?" p. 16.

13. Ibid.

14. Lee, "Continuity and Change in Ireland, 1945–70," in *Ireland, 1945–70*, p. 173.

15. Lee, "Seán Lemass," in *Ireland, 1945–70*, p. 24.

16. Ibid., p. 22.

17. Dáil Debates, 3 June 1959, cited in ibid., p. 22.

18. Lee, "Continuity and Change in Ireland, 1945–70," p. 170.

19. Hugh Leonard, "Drama, the Turning Point," in *Ireland at the Cross-roads* (Lille: Publications de l'Université de Lille III, 1978–79), p. 82.

20. See David C. McClelland, "The Impulse to Modernization," in *Modernization: The Dynamics of Growth* (New York and London: Basic Books, 1966), pp. 28–39.

21. Charles McCarthy, *The Distasteful Challenge* (Dublin: Institute of Public Administration, 1968), p. 21.

22. Lyons, *Ireland since the Famine*, p. 652.

23. *Investment in Education* (Dublin: Stationery Office, 1966), p. xxxiii.

24. Ibid.

25. Ibid., p. 140.

26. Ibid., p. 150.

27. The source for these statistics is the *Statistical Abstract of Ireland* for the relevant years.

28. Paul Andrew, "Ireland and the World Educational Crisis," *Studies*, vol. LIX (Winter 1970), p. 381.

29. See Seán O'Connor, "Post-Primary Education Now and in the Future," *Studies*, vol. LVII (1968), pp. 233–51.

30. *Primary School Curriculum, Teacher's Handbook, 1971*, p. 18.

31. Ibid., p. 12.

32. Ibid.

33. *Primary School Curriculum, Curriculum Questionnaire Analysis* (Dublin: INTO, 1976), p. 24. For a critique of the new curriculum, see Edmund Murphy, "The New Primary School Curriculum," *Studies*, vol. LXII (Autumn 1972), pp. 199–218.

34. For a sympathetic, impressionistic assessment of the National Schools in the 1970s, see Christina Murphy, "The Changing Face of the National Schools," *Irish Times*, 14 January 1980, p. 10; 15 January, p. 10; 16 January, p. 10; 17 January, p. 10.

35. *1979 Census of Population of Ireland: Preliminary Report* (Dublin: Stationery Office, 1979), p. vii.

36. *Irish Times*, 11 September 1979, p. 13.

37. Brendan Walsh, "Ireland's Demographic Transformation, 1958–70," *Economic and Social Review*, vol. III, no. 2 (January 1972), pp. 251–75. See also Brendan Walsh, "A Perspective on Irish Population Patterns," *Eire/Ireland*, vol. IV, no. 3 (1969), pp. 3–21.

38. Brendan Walsh, "Is Marriage Going Out of Fashion?" *Irish Times*, 22 February 1979, p. 10.

39. Basil Chubb, *The Government and Politics of Ireland* (London: Oxford University Press, 1970), p. 142.

40. Desmond Fisher, *Broadcasting in Ireland* (London: Routledge and Kegan Paul, 1978), p. 58.

41. See Damian Hannan, "Kinship, Neighbourhood and Social Change

in Irish Rural Communities," *Economic and Social Review*, vol. III, no. 2 (January 1972), pp. 163–88.

42. Nancy Scheper-Hughes, *Saints, Scholars and Schizophrenics* (Berkeley and Los Angeles: University of California Press, 1979), p. 43.

43. See T. P. O'Mahony, *The Politics of Dishonour* (Dublin: Talbot Press, 1977), pp. 40–42. See also *Magill* (April 1980), special issue on poverty in Ireland.

44. James Downey, "Whose Kind of Country," *Irish Times*, 28 December 1978, p. 2.

45. Kevin O'Connor, "The Irish in Their New Age," *Irish Times*, 7 January 1980, p. 14.

Chapter 9: Decades of Debate

1. E. F. O'Doherty, "Society, Identity and Change," *Studies*, vol. LII (Summer 1963), pp. 130–31.

2. Ibid., p. 132.

3. Gearóid Ó Tuathaigh, "Language, Literature and Culture in Ireland since the War," in Lee, *Ireland, 1945–70*, p. 112.

4. *Commission on the Restoration of the Irish Language, Summary in English of Final Report* (Dublin: Stationery Office, 1963), pp. 37–38.

5. Ó Tuathaigh, "Language, Literature and Culture," p. 117.

6. Nollaig Ó Gadhra, "The Irish Language Revival in 1966," *Eire/Ireland*, vol. II, no. 1 (1967), p. 76.

7. Nollaig Ó Gadhra, "The Language," *Eire/Ireland*, vol. IV, no. 4 (1969), p. 139.

8. *Curriculum Questionnaire Analysis*, 1976, p. 24.

9. For criticism of the effects of the new curriculum on the level of attainment in Irish in the National Schools, see L. S. Andrews, *A Black Paper on Irish Education: The Decline of Irish as a School Subject in the Republic of Ireland, 1967–1977* (Dublin: Gaelic League, 1978).

10. Fisher, *Broadcasting in Ireland*, p. 107.

11. In 1979 such companies as Guinness and Toyota advertised in Irish on television and in the press.

12. *Report of the Committee on Irish Language Attitudes Research* (Dublin: 1975), p. 293. I am grateful to Professor M. Ó Murchú, who made the report available to me.

13. Ibid.

14. Ibid., pp. 293–94.

15. Ibid., p. 294.

16. Ibid., p. 305.

17. Ibid., p. 297.

18. Ibid., p. 298.

19. Ibid., p. 24.

20. Such an identification of Irish with middle-class success was not without risks, however. As the researchers discovered, some working-class feeling was directed against the language since parents of children in inadequate schools in working-class districts felt that Irish was a discriminatory weapon wielded by the middle class against their children, who had little chance of finishing the linguistic obstacle race society set them. Such feeling had received fuel in 1966 when a study had presented evidence (of a highly technical kind, open to question and criticism) that Irish linguistic policy had impeded educational attainment in the National Schools. See John MacNamara, *Bilingualism and Primary Education* (Edinburgh University Press, 1966). The findings of this work were widely broadcast in the late 1960s and early 1970s by a group known as the Language Freedom Movement, and such polemics against the revival policy undoubtedly helped to reinforce for some Irish people the fairly common belief that Irish and backwardness were somehow inextricably intertwined. That some few individuals in Irish society could be seen to have done well while retaining a high regard for the language perhaps did not, in such a context, do much to increase general regard for the language. It may easily have had the reverse effect, in sometimes increasing class resentments of the kind researchers found in the 1970s.

21. *Report*, p. 307.

22. Ibid., p. 308.

23. Ibid., p. 315.

24. Brendan Breathnach, "Not a Revivalist Fad but a Living Music," *Irish Times*, 27 September 1977, p. 1.

25. David Hammond, "The Popular Tradition in Ireland Today," in *Four Centuries of Music in Ireland*, ed. Brian Boydell (London: BBC, 1979), p. 56.

26. See John A. Murphy, "Identity Change in the Republic of Ireland," *Etudes Irlandaises*, no. 1, n.s. (December 1976), pp. 149–50, for a more sanguine view of the significance of such popular expressions of Irish national identity in the 1970s.

27. Seán Ó Tuama, "The Gaelic League Idea in the Future," in *The Gaelic League Idea* (Cork and Dublin: Mercier Press, 1972), pp. 99–100.

28. Michael Hartnett, *A Farewell to English and Other Poems* (Dublin: Gallery Press, 1975), p. 34.

29. Ibid., p. 33.

30. Nationalism, as Wilbert E. Moore has remarked, can supply "a high degree of national integration" which is necessary to "the rapid and deliberate change that forms the contemporary pattern of modernization." It provides "a kind of non-rational focus of identification and rationale for the extensive disruption of the traditional order." Wilbert E. Moore, *Social Change* (Englewood Cliffs, N. J.: Prentice-Hall, 2nd ed. 1974), p. 99. See also Ernest Gellner, *Thought and Change* (London: Weidenfeld and Nicolson, 1965), for

an excellent theoretical study of the role of nationalism in the process of modernization.

31. Donald S. Corkery, *The Irish*, p. 241.

32. What precisely were the components of Irish public opinion in the 1970s on the Northern Ireland question, and on issues related to it, was the concern of various surveys and polls in the period. The fullest of these, and the one that caused the most controversy, seemed to confirm that ambivalence and lack of consistency were implicit in the attitudes of many Irish people to the Northern Ireland question. See "Attitudes in Republic to Northern Ireland Problem," *Irish Times*, 16 October 1979, p. 4. The article summarized the findings of an attitude survey conducted by R. Sinnott and E. E. Davis under the aegis of the Economic and Social Research Institute.

33. One is forced to use this rather cumbersome term to take account of the dual aspect of official Irish ideology in the decades since the Treaty. That ideology had its historic ancestry both in the republicanism of the late eighteenth century and the nationalism of the nineteenth. The ideology has as a result tended to express both an instinct for an Irish republic of diverse elements under the common name Irishman and a nationalist irrendentism in relation to the six counties of Northern Ireland.

34. A classic example of such Jacobite sentimentality is Aodh de Blacam's book, *The Black North: An Account of the Six Counties of Uncovered Ireland* (Dublin: M. H. Gill and Son, 1938 and 1940). This book expressed the republican nationalist ideology in a popular form with the imprimatur of a foreword by Eamon de Valera.

35. "Unhappy and at Home," interview with Seamus Heaney by Seamus Deane, *Crane Bag*, vol. I, no. 1 (1977), p. 64.

36. John A. Murphy, "Further Reflections on Irish Nationalism," *Crane Bag*, vol. II, nos. 1 and 2 (1978), p. 157.

37. Helen Mulvey, "Thirty Years' Work in Irish History," *Irish Historical Studies*, vol. XVII, no. 66 (September 1970), p. 183.

38. Francis Shaw, "The Canon of Irish History – A Challenge," *Studies*, vol. LXI (Summer 1972), p. 117.

39. Ibid., p. 142.

40. Ibid., p. 145.

41. Ibid., pp. 117–18.

42. Conor Cruise O'Brien, "Eradicating the Tragic Heroic Mode," *Irish Times*, 22 August 1975, p. 10.

43. Conor Cruise O'Brien, "Politics and the Poet," *Irish Times*, 21 August 1975, p. 10. See also Conor Cruise O'Brien, "Ireland Will Not Have Peace," *Harpers*, vol. CCLIII, no. 1519 (December 1976), pp. 33–42; Conor Cruise O'Brien, "Liberalism in Ireland," *Sunday Press*, 25 September 1977, p. 2, and Conor Cruise O'Brien, "Nationalism and the Reconquest of Ireland," *Crane Bag*, vol. 1, no. 2 (1977), pp. 8–13.

44. Murphy, "Further Reflections," p. 159.

45. Ibid., p. 160.

46. For an excellent study of the emergence of nationalist historiography and the sense of the past in nineteenth-century Ireland, see Oliver MacDonagh, "Time's Revenges and Revenge's Time: A View of Anglo-Irish Relations," *Anglo-Irish Studies*, IV (1979), pp. 1–19.

47. Liam de Paor, "The Ambiguity of the Republic," *Atlantis*, no. 3 (November 1971), p. 1.

48. Ibid.

49. See F. S. L. Lyons, "The Dilemma of the Irish Contemporary Historian," *Hermathena*, no. CXV (Summer 1973), pp. 44–55. See also F. S. L. Lyons, "The Shadow of the Past," *Irish Times*, 11 September 1972, p. 12, where Lyons criticized Father Shaw for ignoring in his essay on Pearse the degree to which Irish historians had subjected Pearse, and the entire period leading to the Rising, to analytic examination since 1961 when "Professor F. X. Martin published Eoin MacNeill's memoranda of the Rising in *Irish Historical Studies*."

50. T. W. Moody, "Irish History and Irish Mythology," *Hermathena*, no. CXXIV (Summer 1978), p. 23. For a warmly sympathetic assessment of T. W. Moody's contribution to the development of Irish historical studies, see F. S. L. Lyons, "T.W.M.," in F. S. L. Lyons and R. A. J. Hawkings, eds., *Ireland under the Union: Varieties of Tension* (Oxford: Clarendon Press, 1980), pp. 1–33.

51. Moody, "Irish History," p. 7.

52. For information on Irish history in education, I am indebted to Kenneth Milne, *New Approaches to the Teaching of Irish History* (London: Historical Association, no. 43, 1979).

53. Denis Meehan, "An Essay in Self-Criticism," *Furrow*, vol. VIII, no. 4 (April 1957), p. 211.

54. John C. Kelly, SJ, "Solid Virtue in Ireland," *Doctrine and Life*, vol. IX, no. 5 (October/November 1959), p. 120.

55. James Scott, "The Intellectual Life," *Furrow*, vol. XIII, no. 4 (April 1962), p. 204.

56. Peter Connolly, "Censorship," *Christus Rex*, vol. XII, no. 3 (1959), p. 170.

57. Peter Connolly, "Turbulent Priests," *Hibernia*, vol. XXVII, no. 2 (February 1964), p. 9.

58. Adams, *Censorship*, p. 158.

59. That the Jesuit Irish periodical *Studies* since the 1960s published many critical essays on twentieth-century literature was evidence of the new openness to literary insight. Furthermore, the publication in 1969 in that journal of a sternly critical analysis of Professor Magennis's famous Senate speech on censorship was evidence of a new attitude among the Catholic intelligentsia. See Andrew F. Comyn, "Censorship in Ireland," *Studies*, vol. LVIII (Spring 1969), pp. 42–50. This article was in striking contrast to an

454   Notes and References

earlier piece which appeared in *Studies* in vigorous defence of the Irish Censorship Board. See P. J. Gannon, SJ, "Art, Morality and Censorship," *Studies*, vol. XXXI, no. 124 (December 1942), pp. 409–19.

60. John A. Dowling, "Lay Thoughts at Home," *Furrow*, vol. XV, no. 3 (March 1964), p. 160.

61. David Thornley, "Irish Identity," *Doctrine and Life*, vol. XVI, no. 4 (April 1966), p. 181.

62. Jeremiah Newman, "Ireland in the Eighties: Our Responsibility," *Christus Rex*, vol. XXV, no. 3 (1971), p. 186.

63. Ibid., p. 190.

64. Thornley, "Irish Identity," p. 186.

65. Ibid.

66. These studies are reported on and analyzed by Tom Inglis, "Decline in Numbers of Priests and Religious in Ireland," *Doctrine and Life*, vol. XXX, no. 2 (February 1979), pp. 79–98.

67. Reported on in Inglis, ibid., p. 94.

68. Ibid., p. 95.

69. Ibid., p. 98.

70. These figures were supplied by Christina Murphy in a report, "Education, A Review of the Decade," *Irish Times*, 28 December 1979, p. xiii.

71. Tom Inglis, "How Religious Are Irish University Students?" *Doctrine and Life*, vol. XXX, no. 7 (July 1979), p. 412. See also Maire Nic Ghiolla Phadraig, "Religion in Ireland – Preliminary Analysis," *Social Studies*, vol. V, no. 2 (Summer 1976), pp. 113–80, and Michael Paul Gallagher, "Atheism Irish Style," *Furrow*, vol. XXV, no. 4 (April 1974), pp. 183–92.

72. Inglis, "How Religious Are Irish University Students?" p. 419.

73. Ibid., p. 421.

74. Ibid., p. 414.

75. See Eunice McCarthy, "Women and Work in Ireland: The Present and Preparing for the Future," in Margaret MacCurtain and Donncha Ó Corrain, eds., *Women in Irish Society* (Dublin: Arlen House, Women's Press, 1978), pp. 103–17. See also Margaret MacCurtain, "Women – Irish Style," *Doctrine and Life*, vol. XXIV, no. 4 (April 1974), pp. 182–92.

76. A detailed study of these developments in social legislation in relation to church teaching is the Epilogue to J. H. Whyte, *Church and State in Modern Ireland* (Dublin: Gill and Macmillan, 2nd ed. 1980).

77. Republished in *Justice, Love, Peace: Pastoral Letters of the Irish Bishops, 1969–79* (Dublin: Veritas Publications, 1979), p. 128.

78. Ibid., p. 120.

79. An enthusiastic assessment of religious renewal in Ireland in the 1970s is Cahal B. Daly, then Bishop of Ardagh and Clonmacnois, "The Future of Christianity in Ireland," *Doctrine and Life*, vol. XXVII, no. 3 (March/April 1977), pp. 105–24. A less sanguine essay on the same subject is Peter Connolly, "The Church in Ireland since the Second Vatican Council," *Ireland at the Crossroads*

(Lille: Publications de l'Université de Lille III, 1978–79), pp. 87–99.

80. Donal Dorr, "Change – and the Irish Identity," *Doctrine and Life*, vol. XXIV, no. 1 (January 1974), p. 8.

81. The most developed discussion of the concept of pluralism was in *Studies* in 1978.

82. Garret FitzGerald, "Seeking a National Purpose," *Studies*, vol. LIII (Winter 1964), p. 1.

83. Garret FitzGerald, who was perhaps the most zealous in the propagation of the concept, admitted as much in 1976: "In the Republic . . . the concept of a pluralist society has yet to strike deep roots at a popular level; for many people the ideas is an abstract rather than an intellectual one at variance with a traditional inherited value system;" "Ireland's Identity Problems," *Etudes Irlandaises*, no. 1, n.s. (December 1976), p. 142. However, some conservative bishops were sufficiently alarmed by the possibility that it would become a popular notion to preach and lecture against it.

84. Kurt Bowen, *Protestants in a Catholic State: Ireland's Privileged Minority* (Kingston and Montreal: McGill – Queen's University Press, 1983), p. 207.

85. Ibid., p. 208.

Chapter 10: Culture and a Changing Society

1. Bryan MacMahon, "Culture in Rural Ireland," *Christus Rex*, vol. XXII (1968), p. 324.

2. Government White Paper (Dublin: Stationery Office, 1965) p. 10.

3. Information on the Arts Council derived from the Council's annual reports.

4. The membership of the Booksellers' Association of Great Britain and Ireland in 1979 stood at 117 (44 in Dublin and its suburbs). Many of these were not fully fledged bookshops but general newsagents which sold some books. I am grateful to Miss Heather MacDougald for this information.

5. Cited in Maurice Harmon, *The Poetry of Thomas Kinsella* (Dublin: Wolfhound Press, 1974), pp. 11–12.

6. Maurice Harmon, "Generations Apart: 1925–1975," in Rafroidi and Harmon, eds., *The Irish Novel in Our Time*, p. 56.

7. In 1978 the Abbey and the Peacock (the small theatre associated with the Abbey) received £518,000 in subsidy, the Gate Theatre £135,000. As the Arts Council Report for that year stated, however, such support, while a vast improvement on former days, made the Abbey Theatre the poor relation among European national theatres. The figure above scarcely covered the wage bill, and the report found that the low level of subsidy "seriously endangers the Abbey's ability to fulfil its proper role as a centre of dramatic excellence" (Arts Council Report, 1979), p. 16.

8. Christopher Murray, "Irish Drama in Transition 1966–1978," *Etudes Irlandaises*, no. 4. n.s. (December 1979), p. 289.

9. Leonard, "Drama, the Turning Point," p. 78.

10. Murray, "Irish Drama in Transition," p. 296.

11. Ibid., p. 291.

12. In 1978 and 1979 Irish Marketing Surveys conducted a study for the Arts Council on the living and working conditions of artists in Ireland. It reported that the average mean income for creative artists (which included writers as well as painters, composers, and sculptors) for the previous year was just less than £1,500 and that 50 percent of such persons had earned under £1,000 from their artistic endeavours. Three-quarters of all creative artists were found to have more than one occupation.

13. See, for example, Bruce Arnold's chapter "Jack Yeats and the Moderns," in *A Concise History of Irish Art* (London: Thames and Hudson, 2nd ed., 1977).

14. Dorothy Walker, *Modern Art in Ireland* (Dublin: Lilliput Press, 1997), p. 115.

15. Thomas Kilroy, "Tellers of Tales," *Times Literary Supplement*, 17 March 1972, p. 302.

16. Eavan Boland, "The Weasel's Tooth," *Irish Times*, 7 June 1974, p. 7.

17. See Seamus Deane, "Irish Poetry and Irish Nationalism," in Douglas Dunn, ed. *Two Decades of Irish Writing* (Cheadle Hulme: Carcarnet Press, 1975), pp. 4–22; "The Appetites of Gravity," *Sewanee Review*, vol. LXXXIV, no. 1 (1976), pp. 199–208, and "The Literary Myths of the Revival: A Case for their Abandonment," in Joseph Ronsley, ed., *Myth and Reality in Irish Literature* (Waterloo: Wilfrid Laurier University Press, 1977), pp. 317–29.

18. Seamus Deane, "Postscript," *Crane Bag*, vol. III, no. 2 (1979), p. 92.

19. Ibid., p. 94.

20. Ibid., p. 93.

Chapter 11: The Uncertain 1980s

1. Peter Neary, "The Failure of Economic Nationalism," *Ireland: Dependence and Independence, Crane Bag*, vol. VIII, no. 1 (1984) p. 69.

2. See Padraig O'Malley, *The Uncivil Wars: Ireland Today* (Belfast: Blackstaff Press, 1983).

3. *Irish Times*, 23 August 1984, p. 1, citing an EEC Commission Report.

4. O'Malley, *The Uncivil Wars*, p. 392.

5. These figures are drawn from Noreen O'Donoghue and Sue Richardson, eds., *Pure Murder . . . a Book About Drug Abuse* (Dublin: Women's Community Press, 1984), pp. 16–18.

6. See Paul Tansey, "No Sex Please, We're Broke," *Sunday Tribune*, 6 May 1984, p. 16.

7. Desmond Fennell, *The State of the Nation: Ireland Since the Sixties* Swords: Ward River Press, 1983), pp. 15–16.

8. Frank Litton, Preface, *Unequal Achievement: The Irish Experience, 1957–82* (Dublin: Institute of Public Administration, 1982).

9. Joseph Lee, "Society and Culture," ibid., p. 16.

10. David B. Rottman and Philip J. O'Connell, "The Changing Social Structure in Ireland," ibid., p. 85.

11. Thomas J. Barrington, "What Happened to Irish Government?" in bid., p. 107.

12. Tom Garvin, "Change and the Political System," ibid., p. 38.

13. Rottman and O'Connell, "The Changing Social Structure," p. 72.

14. Ibid., p. 73.

15. *White Paper on Educational Development* (Dublin: Stationery Office, 1980), p. 111.

16. Rottmann and O'Connell, "The Changing Social Structure," p. 74.

17. *Irish Times*, 26 July 1984, p. 1.

18. Rottman and O'Connell, "The Changing Social Structure," p. 75.

19. Cited in O'Malley, *The Uncivil Wars*, p. 389.

20. *White Paper on Educational Development*, p. iv.

21. *New Ireland Forum, Report of Proceedings, Irish Episcopal Conference Delegation* (Dublin: Stationery Office, 1984), p. 15.

22. Ibid., p. 20.

23. Ibid., p. 23.

24. Ed Moloney has argued that these discussions did not represent any kind of *volte face* for Gerry Adams, President of Sinn Féin, because he had long been working towards a political settlement. In this reading of their discussions, Adams was open to dialogue with Hume since he had already embarked on a secret process of communication with the British through an intermediary which might have resulted in the earlier ending of violence than in fact occurred. See Ed Moloney, *A Secret History of the IRA* (London: Penguin, 2002), pp. 219–80.

25. *Forum Report*, p. 20.

26. Quoted in O'Malley, *The Uncivil Wars*, p. 407.

27. *New Ireland Forum Report* (Dublin: Stationery Office, 1984), p. 2.

28. Ibid.

29. Cited in Tim Pat Coogan, *Disillusioned Decades: Ireland 1966–87* (Dublin: Gill and Macmillan, 1987), p. 107.

30. I am grateful to Senator David Norris, who made copies of these judgments available to me.

31. Liam Ryan, "Faith Under Survey," *Furrow*, vol. XXXIV, no. 1 (January 1984), p. 6.

32. Ibid., p. 11.

33. See Peadar Kirby, *Is Irish Catholicism Dying?* (Cork: Mercier Press, 1984).

34. Ibid., p. 90.

35. *The Action Plan for Irish, 1983–1986* (Dublin: Bord na Gaeilge, 1983), p. 2.

36. Ibid., p. 3.

37. Ibid., p. 12.

38. Máire Mhac an tSaoi, cited in *Ireland and the Arts*, ed. Tim Pat Coogan (London: Namara Press, nd), p. 80.

39. Alan Titley "Innti and Onward: the New Poetry in Irish," in *Irish Poetry Since Kavanagh*, ed. Theo Dorgan (County Dublin: Four Courts Press, 1996), p. 85.

40. Ibid.

41. Ibid.

42. Theo Dorgan, Introduction to *Irish Poetry Since Kavanagh*, p. 13.

43. *The Irish Language in a Changing Society: Shaping the Future* (Dublin: Bord na Gaeilge, 1986), p. 80.

44. Ibid., p. xxxiv.

45. Ibid., p. 80.

46. Ibid., p. xxxiv.

47. Brian P. Kennedy, *Dreams and Responsibilities: The State and the Arts in Independent Ireland* (Dublin: The Arts Council, nd), p. 221.

48. Ibid., p. 227.

49. See *Cinema and Ireland*, eds. Kevin Rockett, Luke Gibbons and John Hill (Syracuse, New York: Syracuse University Press, 1988). I am indebted to this work.

50. "Editorial," *Crane Bag*, vol. II, no. 2 (1978), p. 5.

51. Richard Kearney, "Between Conflict and Consensus," *Crane Bag*, vol. IX, no. 1 (1985), p. 89.

52. Cited by John Gray, "Field Day Five Years On," *Linen Hall Review*, vol. II, no. 2 (Summer 1985). For a study of the early years of Field Day, see Marilyn Richtarik, *Acting Between the Lines: Field Day Theatre Company and Irish Cultural Politics* (Oxford: Clarendon Press, 1984).

53. Ibid., p. 5.

54. Ibid., p. 7.

55. See my "Translating Ireland," *Krino: An Anthology*, eds. Gerald Dawe and Jonathan Williams (Dublin: Gill and Macmillan, 1996), pp. 137–40. See also Michael Cronin, *Translating Ireland: Translation, Languages, Cultures* (Cork: Cork University Press, 1996).

56. Cited by Gray, "Field Day Five Years On," p. 10.

57. Brendan Kennelly, *Cromwell* (Dublin: Beaver Row Press, 1983), p. 110.

58. Nicholas Grene, *The Politics of Irish Drama: Plays in Context from Boucicault to Friel* (Cambridge: Cambridge University Press, 1999), pp. 235–36.

59. Ibid., p. 236.

60. Michael O'Connell, *Changed Utterly: Ireland and the New Irish Psyche* (Dublin: Liffey Press, 2001), p. 30.

61. J. J. Lee, *Ireland, 1912–1985: Politics and Society* (Cambridge: Cambridge University Press, 1989), p. 521.

62. Ray Mac Sharry [*sic*] and Padraic A. White, *The Making of the Celtic Tiger: The Inside Story of Ireland's Economic Boom* (Cork: Mercier Press, 2000), p. 371.

Chapter 12: Revelations and Recovery

1. Brian Friel, *Dancing at Lughnasa* (London: Faber and Faber, 1990), p. 22.

2. Linda Connolly, *The Irish Women's Movement: From Revolution to Devolution* (Dublin: The Lilliput Press, 2002), p. 193. This useful study shows how the women's movement in Ireland in the 1970s and thereafter had its precursor in the vibrant suffragist activism of the pre-independence period. However, the issue of the rights of women had almost gone into eclipse during the first five decades of Irish independence. See also Mary E. Daly, " 'Oh, Kathleen Ni Houlihan, Your Way's a Thorny Way!' The Condition of Women in Twentieth-Century Ireland," in *Gender and Sexuality in Modern Ireland* (Amherst: University of Massachusetts Press, 1997), pp. 102–26. Daly writes of the "doldrums into which feminism fell after 1920." She acknowledges that this mirrored "developments in other countries where women gained the franchise" but notes "it also appears that Irish feminists found it difficult to replace the pre-war focus on equal rights with an ideology that might have been more in keeping with the culture of the independent state." Daly, p. 119. She also argues that many Irish women working in the home for their large families simply did not have leisure for political activism: "It can be argued that it was only when the fertility patterns desired by Irish couples began to conflict with state legislation, and when a critical mass of suburban housewives existed, that the modern women's movement could emerge in Ireland." Ibid.

3. Linda Connolly, p. 190.

4. Gemma Hussey, *Ireland Today: Anatomy of a Changing State* (London: Viking, 1994), p. 19. See also John Horgan, *Mary Robinson: An Independent Woman* (Dublin: O'Brien Press, 1997), to which I am indebted in this chapter.

5. Hussey, *Ireland Today*, p. 19.

6. Horgan, *Mary Robinson*, p. 177.

7. Greg Delanty, "We Will Not Play the Harp Backwards Now, No!" *The Hellbox* (Oxford: Oxford University Press, 1998), p. 34.

8. See Justin O'Brien, *The Modern Prince: Charles Haughey and the Quest for Power* (Dublin: Merlin Press, 2002), pp. 133–46. O'Brien reveals that a complex strategy within Fianna Fail to oust Haughey was overtaken in

1992 when Haughey was forced to resign because of this old wire-tapping scandal.

9. Michael Peillon, "Carnival in Ireland," in *Memories of the Present: A Sociological Chronicle of Ireland*, eds. Eamonn Slater and Michel Peillon (Dublin: Institute of Public Administration, 2000), p. 140.

10. Ibid., p. 133.

11. Ibid., p. 141.

12. See Tom Inglis, *Moral Monopoly: The Rise and Fall of the Catholic Church in Modern Ireland* (Dublin: University College Dublin Press, 2nd ed, 1998). I am indebted to this volume in this chapter. Inglis observes: "Until 1960 there was homology between the way bishops and priests viewed and understood the world and the way the world was portrayed in the media." Ibid., p. 231.

13. See Emily O'Reilly, *Masterminds of the Right* (Dublin: Attic Press, 1988), pp. 98–125.

14. For studies of the abortion debate in Ireland and its social and legal contexts see *The Abortion Papers Ireland*, ed. Ailbhe Smyth (Dublin: Attic Press, 1992). Taoiseach Bertie Ahern's government sought to resolve this conundrum in a further referendum in 2002, by seeking an amendment to the Constitution which would have excluded the threat of suicide by a prospective mother as grounds for an abortion. Once again the proposition was opposed by those adamantly against abortion in any circumstances and by those who supported the rights of women, which probably accounts in part for the fact that the proposed constitutional amendment was defeated by a small margin. The issue remains confused, with no government inclined to revisit the matter.

15. See Chris Moore, *Betrayal of Trust, The Father Smyth Affair and the Catholic Church* (Dublin: Marino Books, 1995). I am indebted to this work.

16. Ibid., p. 20.

17. Ibid., p. 229.

18. Enda McDonagh, "The Winter Name of Church," *Furrow*, vol. LXIV, no. 1 (January 1995), p. 3.

19. Ibid., p. 8.

20. Mary Kenny, *Goodbye to Catholic Ireland*, revised and updated edition (Dublin: New Island Books, 2000), p. 309.

21. Ibid., p. 314.

22. Patrick O'Brien, "A Letter to the Papal Nuncio," *Furrow*, vol. LXIV no. 1 (January, 1995), p. 15.

23. Inglis, *Moral Monopoly*, p. 217.

24. Ibid., pp. 203–42.

25. Marguerite Corish, "Aspects of the Secularisation of Irish Society," in *Faith and Culture in the Irish Context*, ed. Eoin G. Cassidy (Dublin: Veritas Publications, 1996), p. 151.

26. Ibid., p. 159.

27. O'Connell, *Changed Utterly*, p. 64.

28. This was reported on and analyzed in Bill Cosgrove, "Mass Attendance: Reflections on a Recent Survey," *Furrow*, vol. XLIX, no. 12 (1998), p. 681–89, from which these figures are derived.

29. Inglis, *Moral Monopoly*, p. 212.

30. Cited in O'Connell, *Changed Utterly*, p. 79.

31. Ibid., p. 81.

32. Ibid., p. 82.

33. Ibid., p. 149.

34. See Fintan O'Toole, *Meanwhile Back at the Ranch: The Politics of Irish Beef* (London: Vintage Books, 1995), pp. 275–82. O'Toole's is a lucid account of a murky affair, which by its very complexity lacked the public impact of revelations that were to follow in the 1990s. For succinct summaries of this and other scandals in the 1990s, I am indebted to Gene Kerrigan and Pat Brennan, *This Great Little Nation: The A-Z of Irish Scandals and Controversies* (Dublin: Gill and Macmillan, 1999). See also Paul Cullen, *With a Little Help from my Friends* (Dublin: Gill and Macmillan, 2002).

35. O'Brien, *Modern Prince*, p. 156.

36. Kerrigan and Brennan, *Great Little Nation*, p. 109.

37. Ibid., p. 281.

38. Cited in O'Brien, *Modern Prince*, p. 166.

39. Figures drawn from Central Statistics Office, reported in the *Irish Times* 4 July 2001, p. 16.

40. Mac Sharry and White, *Making of the Celtic Tiger*, p. 360.

41. Ibid., p. 376.

42. Other studies of the "Celtic Tiger" phenomenon are Paul Sweeney, *The Celtic Tiger: Ireland's Economic Miracle Explained* (Dublin: Oak Tree Press, 1998), Michael O'Connell, *Changed Utterly: Ireland and the New Irish Psyche*, and the highly unimpressed Kieran Allen, *The Celtic Tiger: The Myth of Social Progress in Ireland* (Manchester and New York: Manchester University Press, 2000).

43. Figures drawn from the Central Statistics Office, reported in the *Irish Independent*, 5 October 2002, p. 7.

44. O'Connell, *Changed Utterly*, p. 142.

45. Allen, *The Celtic Tiger*, p. 69.

46. Mary P. Corcoran, "Mall City," in *Memories of the Present*, p. 91.

47. Ibid., p. 92.

48. Ibid., p. 103.

49. Figures reported in the *Irish Times*, 24 January 2003, p. 4.

50. Ibid.

51. For a perceptive, amusing account of *nouveau riche* Ireland, see Anne Marie Hourihane, *She Moved Through the Boom* (Dublin: Sitric Books, 2000).

52. Michael Peillon, "Strangers in Our Midst," in *Memories of the Present*, p. 106. See also Neil Middleton and Josephine Olusola, "Home to a Strange

Land," *Furrow*, vol. XLIX, no. 12 (1998), pp. 690–94, for a critical analysis of the state's response to asylum-seekers.

53. In writing on the Irish peace process I am indebted to the following: Paul Arthur, *Special Relationships: Britain, Ireland and the Northern Ireland Problem* (Belfast: Blackstaff Press, 2000); Seán Farren and Robert F. Mulvihill. *Paths to a Settlement in Northern Ireland* (Gerrards Cross, Buckinghamshire Colin Smythe, 2000); Henry Patterson, *The Politics of Illusion: A Political History of the IRA* (London: Serif, 1997); Eamonn Mallie and David McKittrick, *Endgame in Ireland* (Great Britain: Coronet Books, 2001); Fionnuala O'Connor, *Breaking the Bonds: Making Peace in Northern Ireland* (Edinburgh and London: Mainstream Publishing, 2002); Ed Moloney, *A Secret History of the IRA*, and Paul Bew and Gordon Gillespie, *Northern Ireland: A Chronology of the Troubles* (Dublin: Gill and Macmillan, 1993).

54. Farren and Mulivihill, *Paths to a Settlement*, p. 158. Ed Moloney records that Hume had embarked on these talks almost immediately after the earlier dialogue had seemed to run into the sands. See Ed Moloney, *A Secret History of the IRA*, p. 279.

55. O'Connor, *Breaking the Bonds*, p. 277.

56. Cited in John Goodby and Ivan Phillips, "Not Bad: the Spirit Level," in *The Art of Seamus Heaney*, ed. Tony Curtis (Dublin: Wolfhound Press, 2001), p. 260.

57. Seamus Heaney, "Cessation," *Finders Keepers: Selected Prose, 1971–2001* (London: Faber and Faber, 2002), p. 47.

Chapter 13: Conclusion: Culture and Memory in an International Context

1. Patrick Hanafin, "Legal Texts as Cultural Documents: Interpreting the Irish Constitution," in *Writing the Irish Republic: Literature, Culture, Politics, 1949–1999*, ed. Ray Ryan (Basingstoke, Hampshire: Macmillan, 2000), p. 150.

2. Ibid., p. 159.

3. Ibid., p. 161.

4. Declan Kiberd, *Irish Classics* (London: Granta Publications, 2000), pp. 629–30. For a detailed study of the implications for the South of the Good Friday Agreement, see John Coakley, "The Belfast Agreement and the Republic of Ireland," in R. A. Willford, *Aspects of the Belfast Agreement* (Oxford: Oxford University Press, 2001), pp. 225–44. Coakley reckons that a poll of 1999 which showed that 96 percent of "those expressing a view of the matter would like a united Ireland" may be consistent with the 94 percent support of constitutional change in the referendum. This would lend "some credence to the view that the Agreement was seen in the South as a victory for nationalism – or that it was seen at least as being compatible with the traditional nationalist objective of unity." Coakley, p. 225.

5. Kiberd, *Irish Classics*, p. 629.

6. Hanafin, "Legal Texts as Cultural Documents," p. 161.

7. Fintan O'Toole, *The Ex-Isle of Erin: Images of a Global Ireland* (Dublin: New Island Books, 1997), pp. 20–21.

8. Ibid., p. 21.

9. Derek Mahon, *The Yellow Book* (Oldcastle, County Meath: Gallery Press, 1997), p. 15.

10. Christopher Morash, *A History of Irish Theatre* (Cambridge: Cambridge University Press, 2002), p. 269.

11. Ibid.

12. Joseph Cleary, "Modernization and Aesthetic Ideology in Contemporary Irish Culture," in Ryan, ed., *Writing the Irish Republic*, p. 126.

13. Ibid., p. 108.

14. Luke Gibbons, "The Global Cure? History, Therapy and the Celtic Tiger," in *Reinventing Ireland: Culture, Society, and the Global Economy*, eds. Peadar Kirby, Luke Gibbons and Michael Cronin (London: Pluto Press, 2002), p. 97. Gibbons draws here on the writings of Theodore Adorno.

15. Nicholas Grene, *The Politics of Irish Drama*, p. 253.

16. For an acerbic critique of the *Angela's Ashes* phenomenon, see Roy Foster, *The Irish Story: Telling Tales and Making It Up in Ireland* (London: Allen Lane, Penguin Press, 2001), p. 1.

17. Roy Foster, "We Are All Revisionists Now," *Irish Review*, no. 1 (1986), p. 1.

18. Ibid.

19. Ibid., p. 4.

20. Ibid., p. 5.

21. Foster, *The Irish Story*, p. 44.

22. Seamus Deane, General Introduction, *Field Day Anthology of Irish Writing* (Dublin: Field Day Theatre Company, 1991), p. xxiii.

23. Seamus Deane, *Strange Country* (London: Oxford University Press, 1997), p. 193. See also Joseph Cleary, "Fork-Tongued on the Border Bit: Partition and the Politics of Form in Contemporary Narratives of the Northern Conflict," *South Atlantic Quarterly*, vol. XCV, no. 1 (Winter 1996), pp. 233–34.

24. See in particular Edna Longley, "Introduction: Revising Irish Literature," in *The Living Stream* (Newcastle upon Tyne: Bloodaxe Books, 1994), pp. 9–68.

25. See, for example, Tom Dunne, "New Histories: Beyond Revisionism," *Irish Review*, no. 12 (Spring/Summer 1992), pp. 1–12. See also Ciarán Brady, ed., *Ideology and the Historians* (Dublin: The Lilliput Press, 1991) and *Interpreting Irish History: the Debate on Historical Revisionism, 1938–1994* (County Dublin: Irish Academic Press, 1994), for useful general and specific discussions of these issues.

26. See, in particular, Angela Bourke, *The Burning of Bridget Cleary: A*

True Story (London: Pimlico, 1999) and David Fitzpatrick, *Oceans of Consolation* (Cork: Cork University Press, 1999).

27. Luke Gibbons and Kevin Whelan, "In Conversation with Stephen Rea," *Yale Journal of Criticism*, vol. XV, no. 1 (2002), pp. 14–15. I am grateful to Kevin Whelan who made this publication available to me. See also Neil Jordan, *Michael Collins: Screenplay and Film Diary* (London: Vintage, 1996).

28. Quoted in Keith Hopper, "Cat-Calls from the Cheap Seats: The Third Meaning of Neil Jordan's *Michael Collins*," *Irish Review*, no. 2 (Autumn/Winter 1997), p. 2. I am indebted to this valuable article.

29. See Ruth Barton, "From History to Heritage: Some Recent Developments of Irish Cinema," *Irish Review*, no. 21 (Autumn/Winter 1997), pp. 41–56, and Luke Gibbons, "The Global Cure?" p. 98.

30. See Brian Walker, *Dancing to History's Tune: History, Myth and Politics in Ireland* (Belfast: Institute of Irish Studies, 1996), p. 74. Walker is cited by Ruth Barton in "From History to Heritage." For an excellent study of historiography and of history as an institution in Ireland see J. J. Lee, "Irish History," in *The Heritage of Ireland*, eds. N. Buttimer, C. Rynne and H. Guerin (Cork: Collins Press, 2000), pp. 114–36.

31. Barton, "From History to Heritage," p. 53.

32. At some moments it was as if the Famine commemoration had become almost fashionable and had attracted the attention of the media and entertainment world in a way that risked seeming to commercialize the memory of the terrible anonymous sufferings of Ireland in the hungry 1840s.

33. Christine Kinealy, *The Cult of Commemoration: The Great Famine – a Dangerous Memory?* (Dublin: Cultures of Ireland, 1996), p. 4.

34. Luke Dodds, "Famine Echoes," *South Atlantic Quarterly*, vol. XCV, no. 1 (1996), p. 98.

35. Foster, *The Irish Story*, p. 29.

36. See Louis Cullen, "The United Irishmen in Wexford," in *The Mighty Wave: The 1798 Rebellion in Wexford*, eds. D. Keogh and N. Furlong (Dublin: Four Courts, 1996), p. 50. See also Gary Owens, "Nationalist Monuments in Ireland, 1870–1914: Symbolism and Ritual," in *Ireland, Art into History*, eds. R. Gillespie and B. P. Kennedy (Dublin: Town House, 1994), pp. 103–17.

37. Ian McBride, "Review Article: Reclaiming the Rebellion: 1798 in 1998," *Irish Historical Studies*, XXXVI, no. 123 (May 1999), p. 395.

38. Tom Dunne, "Wexford's *Comoradh '98*: Politics, Heritage and History," *History Ireland* (Summer 1998), p. 49. See also Tom Dunne, "1798: Memory, History, Commemoration," *Journal of the Wexford Historical Society*, no. 16 (1996–7), pp. 5–39.

39. Kevin Whelan, "Reinterpreting the 1798 Rebellion in Wexford," in *The Mighty Wave*, p. 36.

40. Ibid., p. 34.

41. Ibid.

42. Ibid., p. 36.

43. Foster, *The Irish Story*, p. 225.

44. Tom Dunne, "Wexford's *Comoradh*, pp. 51–52.

45. Ibid., p. 52.

46. For a critique of attempts in the 1990s to situate Ireland as a present-day post-colonial society from a social and economic point of view, see Liam Kennedy, "Modern Ireland: Post-Colonial Society or Post-Colonial Pretensions," *Colonialism, Religion and Nationalism in Ireland* (Belfast: Institute of Irish Studies, 1996), pp. 167–81. See, by contrast, Carol Coulter, *Ireland: Between the First and the Third World* (Dublin: Attic Press, 1990). The fullest analysis of the post-colonial turn in academic discourse in the 1990s is Stephen Howe, "Colonialism, Criticism, and Cultural Theory," *Ireland and Empire: Colonial Legacies in Irish History and Culture* (Oxford: Oxford University Press, 2000).

47. See David Lloyd, *Anomalous States: Irish Writing and the Post-Colonial Moment* (Dublin: The Lilliput Press, 1993); David Lloyd, *Ireland After History* (Cork: Cork University Press, 1999), and Joseph Cleary, *Literature, Partition and the Nation State: Culture and Conflict in Ireland, Israel and Palestine* (Cambridge: Cambridge University Press, 2002).

48. Joseph Cleary, "Misplaced Ideas? Colonialism, Location and Dislocation in Irish Studies," in Claire Connolly, ed., *Theorizing Ireland* (Basingstoke: Palgrave Macmillan, 2003), p. 93.

49. Quoted by Howe in *Ireland and Empire*, p. 119.

50. Colin Graham, "'Liminal Spaces': Post-Colonial Theories and Irish Culture," *Irish Review*, no. 16 (Autumn/Winter 1994), p. 36.

51. Ibid., p. 41.

52. Howe, *Ireland and Empire*, p. 142.

53. Peter Clinch, Frank Convery and Brendan Walsh, *After the Celtic Tiger: Challenges Ahead*, (Dublin: O'Brien Press, 2002), p. 27.

54. Cleary, "Misplaced Ideas?" p. 95.

55. Stephen Howe draws attention to the Derry origins of Field Day in *Ireland and Empire*, pp. 119–20.

56. Seamus Deane, Introduction, *The Field Day Anthology of Irish Writing* (Derry: Field Day Theatre Company, 1991), p. xx.

57. Ibid. p. x.

58. It was not, it should be stressed, that the emancipation of women in the Republic, the issue of Northern Ireland, and the related issue of national identity could not be brought together in feminist discourse in the period. Rather, the main feminist agenda, at a time of institutional consolidation was addressing matters of immediate import in the Southern state – divorce, abortion, the tax status of women in the workforce and in the home, the prevalence of domestic violence. For a series of pamphlets which engage with feminism and nationalism and with republicanism and the Northern question see Eavan Boland, *A Kind of Scar: The Woman Poet in a National Tradition* (Dublin:

Attic Press, 1989); Edna Longley, *From Cathleen to Anorexia: The Breakdown of Irelands* (Dublin: Attic Press, 1990), and Gerardine Meaney, *Sex and Nation: Women in Irish Culture and Politics* (Dublin: Attic Press, 1991). It is perhaps salient in this context that a pioneering collection of essays by various hands on gender and sexuality in modern Ireland ignored the Northern issue. See *Gender and Sexuality in Modern Ireland*, eds. Anthony Bradley and Maryann Valiulis (Amherst: University of Massachusetts Press, 1997). It is only marginally present in another pioneering work on gender matters – Éibear Walshe, ed. *Sex, Nation and Dissent in Irish Writing* (Cork: Cork University Press, 1997).

59. Theo Dorgan, "Looking Over the Edge," *Irish Poetry Since Kavanagh*, p. 156.

60. See Joan Mc Breen, *The White Page*/An Bhileag Bhán: *Twentieth-Century Irish Women Poets* (Cliffs of Moher, County Clare: Salmon Publishing, 1999).

61. Anne Fogarty, "Deliberately Personal? The Politics of Identity in Contemporary Irish Women's Writing," *Nordic Irish Studies*, vol. I (2002), p. 1.

62. Ibid., p. 3.

63. Ibid., pp. 3–4.

64. Ibid., p. 4.

65. Eavan Boland, *Collected Poems* (Manchester: Carcanet Press, 1995), p. 200.

66. Reported in the *Sunday Times* 12 January 2003, p. 21.

67. Ibid.

68. Clinch *et al.*, *After the Celtic Tiger*, p. 58.

69. Figures reported in the *Irish Times*, 17 February 2003, p. 6. This report of the findings of a government-appointed advisory commission noted that such expenditure had risen to 1.42 percent of gross domestic product. This still lagged "well behind the EU average" and was markedly less than the proportion of GDP spent in a similar knowledge-based economy, Finland, where 3.22 percent is the equivalent figure.

70. See Nicholas Allen, *George Russell (AE) and the New Ireland, 1905–1930* (Dublin: Four Courts Press, 2003), pp. 223–27.

71. See G. T. Wrixon, "Irish Science and Technology: The Changing Role of the Universities," *Irish Review*, no. 17/18 (Winter 1995), pp. 118–26; "'Lords of Ether and Light:' The Irish Astronomical Tradition of the Nineteenth Century," *Irish Review*, no. 17/18 (Winter 1995), pp. 127–41; Seán Lysaght, "Themes in the Irish History of Science," *Irish Review*, no. 20 (Spring/Summer 1996), pp. 87–97; Gretta Jones, "Catholicism, Nationalism and Science," *Irish Review*, no. 20 (Spring/Summer 1997), pp. 47–61.

72. John Wilson Foster, *Nature in Ireland: A Scientific and Cultural History* (Dublin: The Lilliput Press, 1997), p. ix.

73. Ibid.

74. Nicholas Whyte, *Science, Colonialism and Ireland* (Cork: Cork University Press, 1999), p. 6.

75. Ibid., p. 190.

76. Foster, *Nature in Ireland*, p. xi.

77. Dorothy Walker, *Modern Art in Ireland* (Dublin: The Lilliput Press, 1997).

78. Ibid., p. 157.

79. Caoimhín Mac Giolla Léith, "Strategic Representations: Notes on Irish Art since the Sixties," in *When Time Began to Rant and Rage: Figurative Painting from Twentieth Century Ireland*, ed. James Christen Steward (London: Merrell Holberton, 1998), p. 113.

80. Peter Murray, ed., Introduction, *0044* (Cork: Crawford Municipal Art Gallery, 1999), p. 9.

81. Ibid.

82. Claire Schneider, "Kathy Prendergast: Lost Maps ... & Other 'Limbo' States," in Murray, ed., *0044*, p. 129.

83. Ibid., p. 132.

Index

Brown, Terence.
Ireland : a social and

DATE DUE
